Environmental Philosophy

Environmental Philosophy
Reason, Nature and Human Concern

Christopher Belshaw

McGill-Queen's University Press
Montreal & Kingston • Ithaca

ISBN 0-7735-2296-4 (bound)
ISBN 0-7735-2307-3 (paper)

Published simultaneously outside North America
by Acumen Publishing Limited

McGill-Queen's University Press acknowledges the financial support of
the Government of Canada through the Book Publishing Development
Program (BPIDP) for its activities.

National Library of Canada Cataloguing in Publication Data

Belshaw, Christopher, 1952-
      Environmental philosophy

Includes bibliographical references and index.
ISBN 0-7735-2296-4 (bound).--ISBN 0-7735-2307-3 (pbk.)

      1. Environmental Sciences--Philosophy. 2. Human ecology--
Philosophy. I. Title.

GE40.B44 2001   304.2'01   C2001-902162-3

Designed and typeset in Classical Garamond by Kate Williams, Abergavenny.
Printed and bound by Biddles Ltd., Guildford and King's Lynn.

Contents

Introduction

In the second half of his long life the art critic, educator, failed husband and utopian socialist John Ruskin became increasingly concerned about the state of nature:

> This first day of May, 1869, I am writing where my work was begun thirty-five years ago, within sight of the snows of the higher Alps. In that half of the permitted life of man, I have seen strange evil brought upon every scene that I best loved, or tried to make beloved by others. The light which once flushed those pale summits with its rose at dawn, and purple at sunset, is now umbered and faint; the air which once inlaid the clefts of all their golden crags with azure is now defiled with languid coils of smoke, belched from worse than volcanic fires; their very glacier waves are ebbing, and their snows fading, as if Hell had breathed on them; the waters that once sank their feet into crystalline are now dimmed and foul, from deep to deep, and shore to shore. These are no careless words – they are accurately – horribly – true. I know what the Swiss lakes were; no pool of Alpine fountain at its source was clearer. This morning, on the Lake of Geneva, at half a mile from the beach, I could scarcely see my oar-blade a fathom deep.[1]

Anxieties about pollution, climate change and the deterioration of the natural world are not new, even if they are more widespread now than a century or so ago. This book neither describes such changes nor explains in detail why they occur: its aims, rather, are to explore certain of the philosophical questions attendant on changes like these, and to consider in particular how they should be met, which aspects we should welcome, which regret and which, if any, we should try to reverse – or, more bluntly, which changes are good, and which a "strange evil". Its particular focus, then, is on certain issues within moral philosophy. But its scope is not limited to these alone, for underlying these various moral or ethical questions are certain further philosophical concerns about just what the environment is, the nature of value, the kinds of entities of which the natural world consists and the broad shape of our relationship with that world. Hence the title.

To philosophize about the environment is to reason about nature, and about our various concerns and involvements with the natural world. But this isn't a simple one-way procedure, for we are, of course, a part of nature, not distinct from it, and our concerns are themselves an upshot of natural procedures. Moreover, reason itself is hardly autonomous; it, too, is something that has evolved within the natural world, and even if we are able still to speak, somewhat archaically, of the faculty of reason, we only mistakenly believe that it might operate alone in determining what we think, and what we do. There is no reason to think we can or should be wholly reasonable beings. To philosophize about the environment, then, we need to take the complexity of our own natures fully into account.

I

My beginning here with Ruskin is pertinent in several respects, for although this book is written, in the main, from the perspective of what is still called analytical philosophy, that perspective is tempered in various ways. Our thinking about the environment, as indeed about anything else, betrays something of our intellectual and cultural background. As we are not wholly reasonable creatures, so we cannot occupy a wholly neutral perspective. Concern for the environment isn't new, but neither is it, in anything like its familiar form, wholly timeless. Our responses to the problems we face, as well as the problems themselves, are to a considerable degree shaped by our historical location, by what we've been taught, what we've read and what in subtler ways we've come to believe. So there's room, at the outset, for a reminder that environmentalism has a complex and not inconsiderable past.

Ruskin is significant in a further respect. Although he was cosmopolitan, he found a spiritual home, and the place to end his days, in the English Lake District, self-consciously treading Wordsworthian ground, and following the poet in his concerns with the local landscape, the right relationship between that landscape and industry, and the evolution of change.[2] It isn't an accident that I live only a few miles further south, and could, were there not a couple of hills and a couple of hundred trees in the way, be afforded a good view of his house, and a view of the view from that house over to the village of Coniston, and the mountains beyond, lower than the Alps, whose darkening atmospheres increasingly troubled him in his remaining years.[3] It isn't an accident, in that I wanted to live in the Lake District since first visiting the area considerably more than thirty years ago. In the interim I spent a decade in Southern California, which is equally beautiful but in different ways. This was much less a matter of design, although, in giving me many opportunities to travel in the Mojave Desert, to Yosemite and the mountains of the Sierra Nevada, and north along the coast road, not at all to be regretted. Inevitably this book is shaped in part by that mix of New and Old World perspectives and, as a result, by the affecting awareness that there are competing accounts of what sorts of environments we should value, and different understandings as to when and how human involvement might be benign.

I bring in Ruskin here for yet another reason. He is standardly packaged among neither the philosophers nor (or nor yet) among the more familiar environmentalists,[4] so his inclusion serves as a reminder, or pointedly suggests, that the range of influences within this relatively new discipline might well be wide. But as it won't do to attempt the thoroughly distant and dispassionate stance of the analytical philosopher, so also is it inappropriate to approach the environment always recognizably as an environmentalist. A suspicion, and hardly mine alone, is that perhaps too much of the conversation in environmental philosophy has been between members of something like a coterie, concerned to argue fine points of detail between themselves, but too little inclined to take their results into neighbouring fields. Indeed, the very phrase "environmental philosophy" can suggest (and is meant by some to suggest) that we are not so much considering a further subject matter from the broad philosophical point of view, but rather advancing a new kind of philosophy, moderately or radically opposed to the old. Whether such a procedure is defensible is something I go on to consider, but my preference, I might say now, is to emphasize continuities. So this book is informed, I hope in ways some of which are evident, by a fairly broad philosophical background, much of it in the analytical strain, and informed as well by concerns outside the philosophical frame. But analytical philosophy is variously guised. As a student I began with Hume, and his influence, his scepticism about reason and his distrust of theory will be detectable behind some of the arguments, and some of the tempered hopes for arguments, that will be encountered here.

Hume's *Enquiry*, if not his dead-born *Treatise*, could well have been advertised for the specialist and non-specialist alike, and similar claims might be made for this book. It is, in essence, a work that sits squarely within the mainstream philosophical tradition, and I hope that at least parts of it will be of interest and use to those already familiar with that tradition. But it avoids technicalities, I think scrupulously, and assumes no detailed prior acquaintance with either philosophy or the workings of the environment, and so aims to introduce the central problems in environmental philosophy to those as yet unfamiliar with them. It isn't comprehensive, and certain topics are left untouched. My belief is that these topics – and they include decision-theory, eco-feminism and certain issues relating to environmental activism – are the more marginal ones, but others may have a different view.

II

Having noted briefly what isn't included, I might say a little more about what is. There are many more positions covered, arguments considered and details of arguments explored than those mentioned here, but this outline will give the main lie of the land.

There are eleven chapters, each with what I hope are telling subdivisions. Above the level of chapter, no further distinctions are explicitly drawn. Nevertheless, it may be useful to think of the book as divided into four parts. In the first (Chapters 1 and 2) I lay out some of the ground, considering something of the nature, extent and origins of the environmental problems with which we need to be concerned. So Chapter 1 addresses the questions of what the environment is, what magnitude of problem it currently has to face and how its component problems might best be classified. The point is made that in engaging in these clarificatory and classificatory procedures we are already dealing with at least some proto-philosophical activity. And the chapter goes on to consider the respective roles of science and philosophy in understanding and dealing with our environmental problems. It makes the point that while science may well enable us to understand what environmental changes are occurring, much of where they come from and several of their likely consequences, it is unable to adjudicate between competing suggestions as to what should and should not happen, and what we ought to do and desire as far as nature is concerned. Philosophy, and moral philosophy in particular, is critical to the proper evaluation of environmental change. And such evaluation, in turn, is critical to our leading the sorts of lives that, quite reasonably, we want to lead, for our fortunes and those of the environment are to a very great degree intertwined.

Having outlined certain of the major terms, and then allowing that the idea of an environmental crisis is not altogether far-fetched, Chapter 2 goes on to consider whether there is any general explanation of our current situation. While I reject a number of suggestions that have been offered, I allow that modern technology plays a highly important role here, in giving us the means, hitherto unavailable, to massive environmental interventions. But this isn't, contrary to what is often suggested, grounds simply to jettison this technology, or to turn our backs more generally on science, reason and what they may bring. What can be a cause might also be a cure.

In the next part (Chapters 3 and 4) I go on to consider certain familiar strategies for dealing with environmental problems. Chapter 3, after a summary dismissal of some notably poor candidates, looks at democratic and market-based approaches. The principal suggestions here are that although idealized voting and pricing mechanisms would offer highly satisfactory solutions to a wide range of problems, democracies and markets as they currently exist are in several respects imperfect, and hardly reliable means to environmental improvement. There is reason, nevertheless, to suppose that some improvement might be linked with a further commitment to these voting and pricing procedures, and so to think that already well-known political and economic strategies are not without merit where the environment is concerned. In particular, as I resisted, in Chapter 2, the blanket rejection of reason, science and technology – as I gave some support for continuing with what is sometimes called the Enlightenment project – so here I reveal myself unwilling to support a sweeping rejection of the market. Chapter 4 deals with philosophically more familiar territory, outlining consequentialist, rights-based and virtue-centred moral theories, first in general terms, and then in their particular relation to the environment. I rehearse several of the standard objections to these theories while yet again allowing that were any of them to be consistently adopted, the environment would likely fare better than it presently does. But can these theories be ranked in terms of their overall plausibility? I am somewhat sceptical here and, while there is perhaps some discernible inclination to find more in a consequentialist account than in either of its rivals, express reservations as to how any theorized approach to morality can hope to quash our more robust intuitions. Where the environment is concerned, the complexity of the moral phenomena that needs to be addressed is such as to resist any simple solution, no matter how crisp and elegant.

Nevertheless, some progress has been made. The concern thus far has been with approaches to the environment that take as their aim improvements in human well-being. And the argument has been, first, that we ought to understand our well-being in appropriately broad terms, dealing not so much with what we want as with what we need if our lives are to go well. Not only should we be concerned about environmental degradation because it may cost us in terms of material goods, either of an inessential or essential kind – cheaper travel, faster cars, through to food, housing, medicines – but we should be concerned as well because sustaining our relationship with the natural world is a constituent in our psychic health and well-being. A second part of the argument concerns the construal of "we" here. Again, fairly uncontroversially, I argue that we have reasons to consider not only our own needs, but those also of people who are distant from us in both time and space, the satisfaction of whose needs we can, by our own actions, prevent or promote. This demands a somewhat cautious and conservative approach to environmental change: they too are likely to find uses for oil, to want to eat fish, and to appreciate unspoilt terrain.

This, however, leaves certain critical issues so far untouched. And so the third and longest part of the book (Chapters 5–8) deals with one of the central questions in environmental philosophy: that of what sorts of things are of direct moral concern. Many environmentalists claim that even if attention to our well-being will bring to nature substantial benefits, nature isn't here to serve our purposes, no matter how benign. And other living creatures (animals, plants, micro-organisms), along with entities more diffuse and abstract (cataracts, rock formations, species), are all of them things whose moral status is something we need to consider. Do these things matter, not only to us, but in themselves? Supposing they do, what sorts of demands are put upon us? I begin with animals, arguing (in Chapter 5) that they matter at least in so far as they are sentient. We cannot do with them just as we will. And I take pains here to reject denials of this, on the grounds either that sentience is unestablished or that it is in any event not enough to get animals into the moral domain. I want to reject also the contention that my conclusion here is way too weak, and that there are, where animals are concerned, strong constraints on what we might do. Because I have earlier withheld assent from familiar moral theories, so here I am able to resist claims, often encountered, that animals are such that eating, hunting, capturing, enclosing and experimenting on them are all straightforwardly (even if not unconditionally) wrong. The conclusions here, even though various groups will dissent from them, are, I think, still relatively uncontroversial.

As far as non-sentient life forms are concerned, the claim (in Chapter 6) is that even if we agree, as well we might, that such things have a good of their own, are able to be benefited or harmed, and can flourish or decline, still none of this gives us reason to promote their well-being or further their ends. This is a more controversial view. But imagine we are told by God that plants in some distant galaxy are succumbing to disease, and that if we each do a dozen push-ups then (although God doesn't explain how) the plants will recover. This doesn't, I claim, give us a reason to do those push-ups. Nor, I claim, is it importantly different when the plants are much closer to home. Claims to a life-centred ethic are then, as yet, not firmly enough established.

Chapter 7 is something of a mixed bag. This is because, as I explain, two avenues are at odds with one another. A consideration of animals might lead, as it has led here, to plants, or it might in contrast point the way to species. And I consider the moral and (because although important it isn't obvious) the metaphysical status of species in the middle of this chapter. But that is flanked on one side by a consideration of natural but non-living things, such as rivers, mountains and icebergs, and on the other by Aldo Leopold's Land Ethic, with its focusing on ecosystems as the major target for our environmental concern. The argument with respect to all these cases is that while their wanton destruction is wrong, these entities, although a part of nature, are unable, considered in and of themselves, to make any moral claim upon us. The argument, further, is that there is no good reason to insist on any clear distinction between nature and artifice here. As it is wrong wantonly to fell trees, so is it wrong wantonly to knock down towers or chimneys.

The discussion at the end of Chapter 7 leads naturally to that of Chapter 8. Deep ecologists share with Leopold a concern for systems of things, and the complex interactions between the parts of nature, as opposed to this or that individual or kind. They go beyond in wanting first a more thorough reappraisal of the metaphysical basis of both the science and morality of the environment, and secondly, to give their environmental stance an overt political dimension. At the core of deep ecological thinking are claims about intrinsic value, about equality among the different parts of the biosphere, and about our consequent need substantially to limit our presence, reducing both our numbers and the extent of our incursions on the natural world. But deep ecology's claims are not all, I argue, well supported. Its hostility to what it sees as more moderate approaches is wearing. And its own radicalism is, in the end, less than at first it seems.

In the final part of the book I return to certain important issues that are involved in human concern. Chapter 9 comprises a drawing together and further discussion of various claims, both positive and negative, about value. The concern here is to explore the notion of intrinsic value in particular, and to resist the various claims that such value is widespread through the natural world. But giving up on this, I want to insist, doesn't leave us in a position where all values are subjective, human-centred or instrumental. And I attempt in this chapter to develop a dispositional account, roughly on a par with some philosophically respectable views about colour, under which we can claim that something is valuable if it is the sort of thing that human beings would have reason to care about, were they situated such that caring were possible. Such an account will grant us, I claim, a natural world very much as many strong-minded environmentalists would have it, even if it is now differently explained.

The tenth chapter returns, again now in greater detail, to discussions of natural beauty already raised elsewhere. That nature, or parts of nature, can be perceived to be beautiful is a strong motivation to environmental activism, and constitutes one of the most powerful instances of some values not being narrowly instrumental, and yet at the same time being resistant to thorough extrication from a broader conception of human concern. It is difficult to see how we could so much as make sense of the view that something is beautiful just in and of itself, irrespective of how it seems to us. But "us" here is not uniform. And I observe that particular notions of what is beautiful and what is not have varied within nature, as they have without. What matters, I claim, is that we retain contact with beautiful nature. This doesn't straightforwardly license preservation of particular parts. For that we need a conversation at the same time both more piecemeal and sustained.

In the last chapter I look more closely at the place of human beings in the scheme of things. For what was noted much earlier is our need to take the interests and needs of future generations into account. The size and constitution of those generations is not yet determined, but is, to a considerable degree, within our control. One extreme view claims that there should be as many people as possible, while the other insists that the world would be better off without us. I take a middle line here, resisting the grander claims.

III

It has taken longer than expected to write this book. It would have taken longer still were it not for the many people who have given me help. They richly deserve my thanks. Noel Fleming, Rosie Atkins, Gary Kemp, Andrew Ward, Ian Chowcat and Steve Holland have all of them read chapters, and have given me useful and often detailed comments. David Schmidtz, John Shand and Emma Thorlby have read the whole, and have all of them helped me to pull the book into a better shape. I need especially to thank Tom Baldwin at the University of York for very generously giving me the opportunity to teach material which fed into this book, and to my students Andrew Littlewood and Fionn Petch for their thoughtful comments on early drafts of chapters. And I need to thank also my colleagues in the Open University for helping determine that my first and uncertain writings on this topic would eventually result in this book. Finally to John Shand, Steven Gerrard at Acumen and Kate Williams, for patience, encouragement and always intelligent suggestions for change. And to Caroline Mercier, for more than can be listed here.

CHAPTER 1
Problems

Concern for the environment is widespread. Politicians put it high on their agendas, businesses have environmental policies, thousands upon thousands of products are supposed to be environment friendly, green is a favourite colour and countless people describe themselves as environmentalists. But what is the environment with which all these are so much concerned? What makes an issue environmental, as opposed to political, biological or economic? What does someone need to do, believe or want in order to be an environmentalist? There is a need for answers to these questions, but there is a need also to indicate that the answers will be of limited use, and that they cannot always be firm.

Terms

It may seem that the answers here are too obvious to be worth stating. Books, policy documents, government bodies and industries that are concerned with environmental matters often simply assume that the term is understood, and rarely make any effort to clarify just what it is with which they are so concerned. But this ought to be considered unsatisfactory. Although the insistence that key terms be defined before serious discussion gets under way is, in general, rightly resisted, there is in this case reason to hope for more. Talk of the environment is relatively new, a lot hangs on it, and although it can for a while be disguised, it isn't long before evidence of important disagreement as to and misunderstanding of some central terms comes to the surface. Rather than assume that meanings are clear enough, some of the complexities might at the outset be usefully explored.

1

Environment and environments

What the environment is can be understood in different ways. One account describes it as the place or places "where people live, work, move and enjoy themselves".[1] This is very broad, and covers offices and homes, as well as cities, the countryside and many parts of the open sea. It suggests a connection with life: the environment is the area in which life goes on. And it suggests also, perhaps surprisingly, a concern only with human life. So if there are any wilderness areas – polar regions, remnants of desert, the bottom of the sea – from which people are absent, these are just not part of the environment. Other accounts, in contrast, think of the environment mostly in terms of a natural and non-human world, and see human beings, along with their cities, roads, industries and airports, as encroaching on the environment, and competing with it for space. Still others place no particular emphasis on either people or nature: there was an environment, no doubt with its problems, before our species came into existence, and there will continue to be an environment, even if we destroy ourselves, and the environment extends even now to those few parts of the world in which people are still not to be found. But it includes as well industrial conurbations like Dusseldorf, Mexico City, and the Los Angeles freeways. These accounts share, however, an inclination to think of the environment as one thing, spread, more or less, over the surface of the world. Other accounts reject this global approach, and stress the multiplicity of environments, suggesting that there is a large and indefinite number, differently sized and positioned, in the same way as different things or groups of things are located within, and responsive to, different parts of the entirety of the world. An environment, in this sense, and taking etymology seriously, is something like home ground, the territory familiar to and supportive of a particular life or kind of life: hence my environment, the environment of the Navajo Indians in New Mexico, that of wolves, the ticks that live on wolves, and so on. And as different environments in this way overlap, so one individual's environment will itself typically include other individuals. Given the very large number of living organisms, then, it is reasonable to suppose that everything that happens happens in some environment or other, such that nowhere on this planet is off limits, if environments are one's concern. But is there, as I have suggested, a restriction to the earth, and the space or spaces of living things? Or do other planets, even without life, have their own environments, which might themselves be damaged or improved? Several writers have urged that environmental thinking should range this far, so that we might learn more of the environment on Mars, wonder what it is like in different galaxies, and so on.[2]

There are several competing meanings here, then, and they can't all be exactly right. But rather than decide between them, I will suggest first that we think in the main of there being one environment, rather than many, and that we think of this environment as it exists in outdoor places (so excluding the home and the office), whether inhabited by human beings or not (and so including both cities and the few wild places that are left on earth), but inhabited nevertheless (and so excluding, at least until we get there, the distant reaches of outer space). And I make this suggestion for two reasons. First it seems that this is how the term is most commonly used: there just is more talk of the environment than of environments. Secondly this common use does reflect the fact that living spaces do connect together, and affect one another, in a more or less seamless whole. If there were life on some distant planet which, although we might know a little about it, was unable otherwise to interact with life on earth, then we would only misleadingly or improperly speak of one environment with respect to the two places. This would be improper, however, only because it doesn't chime well with how we actually speak. And if my suggestion appears in any way vague, this is first because we speak vaguely, and secondly because there is little other than this vague speaking to go on.

What of the adjective? If the environment is more or less everywhere, and near enough everything that happens happens within it, then it may seem that almost all issues are environmental issues, and that virtually every problem is an environmental problem. But this isn't how we speak. Environmental issues are, as a matter of custom if not of rule, those that figure in a largely natural world, and that occur within, or have significant effects on, public spaces. The question of whether Manchester United should play on grass or Astroturf is not, without some special pleading to the contrary, an environmental issue. Nor is the problem of whether to paint or paper the walls of a museum really an environmental problem. This is not to deny, of course, that these examples, like very many others, have aspects that bear on environmental issues in my sense: some paints are more environmentally friendly than others, and real grass will probably house more insects than a synthetic substitute would. But unless persuaded that this particular insect population in some way or other matters, we are unlikely to think of this question for sport as involving any environmental issues.

Environmentalists

Whereas the environment is something given, and long-standing, which might then be studied or ignored, both environmentalists and environmentalism are of our creation. In the common and relatively recent understanding[3] which I will follow here, an environmentalist is someone who shows a special or marked awareness of environmental issues, and who attempts, within some or other reasonable bounds, to care for, preserve or sustain the environment or some of its parts. The person who tidies the office or puts flowers in hotel bedrooms is not, in this ordinary sense, an environmentalist; nor, although environmentally well informed, is someone who takes it to be their life's work to drop litter in every national park, or to collect, for no good reason, blood samples from members of every endangered species. And environmentalism, similarly, suggests a positive attitude towards the environment, one in which it is assumed that study and care will go hand in hand, or that understanding will bring benefits. There is room for an analogy with certain political affiliations here. A communist typically thinks it not only inevitable but also desirable that there will be, in time, the victory of the proletariat. And conservatism is not only knowledgeable of but also favourably disposed towards the forces of tradition. Similarly, to describe oneself as an environmentalist, or to profess a concern with environmentalism, is to invite certain assumptions about several of one's beliefs, values, attitudes and practices. And when, throughout this book, I refer without any further qualification to the environmentalist, or to environmentalism, it will be this broadly positive or supportive stance that I will have in mind.

These are somewhat loose accounts of these central terms. That is not only good enough, but perhaps better than the alternative. For although we can define any term as precisely as we choose, we can't always do this in a manner that is other than arbitrary. As, to draw a further analogy, there aren't clear divisions between the intelligent and the stupid, or between the hirsute and the bald, so to stipulate meanings for such terms as if there are such divisions is in some ways to distort how things are: similarly for "environment", "environmentalist" and the like. A precise definition would imply a clarity and tidiness that don't exist. What this suggests also, as a corollary, is that there may be disagreement about whether a particular description is well applied. For if there are no specific criteria as to what constitutes an environmental issue and what an issue of another kind, if the appropriate description is to some extent a matter of judgement rather than of rule, then it is possible to disagree with a given characterization. As your freedom fighter may be my terrorist, so your environmentalist may also be my terrorist. But I want to suggest that it won't always matter if we do disagree. Think of art. Even if we seem unable to decide and we disagree about whether something is a work of art, we may be able to decide and agree about how it came into existence, whether it is beautiful or ugly, original or derivative, and so on. And then the further question of whether the thing is a work of art begins to look empty. So, too, with some of the questions about the environment. It is just a mistake to think that we need firmly to settle precisely what sort of issue we are hoping to consider, before we can begin to consider it.

There will be objections to some of this. Consider further the analogy with art. I might suppose it is simply convenient to go with what I perceive as customary usage, claiming that problem cases can be settled as we go along, but others will insist that this already slants things. To think of easel paintings as paradigm examples of artworks, and installation pieces, videos and collage as more or less marginal is certainly to point our understanding of what art is in a particular direction. It will have connections with beauty, tradition, domesticity and class that it might otherwise be without. Similarly, to think of, say, global warming or tropical deforestation as central among environmental issues, and the colour of the houses across the street, or the noise from powerboats on a nearby lake as rather more peripheral, is to incline our grasp of environment and environmentalism one way rather than another. And, as with art, this may have implications for our involvement. If there is one environment, and the pressing problems are global, the temptation to local apathy may in the end be irresistible. I can do something about ozone depletion, but not enough to make much difference. If, in contrast, I tend to think of environment as the space around me, I may be both more motivated to and successful in bringing about change.[4] The one environment view is, then, one we embrace only at a cost.

There is something in this, but not enough to cause any substantial revision in what has been suggested so far. We can, as the slogan suggests, think globally and act locally. And we should consider the larger picture. The big issues need thinking about. Nor need thinking here stunt us elsewhere. Even if there is only one environment, it has, as I have said, its different parts, and it is both natural and reasonable to give some attention to local issues. Putting environment before environments still allows, then, for the focused and small-scale concern and is not in itself a recipe for despair.

There is a further advantage to the less diversified approach. It is implied by what I have already said about seamlessness. To think of environments as living spaces and then, because there are no clear distinctions, the environment as the space in which all the life we know of is to be found is, in this stress on integration, to guard against too pointed a contrast between human beings, on the one hand, and the world of nature, on the other. The environment is in very important respects coterminous with this planet, and is neither the particular places of human habitation, nor the setting for a wild nature that is essentially alien to us. This global and somewhat holistic construal of the key term here has its dangers, as will later emerge, but it does, I think, give a tolerably fair picture of the issues as we have to face them.[5]

Crises, disasters and problems

Many writers refer to the current environmental crisis, to environmental disasters, to our degrading, destroying or damaging this or that part of the environment, to our exploiting the natural world, natural resources, and so on without being at all explicit as to why such descriptions are appropriate. They are hardly neutral terms, suggesting as they do both that things are very seriously amiss and that much of it is our fault. But in many of the cases where the talk is of doom and gloom we might wonder first just what is supposed to be about to happen and secondly what would be so bad about it if it did.

5

Some writers have referred to a crisis, and then offered detailed predictions as to what may be expected (in terms of, say, population growth or ozone depletion) which then gives substance to the crisis referred to. In several such cases, as with bovine spongiform encephalopathy (BSE) or acquired immune deficiency syndrome (AIDS), these predictions have been thus far unfulfilled, and the situation is less bad than expected.[6] In other cases the situation has already occurred, and so information about the upshot is more or less accurate. But in cases of both kinds it is still not always obvious why talk of a crisis or disaster is appropriate. Oil super-tanker groundings, the most recent off the Galapagos, are referred to almost without exception as disasters, although not with evident good reason. Building a few miles of motorway, or a new shopping mall, will cause the death of a comparable numbers of animals and a greater numbers of plants, and lead to an irreversible loss of habitat, but although often unwelcome, changes and developments of this kind are not typically referred to as disastrous. Similarly, people often talk of massive population increases, particularly in the Third World, as seriously threatening to the survival of the planet, but typically without detailing in just what the threat consists. On a smaller scale, there are signs asking people to help the English Lake District by not leaving litter, camping or lighting fires. Perhaps there is not much of an issue about litter, but it isn't explained, and nor is it obvious, why an overnight tent should hinder or harm a national park.

I want neither to suggest that there is no such thing as crisis or disaster, nor to encourage complacency about our present situation. Nor do I propose that we avoid speaking of crises, disasters and the like until offered a precise definition of such terms. There have been disasters enough already – Chernobyl is an obvious example, and the 1999 earthquakes in Turkey another – and there are doubtless more to come. But there are many cases where it isn't obvious, and my point is only that in such cases some account of why a given description is appropriate can quite properly be requested. This is especially important when dealing with the emotive terms that figure so often in discussion of the environment. To label oneself an environmentalist is undeniably to seek to occupy the moral high ground. And to describe some event as a disaster, or a situation as reaching crisis point, is to oblige us to take it seriously, and if possible to attempt change. Given a belief in the pressing importance of some action, those wanting that action have reason to play up their cause, in the hope of winning for it even more attention. Talk of crises can be good for fundraising. Even so, others of us, not yet fully committed, ought, in many cases, to question or challenge the characterization being provided.

An objection that might be raised is that academic hair-splitting, although in other areas innocuous, is here an indulgence that we can ill afford. Given the depth and extent of the environmental challenge (to use a somewhat neutral term), what is demanded of us are deeds, rather than a further finessing of words. But the objection is surely misplaced. There is not one alleged problem, but a range. And no matter how committed they are, environmentalists cannot apply themselves to all of them with equal dedication. Decisions have to be made. It seems reasonable, other things being equal, to tackle the bigger problems first. But to do this correct judgements about the scale and urgency of a problem have to be made. Disasters need sorting from mishaps, risks from certainties, and crisis points treated with circumspection.

I am going to try to avoid some of this emotive language. Instead I will refer to environmental problems. Even that, of course, is a far from neutral term; to describe a situation as in some way a problem will seem immediately to suggest the desirability of change. But we might understand the notion of a problem somewhat differently. Perhaps no change is called for. As long as this isn't clear, as long as there is disagreement, not only about what to do, but also about whether anything at all needs to be done, then there is still a problem. There is, though, a further distinction that needs to be made here. In some cases there will be questions as to the size of an alleged problem. It is said that global warming will make our lives worse, but perhaps little or no warming is taking place, or perhaps although it is real enough it is only temporary, and part of a long-term cycle of change. In other cases there are questions as to a problem's effects. Global warming threatens us. Other changes less obviously have an adverse affect on our lives. We may be persuaded that bad things, even seriously bad things are happening to iguanas in South America, or polar bears, or London sparrows, while not yet persuaded that this will have any consequence for human existence. So although there are problems that could be tackled, we may doubt whether we have any reason to tackle them. How far, within one environment, something else's problems may legitimately be ignored is among the issues to be further explored.

Environment, history and science

The environment has been around for a long time, and human concern with the environment has a similarly long history, but an awareness of environmental issues as importantly distinctive, the belief that there is a particular category of environmental problems at least many of which demand urgent attention, and the self-conscious and widespread use of the term "environment" in something like the sense outlined above are all relatively recent. Not until the late nineteenth and early twentieth centuries did such terms begin to enter common parlance, beginning first, as is often the case, with scientific and academic use, and only later spilling over into the larger arenas of politics and commerce.

The term "environment", however, is not the only one that needs to be considered here. Its introduction and development closely parallels that of an academic discipline to which a concern for the environment is closely related, and with which it is often confused. Ecology, the study of the interactions between living organisms and their environments,[7] was not immediately connected with environmental concerns, and as a science makes no particular commitment to preservation or pronouncement on the value of that which it studies. Yet ecologists have values, of course, and many of them in earlier days saw their role as facilitating particular uses of the environment by showing how to avoid or minimize collateral damage. If ways could be found of felling trees without causing soil erosion, or of spraying crops without letting harmful chemicals into the human food chain, then so much the better. But in so far as environmentalists aim to understand the character of the problems that they detect, and hope to uncover methods for preventing or reversing unwelcome change, then they need to draw on ecology's resources. More recently a particular style of environmentalism and a particular version of ecology have come closer together within the deep ecology movement, which, among its several aims, wants to break down many familiar and apparently firm distinctions, adherence to which, it is said, stands behind many of our current problems.[8]

Why have environmentalism and ecology, as distinctive fields of inquiry, developed so relatively recently? Ask such a question of, say, nuclear physics and the answer refers to the gradual evolution of scientific knowledge along with the equally gradual development of the techniques and equipment with which to pursue such knowledge. But with environmentalism (as perhaps too with psychology) the answer must be less straightforward as, on the face of it at least, the phenomena to be studied, the motivation for their study and the wherewithal to undertake such study have all been around for a very long time. So why only now? One suggestion (and this is something to be further explored in Chapter 2) is that the use of these terms, the development of these subjects, has increased in relation to our growing awareness of an increasing number of environmental problems. As the situation gets worse, so disciplines, specializations and expertise develop in order to cope with it. Yet it is plausible to suppose that there is some degree of reciprocity here. An increase in the number and size of the problems leads to a corresponding increase in the use of the terms. Equally, the wider use of the terms leads to a growing awareness of the problems. And a suspicion here might be (as it might be, similarly, in psychology) that some of our current concerns are simply born of the vocabulary that allows us to voice them.

Philosophy

Issues concerning the environment are many. Whether nuclear power can be made safe, the use of so-called brown-field sites, overfishing of the seas and the benefits and drawbacks of genetically modified (GM) foods are just a few more or less random examples. Each raises a number of detailed scientific, technological, economic and political questions, which have to be answered before an informed decision about what we ought to do can be made. No one book can do full justice to such a range of questions, and the concerns of this book are fairly severely restricted. The focus here is on certain of the most basic and most wide-ranging questions concerning the environment, and what to do with it, and very many of those questions are philosophical. There may be immediate doubts here. Philosophy is arcane, while environmental issues affect everyone. They give rise to the familiar if difficult questions that are addressed by the equally familiar and equally difficult sciences and quasi-sciences: physics, biology, economics, meteorology and so on. Philosophy, abstract, analytical and detached, can't have much to do with it. But this response, although understandable, suggests a too narrow view of philosophy on the one hand, and a too mechanical and practical approach to the problems of the environment on the other. There are two mistakes, then, and I will say something about both.

Philosophy as a highly specialized and distinctive discipline, having its own range of problems and its particular terminology and techniques, inaccessible to other than a few experts, is a relatively recent development, one brought about by increasing compartmentalization within the academic world, and encouraged in English speaking countries in particular by a general distrust of abstract and non-practical thought. For most of its history philosophical inquiry has been thought of as very much more continuous with everyday thinking and everyday problems, and distinguished more by the degree of its persistence with certain aspects of those problems than by any sharp division in the kinds of questions it asks. And it is this second, longer-standing picture of philosophy that is in focus here, a picture that allows some meaning to the claim, often heard, that we are all philosophers, but then offers the reminder that some are more philosophical than others, and that there is undeniable value in the development of expertise.

What, then, philosophy has primarily to offer where the environment is concerned is first a clarification of the many issues involved and secondly the detailed pursuit of a range of moral and value questions that thought about the environment is bound to raise. Some examples of the first of these have already occurred, in the discussion of the meaning of the term "environment", and in the warning against the hope for too many clean distinctions. Clarification involves a deeper understanding of how things really are, and not a merely fictive precision. And there will be several further, and more complex, examples as we go on. It is, though, in pursuit of the second element that philosophy has its most notable and distinctive contribution to make to our thinking about the environment. For not only are these moral questions of fundamental importance, but they are ones that we all need and are almost all able to address, and it is here that the limitations of a purely scientific approach become evident. And just as there is a genuine contrast, even if there are still connections and overlaps, between ecology and environmentalism, so, more generally, is there a similar contrast between science on the one hand, and philosophy, particularly moral philosophy, on the other.[9]

Science and morality

There are countless scientific questions about the environment, and they mostly defy ordinary understanding. Is the nuclear processing plant at Sellafield as safe as British Nuclear Fuels Limited (BNFL) insists it is? Are leaky old fridges really making a dent in the ozone layer and, if they are, what are the likely consequences? Is modern high-yield agriculture genuinely compatible with the survival of much of our native wildlife? Would the dumping of the Shell oil platform at sea be more or less environmentally harmful than taking it back whence it came? There is little many of us can do with questions like these except listen to the confusing and often conflicting advice of experts. What is needed in order to answer them is both substantial amounts of empirical information, which is not always easy to get, and some rather subtle analysis of and reasoning about that information. But answers to these questions, although they will certainly help, will not in themselves tell us how to solve all our environmental problems. If we are agreed that we want to abandon nuclear power unless we can get a risk-free method of dealing with waste, science will inform us as to whether such a method is available. If the plan is to cut fishing until viable populations are re-established, science will tell us how big that population must be, and how far we are from achieving it. And there are examples from softer sciences as well. So if we decide to add lanes to urban motorways only if this will reduce congestion elsewhere, then science – questionnaires to motorists, analyses of journey patterns, comparisons with other road widening schemes – might offer the information we need.

These, though, are not the only sorts of questions to ask. In all of these cases the particular scientific questions become relevant only given certain assumptions about the kinds of concerns we already have, and the kinds of aims we've chosen to pursue. But now those assumptions, while they are often taken for granted, can always and often must be argued about, and in the end agreed on. There are further questions, then, about what levels of risk, and risk to whom, ought to be considered acceptable, about why we shouldn't simply continue fishing until the seas are empty, about the entire point of wanting free-flowing and fast-moving traffic on the roads, and so on. And these further questions are not addressed to scientists of any colour, and don't directly call on matters of scientific expertise. They are, rather, the seemingly less technical questions as to the kinds of things we ought to want or care about, the types of policies and procedures we should hope to introduce, and ultimately are questions about the sort of world we'd like to inhabit. They are, in short, questions of value and morality, demanding that we select from alternatives that which is, all things considered, the best from the moral or ethical point of view. What we need, where the environment is concerned, is not simply knowledge of what sorts of things are happening, and how they can be prevented or encouraged, but also, and as importantly, an understanding of what ought to happen, and of how far we are permitted to go to help bring this about.

There will be objections. A scientist might say that we should, when considering some problem, simply choose the option that involves the least amount of risk, where assessment of risk is seen as a purely scientific enterprise. An economist might suggest we should aim for that which gives greatest net benefit, when all the costs are in. Technologists may, similarly, find it difficult to see how there are questions not only of how some outcome is to be achieved, but also of what outcome should in the first place be sought. There are, as agreed on all sides, difficult questions for science. But there the difficulty ends.

This doesn't, though, undermine my claim about the centrality of moral considerations. The claim is that such considerations are relevant in every case, but not that there is disagreement in every case. Some basic moral values are very generally agreed on – we agree, for example, that human beings are not disposable in the interests of profit, and many will agree that the interests of future generations cannot simply be ignored – but this shouldn't hide from us that such values are, nevertheless, there, or deter us from asking where they come from, and how they gain our assent. Although questions of science are often the most conspicuous, this is only because much of the moral work is already done. And in very many cases the extent of disagreement as to values, and the importance of bringing this to some sort of resolution, is evident.

A further objection is that even if there are other than scientific questions that need to be considered, these cannot be usefully addressed without first having available all the scientific information relevant to their being answered. It is simply impossible, then, to think of scientific and moral questions as being equally basic or important.

There is something right here. Certainly, without any scientific understanding of the world, questions of morality and value will not be properly grounded, or take on any real shape. But this does way too little to justify the thought that the more fundamental questions and problems are always ones for science. First, in the way that there are cases where the moral work is already done, so, too, for science. Scientific understanding is broad, and widely disseminated. We need to know that animals feel pain in order safely to ground our concern over their treatment. We need to know that we can't survive without food in order to worry about the state of crops. But much of this is already common knowledge. So although there is always a need for science, there is less clearly always an ongoing need for scientists.

11

There is, of course, this need in very many cases. There is a great deal that we still don't know. And questions of what to do in this or that particular case cannot be answered unless the appropriate empirical information is to hand. But, and this is the second point, even if we cannot get the right answers, still we can make useful progress when faced with questions of value and morality. We can consider hypothetical situations. We can, for example, ask, *if* the extinction of whales will have no important knock-on effects elsewhere in the environment, should we nevertheless care about their survival? *If* organophosphates present a small but real risk to human health, should they be banned? And so on. These kinds of questions can encourage valuable clarification of our moral beliefs, and can be both asked and answered without recourse to the details of science.

A third point concerns science's independence from morality. The answers we give to various hypothetical questions can themselves provide an impetus to further scientific research. We may decide that if there is any substantial risk to future generations then underground disposal of highly radioactive materials cannot be allowed. And if we so decide then scientists have good reason to investigate these risks. But the link here doesn't pertain only to future research. It would be a mistake to think that disinterested scientific inquiry brings forth a wealth of information out of which moral questions then emerge. What actually happens is that such inquiry is always shaped and given direction by our pre-existing beliefs about what is valuable or important. This should be obvious: science is not cheap, funding bodies are rarely philanthropic, and before putting any effort into answering some scientific question it is always worth wondering why it is considered important enough to ask. And what should also be obvious, of course, is that the influences work here in both directions. Just as our values help shape the direction of science, so science's findings in turn affect our thinking about values, and, in the end, the values we happen to hold. If we are more concerned about animal welfare than many of our predecessors, that is in part because we have more information about the reality of animal pain.

Any serious attempt to consider the problems of the environment will, therefore, raise questions for both science and morality, and neither can be addressed altogether independently of the other. But whereas the need for scientific information is well understood and well known, that for moral deliberation can often be overlooked. The concern here has been first to redress that imbalance and secondly to make clearer what will be the main focus of this book.

Theory and practice

Allowing, then, that many of our fundamental problems are moral, concerning what we ought to do to improve the shape of the world, can the case be made that the problems are thus ones that philosophy, in particular, is equipped to answer? Or are there, as some will suspect, two objections to be made here: first that moral problems are best addressed in other ways, through appeal to tradition, or religion, or, as with much of politics, through a haphazard and piecemeal striving towards consensus; and secondly that philosophy is essentially inert, able to describe and analyse our thinking, but ill equipped to offer any genuine practical advice? To answer these questions I begin with two reminders: first about the need for scepticism over precise definitions; and second about my preference for a broader understanding of philosophy's range of concerns. And so without trying to say exactly what it is, we might well think of philosophy as wanting to apply the methods of reason and argument to those larger moral, epistemological and metaphysical questions – what is the world like? how can we know it? how should we act within it? – with which we are all from time to time confronted. It contrasts with science, economics and history in that its work begins after the empirical information is in, and it contrasts with art, literature and certain forms of mysticism in that its choice of method always puts an emphasis on clarity and reason. This is rough and ready, but enough to make plausible the relevance of philosophy to issues concerning the environment.

Given this, it will appear that in certain respects philosophical inquiry overlaps with some of the alternatives proposed here, and offers procedures for settling disagreement about the environment that, with certain qualifications, will mesh well with those alternatives. Consider tradition. Very few people claim that we should follow the past dogmatically, building, fishing, farming and living together as did our ancestors with no thought as to why this should be so. The argument for tradition is either that the old ways have genuine merits as they stand, or that even though changes are called for, caution is the best policy. Either way, a belief in traditional solutions to environmental problems is defensible, if at all, by appeal to reason and argument. Similarly for religion. Even those who most appear to recommend unquestioning allegiance to some religious perspective do so, usually, because they believe, and think they have reasons to believe, that this will be for the best, either in this life or the next. Faith is rarely altogether blind. And again for politics. Although it is always tempered by considerations of expediency, political debate does centre around wide-ranging visions of the best life, on the one hand, and decisions as to the best strategies for realizing that vision, on the other. And only a cynic will deny that rational conversation plays a substantial role within almost all such debate. So these supposed alternatives to philosophy, as general procedures for addressing questions of value and morality, are not really alternatives at all, but themselves embody philosophical concerns.

One suggestion that might at first appear to scotch this claim about the relevance of philosophy to the environment will turn out not to do so. For suppose that the sceptic insists that although there is the appearance of disagreement about what we should do, and though we undoubtedly go through certain motions designed to settle that disagreement, morality remains for all that an illusion. Environmentalists have certain views about the way they want the world to be, while hunters, developers and profiteers have others. There are differing tastes, but in the end no absolutes of right and wrong. Like many others, I reject this sceptical account, but even if it were true, it isn't obviously true. And if you are to persuade me of its truth, it seems that there is no option but to engage in philosophical conversation in order to get that truth across.

This point is important, not only in showing how philosophy is unavoidable, but also in leading to a distinction, genuinely useful even if less than exact, between normative or applied ethics on the one hand, and ethical theory or meta-ethics on the other. Our practical concern is in knowing what to do. We are looking for some sort of rules to govern our behaviour, to help judge the behaviour of others, and to help settle disputes between us. Familiar examples will include the claim that killing is always wrong, the injunction not to steal, or the suggestion that we should act charitably, justly and in other supposedly virtuous ways. Philosophy often hopes to provide such rules, not simply by fiat, but through reflection and conversation, testing proposed rules against real and imaginary situations, seeing how they fit together, what they individually and collectively imply, and considering their relationship to our everyday beliefs and intuitions. The aim here is to offer a coherent, rationally defensible and viable picture of how we ought to live. But as well as this, and as important, philosophy often wants to explore the several assumptions that lie behind the formulation of such rules, considering the meaning of and relationships between such terms as right and wrong, good and bad; thinking about the general character of moral beliefs; reflecting on the relevance of reason to moral behaviour; and so on. Indeed, for the first half of the twentieth century these highly abstract and theoretical questions were considered the only ones with which philosophy could respectably be concerned; actually telling people what to do was thought best left to priests and policemen. That austere and uncompromising picture of the philosophical enterprise has now very much been abandoned, with most writers doubting the viability of any precise distinction and, even if themselves inclining to one approach rather than the other, allowing nevertheless the validity and importance of both.

This meta-ethical activity connects with the consideration of environmental problems in at least one very important respect. Consider first the rather general question of what morality is directed to or concerned with, or, more generally still, what a worthwhile world will contain. Typically, and traditionally, what has been thought to be of value is human happiness, or well-being (and perhaps also certain activities not directly connected with well-being, such as truth-telling, acquiring knowledge or being in touch with reality rather than a simulation). And this view has the consequence that what matters, morally speaking, is only that which bears on our happiness or well-being. Such a view has several implications where the environment is concerned. The extinction of species, for example, will not matter unless it matters in the end to us. And the preservation of wilderness would be of no consequence, if it were not for people who valued its preservation. Certain problems can be ignored. But now some of the most important and highly developed thinking about the environment has urged that this view be abandoned, insisting that things other than human well-being matter, not only to us but in themselves. So even if there were no people in the world, it could still be a better or worse, a more or less valuable place, depending on what else is within it.

Thus a great deal of important philosophical activity has been directed to these questions of value, and in particular to the question of how widely the net of intrinsic value, or the value things have in themselves,[10] can be cast. And this activity, although itself abstract and theoretical, has important practical consequences. If, for example, the existence of desert is intrinsically valuable, then we won't have an untrammelled right to cultivate, build upon or in some other way obliterate it. If a species of snail is intrinsically valuable, then road building that threatens the snail's habitat will need to take this into account, quite irrespective of how people feel about snails. Certain development programmes may have to stop.

Major parts of this book will, then, explore the philosophical contribution to these ethical, meta-ethical and value debates. What will need to be explored also is the claim that the contribution works in two directions, for it is often insisted that consideration of the environment has brought about a radical overhaul of philosophical thinking, whereas in areas like business or medical ethics, where the point is to apply philosophy as it is to a given set of problems, the complexity of our relationship to the environment has demanded very substantial revisions to a number of fundamental philosophical beliefs. I have mentioned only questions of morality and value, but it has been insisted that environmental problems necessitate similarly radical reappraisals of other areas of philosophy as well. Environmental philosophy, then, is seen not simply as the bringing to bear of an established discipline on a particular subject matter, but rather the forging of a new programme of study, demanding a different kind of expertise. What substance there is to such claims, and how, if at all, they are to be made out, are among the central concerns of this book.

Further terms

Philosophy has a bearing on the environment in several ways. One of them, as I say, is in encouraging, where possible, the drawing of clear distinctions. It isn't always possible. The distinction between an environmental problem and some other sort of problem is not always clear-cut. Even so, this doesn't prevent us from recognizing, in very many cases, that we are faced with what is indisputably an environmental issue. And now within this complex network of issues certain further distinctions, even if not always perfectly clear, can usefully be drawn. Then, when we have drawn them, it can be asked how they might relate, first to one another, and secondly to some of our characteristic environmental concerns.

First, there are problems of pollution. These occur when some part of the environment is degraded or spoiled by the presence of an excess of alien material. The damage caused by oil spillage, such as that caused by the 1989 grounding of the *Exxon Valdez* in Prince William Sound, Alaska, is a prime example, as too, although often less visible, is the pollution caused to water supplies when, as in a notorious situation in Cornwall, poisonous chemicals somehow get into the reservoirs. When people think of pollution they often think first of dirt. But these days many people are prepared to talk as well about noise pollution caused, perhaps, by air force jets on training missions, or even light pollution, as when a completely dark night can no longer be experienced near cities.[11] Pollution can harm human beings, as in the case above, but it can also harm animals or plants, as when fish are killed by some spillage of poison into the rivers or seas. Evidently the identifications here presuppose some quasi-moral evaluation of both the alleged pollutants and the environment that is affected. That there is such a thing as light pollution, for example, is a relatively recent idea, and demands not only an understanding of the effects of light on the behaviours of plants and animals (including human beings) but the judgement that these effects are adverse, not only on certain individuals, but in some way on the environment as a whole. It has to be understood thus, surely, for the alternatives are too narrow or too wide. We don't think of pollution as affecting only human beings, but recognize its consequences for animal and plant life as well. But we don't think of all alien materials as pollutants, even though they almost all have negative effects somewhere or other. Organic insecticide, good for roses but bad for greenfly, is only tendentiously described as a pollutant.

Secondly, there are problems of conservation. It is often said that we are using natural resources – materials such as zinc, copper or oil, and living, and so theoretically renewable, resources such as trees or fish – at an unacceptable rate. We have current need of such resources, but as both we and our descendants will have similar needs in the future, so we are required to conserve stocks. With renewable resources the hope is that their depletion might be indefinitely delayed, while with finite resources it is rather that they will last until an alternative is found. Otherwise our descendants will have no such resources available. Conservation, as I have described it here, and indeed as the term is typically employed, refers to those things that are of use to human beings. But nothing stands in the way of our choosing to conserve resources for the sake of a species other than our own.

Thirdly, there are issues concerning preservation. In contrast to the managed use of resources, preservation is desired for things that should be saved, not for later use, but just because it is good that they continue to exist, either for essentially aesthetic reasons, or in relation to their scientific interest, or – although perhaps this is in the end deeply mysterious – simply for their own sakes. In most cases, those who object to land development are not proposing that the land be used in a different way, or set aside for later use. They want the land preserved in its present state because they believe it to be valuable just as it is. And closely connected with preservation is restoration. Sometimes it seems not enough to keep things as they are; we have to try to turn the clock back. In many of Britain's national parks invasive and alien plants, such as rhododendrons and various conifers, are being replaced with indigenous species in an attempt to restore habitats to something closer to their natural state.

These distinctions are real enough, but the terminology as outlined here is not always consistently applied. In particular, conservation is often used with a wider meaning than that given above, covering ground for which preservation might be a more appropriate term. It has, too, in its broader sense, the longer history, for some sort of concern for future resources, putting aside seed for the next year's harvest, keeping enough cattle, sheep or hens for breeding purposes, has always been an essential feature of agrarian and post-agrarian life. But conservation as a self-professed activity, a distinct aspect of land management, became established only relatively recently, and particularly in North America when, once it was discovered that frontiers are finite and that there are not always new lands to discover, a rapid depletion in natural resources became very quickly evident. Both the redwood forests and the buffalo herds of the plains were, particularly during the last years of the nineteenth century, being destroyed at a wholly unsustainable rate. And conservation has the more evident rationale. That a country should want not to run out of gas or water, that it should seek to maintain fish stocks, or a supply of wood or clay, can all seem to be perfectly comprehensible concerns. Only if there is good reason to think that demand will cease is it sensible to fail to attend to supply. This is not to skate over an assumption. If conservation issues are to become pressing, then this is because of a belief that we do have duties to future generations. It may seem obvious that we do, but that assumption can be challenged.

Preservation, in the West, a still more recent concern, raises more evident and less tractable problems. Although in many cases the results will be the same – both conservationists and preservationists will have an interest in fish stocks, both will be concerned that forests are maintained – the rationale is different. Conservationists are concerned usually with longer-term human benefit, while preservationists have their sights elsewhere. But where, exactly? A concern with landscape, like a concern for architecture or painting, might be explained in terms of human satisfactions of the non-material kind, but in many cases there are conflicts between preservation and access, with only handfuls of people being permitted to enter some wilderness area. But the idea of preserving land for its own sake, rather than for ours, raises a number of deep questions as to the sorts of values things can have, and the extent to which we should want to sustain these values. And these questions are especially troubling where aesthetic values are concerned. It can appear that certain areas are first singled out because they appeal to us, but are then claimed to be independently valuable.

This distinction between conservation and preservation – managing for our benefit, and leaving as is – shouldn't be confused with another distinction with which it might, but need not, overlap, and that's the distinction between radical and minimal, or even zero, intervention. Early in the twentieth century, a series of environmental problems persuaded some scientists that our ability to manage the environment had been greatly overestimated. The unforeseen consequences of large-scale eradication of so-called bird and animal pests, the 1930s dustbowl in the Midwestern states of the USA and the overuse of insecticides such as DDT all did much to undermine faith in the quick technological fix. Although many influential scientists continued to believe that we had merely to refine the science and technologies needed, an increasing number of environmentalists and ecologists began to argue that nature is best able to manage itself, and that human intervention is always counterproductive. But the hands-on and the hands-off approaches are each consistent with both conservation and preservation. Someone concerned to best manage future renewable resources, aimed at the long-term human good, might well argue that the minimalist intervention will work best. Less plausibly, but still possibly, it might be claimed that a fairly heavy dose of science and technology is needed in order to best serve those things that should be preserved for their own sake.

These particular varieties of environmental concern, as I have outlined them so far, pay less attention to the situation of animals than might be expected. So two further issues might be mentioned here. There are, first, several concerns about extinction. Plants, insects and even simpler creatures are becoming extinct at what appears to be an alarming rate, but much of the popular concern is focused on higher, and larger animals. How is this to be understood? It is sometimes a conservation issue, for example when people are concerned about running out of some tasty fish. More often it is a matter for preservation: people want to save whales, or tigers, or skylarks to look at, rather than to use. And sometimes it connects with pollution, as when we take extinction as a sign that we are degrading natural habitats. It is a mistake, then, to think of all our concerns about extinction as having the same sort of rationale.

Secondly, there is a growing concern for animal liberation, as increasing numbers of people oppose the sorts of conditions to which we habitually subject many different kinds of animals, by breeding and keeping them in factory farms, laboratories and zoos, on the one hand, and also by hunting, shooting and fishing, more often in the name of sport than of food, on the other. Whether these concerns are properly thought of as environmental is a much debated point, and I consider this in greater detail later in the book. My conclusion, perhaps by now predictably, will be that the attempt to draw a sharp distinction here is ill judged. Nevertheless, there are certain differences between this sort of concern for animal welfare, on the one hand, and many of the more obvious environmental concerns, on the other.

Clarity and action

The major aim of this book is to encourage an understanding of environmental problems. It is not a manual for solving those problems. And this is not simply because the book is in certain respects incomplete, lacking any detailed advice on how to put its precepts into practice. It is for further reasons.

First, as will emerge, while I don't claim any principled scepticism about practical philosophy, and have no worked-out theory as to why this should so often be unsatisfying, I do have doubts as to whether many of our real-life moral problems have any clear or straightforward solutions. The aim here is to show something of how far we can go towards such solutions, believing that the effort is worthwhile, and that much of importance will be uncovered along the way, even if in the end the pickings are thin. Secondly, I have doubts about the overall value of reason, argument, clarity, level-headedness and other supposed intellectual virtues where much of ordinary life is concerned. This doubt is at one level very easy to defend – it is surely clear that if we were all to succeed all of the time in being rational the world would be a seriously impoverished place, with little in the way of music, poetry, football, glitzy shops and the like. But the doubt is perhaps much more widely defensible than this. Consider morality. It isn't reason that causes mothers to care for their children, or the bereaved to show respect for the dead, or most of us, most of the time, to obey the law. Nature, custom, habit and tradition play the more dominant roles. Now it might be said that even if reason doesn't explain why we act as we do, that it doesn't motivate us, still what we do, when we do the right thing, is compatible with reason. If we were to think long and carefully about it we would still continue to tell the truth, obey the law, be less than thoroughly selfish. But scepticism about such a claim has a long and impressive history. It is far from clear that we have reasons to behave morally. And what we might reasonably want, a world in which families stick together, where there are people prepared to tend to the sick, and where keeping promises is very much the norm, may well be a world less likely to obtain if people were always reasonable.

How exactly does this connect with the environment? Go back to the distinctions above. They are real enough. And in certain cases it will be clear as to what type of problem a given situation presents. But in many cases it will be less clear. There is little reason to expect such distinctions to map onto environmental concerns in any straightforward and evident way. First, many cases are complex, and involve a range of concerns. Pollution of the atmosphere by acid rain has widespread effects, and will interfere with both conservation and preservation programmes. Attempts at the restoration of natural forest, as in Scotland, can undermine conservation efforts directed at indigenous wildlife. Should we nevertheless be as clear as we can be about such distinctions? Consider one case: the protracted dispute about the Newbury by-pass in Berkshire. Some people argued that road building offered only a short-term solution to a long-term problem, and that benefits to local people and local businesses would be negligible. Others, closer to the proposed route, objected to the pollution caused by increased traffic, while still others wanted to preserve the area, either for its own sake, or for the sake of the animals living within it, or as one component in a wholesale objection to the politics of development. And it often seemed as if those involved were both confused and confusing about the exact nature of their objections. Perhaps, though, there are reasons for preferring this. You might think that a vague and muddled objection, rather than one that is precisely focused, will draw on different kinds of support. A thousand votes against some policy might seem more powerful if it never emerges that those objecting have different and sometimes conflicting reasons to object. You might also think that if protesters are altogether clear about the complexities of the situations with which they engage, they will be less enthusiastic about, or committed to, their protest. The arguments against GM foods, nuclear power, or fox-hunting, like those against roads, are rarely as straightforward and decisive as many objectors seem to believe, but we may value their resistance never-theless. Getting clear, making distinctions and being philosophical can encourage inertia.

Summary

One danger in considering such a big and seemingly pressing issue as the state of environment is that you never get started. Another is that you jump straight in, paying no attention to the preliminary issues that ask to be addressed. In this opening chapter I have wanted to defend the idea of a middle ground. We can adopt a working account of the key terms – environment, environmentalism and the like – while acknowledging that several variant accounts are not without merit, and cannot be proved to be wrong. Similarly for further terms, such as preservation, conservation and pollution, which then give structure to discussion of the environment, providing something like a taxonomy of its problems. Again, the main point is to uncover certain distinctions that might usefully be made, even if these distinctions are not always precise, and even if the mapping between terms and distinctions might be differently construed.

I have wanted also to say something of the relationship between science and philosophy, where the environment is concerned. Although there are countless questions of a scientific kind, many of which need to be pursued if our understanding of the environment, and its changes, is to be at all secure, we cannot address these alone. For we want also to know how to respond to these changes, which to welcome, which to regret, which we should try to avert, and science cannot answer moral and value questions like these. Nor can we be rightly persuaded that they have no answers, such that beyond the boundaries of science everything is a matter of taste, or feeling. The role for a philosophical approach to environmental problems is, I have argued, both real and substantial.

What would the environment be like if we were all, as philosophy would have us, highly reasonable in the attitudes we take towards it? As will emerge, it is far from clear that it would be in all respects more as environmentalists would prefer it. Further, and more bluntly, it is far from clear that it would be in a better shape. Perhaps there are things that we ought to want, and that would benefit the environment, but are less likely to want if we are thoroughly reasonable. But this book isn't intended to benefit the environment: it is intended to get us to think more clearly about it.

CHAPTER 2

Causes

.

There are problems for the environment. We might argue about how many and how serious they are, but global warming, damage to the ozone layer, destruction of the rainforest, mass extinctions and running down of fish stocks in many of the world's seas are incontrovertibly cause for concern. So, too, are a range of more local problems: tankers run aground; dangerous chemicals leach into the water supply; the countryside continues to fall to the bulldozer, giving way to yet more shops, houses, roads and storage depots; and sparrows, thrushes and skylarks disappear. There are vastly fewer butter-flies. Almost no one is complacent about all this.

We can ask about causes. Particular situations are brought about in particular ways. And although in some cases at least an important part of the cause is evident – ships sink because someone was asleep, and cutting down rainforests is at least in part caused by short-term agricultural demand – in others, as with the disappearance of sparrows, technical and scientific work needs to be done. Suppose, as many believe, that these and other problems coalesce into something like an environmental crisis. This may not be quite the right word, but it ought not to be denied that there are a number of seemingly serious and often interconnected problems facing the world today. We can ask a further question about causes. Is there any underlying explanation for this present wide-scale predicament? Any answer here will not be couched in purely scientific terms. It will need to refer to certain complex phenomena within human history. And there is a further question. It is undeniable that there are problems facing the environment. It is even more undeniable that there is widespread belief that there are such problems. We can ask, how are these current levels of awareness, how is this environ-mentalism, to be explained? The answer here, too, will refer to human history.

History

How long has this situation been going on? It is often suggested that the so-called environmental crisis is a peculiarity of our own time, and in large part generated by the habits and attitudes of our modern, often materialist lives. It is very different from how it was. Until recently most of the population lived in close proximity to the land, and were obliged to understand, care for and respect it. They lived in smaller communities, moved less often and had a sense of place, a respect for the past and a concern for the future. The rhythms of the day and of the year played a much bigger part in everyday life, as limitations in lighting, heating and food production in particular demanded a closer connection between the human and non-human worlds. But since the nineteenth century, the growth of industrialization, and the subsequent shifts of populations from the countryside into cities, and then, increasingly, further shifts from city to city and from country to country, have severed these links with the natural world, and left most people with little sense of their relationship to the land, and to the sources of their food, power and other materials of their lives. Severed too are the links between people themselves as the rootlessness endemic in modern urban living fosters involvement only with oneself and one's immediate family, undermining identifications with and concerns for the larger community. Nor are such changes confined to urban life. The countryside itself is altered almost beyond recognition: depopulated; managed by only a handful of, usually, men, and viewed by them as just another business, a food factory, to be run as efficiently as possible, with whatever technological and biotechnological means are to hand.

Many of these changes, or so it is said, encourage and are encouraged by a global economy, as the increasing sophistication both in methods of manufacture and products themselves reduce the opportunities for small-scale and local initiatives to make any significant contribution to satisfying our most basic needs. As goods and services are increasingly brought in from afar, as it becomes cheaper to holiday in Malaya than in a local hotel, as the food in supermarkets betrays little evidence of the changing seasons, as building design and materials lose touch with local styles and traditions, our understanding of time, our loyalty to place and our concern for strangers are all systematically eroded.

No blame is put on individuals. There is neither the motivation nor the opportunity for us to acquire knowledge of and concern for our local environment. We can hardly be expected to be other than indifferent to nature's misfortune. But as we cannot be held responsible, so, too, can we not be expected to do much to remedy the situation. We inhabit, precariously, a world we little understand and are unable to control. Only recently have such changes taken place, and only recently has the environment found itself in such a mess.

This is too neat. Certainly many of these changes have occurred, but not enough of them to explain our current problems. It is clear that the material living conditions for most people have changed immensely, although in ways that many would argue are very much to our benefit. It is less clear that attitudes to the natural world have altered to any marked degree. Ours is not the only age in which people have shown themselves insensitive to the environmental consequences of their actions, nor the only age in which, as a matter of course, the most economical, cost-effective course of action is the one most likely to be pursued.

We worry about the extinction of species, but it was not we but our very distant ancestors who, it seems, wiped out the mammoth. New Zealand has no indigenous mammals, but this is because the Maoris, within the past thousand years, have exterminated them. It is a similar story where other forms of life are concerned. Easter Island is notorious for its lack of trees. But it wasn't thus until warring tribes lost their sense of a nature in balance, and cut them down at an irreplaceable rate.[1] Less dramatic but no less substantial change has occurred much closer to home. Wolves and wild boar were hunted to extinction in Britain not recently but centuries ago. And the shape of the English countryside, those aspects that we most admire, and much of which still remains, are the results of long-term human intervention. The Yorkshire Dales were once impenetrable forest, cleared, in the main, in the Middle Ages. Their character, like that of the Lake District, the Sussex Downs and much of Wales, is shaped by free-enterprise farming. Mixed woodland, dry-stone walls, hedgerows, vernacular architecture, the patchwork of fields that, although constantly under threat, continues to be a characteristic of so great a part of the English countryside[2] – all these things exist not so much because people were following environmentally sensitive policies, or were in dogged pursuit of the picturesque, but because they were the most cost-effective ways of increasing production, and of accumulating wealth. If today we grub out hedges, plant conifers and rape, or sell off land to developers, we are pursuing the same sorts of policies and betraying the same general attitudes as those of our distant ancestors.

We worry about pollution. But the world is not obviously a dirtier place today than it was four hundred years ago. Towns, rivers and the air we breathe are all, in many areas, much cleaner now than they have been for hundreds of years. Our food, in spite of recent and well-publicized scares, is today much safer to eat. Pollution is more widespread today than it was, but this is because there are more people and more cities than there were. Even so, in many of the industrialized countries there is less pollution. This reduction in pollution is brought about largely by legislation, but even if there is more litter in the streets than there was in the 1950s, there is no reason to think that general attitudes have changed for the worse in the past two centuries or so.

We suspect ourselves of having short-term and self-interested concerns, in contrast to those of the past. People used to plant trees for the future, but now we dig them up. This too is a gross distortion of the facts. Even though, because of roads, cities, airports and so on much less land is available, there are more trees in England today than there were in the eighteenth century.[3] Admittedly, many people will argue that they are of the wrong kind and in the wrong place, but this is arguably a subtlety, and the bigger picture is nothing like as bad as is often supposed.

There is, in short, no sea change from the love of nature. Indeed, quite the opposite can be argued. Our recent times are remarkable for our concern with preserving the past and resisting change, and with an increasing worry over the balance between our material and spiritual concerns. Rather than an occasion for gloom, the current widespread concern about the environment should be cause for cautious optimism.

This is not to suggest that all is well, nor to deny that deeply significant changes have occurred during the past couple of hundred years, but they concern technology rather than attitudes. Earlier human interventions within the natural world were on the whole localized, modest and impermanent. There have been very many exceptions to this,[4] but in general the means for the more blatant intrusions on the natural environment were simply not available. Building, mining and farming had no option but to take account of local conditions and local materials. Roads, canals and even railways had to find an accommodation with the land that they wanted to cross. And because transport was expensive and slow, and mass-production techniques were unavailable, whole ranges of goods had to be produced locally. Hence the variety within the landscape – woods, coppices, mixed farming, small but complex villages, watermills, fishponds – that we still admire.[5] Hunting, shooting and fishing were similarly inconvenienced by the modest equipment available, and in most cases it just wasn't possible to kill at a rate that would threaten the future viability of the resource. Waste products tended to be organic, moderately toxic at worst, and to degrade fairly quickly back into the environment. Virtually all of this has now changed. The fallout from Chernobyl, the scale of tree felling, both in tropical rainforests and western USA, and the rate at which fish stocks can be depleted are just three instances of how modern technologies can allow us to make an unprecedented and immediate impact on the natural world. The ease of transportation leads to a stultifying uniformity the world over. And complex biochemical materials, in fertilizers, herbicides, plastics, paints and so on, make pollution problems both longer lasting and at times less immediately evident than previously they were.

So although modern life presents undeniable dangers to the environment, these derive more from the sophistication of the technologies available than from any increase in short-sightedness, irreverence or plain greed on the part of human beings. We are probably not more wicked than our ancestors, but we are more dangerously equipped.[6]

Culture

There is a second, in some ways competing, account, and that is to contrast not the present with the past, but our own Western or European culture with others that have shaped thinking elsewhere. On this account fairly large parts of the world have for a long time adopted the wrong attitude towards the environment, while in other larger parts, different cultures have had different, environmentally more beneficial effects. If there has now been a recent and large-scale turn for the worse, this is simply because European culture has been so successfully exported, taking its evils with it. There are the same problems to confront, but their origins reach much further back.

Religion, science and philosophy

In particular, first Christianity and secondly the European philosophical tradition are held to stand behind and generate our fairly systematic disregard for the condition of the natural world. Other traditions, deriving from different religions, and having, as a result of that, different attitudes to both philosophy and science are, in contrast, friendlier towards the environment, and are better able to promote its well-being.

Some of the detail of this account, initially and most influentially advanced by the American historian Lynn White,[7] is worth exploring. Although he thinks that the "ecologic crisis" is only recently upon us, White attributes this to the synthesis, in the mid-nineteenth century, of the hitherto effectively separate disciplines of science and technology, and connects this, in turn, to that century's increasing democratization. The upshot is to collect together and release into the world a series of forces that, while remaining separate, were unable to effect the sorts of massive and potentially devastating change with which we now have to deal. But much of the interest in White's account is in the story he tells of why science, technology and democracy should figure so much larger in the West than elsewhere. The dominance of North European models of science and technology in particular is, as is well known, hardly recent, and is commonly linked with the Renaissance and secularization, but in tracing much of this back to the first millennium White is able to argue for a much closer connection between these successes and religious, specifically Christian thought than is normally suggested.

How, though, are religion and science coupled together? On White's account, science can be seen to gets its blessing, and nature its downfall, even within the creation stories at the beginning of the Bible, for the claim there is that God created man in his image, to "rule the fish in the sea, the birds in heaven, the cattle, all wild animals on earth, and all reptiles that crawl upon the earth".[8] And God tells Adam and Eve that ruling in this way is required of them, but not them alone, for they should "Be fruitful and increase, fill the earth and subdue it".[9] What we might learn from this is that we are close to God, distant and different from nature and, so far as the earth itself is concerned, more or less in charge. We learn also that people are good, and that more are better. It is unsurprising, then, that we believe ourselves warranted in developing and using science and technology to control and populate the natural world. To do this is to do God's work.

It is not yet clear that there is anything specifically Christian in all this, but Christianity rather than Old Testament Judaism features in White's account in relation to the third element in the amalgam. It is specifically Christianity, with its emphasis on the intrinsic worth of all people, and our equal value in the sight of God, that helps explain the eventual triumph of democracy. That, in turn, leads to a further increase in scientific and technological change, as impediments to developments are eroded, and markets for alleged improvements expand. With all three elements in place, and with their ongoing endorsement by the major religious traditions, the prospects for the environment are poor. Nor have we much hope of dismantling only the superstructure; what we need, White insists, is nothing less than a new religion.

The focus in White's account is very much on the connections between science and religion, but other writers, in a line of thought that complements his, have identified the dominant philosophical tradition as a companion in guilt. Western philosophy starts, and first flourishes, with the pagans of ancient Greece. But there too, in initially different ways, views are put forward that permit or encourage environmental double standards. Socrates, Plato and, perhaps particularly, Aristotle insist on rationality as marking a clear and significant difference between human beings on the one hand, and the rest of nature on the other. Here too we stand apart. As is well documented, the two traditions coalesce, and just as Platonism affects Christianity, noticeably in relation to Pauline doctrine, so also do Christian ideas very soon exert their influence over philosophical thinking and concerns. This occurs most notably first with Plotinus, is significantly advanced by Augustine and, with Aquinas, issues in a system of views that insists both on the hierarchy of God, man, animals and plants and also that we, ensouled and rational, are distinct from the rest of nature.

Renaissance and post-Renaissance thinking, although increasingly less full of God, is nevertheless unable or unwilling to set itself free of this Christian doctrine. Bacon's optimism about technology, and Descartes's account of the mind and consciousness, represent two different but complementary and deeply influential ways of marking the distinction. The non-human world throughout consists of a fundamentally different sort of stuff, and a stuff that presents no moral impediment to being fashioned and manipulated as best suits us. So dualism is not a feature of the Cartesian philosophy alone, but has both a long history and a range of current influences. We are encouraged, the story goes, first to distinguish between the mind and the body, secondly to rank the former above the latter, and thirdly to deny that mind is possessed of by things other than God on the one hand, and the images of God, namely ourselves, on the other.

This story too has, in all its major strands, certain shortcomings. We can, first, match text for text, and counter those biblical passages with others that sustain a different interpretation. John Passmore, in particular, in one of the earliest full-length treatments of our relationship to the environment, has argued that White's reading, in which we have dominion over nature, has no better warrant than an alternative stewardship account.[10] Certainly we are to look after and care for the natural world, but this is not at all to suggest that we can do with it as we will. And not only are the texts ambiguous, but their hermeneutics is rather less consistent than might be supposed. White himself offers St Francis of Assisi, hardly a marginal figure within the Christian tradition, as an alternative exemplar, proposing that he become the patron saint of ecologists.[11]

Nor can the later philosophical tradition be presented as quite so uniform as this suggests. I will need to return to certain details, but here make just a pair of points, and briefly. While some point to the Renaissance as a critical turning point, others fasten on the Enlightenment as the juncture at which an atheistic, rationalist and materialist philosophy left the academy to be disseminated among the wider world (which, with eighteenth- and nine-teenth-century exploration and colonization, was getting wider all the time) with, for the environment, seriously negative results. Again, this is too simple. First, utilitarianism, which insists on the moral relevance of all pleasures and pains, can itself be traced back to the Enlightenment. That philosophy gives hope to animals. And secondly, it is precisely around the time of the Enlightenment that a substantially deeper interest in and respect for nature begins to characterize much of Western thought and practice. Mention might be made of English landscape gardening and its respect for natural form; Burke's analysis of the beautiful and the sublime and the relation of that analysis to the growing interest in, for example, the Alps and the English Lake District as places to linger in rather than hurry through; Wordsworth's pantheism; and Goethe's painstaking studies in biology and botany in particular.[12] Linnaeus, Lamarck and Lyell are of the period, and then Darwin, and a profound rupturing of the distinction between human and non-human nature, is not far behind. So again, the idea that there is some simple connection between our cultural beliefs and environmental exploitation cannot long be sustained.

There is a deeper issue here. Implicit in White's critique is the suggestion that alternative cultures might do things differently, and better, with respect to the environment. There are many questions of detail as to actual practices here, but allow for the moment that Hindus, Australian Aborigines and South American Indians have in general a closer and more sympathetic relationship with the natural world. We can still ask, do they get this relationship right? What the monotheism of the Judaeo-Christian tradition insists on, as against most polytheistic religions, is that the natural world is not divine, is not infused with spirit, and is not appropriately given the same sort of respect and reverence that we show to human beings and to God. It is often observed that without this distinction not only would we have avoided many of our environmental excesses, but we'd be without most of the benefits of medicine, reliable harvests and the raw materials for clothing, power and homes.[13] But benefits are one thing, and truth is another. One thought is that in drawing just this distinction between man and nature, monotheism has it exactly right. That might be to give the insights of religion more credit than they deserve. Another, more defensible thought, is that there is a fair bit in the distinction to begin with, and, once we have made it, the wherewithal for further refinements. If we now know that the line between human beings and other animals is less sharp than was previously believed, that is because we've been able to investigate, without risking the charge of sacrilege, the true nature of the animal mind. White seems to want to throw a lot away, and his call for a new religion is either to suggest that we bury our heads in the sand, or that there is no real truth to be had, and just different ways of going on.[14]

To suggest, however, as I am suggesting here, that there is something importantly right about the overall picture of the world given to us under the philosophies and religions of the West is not to suggest that nothing can therefore be wrong. As Passmore observes,[15] our underlying modes of thought do encourage the beliefs that we should improve on nature, and that radical intervention to bring about such improvement is, in principle at least, never inappropriate. These views, as is evident, have on occasion proved costly. Still, many will believe that the remedy for our current ills lies within and not without the prevailing culture, which does, after all, always permit and often require a reasoned response to any situation that we might encounter. How can anything other than this be preferred?

Human beings

Something of both these views can be salvaged if we give up on the distinctions between now and then, or us and them, and blame all cultures, all periods for our quandary. The problem lies in something rather more pervasive: human beings.

There are pessimistic and even more pessimistic versions of this account. On the moderate version, environmental problems are always caused by contingently existing human failings, or errors, or greed. These are associated with no particular times or places, even if it is allowed that some circumstances and structures are more encouraging and tolerant of such ills than others. One way of looking at much of modern environmentalism is as arguing for significant changes in our contemporary lifestyles – less competition, less waste, more interaction and communication between different groups of people – without, however, urging any blanket rejection of either the present, or the West. Human beings are a problem, but we might do better. On the gloomier view, these failings are an ineradicable part of human nature, such that our dealings with the environment will always be to its detriment.

Such accounts oversimplify. Environmental problems can emerge quite independently of human beings. We may still be uncertain as to its cause, but there is little denying that things went wrong in the world as far as the dinosaurs were concerned. Some will reject this, insisting that unless human beings are adversely affected, no genuine problem can have occurred. Dinosaurs died out, but there was nothing amiss in this. That, though, is a troublesome view with, as will emerge, many implications that are not easily swallowed. But suppose for the moment that it is right. Still, even the more moderate of the views outlined here is untenable as it stands. Although many problems are indeed attributable to human activity, others are not of our making. It is unclear to what extent recent climate changes have natural causes, and unclear, too, just what hand we have in the current cycle of extinctions. Nevertheless earthquakes, volcanoes and the disappearance of parts of Yorkshire into the North Sea are, more or less incontrovertibly, environmentally damaging occurrences the responsibility for which does not lie with us.[16] To assign all the blame to human beings seems, then, to be an obvious mistake.

The gloomier account fares, of course, even worse. Although there is nothing at all wrong in insisting on the variability of human nature, and in being alive to the evils we can produce, there seems no good reason to paint a wholly one-sided picture. We do bad things, but we do good things as well. No good reason is not, however, the same as no reason at all. And it is worth noting that residues of the second account are probably in play here. For the same Judaeo-Christian story that puts us very close to God, that allegedly encourages our wholesale interventions within the world and that (according to White) is alone among religions in presenting a picture of ongoing progress and perfectibility,[17] also promotes the view that we are all sinful, worthless creatures who, since our justified exclusion from paradise, are destined to fit uncomfortably within the world, suffering under our inherited guilt, steeped in wrongdoing and receiving only the punishment we deserve. There was a golden age, but it is very long ago and irrecoverable. We are fundamentally wicked, while the natural world, even if morally neutral, is, as God observed, good.

There is a profound irony in that some of the most severe critics of human intervention, who lay the blame for that intervention squarely at Christianity's door, can themselves be seen as falling under that same religion's sway. And our understanding of our present situation will not be well served by too heavy a dose of puritanism and self-loathing.

Awareness

Why, then, if in the end there is no deep distinction between some pastoral golden age and our current post-industrial morass, or between Eastern harmony and Western despoliation, or again and more resolutely between human beings and the rest of nature, is there such a widespread concern about the environment and its crises? How is this to be explained?

It is in some parts straightforward. There are problems, we are aware of them, and we, or some of us, respond appropriately. And the present situation is different, even if not deeply different, just because both the extent of the problems – in particular their implications for the whole planet and their other than temporary nature – and our levels of awareness are both greater than they were in the past. Now this is perhaps right enough as it stands, and nothing that has been said about some of the very clean-lined accounts of our difficulties should be taken to suggest otherwise, but there is certainly more to the picture than this. And it is worth making a few more comments here, not so much on the problems we face, but on our current manner of facing them. For if, as I will suggest, that is to some degree without a rational foundation, then it may be that some of the suggestions for remedies will be ill conceived.

The broad shape of this awareness is clear enough. In the first half of the twentieth century, and particularly in the USA, where there was both the finance and the initiative to foster new technologies, and also fewer constraints on their widespread deployment, there occurred a number of events that brought about serious doubts as to technology's efficacy. Most notable among these were the 1930s dust-bowl phenomena in the Midwest, and the overuse, in the 1950s and 1960s, of DDT, with its highly damaging and wholly unexpected consequences for plant and bird life. It was the latter, in particular, once the wider public had become aware of it,[18] that did much to encourage the growth of modern environmentalism. The link between new technologies and big business was, of course, nothing new, and had for a century or so earlier stood behind the industrial successes and imperial ambitions of a number of Western countries, including Britain, Germany and Japan as well as the USA, but what is particularly salient here is the wholesale employment of relatively complex biochemical materials over very large areas in connection with domestic food production. Mistakes here have, inevitably, profound consequences for public confidence in the scientist's word. Salient, too, is the growing belief, particularly in a country as committed to democratic processes as the USA, that the public has a legitimate interest in being informed about and, where appropriate, objecting to all those practices that impinge on their health and well-being.

Other factors, in various ways connected together, helped to stimulate environmental awareness. America's Cold War with the USSR, the subsequent development of nuclear weapons and the testing of such weapons on

Bikini Atoll and elsewhere[19] did much to raise awareness of how precarious was our continued existence on this planet; and the levels of secrecy and distrust surrounding such weapons, along with the increasingly blurred lines between military and industrial technologies, served only to increase scepticism in governments' and science's insistence that all was well. The Vietnam War, targeting mostly peasants in the open countryside, much of it undeniably beautiful, only reinforced doubts about technology's ability to remedy perceived ills. Photographs of our planet taken from space in the 1970s merely underscored the fragility of our situation. Much of the concern here, although now aired in many of the industrial countries of the world, begins with the American experience, and much of it is directed to human involvement, or overinvolvement in nature's ways, but particularly and more recently important in Britain has been the reaction, soft-voiced but long-lasting, to the great storm of 1987. There had already been serious and highly evident losses to Dutch elm disease, but this overnight destruction of thousands of trees, many of them ancient, and most of them concentrated in the south east, led to a quite remarkable resurgence of interest in the natural world.[20]

This is, so far, to mention issues in which our interest is appropriate, and our judgement as to alternatives, even if not methods for realizing them, is often sound. But environmentalism has further interests, some of which may be less legitimate.

There is, first, an increasing awareness of conditions and situations elsewhere in the world. Global tourism is a real option for many in the West, and even for those who don't want or can't afford two weeks in Cuba or Thailand or the Seychelles, colour photography in magazines, film or television makes some knowledge of and interest in distant events very widely available. Indeed, it is often considered a moral duty to be informed about world events, even if one is not expected to do much about them. This knowledge is, however, typically superficial, and often, because of the manner of its presentation, emotionally coloured. And so there is at least a danger that we are led to make judgements about situations that we fail fully to understand, and to underestimate the many differences between distant conditions and those closer to home. Nor is this merely speculative. As is well known, although many of the problems are allegedly global, and information about these problems is available globally, environmentalism has typically local manifestations, most often among educated elites in prosperous Western democracies. Further, our proposals for tackling these problems often involve imposing greater burdens on others than on ourselves. This quite understandably leads to the suspicion that we are either exaggerating the problems or, if they are genuine, offering a too half-hearted response.

The danger here comes from too shallow an understanding of different places. There is a similar danger concerning different times. We have, of course, and perhaps with good reason, lost confidence in the inevitability of progress, and are disinclined merely to assume that the present is better than the past, with the future promising to be better still. But our confidence in and comfort with our current situation may now be at too low an ebb, leading to too great a preoccupation (and one that is wholly new)[21] with times other than our own. Certainly a pronounced concern with the future has been an evident characteristic of much of twentieth-century Western thought, both in academic and popular veins. This may have been in part encouraged by our position at the end of the second millennium, but to explain is not to justify. The future is of concern, and environmentalists are right to insist both on our responsibilities with respect to it, and the potential we have for creating damage that can only with difficulty be undone. Nevertheless, there are reasons for treading very carefully where detailed predictions are concerned, both as to the kinds of needs and desires future generations will have, and the general situations that are then, as a consequence of events now, likely to obtain. There are dangers in crying wolf.[22]

There is also the past. The levels of interest in and respect for the past ought in many ways to be seen as a quite disturbing feature of the present time. We almost certainly know more about the architecture, music, literature, painting, science and philosophy of the past than did any previous age. As with different places, this is encouraged by technologies that permit access to and preservation of the past on a scale unimaginable only a generation or so ago. But it is encouraged also by dissatisfaction with the products of the present, which in relation to past achievements often appear simply pale. Again, however, there is a danger that much of this is ill informed, uncritical and ultimately stultifying, as when it becomes almost impossible to demolish or alter an otherwise nondescript old building, or when a programme of popular classics will steal both audiences and funding from less familiar but more challenging contemporary works. And where the environment is concerned this rose-tinted and underinformed vision of past life can seriously distort our understanding of what ought to be done, and why. This bears on preservation and restoration projects in particular. At least in Britain, almost all of our efforts, and almost all of our interest, are directed to sustaining or recovering a somewhat sanitized picture of rural life of, at most, a couple of hundred years ago.[23] No one wants the countryside as it was in the Middle Ages. It may seem different in countries like the USA and Australia, where environmentalists' concern is often directed to supposed areas of wilderness, but it should be remembered, first, that those countries too have been populated, although sparsely, for thousands of years, and secondly, that even wilderness undergoes change. So either we select, for reasons having more to do with familiarity or nostalgia than ecological good sense, some otherwise arbitrary time-slice, or we fashion an essentially fictitious vision of nature's past, and set about its creation.

Do causes matter?

I have sketched out three accounts of the origins of our current environmental problems, and suggested that all of them are in some ways wanting. But why bother? What if they were true? It is worth considering why, other than for reasons of historical curiosity, we should care to make discoveries about causes.

It may appear a luxury. Imagine that we discover an asteroid is on a collision course for earth. The important thing is to try to prevent this; it doesn't matter why the asteroid is where it is. Or consider a real case. When the *Exxon Valdez* ran aground, the pressing problem, for environmentalists, was to counter the effects. Those effects could be addressed without any understanding of why the ship had sunk. But these are special cases for two reasons. First, it is often not clear exactly what the nature of a certain phenomenon is, unless there is available some explanation of its origin. There are medical analogies. Although it may appear unnecessary for a doctor to discover just how I broke my arm, backache can have many explanations, and appropriate suggestions for its remedy will require investigation into its cause. The same is true for many environmental problems. There is simply nothing that can be done about the disappearance of sparrows unless we can discover why their numbers are falling, and there is little to be done about rising sea levels (we can build sea walls, the equivalent of bringing a sticking plaster to suppurating wounds) unless we can understand what is bringing this about. Secondly, there are cases where, although we can already take effective action to prevent the occurrence, or counter the effects of a particular phenomenon, a knowledge of causes will help gauge the chances of a repetition. It is important to know why tankers founder even if, in the immediate aftermath, there are more pressing concerns.

I have been discussing here only the immediate and near immediate causes of particular phenomena. But the overall concern in this chapter has been with the underlying causes, if any, of the current spate of problems. Nevertheless, the last of the above points is relevant here. Even if in every case where a problem comes to notice there is reason to address that problem directly, there is still value in considering whether there is any deeper pattern to this and to further, perhaps seemingly unrelated, problems. A good doctor will take this approach to their patient, and an epidemiologist will do likewise when clusters of patients present with similar symptoms or diseases. And one benefit here is that hitherto unnoticed problems might more easily be detected, and further problems might be prevented. Similarly for the environment: if we find that a host of apparently disconnected problems are similarly explained, then in addressing this we will reduce the incidence of such problems.

There is, therefore, no principled objection to this interest in an underlying explanation of our present environmental concerns. But there are reservations that can be aired about some of the particular arguments that are employed here. Consider White. He identifies science and technology, and behind them Christianity, as leading to our current problems. To avoid the effects we must look to the cause. And so we will find no remedy in further applications of science. And Christianity has to go.[24] This is a familiar line of argument among environmentalists, insisting, as here, that as science got us into this mess, so it cannot show us the way out or, alternatively and more generally, that as a faith in reason has brought things to a head, so that faith must now be abandoned.

The argument is, however, no good. There is a quick response, and one that takes a little more time. The quick response is to point out that there is bad science, and faulty reasoning. We must try harder. The longer response considers causal connections in a little more detail.

Suppose we understand causes in terms of sufficient conditions. President Kennedy's death was caused by gunshot wounds to his head. Given certain background conditions, such wounds are enough to bring about death, but it doesn't follow that were it not for these wounds he would have lived; there might have been further gunmen waiting, the car might have crashed, and so on. If we are thinking in terms of sufficient conditions, we cannot say that to avoid the effect we must avoid the cause. Some further sufficient condition might be present.

Suppose instead we think of necessary conditions. An explosion was caused by a build-up of gas. Still, this doesn't guarantee the explosion; if it hadn't been for the match, no explosion would have occurred. If we are thinking of necessary conditions, then, we similarly cannot say that to avoid the effect we must avoid the cause. Some further necessary condition might be absent. In many cases our understanding of causation is looser than this. The claim that smoking causes lung cancer is widely understood and widely believed, but it is implausible to suggest that smoking is either necessary or sufficient for lung cancer. Some non-smokers contract the disease anyway, and many smokers die of other causes. Only if we understand a cause as being both necessary and sufficient for its effect can we rightly claim that to avoid the effect we must avoid the cause. Very few, if any, standard claims as to causal connections can be understood this way and certainly not the relationship between Christianity and our current environmental problems. And equally certainly not the relationship between science and technology and those problems. Because the whole notion of causation is somewhat vague, and because the aetiology of our environmental problems is manifestly complex, we ought to resist any pat solutions.

Summary

Set aside the question of whether our current situation is really one of crisis. Still, many things, perhaps very many things, are wrong. Is there any general explanation for this? Several well-aired views have been rejected. We are not conspicuously more greedy, more thoughtless or more hostile to nature's well-being than were our ancestors. We can't blame religion, or philosophy, for instilling in us the false belief that nature is there to be exploited. And we're unable reasonably to suppose that human beings are somehow responsible for all the world's ills as if, were it not for us, all would be well. This is to deny neither that there are a number of serious and often related issues – climate change, extinctions, deforestation, energy sources – facing us today, nor that there is something useful to be said in accounting for them. And it has been suggested that modern technology, and the technology that then allows for technology's spread, although it has in many ways brought improvements to our lives, has also led to a proliferation of environmental problems. Change, much of it unwelcome, and much of it wide-ranging, occurs now at an unprecedented rate.

There are, however, two sides to the picture, for the science and technology that enable us to create and export these several environmental problems also lead us to be more fully aware of them than would previously have been possible, and may also offer the means to their solution. Only a simple-minded view of causal connections, I have suggested, will lead us to deny that something akin to a cause cannot also be a cure. We must not be ostriches.

CHAPTER 3

Solutions I: Voting and Pricing

Suppose we agree that, even without a definition, and even without tidy margins, we have a reasonably secure grasp of what many environmental problems are like. Some of these problems are technical: we agree on the solution needed but so far lack the means for its implementation. Others involve disagreement either as to whether a problem exists or, if it does, the shape of its best solution. My focus is on problems of the latter kind, in which there is disagreement as to values. How are such problems to be solved? There have been a number of suggestions. I will consider two in some detail, but need first to mention two more, which can be soon dismissed.

Poor solutions

They can be dismissed because, at least as they stand, they fairly clearly offer no satisfactory response to our problems with the environment. There are, though, components within these familiar if inadequate responses that will surface again in later discussions.

There is no answer, so nothing should be done

Some people believe that although scientific questions have answers, moral questions do not. And so the kinds of environmental problems that we are interested in here, questions of what we ought to do, how we should think about some alleged calamity, whether we're obliged to resist or welcome a pattern of change, similarly have no answers. Different people have different opinions, but neither side is right and neither side wrong. And so there is no point in trying to decide between them.

There are two ways in which someone might reach this position. They might be faint-hearted. Some people are just overwhelmed by the size and the intractability of many of our present-day environmental problems. They see merit on both sides, hear the pros and the cons of argument, and yet find that, as far as they can tell, neither camp has any convincing answers, and neither can muster a compelling case. So they despair. If the answers are this hard to come across, perhaps there just are no answers.

This is one kind of scepticism. There is no commitment here to any kind of theory, the consequences of which are that our environmental problems are unreal, and that there just cannot be solutions to the questions that, at least at first, they appear to raise. Indeed, it may well be acknowledged that there are genuine problems as to what to do, and that answers are, in principle, possible. It is just that we seem unable to discover any.

Others are more robust, insisting that not only are there not, but also there cannot be, answers to moral problems of this or indeed any other kind. Further, the very idea of there being any real problems here is misguided. Morality is, at bottom, a matter of taste or opinion. And while I may have some kind of problem in knowing just what I want, or what my tastes are, and just as we may together have a practical problem of deciding what we will do when our tastes or opinions conflict, there is not, contrary to what the believer in morality seems to hold, any further problem in deciding what really is the right thing. So whether or not lying, stealing and killing are wrong is just a matter of opinion. So, too, is whether women should have an equal place in society as men, the relationship between punishment and crime, issues about abortion or euthanasia, and so on. And so, too, are questions about the environment. Some people want to preserve the countryside, save whales and eat organic food, while others favour development, hunting and hi-tech food. There are different values here, but no way, even in principle, of deciding between them. So the distinction made earlier is even more important than it has so far appeared. Questions of science are real, and have answers. Questions of value are less real, and don't.

This is a stronger kind of scepticism. Indeed, it is sometimes suggested that it isn't really a sceptical position at all. Some people have doubts about morality, but the people described here have no doubts; they insist that morality is a kind of illusion. Theirs is better seen as a dogmatic position.[1]

Should either scepticism or dogmatism be accepted? Philosophers have engaged in long and complex debates arguing for and against these positions. We should not enter into these debates here. Perhaps one or other of these positions is right, but neither is obviously right. It looks as though there is hope of answering at least some of our questions about the environment. And I am going to suppose that hope should be generously entertained, at least until it proves to be vain. Scepticism and dogmatism should, at least for the time being, be put well to one side.

Let the law decide

Some people are impatient with the roads protesters. And they are impatient, too, with many of the demonstrations against logging or nuclear energy, with hunt saboteurs, with the actions of Greenpeace in the Pacific Ocean and with those involved, recently, in destroying genetically modified (GM) crops. They think that breaking the law in pursuit of a cause is rarely, if ever, defensible. And they think that the law has already decided the rights and wrongs of environmental questions. If the law permits us to cut down trees, or spray crops, or take limestone pavement and sell it to garden centres, then there can be no legitimate objections to our doing such things. There is no wedge between the law, on the one hand, and morality on the other.

There are, however, two things wrong with this. First, there are bad laws. Perhaps there is always some objection to breaking the law, and some reason, especially within those democratic states that encourage free and open debate, to keep protests within legal limits. But even if breaking the law is both morally and legally wrong, it doesn't follow that what the law forbids or requires of us is just what it ought to forbid or require of us. Laws supporting apartheid, whether in South Africa or the USA, were bad laws. And the same might be said of laws governing the emission of greenhouse gases, or allowing whaling, or inhibiting peaceful protest to suspect environmental policy. Of course, there are reasons for hoping, especially in a society where lawmakers are intelligent, decent and impartial, that the correspondence between law and morality will be close, but then it is so as a result of good practice, and not as a matter of principle.

Secondly, even good laws don't map perfectly onto morality. Very many people believe both that lying is wrong and that lying ought not to be illegal. Many believe that the same is true for abortion, hunting and drinking to excess. For there ought to be an area reserved for private morality, open, of course, to public approval or disapproval, but protected from the diktats of the state, within which good and bad, right and wrong decisions might be made. To think otherwise is to think as a totalitarian.

On two counts, then, we cannot settle moral disputes, disagreements about how things should be, by a simple and straightforward appeal to law. What the law permits may nevertheless be wrong. And what the law forbids may nevertheless be permissible, or even required. Moral questions resist this easy solution.

Voting

Many people believe that environmental problems are a symptom of the failure of political systems. In particular, if democracy functioned more effectively, allowing the popular voice a greater say, then the environment would benefit. As it is, the thought goes, problems are often caused when factional groups, individuals, businesses and non-representative governments are permitted to pursue their own private interests at the expense of the public good. It can seem as if there is some evidence to support this claim. Environmental problems are worse in those areas of the world where democratic institutions are most poorly developed, and were, until recently, particularly pronounced in countries of the communist-governed Eastern Bloc. And giving an even stronger voice to the people through increased access to information, more consultation, greater accountability and so on can be seen to have brought further benefits even in countries where democracy has long been the norm. Where the environment is concerned, voting helps.

There are stronger and weaker versions of this claim. On the strongest account, an effectively run democracy would offer to solve all our problems. On weaker versions, some problems will remain, but still significant improvements can be brought about by increasing our commitment to the democratic process. I think this weaker position is right. But we need to look in more detail at just why and to what extent benefits may be expected to accrue. First, though, we need some clarification of the nature of democracy. And we need to highlight certain of the difficulties democracy has to face in dealing with the environment.

Three puzzles

The democratic solution will, in outline, appear simple and straightforward. We count heads. We simply discover how many people, or adults, or adults who are not in prison or insane or in ermine, are in favour of one course of action, and how many support another. The policy with most votes wins. The procedure is relatively easy to introduce, delivers results and, it seems, is fair. And if the results are other than satisfactory, the claim goes, then this is because of particular shortcomings in the details of application. These can be fixed. Easily said, but there are a number of problems here that admit of no simple solution. While some have a close connection with environmental questions in particular, others are more general. I will start with those.

First, it isn't immediately clear just what, in a democracy, one is supposed to do. Is the idea that you should vote for what you want for yourself, or that you should vote for what is best overall? Clearly there will be differences. It is best for me if there are tax cuts, and if the motorway is sited elsewhere, even though I realize that revenue is needed, and that roads just have to be built. I have a choice in such cases as to whether to promote the private or the public good, and it is perhaps not obvious which choice I am supposed to make, if democracy is to function effectively.

There are cases where this choice doesn't arise in practice. For there are certain hotly debated questions of principle in which individual interests are not usually at issue. Only a handful of people have any direct involvement with capital punishment, and although many more are or will be themselves affected, arguments about abortion and euthanasia typically centre around moral principle, rather than what one individually stands to lose or gain. Where the environment is concerned, the dispute about foxhunting offers a recent example in which the vast majority of people are not directly involved.

This puzzle about the sorts of goods one is supposed to promote connects with another concerning the differences between two contrasting forms of democratic government. This is not Athens, and no such ancient model of democracy (revamped to include women and those who would be slaves) is today workable in practice.[2] We cannot gather together in the marketplace and vote on every issue. But this distinction between a representative and a direct democracy perhaps isn't wholly clear. On one account, the difference is simply one of convenience: as it just isn't possible to discover directly what everyone thinks, a representative is elected to do his or her best job in reflecting the majority opinion. On a second account, however, the difference is more significant. And on this account the representative is understood to pursue the best interests of the electorate, where these are not necessarily coincidental with the majority wishes. In Britain, the votes on capital punishment best exemplify this distinction in practice, where the conscience or judgement of members of parliament (MPs) typically goes against the brute majority wishes of the electorate. The justification here, presumably, is that the member believes that the absence of capital punishment is, in some suitably broad terms, better for the country as a whole, and better also for his or her proportion of the electorate, whatever individually or collectively they may happen to think about it.

There is also a third puzzle, which connects with but is nevertheless distinct from the other two. Is democracy thought to function effectively only when the electorate is both well informed and rational, and so able presumably to see what really is for the best,[3] or are there no such constraints, and the need is only for people to vote in accordance with what they most want? The question here is not a rerun of that about public and private concerns, for one can be well informed or badly informed about either, neither or both. Although some will benefit from tax cuts, a majority who vote for such measures are in fact not furthering their own interests, even if, when successful, and their take home pay is marginally increased, they do manage to satisfy their immediate short-term desires. And the question is distinct from that about direct versus indirect representation. Suppose that MPs do what they think is best. There are presumably times when they are apprised of the relevant facts, and times when they're not, but their conviction about the rightness of choice might not vary. It may be thought uncharitable to suppose that MPs might be other than well informed, but we get the government we deserve, and so their level of competence will to some degree reflect ours, in voting for them.

In these several respects, then, what democracy involves can be further explored. Without elaboration, a belief in democracy is somewhat empty. Suppose that in any of these respects we construe democracy one way rather than the other. We are highly likely to get different results. How can we support a system that, unless its character is further clarified, can issue in so many different outcomes?

There are two responses here. Both take as their starting point the observation that however democracy is organized, and by whatever principles it is underpinned, it is certainly the case that counting heads will, in very many cases, deliver some result as to what should be done. It won't do this in those cases where there is an exact tie, and it won't always do this in a satisfactory way when there are three or more options from which to select. A policy might have more support than its rivals while still lacking the support of the majority. Set such cases aside.[4] And now the first response insists that the policy that has majority support is the right policy to follow. So if the majority vote to save the whale, then saving the whale is right, almost by definition, and if they vote to return to hunting, and are indifferent to extinction, then that in turn is right. Voting for a particular policy simply and straightforwardly determines that that is the right policy to follow. The second response, in contrast, allows that we might get things wrong, but nevertheless insists that voting is generally a highly reliable method of discovering what is independently the right thing. If we change our minds about whales, or slaves, or executions, then we are either making or rectifying a mistake.[5]

There are, however, problems either way. To opt for the first suggestion here is in effect to endorse that scepticism about morality that I wanted, at least for the time being, to dismiss. Just as it is implausible to suppose that what the law demands is right by definition, so, too, for the majority vote. And this is a sceptical position, I suggest, just because putting this much faith in the majority is in effect putting no faith in them at all – faith is not quite the word when there is simply no chance of things going wrong – and is tantamount to a denial that morality can have any independent foundation. Because scepticism is difficult to believe and difficult to argue for, this first suggestion can be rejected.

The other option is little better. If we believe that there really are right answers to questions about abortion, or foxhunting, or redistributing wealth, or the levels of risk we might impose on future generations, then we must give up our confidence in simple majority voting as a way of uncovering those answers. No one thinks that we should just put to the people some of the difficult questions of science, say whether smoking causes cancer, or whether nuclear power is safe. It is acknowledged that considerable expertise is needed. Why think they are better equipped to tackle the equally difficult questions of morality?[6] It is very hard to see why anyone should believe both that there are genuine moral problems that need to be addressed and that simple majority voting can be relied on to answer them.

A defender of democracy might now back-pedal. One well-rehearsed suggestion is that even if voting isn't exactly a good way to settle the problems of morality, it is still the best way we have. Any serious defence here will require a more detailed listing and consideration of the alternatives than is usually given. And a further suggestion takes an even more evidently pragmatic stance, claiming that no alternative to democracy would for long be tolerated, however decent and efficient it turned out to be. Again, justification for this is hardly straightforward. Both suggestions will, if elaborated, draw on more claims as to the facts, about human psychology and the history of politics in particular, than can here be explored. And I will say no more about them.

A third suggestion is perhaps more promising. For it is a view of many, including, in the nineteenth century, J. S. Mill, that democracy is able to encourage a considered response to both public and private life, and so can help develop in all of us certain virtues of character that we would otherwise lack.[7] But this view cannot be satisfactorily advanced willy-nilly, and depends, at least in part, on settling some of those earlier puzzles one way rather than another. And there is a degree of reciprocity here, for the more plausible it is to suppose that democracy might in this way be to the benefit of its citizens, the more likely it is that those citizens might be brought to act in such a way that the relationship between voting and moral truth starts to become clearer.[8]

Ideals

A critical distinction is that between uninformed and well-informed desires. In so far as either individual voters or their representatives genuinely know about and understand the issues in question, then democracy's results will be more easily defended. Suppose that abortion is either right or wrong. If we understood the nature of fetal development, knew what the procedure involved, had insight into its various effects on mothers, doctors and family members, had some knowledge of the pros and cons of alternatives to abortion, then we would be more likely to identify what is right and what is wrong, and vote accordingly. Similarly in other cases. The greater our access to and understanding of the relevant information, the more likely we are to vote appropriately on issues such as capital punishment, foxhunting, GM foods, rainforests, and so on.

There will, though, be two objections here. The first is that in suggesting that information is connected with morality I seem to be going back on what I said earlier about science's inability to answer all our important questions. I am now suggesting, apparently, that moral facts are straightforwardly implied by sets of physical facts, such that morality is some sub-branch of science after all. Because the issues here connect with some of the deepest and most intractable problems in moral theory, I am unable to answer this objection in full here, but, and briefly, a defensible position can have it that even if moral facts somehow sit upon physical facts, they might still be a different kind of fact.[9] Further, even if they don't depend altogether on physical facts, it seems there must be some close relationship between them. It is most implausible to suppose that the facts about fetal development, the psychology of motherhood and so on might be completely irrelevant to the moral question about abortion, and similarly implausible to suppose that facts about animal pain should have nothing to do with foxhunting. So even allowing that the detailing might still be obscure, it is surely reasonable to suppose that the moral is far from independent of the physical. And this is why information will, at the very least, be of help.

The second objection, similarly, drags us into murky waters. Perhaps the better informed we are the more likely we are to know what is right, but we still won't vote for what is right unless either we are persuaded that there is something in it for us, or we just happen to be altruistic, inclined for whatever reason to promote the greater good. So even if information helps, more than information is needed. But, although again briefly, it has often been argued that a genuine grasp of the moral facts will itself lead us towards certain courses of action, and away from others. No further or external motivation is needed. Rather than take sides here I might simply allow the objection to go through, and so allow that for democracy to function properly we might need not only to be well informed but also well disposed towards the concerns of others.

Nevertheless the distinction between being well informed and badly informed remains critical, for it makes the others less pressing. Consider again the distinction between voting for self on the one hand, and for the overall good on the other. There are real differences here in the case where I am not well informed about the situation, but these will tend to disappear the more knowledgeable and reasonable I become. First, if, lacking altruism, I favour self, I will vote for what is in my genuine best interest, rather than the immediate object of desire. I am now less likely to vote for lower tax on cigarettes. Secondly, if others similarly vote for self, then even if, because we have different interests, our votes conflict, the winning vote will nevertheless be for the policy that has the greatest support. And because it has the greatest support, this, in many cases, is what I would vote for if, rather than for self, I was voting, again knowledgeably and reasonably, for the greater good.

Similarly, the distinction between direct and representative democracy becomes less important. Representatives, when well informed, will be neither more nor less adept at selecting appropriate policies than the equally well-informed average voter. They will, presumably, vote in favour of the overall good, rather than for themselves, if only because this is part of their job. But if the argument above is correct they will, in this, vote for what would be selected anyway.

Suppose that we are to some degree well informed, rational, impartial and seeking to promote the greater good. Then democracy will to some degree prove a useful tool for uncovering moral truth. But suppose instead that we are perfectly well informed, rational, impartial and good-promoting. Then, first, democracy will be the perfect tool. There will no longer be the possibility of our getting things wrong. This is not, as previously, because the right thing is defined in terms of our choices. It is, rather, because a condition on our being counted as perfect is that we always choose the right thing. So, given perfection, certain standard objections to democracy will collapse. It is often complained that it focuses on the short term, but, given perfection, voters will either consider the longer term or be able to justify their merely short-term concerns. Similarly, it is often thought that democracy gives insufficient protection to minority interests. Unless there are suitable checks and balances, democracy becomes the tyranny of the majority. But this concern, although well founded in practice, will have no grounding where idealized democracy is concerned. Suppose a minority interest is one that ought to be protected. The ideal voter will recognize this. If he or she affords this interest no protection then it is presumably because none is warranted. Secondly, democracy becomes redundant. Ideally informed rational voters, seeking to promote the public good, will just not disagree. So if there is one such voter, the rest of us might simply relax, and let him or her get on with it. We can give up on elections, parliaments and spin, and follow the single voice.

Of course we remain very far from this ideal. We cannot identify any god-like figure, of either the Christian or the Rousseauian variety, whose voice we can with confidence listen to, and who will always be able to tell us what is best. Nor is there a second version of the ideal. We cannot listen to and then confidently follow the majority voice of self-interested voters who, while not altruistic, are both well informed and rational. But in so far as it approaches this ideal, an effectively run democracy will, to a significant extent, help uncover the truth about morality.

Democracy and the environment

Forget, for a moment, the ideal, and consider democracy in practice. Some voters are reasonably knowledgeable about a range of complex issues, while others are to varying degrees ignorant. Some are blatantly self-interested, while others seek to promote the greater good. Why believe there is much help in all this for the environment?[10]

I might make a few commonplace observations. First, even given self-interest, there are benefits to be had. Private companies, businesses and individuals may well pursue their own interests, typically in terms of profit, without having regard for the condition of the environment in which their businesses, factories, quarries, mines, farms or forests are located. Those adversely affected by these environments will, if their voice can be heard, seek improvements. As bosses are typically outnumbered by workers, so conditions will improve. Secondly, there is among the public at large a tendency in general towards conservatism and suspicion of change. This may, as with GM crops, be irrational. Even so, there are reasons for thinking that an overall cautious approach to technological change is desirable. And democracy may encourage this. Thirdly, it will also encourage conversation and debate. We may be sceptical about the levels at which this is pursued, and what it achieves, but we are not altogether without grounds for thinking that democracy, education, rationality and knowledge are connected. Reasoned responses and a concern for others are both desirable, and democracy will go some way towards their promotion. But even if, in very general terms, there are grounds for having some faith in democratic solutions, there are several respects in which this faith must be tempered. Given human nature, democracy is imperfect. And it is, arguably, noticeably imperfect where the environment is concerned.

Places

Even if there is one environment, it has its somewhat separate parts, and there are often questions as to who has an interest, or enough of an interest, for their vote to be counted on particular environmental issues. Consider roads. Who should have a say in the reconstruction of the San Francisco freeways? Very many more people have some interest in the outcome than those living in the immediate vicinity of planned and projected roads, and taxpayers, those travelling through or around the city, conservationists and businesses elsewhere can all claim to be affected by the decisions that are reached. There is no easy way of drawing lines here, yet it is far from obvious that it should be considered a national or even a state problem, in which all voters get an equal say. Some of these interests are marginal. The difficulties are if anything even more pronounced where a seemingly national issue has considerable international consequences. Consider the radioactive waste from the reprocessing plant at Sellafield. Many of the residents of West Cumbria are in favour of nuclear power. Theirs is a depressed part of the country, and many jobs, and thus many incomes, depend on the plant's staying open. They are, understandably, fearful of change. Other people feel differently. Should we consider the likes of people like me, living some thirty miles away? And what about the people in Hampstead, or Islington? Governments are under some obligation to consider the views of the whole of their electorate, even if they don't believe their interests are seriously compromised by the issue to hand. But now what about the Irish? They are concerned, again understandably, about the effects on fishing, wildlife and ecosystems along their east coast if dumping in the Irish Sea is to go ahead. But the British government has not, so far, appeared to take much note of these concerns.

It is clear, therefore, that establishing the constituency of those who should have a say on particular environmental issues is not easy. There are, first, varying degrees of concern within a given electorate, such that allowing everyone a say can seem inappropriate. And there are high degrees of concern without a given electorate, such that denying these people a vote can also seem inappropriate. A faith in democratic solutions is to some degree unreasonable until some indication is given of how to settle these constituency issues.

Times

There are, as I have noted, many cases where the electorate as a whole is underinformed. But there is often some incentive to become better informed. Decisions on Britain's role in Europe will affect almost all of us, but because of the very long-term nature of many of the problems, a similar incentive is often lacking where the environment is concerned. Problems with the ozone layer are unlikely to impinge significantly on human lives for at least a half century or so. And it is a similar story, often, for nuclear waste. We are not strongly motivated to find out what best to do with it. There are two closely related issues here. First, our view may simply be that this is someone else's problem. We may, however, be wrong to think this; perhaps we should be concerned. Secondly, even if we are concerned, and want to do the right thing for the future, we might come to the wrong decision. But because there is no evident cost for us in getting things wrong, there is no obvious incentive to try harder, first to discover whether we have responsibilities here, and secondly, to work out how they might best be fulfilled.

Creatures

With problems of the first sort we recognize that people elsewhere have interests in what we do to the environment. Although there are difficulties both in weighing this interest and in crossing national boundaries, we could give these people a vote. If they had a vote, then whether or not we were concerned on their behalf, their interests would be represented. The second problem involves future people who cannot be given a vote, although we might recognize that they have interests and decide to take them into account. They cannot, because of their temporal location, represent themselves within any current election. But now there is a third problem. An appropriate concern for the environment demands, it is often alleged, a concern for creatures other than ourselves. For as human beings have interests, and can be benefited or harmed, so, too, do animals. So too, according to some, do plants, rocks, deserts, ecosystems and distant planets. Whether and to what degree there is substance in any of these claims is, of course, a big issue for later chapters. But whatever the results there, one thing seems clear enough now, namely that these non-human creatures and things just couldn't, even in principle, be given a vote, and so just couldn't represent themselves, or their wants or needs, in any election, at any time. Unlike with future people, the problem is not one of their relationship to us, here and now. It is internal to the sorts of things they are.

Voting, interests and concern

Go back to ideals. It can often seem unclear whether we are supposed to vote for ourselves, or for the greater good. But perhaps this doesn't matter. If we are supposed to be ideally well informed and rational, then a vote for ourselves is a vote for our own interests. Suppose others vote similarly. Then even while no one is concerned for others, there will be here the victory of the greater interest. What more could we want?

We could want to make sure that all self-interested parties are able to vote for themselves, for otherwise this victory is not guaranteed. National boundaries must not prevent this; nor must temporal location; nor must a general inability to vote. But only in the first of these cases can we enfranchise those other than ourselves whose interests, we may believe, should be taken into account.

Assuming only self-interest, democracy can be engineered to generate real benefits for people living together, at the same time. But to bring about benefits for people living at different times, or for creatures who are unable to vote, more than self-interest is needed. We will need, as well, appropriate levels of concern for those people, or for those non-human creatures. Assuming we are ideally informed and ideally concerned, we will without a doubt hit on the perfect solution to all our environmental problems. But this is pie in the sky. Given any realistic assessment of our levels of ignorance, on the one hand, and self-concern, on the other, and given that many of its problems bear on other times, or other creatures, then democracy's benefits, where the environment is concerned, will, although real, be limited.

Pricing

A further procedure appears to some to be fundamentally opposed to a system based on voting. To speak in currently unfashionable terms, whereas a belief in democracy originates in and is still somewhat the province of the politically left, a commitment to the market as a means for regulating and furthering society's ends is associated with the right. But if this is unfashionable, it is in large part because old oppositions have been eroded. There is now a widespread belief that market considerations should very much take the lead in determining public policy, with the direct hand of government playing a lesser role.[11] Democrats have a choice. They can either acquiesce in this substantial role for the market, or they can argue that genuinely democratic processes are thereby systematically subverted and distorted: we are either hoodwinked, thinking quite irrationally that it is best for all, or we are persuaded to gamble and, while acknowledging that there are winners and losers, led to believe that we stand a good chance of coming out on top. Either way, as still many would have it, what is good for the market is good for handfuls of shareholders and bad for the rest of us. Where environmental issues in particular are concerned, many of those most anxious for solutions are terminally ill disposed towards an approach centred on economic considerations.

Is this scepticism, however, well founded? Is the free play of market forces antithetical to environmental protection? Or is it, as some suppose, merely the vestiges of state control that, in distorting markets, bring about those situations in which the environment suffers? I will argue here that market considerations can and often do promote acceptable and coherent environmental policies. Further, there are reasons for thinking that if the market were in certain respects freer, the environment would benefit even more. But there are limits. As with democracy, a market approach cannot, in practice, solve all our problems.

Letting the market decide

One of the problems with counting heads is that the degrees of interest and involvement will vary. Consider the individual. I can vote for many things, without ever having to think about which I value most. And consider society as whole. One worry about democracy is that greater numbers don't have to mean greater concern. Why permit the majority to outweigh a minority when, conceivably, the minority cares much more? Why, when people are involved to different extents, should they have a say to an equal extent? One way of solving this problem is to look to the individual purse. How can we measure the degree of interest someone has in a given outcome? Find out how much they are prepared to pay to achieve it. People's interests are considered to the extent that they are prepared to back them with hard cash. Money can allow us to rank preferences. Who pays wins.

What, in a little more detail, such an approach involves is first measuring and then weighing the various costs and benefits involved. A choice between policies is rarely straightforward, with the various options each presenting a complex mix of advantages and disadvantages compared with others. What will count as the best solution to a given problem is to choose and implement the policy that makes for the greatest net benefit overall. There may be no perfect solution to the energy problem – nuclear energy, fossil fuels and solar, wind and wave powers all have some disadvantages – but there is a best solution. Similarly in other cases. There is both support for and opposition to a 10 mph limit for boats on Cumbria's Lake Windermere, with business and environment playing key roles in the debate. Whether or not to impose such a limit involves, on this plausible account, an assessment of the various costs and benefits involved. But now to do this some yardstick is needed: we cannot directly weigh cheaper energy against waste disposal, jobs against traffic build-up, or the thrill of speed against the unhurried pleasures of the fells. And money provides the yardstick: if the costs and benefits are given a monetary value, then they can be more easily balanced against each other. How to assign these values? The preferred method, under the approach canvassed here, is to leave it to the market. If all the considerations that bear on a particular problem are allowed to find their proper market price, then opting for the cheapest solution must be to do what is best. As one writer has put it:

> To assert that there is a pollution problem or an environmental problem is to assert, at least implicitly, that one or more resources is not being used so as to maximize human satisfactions. In this respect at least environmental problems are economic problems, and better insight can be gained by the application of economic analysis.[12]

That is the story in a nutshell. Cost-benefit analysis aims to solve environmental problems by economic means. Everything is priced, and every price is determined by willingness to pay, either to get something new, to keep what we already have or to compensate for some loss.[13] Take the market seriously, and our problems will be solved.

However, it is obviously not straightforward. Consider the boats again. It might be fairly easy to calculate potential losses to the local businesses that benefit from boating. It is less easy to put prices elsewhere, and assess the costs of continuing with the status quo. Yet this has to be done. Otherwise the boat owners too easily win the argument. Supporters of cost-benefit analysis agree that existing market and market operations are often seriously flawed. They have to be substantially refined in order to gain both in efficiency and in the benefits they deliver. There is always the need for such refinements but, because of the complex character of many of its problems, this need is particularly pressing where the environment is concerned.

Refining the market

Consider pollution. Everyone agrees that smog, filthy beaches and poisoned rivers are things we would be better off without; the difficulty is in knowing just what to do about them. As long as businesses are free to belch out smoke and fumes into the atmosphere, they will continue to do so. Although there are obviously costs involved – damage to buildings, crops and trees, illness and disease, poor air quality – these are, first, not given in economic terms, and their remedy, secondly, doesn't fall to the businesses that directly enough are their cause. Because these spillover costs, or externalities, don't figure in the company accounts, their goods are cheaper than they would otherwise be. But how to fix the price, address these imbalances in the market and cut pollution? There are different ways.[14]

Governments or their agencies can directly impose limits as to acceptable pollution levels, typically on an industry-wide basis, with a system of penalties designed bring about compliance. And pollution will fall. But it can be objected that such a system is expensive and inefficient. Smaller businesses often have difficulty in sticking to the limits while retaining competitiveness, while the companies that can fairly readily meet the standards have no incentive to go further, and develop or back new technologies designed to further reduce pollution.

So market forces can be given a greater say. Rather than impose uniform standards across industry, governments can decide on what are overall acceptable pollution levels and then encourage the operation of market forces to bring these about. Such a system requires two main components: first, a range of incentives that promote industry's responsiveness to anti-pollution measures; and secondly, systems that encourage flexibility as to how and where these cuts are achieved. Government still fixes pollution levels, and itself imposes charges on industry. But market forces then determine how particular businesses respond.

There can now, however, be a further reduction in the government's role, so that greater reliance is put on those who actually suffer the effects of pollution to demand, via the courts, financial redress. This can involve industries, as when a business downstream seeks to recover some of the costs for clean water from polluting businesses upstream, and it can involve individuals, as when an employee or consumer or passer-by sues for illnesses caused by nuclear power, smoking or asbestos. And, if there are enough teeth to international law, it can involve different countries.

The first of these models, often associated with older-style "command and control" economies, is now very much out of favour, and it is widely acknowledged that market forces can play a considerable role, and play it very effectively, in reducing pollution. It isn't only here, however, that the market might be brought to bear, with noticeably good effect, on certain of our environmental problems.

One way to think of the air we breathe is as a public good, which, though of value to all of us, is owned by no one. We take for granted that it will be of good quality, without recognizing that there are costs attached to this. The pollution problem arises because, though almost everyone is affected, no one has any direct claim on the polluting companies as they would, say, if identifiable dirt and waste materials were to settle on farmland, or in gardens. But there are further goods of this non-private kind, and not only might they be polluted and abused, they might also be overused. Again the market can help. Consider water. This has long been thought of as something to which we should have free and unlimited access, so it is squandered, particularly by business and agriculture, but also by individuals at home. But if charges are made, consumption will fall, and the demand for new reservoirs, with their consequent environmental damage, will be reduced.[15] Or consider the countryside. If there is no financial cost attached to a day on the beach, or in the park, or climbing mountains, then, especially when the alternatives are expensive, such activities will pull in considerable numbers of people who, by eroding footpaths, leaving litter and demanding car parks, toilets and cafés, will then bring about environmental damage to some significant degree.[16]

A similar hard-headed approach, promising similar beneficial results, might be adopted elsewhere. As fish stocks continue to dwindle, it has been argued that the seas should be effectively privatized, with different countries or different companies owning the rights to fish different parts. Only then, it is claimed, would there be a real incentive to preserve and manage stocks effectively. At the moment, with virtually open seas, anyone not catching as many fish as possible is just leaving the way open for others to take them.[17] Within this free-for-all, any individual effort at conservation is simply irrational. More exotic species can also be helped. For many years, people, particularly in so-called developed countries, have urged the preservation of wild species, but their habitats have increasingly come under threat. Local people have had no good reason to give up their own country for animals. Even when hunting has been made illegal, a blind eye is often turned, and there has been no real incentive to catch poachers. But the growth of so-called eco-tourism has changed this. Wealthy Europeans have made a difference. There is now a charge for looking, so the future is more secure.[18]

In all these cases, government intervention is needed to correct market distortions. In other cases, government has itself introduced those distortions. State subsidies, when inappropriately applied, can generate environmental damage by reducing production costs beyond their proper market rate, and thus bringing about levels of pollution that market forces would otherwise proscribe. Notoriously, food production in Western Europe is heavily subsidized, and many of the unwelcome changes to the agricultural landscape – fields like the Canadian prairies, reduction in the range of crops, intensive meat production – would arguably not survive without government support. Competition is undermined, with, for example, organic foods being priced out of the market by subsidies offered to conventional production.[19] Nor, in light of the covert support they get from government, are GM foods competing on a level playing field. The remedy here isn't simply to cut subsidies. Many people are still in favour of subsidies for public transport, believing they will help the environment. And so they will. But it might be more effectively helped if we drop subsidies on the one hand and insist, on the other, that road users pay for their system at a real market price, with the full costs of road building, public inquiries, road-related injuries, noise and air pollution, effects on business and property prices all factored in.

While the emphasis so far has been on underpricing, the market suffers distortions also when goods are overpriced, and so underused. There are, first, cases where although the aim is to maximize profit, this is achieved without maximizing efficiency. Monopoly and near-monopoly situations can permit business to price its goods above the genuine market rate, such that while profits are high, they sell less than would otherwise be the case. And this can discourage innovation. A business with a monopoly on pollution-reducing equipment can offer outdated equipment at a rate that discourages high volume sales. A company owning a toll bridge or road can make money while encouraging traffic to take the longer route, congesting and polluting the city centre. And there are, secondly, cases where profit isn't the major concern. Property and land owners, ignorant of or indifferent to the real value of their assets, can offer them at too high a price. The result is overdevelopment elsewhere.

Scepticism about market solutions to environmental problems is often well founded. Supporters of cost-benefit analysis recognize this, but argue that this is because in almost every case our markets are imperfect, with many costs being inappropriately assessed. No one pretends it will be easy, but what we need to do is enhance the market's role and increase its efficiency, rather than, as many environmentalists believe, guard against its effects.

Refining the trader

This is only one half of the story. Not only do we need to acknowledge and then seek to counter defects in the market, but we have to do the same for those – all of us – who are buying and selling within it. The market will only function effectively, generating maximum benefits at the minimum cost, if goods are properly priced and those prices then appropriately responded to. Incompetent trading will mess up the system as a whole. So how must we be refined?

Cost-benefit analysis requires, first, that we are fully aware of the choices available, and understand the costs and benefits associated with each. Suppose that we simply don't know the price of petrol. We are hardly certain to make the right choice between road and rail. Or suppose we are unaware of traffic conditions near our destination, or the effects of driving-related stress on our health, or marriage, or efficiency at work. Again, our choices may be skewed.

It requires, secondly, that we are rational. It is not enough to have the information needed for the right decision unless we are able to make use of this information in appropriate ways. We need the wherewithal to discover what it implies, and then the willingness to act on it. Suppose I value health. I need, first, to be able to make the connection between the stress of driving with my longer-term well-being, and secondly, I need the strength of will to leave the car in the garage when, because it looks like it might just rain, I am tempted to forego the short walk to the station.

Because we are neither perfectly well informed nor perfectly rational we cannot, in fact, rely on the workings of the market to deliver optimal results. The cost-benefit approach recognizes that human failings distort market operations, with the result that we make choices that are bad for us, bad for society as a whole and bad for the environment at large. But, having identified the sorts of failings involved, we can now make efforts to correct and compensate for them.

Are there further ways in which human nature needs to be refined, if the market is indeed able to help with environmental problems? Two suggestions can be aired. The first might be fairly quickly rejected while the second needs a fuller consideration. First, then, what is to be rejected is the suggestion that we should be altruistic, given to taking the welfare of others into consideration. Driving hurts others in various ways, but I don't need to know, understand or care about this in order to come to the right transport decision. It is enough that this hurt is translated, by market operations, into a cost that, in terms of fuel prices or road taxes, I then must bear. Indeed, it is considered a particular virtue of the market approach (as with democracy under certain of its construals) that it generates results that further the good of the whole, while not requiring of any of us that we are ourselves directly concerned to promote that good.

What, though, should be our concern? There is, so far, some ambiguity with the notion of rationality. Is the requirement that we are rational in choosing the means to given ends; that I understand, for example, that if I want a cactus garden I would be advised to move south? Or is it, further, that we are rational also in our choice of ends; that I occupy myself with something less frivolous than the prickly pear? Does cost-benefit analysis, in other words, require, as part of its understanding of perfect market operations, merely that we have some or other desires, no matter what for, or does it further require that these desires are rational, such that if they are appropriately pursued they will give us, not only what we want, but also that which will genuinely do us good? It makes a difference. If we happen not to like, not to value, and not to want to pay for the High Sierra in something approaching its natural state, then there is no objection, on the preference account, to covering it with ski-lifts and mountain-bike trails. But an account focused on genuine good may well guard against this result. There are complications here that cannot be pursued in detail;[20] suffice it to say that although such analysis is often concerned with mere preferences, there are reasons for and no reasons against connecting its ideal form with a narrower understanding of welfare, one that refers to self-interest and what is really good for us.

A further refinement is critical, although it is concerned not so much with our natures as our pockets. The central idea behind cost-benefit analysis, and its particular advantage over a simple voting system, is that it proposes to measure the precise degree of our preferences, or interests, by looking to our willingness to pay. Thereafter, assuming information and reason, there emerges a proper ranking first of individual preferences and then, by setting these against one another, a result for the whole. But this is quite hopeless as its stands. It is no good at all asking the rambler how much he would give for peace and quiet above Windermere, for he might well reply, an awful lot if only he had it. An individual's preferences may be ranked by how he or she would spend, if everything were priced, but no worthwhile comparison across individuals is possible unless it is assumed that they have equal amounts of money to begin with, which is patently not the case in real life. Some of us, indeed some groups of us, are better off than others. And as speedboats will win over fell-walking, so, more generally, commerce rather than the environment will flourish, just because purchasing power is not equitably distributed to begin with. Idealization of market conditions needs to take this into account.

Objections to a market approach

Several objections have been made, but none of these is fatal. Cost-benefit analysis already recognizes that actual markets are flawed. Its argument is about the relationship between a perfect market and the elimination of environmental problems. Nor need we wait for perfection. As with democracy, having identified the ideal we can attempt to move towards it. And if we move towards it, our situation will be improved.

There are, however, further objections to the market approach that cannot so readily be countered. If telling, then, while certain benefits may continue to be felt, they will be considerably reduced. More important, there are challenges here to the theoretical success that a perfected market claims for itself. I consider three such objections here. The first alone is easily dismissed.

Money

Cost-benefit analysis requires that we put a price on everything and see everything in monetary terms. But money is not the be-all and end-all; it is not the only or supreme value. The project is doomed from the start.

However, this is to misunderstand the exercise. Such analyses need no elevated views as to the value of money. In particular, there is no need of divergence from a commonly held and commonsensical view that money is valuable not as an end, as something worth having for its own sake, but only as a means, or tool, or device for securing further goods. Misers may disagree, but most of us want money only for purchasing power. Its use in the market is merely as a convenient measuring rod by which the worth of other things, many of which are valued for their own sake, can be compared.

Not playing the game

This wrong-headed objection leads to another. Even given assumptions about available funds, many people express reluctance to put a price on certain goods, seeming to believe that to do so suggests, wrongly, that such goods are among the sort of things that can, with perfect propriety, like so many pounds of apples or sacks of sugar, be bought and sold.[21] But certain goods ought not to be thought of in such terms, for they are priceless, beyond such ordinary valuing, indeed perhaps only mistakenly thought of as goods at all. Such is a widely held view. In defence of the market approach, the authors of the *Blueprint for a Green Economy*[22] argue against this, claiming that pricelessness can be understood in two ways:

> The first is that priceless objects are of infinite money value. When art experts speak of priceless works of art, however, they do not mean that they have infinite values. They mean that they are unique and irreplaceable, but that, in auction they would fetch very high prices indeed. A moment's reflection will indicate that no one can or would pay an infinite price for them. So it is with the condor and the rhinoceros . . . The equation of "priceless" with "infinite value" is illicit. The second interpretation is more appealing. This says that there are some things in life which simply cannot be valued in money terms – there is somehow a compartment of our thinking that refuses to place money values on, say, human life. While this is a more reasonable interpretation of phrases such as "beyond price" care needs to be taken in applying it. We do not act as if human life, for example, is outside our capacity to value things in money terms. We quite explicitly draw boundaries round the kinds of expenditures that we are prepared to make to save life. Thus, while there remains a quite warranted suspicion that the process of money valuation is illicit in some contexts, the reality is that choices have to be made in contexts of scarce resources. Money as a measuring rod is a satisfactory way of proceeding.[23]

This is on the right lines, undoubtedly, but it may be better to acknowledge even more clearly that both varieties of pricelessness are in the end illicit. A suspicion about monetary valuation is surely understandable but hardly warranted or justified in that, as the authors note, not even human life can stand outside such evaluations. Hard decisions have at times to be made. And human life, the condor and summer evenings are all things on which a price can be put. To deny this is in effect to deny that there can be a ranking of values – to deny, for example, that we might decide that human life is worth more than the condor.

This isn't yet to silence the market's critic, for what might still be said is that we may well be justifiably suspicious of someone who is in the habit of viewing everything in monetary terms, or of thinking about what would compensate him or her for abandoning a certain good; and that much is right. But what one does as a matter of habit can nevertheless be distinguished from what one does, on occasion, when pressed. So a further powerfully expressed rejection of this component in the market approach can, I think, be seen to fail. John O'Neill suggests that just as Iscariot's betrayal of Jesus is indefensible, so, too, is our willingness to put a price on certain environmental goods, say a justifiably admired landscape. In both cases, what ought to be an unconditional commitment is abandoned, even before the going gets rough. But again, the argument depends on some slippery language. Is it true that a "person who would be willing to put a price on a friend simply has not understood what it is to be a friend"?[24] Yes, but there is an onus on "willing" here.

Consumers and citizens

In an important and influential treatment of this topic, Mark Sagoff argues that although there is a considerable role for the market to play in pricing consumer goods and, in playing that role, substantial environmental benefits to be had, it cannot, even when perfected, solve all our problems. For there is an unbridgeable distinction between those goods well enough suited to economic concerns, and those better reserved for political interests. Even though it doesn't standardly figure in the marketplace, clean water, for example, is appropriately viewed as the sort of good to which market considerations are eminently suited. There are some qualifications, but, broadly, its availability ought to depend on willingness to pay. Noise pollution should figure in an analysis of transport costs. And so on. But education, sex and race equality and our treatment of refugees present, on Sagoff's account, different sorts of problems, the solutions to which are discovered through the political process and reasoned debate, and not through our preference, backed by hard cash, for one option rather than another. Similarly for much within the environment. A decision to turn a wilderness area into yet another theme park cannot be justified in terms of the market outcomes, for the market, in

59

its concern with willingness to pay, is blind to the deeper ethical and aesthetic considerations that are of crucial importance in issues such as these. What being a citizen requires, and being a consumer more or less ignores, is close attention to the sort of society we want to build for ourselves, to live in, and then to leave behind. And this the market can neither replace nor provide.

There is, however, a response. It runs along lines similar to those outlined above, when I suggested that idealization of the market might well require that we replace untutored preferences with a notion of well-being that gives central place to our genuine interests and needs. Sagoff anticipates the response, but finds it inadequate.

There is, first, the distinction between a narrow and a wider view of externalities. Costs of building a theme park relate not just to building car parks, hamburger stalls and rides, but must reflect the consequential damage done elsewhere. The closure of farms and small businesses, rehousing of families and losses sustained by eco-tourism have all to be taken into account. But given the demand for entertainment, this may well be insufficient to protect the environment. Market advocates might now respond by suggesting a still wider understanding of spillover costs, whereby the objections of those not directly involved are also taken into account. But:

> When analysts expand the notion of an externality in this way to embrace the opinions and beliefs of the citizenry, which are central to environmental legislation, they make a bald attempt not to inform but to replace the political process, an attempt they may not acknowledge. It is for the political process – not for economic analysis – to gather and judge these opinions and beliefs.[25]

So in attempting the wider purview, cost-benefit analysis gets beyond itself, treading on ground to which its character and procedures are ill suited. Judgement of opinion and beliefs certainly matters, but it is not for the market to offer these judgements. Sagoff continues:

> Policymakers need to know which beliefs about facts are credible and which arguments about values are sound. The credibility of a belief (e.g. that the earth is round) depends on evidence and expert opinion, not the amount that people are willing to bet that it is true. Nor does the soundness of an ethical argument depend on willingness to pay, although economic information, of course, may be relevant. Thus cost-benefit techniques, when they go beyond determining efficiency in the narrow sense, do not provide useful information. Rather, they confuse preference with ethical and value judgement.[26]

Although its heart is in the right place, there is something not altogether satisfactory about the argument here. The difficulty, I think, is that Sagoff takes too little note of the distinction between actual and improved or perfected market operations. On any reading, traders need more than mere preferences if results delivered by the market are to carry any weight. They need to be well informed about, at least, the facts relevant to their choices. Otherwise they won't even get what they want. So there is already more to take into account than mere beliefs and opinions. My suggestion, that we should discriminate between mere preferences on the one hand, and those preferences guided by appropriate beliefs as to a range of values on the other, is then only a further step in a direction already taken. Of course, just as the market itself is not asked to judge between true and false beliefs, so it isn't itself required to favour interests above mere preferences, as if we somehow put a block on badly informed people buying frivolous goods. But as we can encourage consumers to know the truth, so we can encourage them to recognize the good. And nor is this step illegitimate, taking cost-benefit analysis on to territory that should be set aside for politicians. It can be conceded, of course, that the procedures of democracy, in particular, will encourage, as a market alone will not encourage, sound ethical arguments to emerge. But the market can readily allow space for this.

Summary

I have needed to discuss these supposed political and economic solutions just because in many countries there are widespread beliefs that our lives, the lives of others and the wider environment can all be made better by an increased commitment to the democratic process on the one hand, and the free and unfettered operations of a market economy on the other. Because these beliefs are influential, informing political and media debate, and so already affecting the way we live, they demand to be taken seriously. Are they true?

Actual voting and pricing procedures leave much to be desired. Suppose, without introducing any further changes, we elect to base every decision on one or other of these procedures. It is plausible to suppose that things would get worse.[27] Suppose, instead, that we consider democracy, or the market, in its ideal form. My claim is that then every problem would be solved. But this is not of profound significance. For suppose that we ought to save tigers, or develop wave power, or scrap GM food. In a perfect democracy we would, with respect to such issues, have, understand and draw the right inferences from the relevant information. And if we understand the perfect democracy to be one in which we vote not for ourselves but for the general good, then we would vote accordingly. If there are powerful reasons to save tigers then tigers would be saved. Similarly for the perfect market. It would be configured in such a way as to generate the best outcomes. Allow that we cannot do everything. We can save the tiger, or the rhinoceros, but not both.

If there is reason to save the tiger over the rhinoceros we would see this, and back our choice with cash. There is nothing of profound significance here, because the conditions for a perfect democracy, or a perfect market, just are those that give us the best outcomes. And the nature of these conditions and outcomes isn't determined by democracy, or by the market. They are given antecedently. Without some prior moral notions we would not, for example, require of the perfect democracy that everyone has a vote, or insist that in the perfect market everyone has equal amounts to spend. And so it is these prior notions that are doing much of the work within our understanding of the ideal.

Even if we cannot reach perfection we can aim towards it. On the suggestions I have made here, that will involve more education, greater equality between people, more dialogue, and a transparent mechanism for ranking our fully informed preferences. It is often supposed that democratic and market-based processes work in opposition to one another, but I have suggested that they can operate in tandem, with, for example, the conversation of democracy helping shape a system of prices on the one hand, and then a visible and comprehensible structure of costs giving substance to our choices on the other. Is there any reason to suppose that, so enhanced, democracies and markets will aid the environment? I have suggested there is such reason. Perhaps we can imagine that some quite different systems might be compatible with environmental improvements. So might they be. But in a highly populated world where there is already a fair amount of freedom, and a good deal of trade, improvement to systems and procedures already in place is likely, or so I have claimed, to be beneficial. That, too, is a claim of hardly profound significance.

CHAPTER 4

Solutions II: Moral Theory

We want to know what to do. Should we save the tiger, permit more roads or believe in nuclear power? More exactly, we want to know what most to do when there is a range of options, all of them attractive to some, but not all of which can be satisfied: safer or cheaper power, easy access to the countryside or its preservation, tea or tigers. We want to know how policies should be arrived at, and how decisions should be made. Two procedures have been considered, but in their actual forms both democratic and market forces are imperfect mechanisms, delivering results that often seem unacceptable. Of course, it is possible simply to stipulate that the policy that gets the most votes, or the one that wins out on a cost-benefit analysis, is then straightforwardly the one that should be put in place, but this is a view adopted only by a handful of die-hards. Most people recognize that these institutions as we have them are deeply flawed. But what of ideal forms? If we could perfect our voting or pricing mechanisms, then we could have much more confidence in the results they deliver. But, I argued, there is an important sense in which we are here in danger of getting things the wrong way round. For there is no independent notion of what the ideal form of democracy or the market would be, which might then be seen to generate, as a matter of routine, an unbroken series of acceptable verdicts on policy decisions. Rather, our assessment of a system's worth just depends on how effectively it generates the results that we have already decided we want. Our ideals are formed by, rather than themselves forming, the verdicts they deliver.

There is a further important objection that can be levelled against the market-oriented approach to environmental problems. Perhaps this objection could be glimpsed at the outset, when I suggested that the depth of people's pockets isn't an obvious measure of their degree of concern. And perhaps it becomes clearer later, in worrying about how both income differences, and the difficulty in properly pricing certain goods, bears on the market approach. The objection is this: the market is at best a reasonably accurate pointer to what we are really interested in. We are not really interested in what people will pay for such and such a thing; we are interested in how important, or valuable, the thing is. The market certainly helps gauge that importance. But the two things, its market price and its real value, can, and often do, drift apart.

The objection can also be made against an approach centred around voting. For again, our predominant interest is not in the crude numbers favouring a certain policy against its rival; it is, rather, in whether the former policy really does offer more advantages than the latter. There is very probably going to be some relationship in general between the degree of popular support and a policy's real advantages, but for particular cases in the actual world this relationship will not always be close.

What needs to be more fully considered, then, is just what the important thing is that the approaches considered so far are trying, with limited success, to pick out. What is it that is good, or valuable, and how does this good or valuable thing require that we act? In place now of the kinds of practical solutions to environmental problems that have been considered so far, I want to turn to certain highly general and rather more theoretical accounts of what we should do.

Consequentialism

I can begin with a relatively familiar moral theory. Rather than trying to use the law, votes or money as an indication of how to settle disputes, consequentialism offers a seemingly more direct method, and one that, provided it is properly applied, is certain, at least by the theory's own lights, to deliver the right results. For consequentialists hold that the right thing to do in every case is to choose the action that maximizes net benefits over drawbacks. If I am deciding whether to buy my girlfriend a new sports car, or to give money to the Green Party, I should, if I want to do the right thing, work out both the good and bad consequences of each proposal, weigh them up and then choose that which, all things considered, will be best. If a government is deliberating between peace and war, it needs to assess the full consequences of each course of action, and then determine its policy accordingly. So consequentialism holds first that there is a way of comparing outcomes, and secondly that we ought to bring about the outcome that offers the greatest overall benefit. I have assumed that in many cases environmental disputes centre on different beliefs about what is best for people. Given that assumption, consequentialists will argue that what is best is that which produces the greatest net benefit for the people involved. If we can assess the various benefits, we can decide what to do.

There are two sorts of problem. Consequentialism can seem to be too straightforward, and then it can seem not straightforward enough. The first problem, then, is that it may be unclear what sort of contrasting or rival account is being displaced. Isn't it just obvious that we should do what is best overall? And if this is just obvious, how can it be any kind of advance, and how can it help to solve any problem, to be reminded of it? Most people, and certainly most politicians and policy-makers, claim to be concerned with doing what is best; they disagree not about this, but about what the best consists in, and how to achieve it. Maybe consequentialism is just too appealing to be any good.

Not so. For in several respects consequentialism, when unpacked, is quite clearly distinctive enough for its acceptance not to be a matter of course. It isn't an uncontroversial theory, and certain of its demands are far from easily satisfied.

Some details

Consider its demand that we be concerned to produce the best overall consequences. While every plausible view requires that we take consequences into account, many of them leave some room for other considerations as well. But not consequentialism. So, suppose we compare two states of affairs. And suppose we agree that it would have been better overall if Saddam Hussein had been killed, either by accident or by assassins, prior to the Gulf War in 1992. We might still disagree about whether it would have been right to kill him.[1] Or suppose I can pass my exams, become a doctor and save lives only by cheating. Most people will think that cheating is still wrong. But consequentialists are not moved by such scruples. They think that we should always do that which will have the best consequences, even if it means that we should act in ways that conventional morality, often apparently with good reason, disapproves of.

In other situations, although doing what will have the best consequences is certainly permitted, it isn't clearly required. My girlfriend has had a rough day. I can buy her flowers, or I can send the money to Kosovo. Flowers will make her smile, while money to Kosovo will buy food for people who are starving, or shelter for the homeless and dispossessed, or medicine for the sick. May I buy her flowers? Although almost everyone will agree that there is some obligation to help in cases of real and immediate need, many fewer agree with the consequentialist that I act wrongly whenever I fail to produce the greatest net benefit overall. I will do this, in such a case, if I send the money to Kosovo. But is it really wrong not to do this, and to put friends, or family, or even yourself, first?[2]

The difficulties here are related. In insisting that we always do that which will produce the best consequences, that will maximize the overall good, consequentialism seems to require us to become simple benefit machines, forever guided by external demands over which we have virtually no control. And as a number of philosophers have argued,[3] our autonomy and integrity as agents seem by such insistence to be systematically undermined. Critics have spoken here of consequentialism's denial of agent relativity; we are not allowed to distinguish between what would be best from a wholly impartial view, and what we, as occupiers of a partial perspective, might or might not do. And this agent relativity has, as I have indicated in the examples above, two forms. In the first case it can seem as if there are agent-relative constraints: although it would be best if a certain outcome obtained, it is still wrong for me to produce that outcome. In the second case there are agent-relative permissions: although it would be best if a certain outcome obtained, and it would not be wrong for me to produce that outcome, still it would equally not be wrong if I failed to produce it.[4] In ruling out agent relativity in both its forms, consequentialism is at odds with some deeply entrenched moral intuitions.

A related point might be mentioned here. The theory gives no credit for good intentions. One person tries to do good, and fails. Another tries to do evil, and by a fluke ends in doing good. The second person does the right thing. In this unadulterated emphasis on outcomes, and its lack of concern with motive and character, consequentialism, once again, reveals itself as indifferent to the interest in persons that figures so large within our everyday moral notions.

There is a further difficulty, for in its insistence that we be concerned only with maximizing overall benefits, consequentialism reveals itself as wholly indifferent to where these benefits fall. Many people believe that this indifference is inappropriate, and that distribution matters. They think either that benefits should be handed out equally, so that there are fair shares for all, or that the greater benefits should go to the worse off, so that they can begin to catch up. But consequentialists have no such concerns. They will allow, if maximizing requires it, that the badly off can be ignored, in order to further improve the lot of those already well off. They will even allow that those already badly off can be made even worse off, if that will produce the greatest benefit overall. Consider an extreme case. The poor are already miserable. They live in slums, but on an extremely valuable riverside site. We can give them some assistance, or we can throw them out, rehouse them miles away at the city's edge, and redevelop the land, building houses and sports facilities for the rich. If we throw them out they will be even more miserable, but not much more. But the rich will be very much happier if they can do lunches, collect art, and play racquetball near the water's edge. Consequentialism says we should throw out the poor, and redevelop the land.

Perhaps consequentialism is right to say that we should have killed Saddam Hussein, that we cannot buy flowers if we could do more good elsewhere and that we should in the above case redevelop the land. Perhaps the only thing that matters is maximizing benefit. I don't want to take sides here. The point is simply to show that in spite of first appearances, consequentialism isn't obviously correct. Everyone thinks that doing that which has the best consequences matters, but very few think this is all that matters.

Some more details

In the areas discussed above it is clear enough what consequentialism requires, even if it is difficult to believe that what it requires is right. In other areas the difficulty is in seeing just what the theory demands of us. Construe its details one way, and the theory becomes more plausible; another way, and it loses ground.

There are going to be problems, first, in discovering the various consequences of our actions. Perhaps I know that if I send flowers I will bring a smile to her face, but then I don't know, if one thing leads to another, whether in the end we will be right for each other. And then there will be further problems in bringing to these consequences some sort of measure so that we can rank one action against alternatives. Maybe this somewhat grubby life is the best I could have had. Consequentialism doesn't shirk the problems here: it doesn't, for example, say that we need concern ourselves only with the most obvious and most immediate consequences, or that rough and ready measures are good enough. But it insists that difficulties in practice do not spill over into principle: what makes one outcome better than another is its maximizing of benefit, and this holds whether or not those benefits can be measured.

Even allowing that we are concerned with theoretical requirements, however, there are further difficulties relating to measurement. Assume that we have correctly allocated some numerical scores for both the benefits and the drawbacks of competing projects. It still need not be straightforward as to which we should choose. Setting aside the possible case in which these scores exactly tie (the right thing here would be to toss a coin), there could be cases in which the net difference is the same, even though the initial scores are different. One project might offer vast benefits along with considerable draw-backs, while its rival promises much less of both. The net gains are, however, the same. So it is either an exciting world or something rather more bland. Which should we choose? Consequentialism doesn't say. Whether, other things being equal, we ought to maximize pleasure or to minimize pain is not stipulated by the theory.

Consequentialism also appears to be silent in a related area. I mention this here, although it is a difficulty that will demand a fuller discussion in Chapter 11. Consider actions that offer different amounts of net benefit. I can marry Susan or Caroline. If I marry Susan there will be more overall happiness than if I marry Caroline. Is it then obvious whom I should marry? Only if we have no interest in the number of people claiming a share of this happiness. Susan wants children, while Caroline wants her career. So although there will be more happiness if I marry Susan, it will, because of the children, be shared out more thinly. Or consider a more extreme example. A scientist can either help her father enjoy his 75th birthday, or she can produce ten clones of everyone now alive, and parcel them off to form exact replicas of our world on a series of distant planets. In the former case there is just a little bit more happiness in the universe, while in the second the current level of happiness is increased tenfold. Still, it isn't obvious, I think, that the scientist should produce these clones. Although the amount of happiness increases vastly, no one who exists is even a tiny bit happier. So is there any real benefit? Even allowing that we are concerned with happiness, consequentialism just doesn't tell us, as Jan Narveson has put it, whether we should want to *make happy people* or to *make people happy*:[5] whether we should add to the happiness of existing people (and so increase the average levels of happiness), or whether we should add to their number (and so increase the total level of happiness, even if the average level remains the same, or goes down).

I am assuming here that in wanting to maximize overall benefit, the consequentialist is concerned with happiness. But is this assumption fair? Consequentialism is precise, in that it insists we be concerned only with the consequences of our actions. But it is imprecise, in that it doesn't in itself tell us which aspects of those consequences are of concern. It is a moral theory, and so is concerned with the good, but it doesn't say what the good consists in. And in fact there are several plausible suggestions that can be made here. Different versions of consequentialism bring different ones to the fore.

In the theory's most familiar form, that of classic utilitarianism, the relevant consequences are those that generate pleasures and pains. In another, and very closely related, form, utilitarianism is concerned instead with happiness or unhappiness. But two further forms of the theory should be noted. One is concerned with the satisfaction of preferences or desires. Another is concerned with well-being, or welfare. Both forms, and their relation to classic utilitarianism, need here to be considered in a little more detail.

There are many things that people want. And our different wants can, at least often, be ranked in order of preference. At breakfast, I prefer tea to coffee. I prefer the countryside to the beach. And I prefer, other things being equal, to travel by rail rather than by road. A concern with preferences is of interest here because it connects, in many ways, with the two approaches to problem solving discussed in Chapter 3. Both the ways in which I vote, and the ways in which I spend, are in large part determined by, and so indications of, my preferences. Because I prefer security for those badly off to opportunity for all, I vote accordingly. And because I prefer to travel by rail than by road, I will pay at least a little more in order to use the train.

As well as the things we want, there are the things that do us good. The idea of our well-being is not unfamiliar. It is the idea of our leading a good life overall, where that is understood in neither conventionally moral nor material terms (for I could do a lot of good or have a lot of money without myself living a good life) and where some reasonable stretch of time is involved (for I am not living a good life if things simply go well over the odd weekend).[6] Many things contribute to human well-being, including, as well as obvious things like food, health and shelter, the slightly less obvious, such as friendship, satisfying and worthwhile work, or exposure to good books, music or conversation.

How are preferences, on the one hand, and well-being, on the other, connected? It would be a brave world if getting what we wanted could be relied on to do us good. But we all know that only too often getting what we want leaves us disappointed, unsatisfied or ill at ease. I very much wanted a different guitar, but, when I got it, it seemed little better, if at all, than the old one. Some people save and save for a new car, which in the end makes hardly any difference to their lives. A holiday, planned for months in advance, can fail to live up to expectations. In many cases, getting what we want does little for our well-being. And the converse sometimes holds. Some of the things that are good for us are things that we prefer not to happen. Suppose the overseas holiday is cancelled. It might turn out that, although it is not at all what we wanted, two weeks at home benefits us in countless unforeseeable ways.

There is a further important distinction to be made here. Wants and preferences vary widely from person to person. It is just a fact about me that I want a bigger garden, and a further fact about me that I get pleasure from mountain biking. Other people want different things, and get their pleasure in different ways. But well-being does not in this way vary from person to person. Some people long for while others detest dry martinis at sunset. But in neither case does a martini make a genuine contribution to our well-being. Conversely, some sort of exercise, or some sort of exposure to art and music, or some manner of close relationship to other human beings does add to well-being, whether or not we want such things, and whether or not we believe they will do us any good. And the distinction here is often, and usefully, couched in different terms: we might say that it is an *objective* fact about us that certain things contribute to our well-being, while it is a *subjective* fact about us that certain things are what we want, and cause us pleasure.[7]

This distinction, between objective and subjective accounts of the good, has a bearing on different versions of classic utilitarianism. This best known consequentialist theory, promoted by Jeremy Bentham, refined by J. S. Mill and then lampooned by Dickens, construes the good in terms of pleasure or happiness,[8] but these are not evidently the same. The sources of pleasure, like the objects of desire, vary significantly from person to person. Pleasure is, in terms of the distinction made above, a subjective state. And so a theory that sees pleasure as the good offers no hard and fast rules as to what sorts of things the good world will contain. Some get pleasure from art, theatre and profound conversation, while others enjoy lager and magazines.[9] Which should we choose? It depends simply on the intensity of feeling and the numbers of people involved.

What about happiness? Whereas I am experiencing pleasure if I feel a certain way on a certain occasion, many people believe that happiness is considerably more complex, involving reference not only to feelings, but also to beliefs about one's situation, and to the matter of whether those beliefs are true. Someone being brainwashed into thinking they are in Hawaii, with coconuts and girls, may well be experiencing pleasure but, if they are in fact prisoners of war in Korea, they will not be genuinely happy. Conversely, being unhappy is not the same as being in pain. Drilling and filling causes pain, but it is far from clear that I am, while at the dentist, genuinely unhappy. Yet it is worth stressing that what, if anything, is unclear here is not some deep fact about the true nature of happiness, but, more prosaically, just the way in which the terms "happy", "happiness" and the like are standardly used. The critical and substantial distinction is between subjective pleasure on the one hand, and objective well-being on the other; the difference here doesn't depend on how terms are used. And although I think happiness is more strongly connected with the latter notion, it doesn't matter that much if someone disagrees over this terminological point.

Consequentialism itself is neutral between these different accounts of the good. Some of its supporters do insist that what matters are pleasant states of mind, however produced. But others claim that the important good is well-being, adding that there are objective criteria by which well-being can be assessed.[10] When, as often happens, consequentialism is criticized as being too hedonistic, or materialistic, or concerned with crude market-value thinking, it is typically the simpler and earlier versions of utilitarianism that the critic has in mind. Other versions are well able to resist such criticisms.

Consequentialism and the environment

To what extent does consequentialism offer a method of solving our various environmental problems? Does it tell us what to do? Does it provide an acceptable means of adjudicating between rival proposals? Does it have advantages over the methods canvassed earlier?

Suppose we get a grip on the basics of the theory. And suppose we fill in the details, to do with the sort of good being measured, the issue of actual or possible people, more pleasure or less pain, in seemingly appropriate ways. Then consequentialism will dictate the solution to environmental problems, just as it dictates solutions wherever they are required. Whether its verdicts are acceptable is a more difficult question, and will depend in part, but I think only in part, on just how those details are filled in. Its advantages? In contrast with the simple majoritarian picture, consequentialism attends to the degree as well as the number of concerns. A patch of waste ground could be cleaned up and turned into a park. Most people want this. A few realize that the ground is home to certain rare dragonflies. Should there be a park? The clear majority think so, but they won't lose any sleep over it. But the few care desperately that these insects are protected. Consequentialism, in contrast with head counting, may decide against the park. And it has advantages over the economic model. Consequentialism takes into account the interests we actually have. It doesn't take these interests into account simply in so far as we are able to back them with hard cash. A few want more skiing in the Scottish Highlands and a vast majority are opposed, but the few have money, while the many are mostly students or unemployed. In brute market terms the few will win, while under consequentialism they will almost certainly lose.

Remember, though, that consequentialism has its downside. First, it is not eminently practical. Neither long-term nor immediate benefits are easily measured. And so we may have difficulty in assessing, for example, whether a relief road should be built. Secondly, it isn't eminently fair. Perhaps nuclear power does offer substantial benefits for the country as a whole. Still there is a considerable cost to be paid by those who live close to reactors in terms of health risks, a drop in property prices and attendant poor amenities. These costs may be outweighed by the benefits, but it can seem unfair that they are borne so heavily by so few. A third difficulty is perhaps less pressing here. I noted above that consequentialism can seem to be impossibly demanding, urging, as it does, that we are always concerned to produce the best outcome, and allowing us no freedom just to pursue our own lives and projects. But perhaps we can focus on the theory's relevance to public policy, rather than private decision-making. Certainly Bentham's major concern was with the advantages of utilitarianism to legal and political decision-making rather than its offering a basis for everyday life, and in this restricted form the theory is less objectionable. Perhaps as individuals we don't need always to do our best, but governments and lawmakers surely do.

As well as these general considerations, there are certain respects in which the special features of environmental problems impinge on consequentialism in particular ways. I will mention some such features now, even though parts of what is suggested here can only be pursued in any detail much later.

Space

One of the characteristics of consequentialism is that it considers everyone equally. It doesn't allow that I can count my interests, or those of my family and friends, or those of the people who live nearby, or speak the same language, or have the same colour skin, for more. People are scattered over most of the surface of the earth, and consequentialism requires that they be given equal consideration. It is indifferent to spatial location.[11]

This must be considered an advantage of the theory, as far as this book's topic is concerned. We are increasingly used to seeing many of our problems as global. Because we have to consider the global effects of our actions, because we cannot ignore effects on people who live elsewhere, have less power, or less influence, consequentialism will appear well suited to environmentalism. We will be prohibited from pursuing the national interest at the expense of the rest of the world. The inability to ignore distant effects will act as a brake on innovative technologies that offer local benefits. And we will be discouraged from cleaning our own backyard while things are dirtier elsewhere.

However, it would be a mistake to suppose that all evidence of global thinking indicates that consequentialism's indifference to space is taken seriously. Politicians seem often to be concerned with global issues. They profess to understand and to care about the effects of rainforest destruction, the use of old fridges in places like China and overfishing of the seas. But consequentialism demands that we treat people living in different places in the same way. And there is reason to think this isn't happening. It is easy enough to warn against the effects of old technologies in distant countries. It is harder, at least for politicians, to call a halt to the equally damaging effects of new technologies here at home. Global thinking, the consequentialist will insist, should not be used as an opportunity to pass the buck.

Time

Environmental thinking deals, more frequently and more seriously than do many other areas of moral concern, with issues involving long stretches of time. There is considerable anxiety about the future consequences of present policies, worries about how, unless we change, the seas will become empty of fish, about deterioration in the ozone layer, the effects of which will become increasingly noticeable decades hence, and about the painfully slow rate, lasting over thousands of years, at which spent nuclear fuel might become marginally less dangerous. We are almost all, to a greater or lesser extent, concerned about the unhappy state of the world we are leaving for others to inherit. It might be said that people have always had such concerns, but until relatively recently, the concern was primarily for one's own family. They could be affected by our actions, by whether we saved, and looked after our property, or whether we let things go to rack and ruin, hocked the silver and turned to drink. And the concern was to benefit them. Other people, except in rare cases, were not so much considered. Our concerns these days are different. We are aware of global responsibilities, and are much more likely to consider how people the world over will benefit or suffer from the long-term effects of what we do. There is a further difference. Only in recent decades have scientists, economists and statisticians been able to offer long-term predictions about the state of the world. They often get things wrong, but their arguments cannot simply be ignored. And as we have this information about the future, it seems we are required to do something about it.

Consequentialists want to consider the fortunes of all those affected by our actions. Some of those who will be affected are still children. They don't have the vote. Nor do they have much money. This, for the consequentialist, gives us no reason to discount them. Their interests have to be taken into account. Some of those who will be affected are not yet born. Again, consequentialists believe this fact to be of little moral relevance. People will be born, they will be affected by what we do, so their interests have to be considered along with the rest. In that it demands we consider all those who will be affected by our actions, consequentialism is indifferent to temporal location.

The requirement that we consider people wherever they live is one that is likely to help the environment. So, too, is the requirement that we consider people whenever they live. If we needn't consider future generations, we might believe that we can squander resources, ignore long-term environmental risks and trash the planet. But if we are persuaded that the interests of the unborn need to be taken into account, our attitudes may change. We will reduce our consumption of limited resources, demand more information about long-term risks, and generally adopt a more cautious approach. Environmentalists will welcome changes like these.

This welcome should, however, be cautious. Considering people whenever they live is noticeably less straightforward than is considering people wherever they live, for at least two reasons. The first concerns ignorance. Consequentialists say that we have to concern ourselves with the happiness or interests of future generations. This is all well and good, but how are we to do this? How can we tell where their happiness or interests lie? We cannot ask them what they want. One suggestion is that we should assume their desires, interests and concerns will be (roughly) similar to ours. And so there will be an ongoing need for copper and aluminium, a persistent concern about the spread of nuclear fuels and a continuing demand to save the tiger and the whale. Then, as now, there will be disputes between developers and conservationists as the different and conflicting interests of various groups prevent any easy solution to environmental problems.

These assumptions are not of a piece. One assumption is that the technological problems will be the same. But perhaps they will be different. People in the past did not save flint or bronze for us, and we do not mind, so perhaps people in the future will not share our need for copper, oil or coal. We cannot, it is said, simply assume that the present technological problems will be replicated in future times. A second assumption is that our successors will be roughly the same sorts of people as ourselves, with roughly the same sorts of interests and concerns, and looking for the same sorts of things in life. But perhaps this, too, is far-fetched. Two hundred years ago most people had no interest in mountain scenery. Before the nineteenth century the alpine peaks, glaciers and the American West were seen as challenges to human ingenuity, places to be civilized and tamed. Even the English Lake District was feared, and seen as a miserable and difficult part of the country, to be avoided whenever possible.[12] Tastes change. Perhaps, in a thousand years, people will have tired of whales.

There is a problem either way. If we accept that we don't know what future people will want and need, we have to accept that it becomes impossible to plan. Perhaps we can make some sorts of predictions as to the effects of our actions over the next few hundred years, but we will not be able to tell how these effects will be greeted by the people then alive. Consequentialist thinking is handicapped. But suppose we assume that in the future people's needs and interests will be broadly similar to ours today. Then a different problem emerges, and we encounter the second reason why considering future generations is difficult.

This reason concerns numbers. Just as we need to consider those living in different places, so, too, we need to consider people living at different times. And this generation shouldn't pursue policies regardless of the costs on future generations. Although they don't live now, their happiness has to be taken into account. It is unfair to land the unborn with more than their share of dirt, to offload on to them our unwanted risks, and to deny them their fair share of resources. But this ties our hands in what many see as unacceptable ways. For suppose, as seems plausible, that the human species will be around for another thousand, or another ten thousand, years. There are billions of people now alive, but there are trillions to come. Our generation represents a tiny proportion of all the people who will have lived their lives on this planet. And they are all, we are supposing, entitled to their share of the earth's resources. How big is our share? How much copper, or coal, or uranium, or marble can we use before we encroach on others? On the assumption that there are fair shares for all, and that fair here means equal, then almost none.

This difficulty is serious, but perhaps it isn't devastating. There isn't space here to go into philosophers' attempts to solve the problem,[13] but I can point out that it is most acute where finite and non-renewable resources are concerned. The more people there will be, the less our share of coal. It doesn't concern renewable resources in the same way. If we can grow, use and replant a forest, so too will future generations be able to do this. Nor does it in the same way concern pollution, for it is unlikely to be true that the more people there will be, the worse it is for us to pollute. (If the dirt will be around forever, and threaten everyone equally, then this could be true. Nuclear waste is the nearest example. But most pollution is not like this. The next generation can clean up our mess.) Does it in a similar way concern preservation? Arguably it does. The wrongness of allowing tigers to become extinct gets worse, the more generations there will be to regret their loss. But we might suppose the generation that experiences the loss feels it more. We don't miss mammoths.

Scope

The third consideration is of a different kind. Consequentialism in all its varieties requires us to consider people wherever and whenever they are. Because of the large scale and long-term nature of our problems such requirements may be environmentally beneficial. Whether the environment can benefit in a third way will depend on the version of consequentialism we choose to adopt.

The sorts of objections that are often brought against consequentialist thinking, even if they are not always coherently articulated, are that it is anthropocentric, overly rationalistic, and materialistic, concerned typically with fairly base sources of human happiness. Now it is the third charge that I am concerned with here. Perhaps if we are concerned simply with pleasure, with what people happen to want, or with a crude understanding of happiness, then it is likely that the environment will suffer. Wetlands will be drained and turned into theme parks, deserts will offer scope for retirement homes, plants and animals will become extinct whenever their survival conflicts with our pleasure.[14] But, as I have suggested, consequentialism tolerates various construals of the good, and if we are, instead, concerned with well-being, with happiness more richly understood, and the conditions under which we and our kind might thrive, then the prospects for the environment are arguably much improved.

Many will claim that our living well is just not possible without a certain kind of concern for our surroundings, and as we are natural creatures, living as part of the natural world, this concern needs to take into account the world's own well-being, its overall state of health and its beauty, as well as its utility. Our living well requires that not only material, but also psychological and spiritual needs are satisfied, and these are seriously compromised, the argument goes, in any attempt fundamentally to detach ourselves from the natural world, to see it purely as a resource, each part of which is valueless unless it offers a direct contribution to human happiness. Thus much that is not of immediate concern is of concern nevertheless; much that doesn't contribute to our pleasure can still add to long-term satisfactions; and much the point or value of which we fail to grasp can be argued to have a value, and to provide for the deeper of human needs. Even if we never visit wilderness, it is good for us to know that it is there; even if the threatened plants cannot be used for food or drugs, we should still regret their disappearance; and even if we were to find a concrete and plastic world easier, cheaper and more fun to inhabit, we would still be mistaken to create such a world for ourselves.[15]

So, the more subtle our notion of human well-being, the more we veer away from a purely subjective concern with pleasant sensations, and towards an objective account of happiness, the more scope there is for insisting that people's actual preferences don't always line up with their real interests. Then it can be argued, not implausibly, that a range of pro-environmental policies that are otherwise difficult to justify find their rationale. If we were consequentialists, and were concerned to do the best for our own and for our descendants' well-being, then many of the world's environmental problems would be better handled.

A rival account

A major objection to consequentialism is its denial of agent relativity. One form of that objection, that it refuses us permission to pursue our own projects, can, I suggested, be set aside. It finds its target if it is claimed that we have here an all-embracing theory that tells everyone, in every instance, how they should decide what to do. But if consequentialism is restricted to legal and political decision-making, then this objection has less force. Although individual action will certainly make a difference to the environment, it is not unreasonable to think that today's large-scale problems stand in need of large-scale solutions. The other form of the objection remains critical. Consequentialism often requires us to perform actions that, on an intuitive level, it seems should not be performed. In endeavouring to maximize the overall good I might need to steal from the supermarket in order to feed my children; a doctor might need to kill one patient in order to use various organs to save many lives; a judge might need to send innocent people to prison in order to relieve public anxiety about crime and the causes of crime; and a government might deliberately bomb innocent civilians, in order to bring an end to a war that would otherwise drag on with an overall greater loss of life. Although overall happiness might, by acting in these ways, be increased, so acting can still seem straightforwardly wrong.

Must this objection to consequentialism remain at the level of intuition? Not according to rights theorists. For they want to put forward an account under which these objections are appropriately explained; it is because individuals enjoy certain rights that these restrictions to our maximizing the overall good come into play. We are permitted, and perhaps sometimes required,[16] to produce best outcomes until the point where rights are about to be infringed, at which point this concern for consequences must give way. So it is because shopkeepers have certain property rights, because patients have a right to benefit from and not unwittingly to contribute to medical treatment, because the accused have a right to a fair trial and due process, and because civilians have a right to be distinguished, in war, from combatants, that, in cases such as those above, the consequentialist programme begins to come unstuck.

Notions of, and appeals to, rights are widespread. Further, many people believe that such notions, and such appeals, can be fashioned into a wide-ranging moral theory which then forms a rival to consequentialism in accounting for what we might and might not do. And certainly, where the environment is concerned, appeal to rights will make for substantial differences in the kinds of activities that are permitted, and proscribed. But although rights talk is familiar, certain of its challenges to consequentialism effective and belief in its overall coherence not uncommon, it is far from clear that it can in the end fully deliver on its promise of a theory.

Some details

Certain distinctions can be introduced. In each case, although the distinction will seem straightforward enough, and the rationale for drawing it tolerably clear, there are problems in its wake. These problems are perhaps not insoluble, but they do eat away at the alleged theory's initial appeal.

First, it will be fairly clear that what is under question is the existence and status of moral as opposed to legal rights. That there is a battery of legal rights is not under dispute, nor can there be disagreement about certain basic features of such rights. These legal rights are established by and dependent on statute, and thus can and do vary from place to place, time to time, and person to person. And although there are occasions on which lack of clarity within the law can make a particular case problematic, in most situations disagreement about which rights one has can be easily settled. But, as I suggested earlier, it is often thought that the law itself should be guided by moral considerations, so that one ought on the one hand to have this or that legal right, which is as yet denied, or ought not on the other to be allowed to do that which the law so far permits.[17] Appeal here to an underlying moral framework – which on most accounts doesn't vary, or vary much from place to place, time to time, or person to person – means that evaluation might be made of two discrete and internally coherent systems of law, in which various legal rights are embedded, with the result that one of them is, on moral grounds, to be preferred. No mention yet, quite, of moral rights, but it often comes close behind, so that it is claimed not only that one ought to be permitted to do such and such, but that one has a moral right to do it, that one government shows, in its system of laws, greater respect for moral rights than another, and so on.[18]

Yet whereas the existence of legal rights is uncontroversial, that of moral rights is hotly disputed. Are there really such things? If they exist, they can neither be created nor destroyed, they can in no straightforward way be perceived by either direct or indirect means, and when asked to furnish a list of such rights, sane, intelligent and well-meaning people will typically and persistently disagree. That one has this or that moral right is often asserted quite dogmatically, with little attempt at justification, and it is not at all difficult for the sceptic to worry that the entire edifice is built on air, and that rights have a place in a well-structured universe akin to curses or spells. It is just such worries about their ontological status that caused Bentham, famously, to refer to rights as "nonsense upon stilts", displaying there a predilection for metaphysical austerity that is echoed, more recently, in John Mackie's more wide ranging critique of moral realism as a stance that posits various "queer entities" – things whose ontological status is irredeemably suspect, and whose alleged existence we can well do without.[19]

This is to target rights understood as real, independent and non-physical items within the world's furniture, but there are arguably other, and more acceptable ways in which they might be construed. One is suggested by utilitarianism itself, which, developed in a certain style, can accommodate some notions of moral rights within the consequentialist frame. For while in its fundamental form the theory insists that with each act we produce the best overall consequences, the practical difficulties here encourage a variant that requires us to follow the broad principles that do best for consequences overall. A shift in focus from acts to rules renders utilitarianism rather more plausible, and at the same time countenances some reference to rights: to say that people have a right to a fair trial is to say no more than that following the rule "give everyone a fair trial" will produce overall better consequences than will either following a rival rule, or deciding each time on a case-by-case basis. There are, though, real dangers here of falling between two stools. Rule utilitarianism, notoriously, collapses back into the earlier act version, and most rights theorists see this nod in their direction as little better than a wink. The reason is this. Even if utilitarianism can find some space for rights, and even if it might in the end bestow virtually the same rights on people as will a rights theory proper, the rationale remains importantly different. For the utilitarian has always an eye to aggregate welfare; we grant people individual rights just because that is in the end better for the overall good. This certainly makes the existence of rights less problematic, but it also undermines their distinctiveness. Rather than an unchanging and authoritative given, rights are now seen as a means to an end and, importantly, can change as circumstances render one means more efficient or effective than another. Many rights theorists see this as an inversion too far, believing that it is something about the individual, and what he might and might not both do and suffer, that should come first, rather than a concern for the collective.[20]

Fixedness is important here, and it is just this notion of absolute, unconditional restrictions on what we might do to one another that the rights theorist focuses on. And although there are, of course, many questions as to what these restrictions are, and why they should be thought to hold, it isn't clear that they need be grounded in some metaphysically suspect entities. To say that one has a right not to be tortured is just to say that torture is absolutely, unconditionally wrong, and not (as the consequentialist would have it) wrong only as long as torturing will fail to produce some net benefit overall. That seems to make sense, and doesn't (*contra* Bentham and Mackie) appear immediately to be too much in the ontological fast lane.

What, though, underlies this whole approach? Why should we think an individual has, in this way, certain moral rights? Why, conversely, should there be these allegedly unbending restrictions on what we may do? There are some reasonable general considerations that need to be brought to light here, and then two contrasting ways in which this general account might be unpacked.

In the background is Kant, and the broadly Kantian distinctions between, first, means and ends and, secondly, categorical and conditional imperatives or rules.[21] What consequentialism appears to condone, and even at times to encourage, is the use of another person as a means to some greater good. The stock example is the unfortunate down-and-out who enters hospital for some minor operation, only to be killed, cut up and his parts used for a number of life-saving or merely life-enhancing procedures. The raw intuition that this is wrong is elaborated, within a Kantian account, into the insistence that it is impermissible to treat people merely as means, and that we are required instead to see them as ends, as things that matter, deserve respect, have a value in themselves, independently both of any good they might do, and of any localized or contingent properties they might have. Brain surgeons and beauty queens are not to be the only people guaranteed safe passage through our hospitals. Prohibitions are thus categorical, deriving from a thing's unchanging status as an end, and not conditional, normally in place but over-ridden when greater goods are in sight. Although the emphasis might so far appear to focus on what we can't do, the whole structure here can be readily inverted, bringing rights to the surface. Killing the down-and-out is wrong: he has a right to life. Lying is wrong: we have a right to hear the truth. Using people is wrong: there is a right to freedom, to respect. Nor is there a need to decide on priorities here. Rules, obligations and rights are intimately linked in a moral framework that elevates an unbending commitment to principle above a concern with outcomes.

Details of this rule-based or deontological account are not, and cannot here be, clear,[22] but the notion that certain things should be seen not as means but as ends can connect with two broad lines of thought. The first emphasizes autonomy. It has been argued, most notably by H. L. A. Hart,[23] that to recognize an individual's moral rights is to recognize the overarching importance of their being able to take charge of their own life, to make certain choices, whatever they may be, and to pursue their own plans and projects. The Kantian perspective is here very firmly in frame. A second approach focuses on interests. As we have, independently of our often fleeting and irrational desires and preferences, certain interests, things that will contribute to our well-being or good, so there are important restrictions on what others may do in our regard. At least some of an individual's genuine interests cannot be overridden for the sake of some greater good elsewhere. The distinction here has a bearing (and this becomes increasingly important in later chapters) on the size and nature of the constituency of those having some or other moral rights. Under the former of these accounts, rights will be restricted, more or less, to rational and self-conscious beings, those able to exercise genuine choice, to plan for themselves a life and reflect on its changing shape. Perhaps some human beings and certainly most non-human animals will thus fail to have any rights at all. The interest account is less parsimonious, and as the range of things having interests is much wider, bestows rights on a considerably larger scale. To take what I hope is an uncontroversial example, a new-born child is hardly yet an autonomous being, but it has a range of interests. It has rights on the latter account, but not on the former.[24]

The distinction has a bearing, too, on a further, related issue concerning the constituency of those having rights. For it is often, and often unthinkingly, said that rights are correlative with responsibilities or with duties, and that morality always wears two hats, concerned to free us to pursue our own lives, on the one hand, and restrain us with respect to lives elsewhere, on the other. What is surely correct in this is the idea that rights, whosoever has them, do generate duties or responsibilities in others to act, or to refrain from acting, in certain ways. If I have a right to free speech, you have a duty not to interfere with my exercise of that right. You ought to let me speak. It seems clear, then, that if there are rights anywhere, there are duties somewhere. What is not obviously correct is the further suggestion that anyone having rights must thereby incur some duties or responsibilities; that rights and duties fall in the same place. This second claim will be correct on Hart's account, for those self-conscious, autonomous and rational agents who enjoy rights will be precisely the kinds of things that have duties or responsibilities, and are constrained by morality, with respect to others. But consider the alternative model. It seems perfectly possible for something or someone to have interests, and thus rights, and still not have the requisite intellectual make-up for the notions of duties or responsibilities to find their proper home. A storm, a tree, a virus, a snake and an infant have no duties – they can damage or injure things, but they cannot do wrong in the moral sense – but it doesn't straightforwardly follow from that that they have no rights. And as it isn't clear that the autonomy model is the one to follow, so it isn't clear that rights and responsibilities are so closely connected as many seem to believe.

There may yet, however, be reason for preferring the former model over its rival, for if rights are not already stacked in rows in some Platonic heaven, where do they come from? Contractarianism holds that rights are uncovered and established in some sort of give-and-take discussion among free and rational agents, who see that although there will be some losses to individual freedom in recognizing the rights of others, there will, as far as their own security is concerned, be outweighing gains. This social contract model again restricts rights to those who might be a party to the contract. There is no incentive to make promises to or respect the freedoms of creatures who can offer nothing in return.[25] But this marked reciprocity within the contractarian account is considered by some to be a defect: given the depth of our intuitions that one can do right or wrong to creatures other than those with whom we bargain, there is within such an account only a part of morality at best.

Even if there is here no need to decide finally between these different accounts, there is still need to draw out a further distinction that figures in most of them, and that, again, has bearing on environmental matters. Start by noting one major difference between rights-based and consequentialist ethical theories. Only the latter purport to tell us what to do in every case, for only the latter insist that what we ought always to do is maximize the overall good. Rights theories are less ambitious, and not in this way at odds with the intuition that some of what we do is up to us. Indeed, it may well be thought that to provide a sound basis for that intuition is one of their principal aims, for again, if we focus not so much on the rights and rights holders themselves, as on the duties they lay on others, it becomes clear that what such theories emphasize is the proper limits on the freedom of rational creatures. I am at liberty to exercise autonomy, live my own life and pursue my own projects just as long as I don't infringe the rights of others.[26] How far this requirement, this duty-doing, interferes with my own existence depends, then, on the nature and number of rights that others enjoy, and the extent to which our circles overlap. And traditionally, rights have been construed as falling into two main kinds, which then impose on me correspondingly different duties.

There are first, then, negative rights, which imply duties not to act in certain ways. Your right to life, as it is typically construed, demands that I refrain from killing you, rather than that I provide the means for keeping you alive. Your right to liberty similarly imposes duties not to restrict your movement, rather than positively to assist you in getting around. Such rights figure large in the liberal tradition, and constitute generous parameters on the scope for individual activity. It is, for most of us and for most of the time, relatively easy not to infringe rights like these, as the duties they impose are easy to fulfil. And these duties fall, at least in principle, indiscriminately on all those capable of having duties of any kind. It is academic at the moment, but nevertheless true that I ought not to steal from vineyards in Chile.

There are also, however, according to many, positive rights, which generate duties of a more demanding kind. The positive right to education requires that the means to education be provided, as similarly does the right to healthcare imply that there is a duty to provide and maintain a system of doctors, hospitals, medicines and the like. Duties here, unlike negative duties, do not (and evidently need not) fall on everyone; it is enough that someone, or some body, provides the requisite assistance. The difficulty here, of course, is that it is more tempting to agree that such rights exist as long as one is not inconvenienced by the corresponding duties falling on one's own shoulders. Where exactly they do fall is, notoriously, a matter for some debate.

Two problems

Although, or perhaps because, ordinary talk of rights has the edge over consequentialism so far as intuition is concerned, there are greater difficulties in putting together a developed theory of rights. I will mention two well-known problems here.

First there is the question of what to do when different rights conflict. My right to freedom of expression, supposing I am given to racist invective, will clash with your right to a life free of gratuitous offence; the fetus's right to life will conflict with the right of a woman to do with her body as she will; and the right of countries to settle their internal disputes may be at odds with the rights of groups of citizens to self-determination. Some of these conflicts can be avoided by denying that the alleged right really exists, but although on occasions entirely legitimate – people just don't have a right to play loud music at three in the morning, whatever they say – this is a move that can at times appear *ad hoc*, and will, if pursued consistently, severely prune the number of rights any of us might enjoy. A more promising strategy is to devise a hierarchy of rights, a way of ranking them so that it becomes clear, in conflict cases, just where the priority lies. And one often made suggestion here has been that negative rights take priority over their positive counterparts, so that, for example, your right to bodily integrity takes priority over my right to healthcare. I cannot demand your kidney even if you, but not I, can live without it. But this can leave positive rights in an invidious position. Construe the right to property negatively, such that we can keep what property we have, make this right one that takes priority over any positive right, then the legitimacy of the tax system, and with it the means to provide those in need with the staples of existence, is fatally compromised.

The problem here derives, in part, from the underlying idea that rights are absolute – your right to life, for example, doesn't depend on there being no one with some seemingly better use for your body, and the right to liberty is not one that governments should set aside whenever it is expedient to do so – and that idea is deeply problematic even before conflicts between rights come into play. The consequentialist's apparent ease in proposing the sacrifice of the one for the many may well be counterintuitive, especially when the net gains resulting from such sacrifice are relatively small. But when it is insisted that the individual's rights are sacrosanct and that it would be wrong, for example, deliberately to kill an innocent person, even if that were the only way of saving a whole city, then intuitions can veer the other way, and rights theorists finds it considerably harder to defend their position. Supposing there does in this case appear to be a defence, the critic can simply up the ante. If the survival of an entire country, the entire world, depends on killing this innocent person, would it still be wrong to do so?[27] And if it depends only on twisting that person's arm, or hitting them over the head with a briefcase? To answer negatively here is not simply to endorse consequentialist thinking, for the thought may be that while killing the innocent is not justified whenever a greater good will thereby ensue, some goods are so great that such killing might be permitted, or even required. And so even without a precise answer as to which size goods warrant such action, there is enough here to worry at the fundamentals of the rights account.

Rights and the environment

These problems in constructing a well-formulated theory of rights cannot simply be ignored. Even so, we might wait for their final solution, and in the meantime consider to what extent a rights-based approach could help with the environment.

There are likely to be benefits. If we offer even an unadventurous account of the rights people have, and then endeavour to respect those rights, some of the more evident environmental problems will be, to varying extents, alleviated. For this unadventurous account may well refer, among other things, to such public goods as clean air and water, to living free of hazardous substances, and to food's being safe. If it is suggested that people have rights in respect of such goods, then in so far as those rights are taken seriously, various forms of environmental pollution will have to cease. And if the account then goes on to propose further rights, for example to security of housing, access to the countryside, or concerning the state of the world to be left for one's children, then there will be correspondingly further benefits. And this is still so far a cautious list of negative rights; the suggestion is not that one has a right, for example, to be provided with housing, but only that if one has a house, it cannot simply be taken away as a result of some government's motorway construction or dam building or weapons testing scheme. Even some very basic rights, to freedom of speech, liberty and education, might be considered environmentally friendly, at least in so far as it is reasonable to believe that democratic processes and open government with which such rights are connected will do more for the environment than will the alternatives.

Although there are many ways in which rights talk can acquire a radical edge, the picture I am giving here is one in which appeal to rights is in several respects importantly conservative in tendency. And as many environmental problems might seem to result from an overenthusiasm for innovation, this appeal will take shape as a restraining force, holding back unwelcome and untested development and change. But this is only one side of the story. Certain of the problems that we face result from carrying on in the old ways when, as circumstances have changed, a new approach is called for. Consider, for example, the right to have children. Even if, plausibly, we construe this as a negative right, such that there is no entitlement to assistance with reproduction, or with financing a family, it may still seem that the free exercise of such a right is at odds with long-term environmental stability. Similarly, the claims that are often made to having a right to continue with some long established ways of life – logging, foxhunting, whaling, or simply continuing with traditional access to the countryside[28] – can hold back legislation necessary to meet the problems of a changing world.

If appeal to rights might in this way run foul of what is needed regarding present populations, the problems become more difficult where future generations are concerned. Some of these problems have been visited earlier: on the assumption that there will be many more generations of people on earth, then fair shares for all might leave us with impossibly small allocations of finite resources. Social contract theories have a quick way with this, of course – as generations as yet unborn have made no deal with us we can hardly steal from them – but this is only a make-believe solution to a problem that is all too real.

That is a particular problem, but the overall conclusion might be, although unexciting, somewhat less pessimistic. Setting all the difficulties in fully articulating a rights theory to one side, it seems reasonable to believe that if we gave greater acknowledgement to people's rights the environment would benefit in several significant respects, even if in certain others there might be no improvement, and even some harm. I suggest that this is true, even without giving a precise account of what rights people might most plausibly be thought to have, and even without offering any detail on what environmental benefit and harm might amount to. Achieve greater precision on both sides here and still I doubt whether this bland conclusion would be either improved upon or withdrawn.

The virtues

Opposition to both consequentialist and deontological approaches to moral theory has, in recent years, led to a revival of interest in virtue-based accounts of what we should and should not do. I can only sketch some of the basics of such accounts here, but hope nevertheless to show how they differ in important ways from those more familiar approaches considered so far. The virtue approach has, as will emerge, evident merits. Whether it can justifiably be considered a viable alternative to the more standard theories is, however, another matter.

At the heart of the virtue approach is attention to the notion of character, and to the sorts of character traits or settled dispositions by which someone will be habitually guided in both action and thought. It is objected that rival theories neglect this, and either systematically undermine the consistency necessary for character, as when utilitarian and other consequentialist accounts demand that we do whatever is needed to maximize outcomes, or give to character more or less free rein, as when rights-based accounts appear indifferent to what we do, as long as we don't infringe the rights of others. Thus virtue-based accounts put more of an emphasis on the kinds of people we are, rather than the particular things we do, with, of course, the very reasonable assumption that good people will tend to do the right thing.[29] And they will tend to do the right thing often unthinkingly, for someone of good character, having acquired the appropriate dispositions, is thereafter only seldom required to reflect long and hard as to how to act. Such a person will be generous, honest, reliable and kind as a matter of course, and not only when it is expedient, or otherwise appropriate, to be so.[30] What is the upshot? Virtue theorists look on the moral world as importantly coherent and unified, and so step around many of the questions about what motivates us to morality that so bedevil alternative accounts. Having the virtues, acting virtuously, is good for others but good, too, for oneself. It may not always be obvious to someone not yet on the right road, but the life of virtue is also likely to be the happy life.

Virtue theorists propose, moreover, that the very existence of people of good character can provide solutions to a range of moral dilemmas. For if one wants to know what would be the right thing to do in some particular situation one should take a virtuous person as an exemplar: what they do, along with their reasons for doing it, provides a model that one may well try to emulate.[31] What one will learn by such a procedure is, as the theory readily acknowledges, subtle and complex, for the virtuous person's response to the morally problematic situation is guided by and sensitive to the precise details of that situation, and not by a simple and quasi-mechanical application of a formula or rule.[32] And this has bearing on how good character might be acquired. Long-term education, serious engagement with the array of life's problems and becoming habituated to the right responses are essential. And the ethics of virtue, as many of its proponents have pointed out, is more likely to be learned, its implications more fully understood, from reading a good novel than from plodding through some academic tome.

Now there are undoubtedly merits in the virtue approach. Contrasting theories do very much neglect the role and importance of character within our moral thinking, and they do often appear to brush aside the complexities within many ethical dilemmas. Virtue accounts are more supple. Utilitarianism, for example, appears to claim that in lying, cheating or killing in order to maximize overall good, one does nothing wrong at all. Deontological accounts, in contrast, issue flat prohibitions in such cases. The virtue approach, uniquely here, gives conventional morality a strong but not impregnable place in our moral thinking, acknowledging that there are times when we might properly choose the lesser of two evils, and in connection with that, allowing for, and showing interest in notions such as regret, conscience and bad luck.[33] And there is substance. Depending on which approach we choose, the outcomes may differ. A virtuous person will be consistently benevolent, while the consequentialist will assess benevolence's effects from case to case, and while prepared to recommend acting in accordance with the virtues as a rule of thumb, believes that there are times when what appears to be vice is called for. A virtuous person may refrain from some activity, telling cruel jokes about the dead, for example, where a rights theorist might find it difficult to recommend anything other than a free hand, holding that as the dead have no rights, no harm can be done to them.[34] But ought we to be fully fledged virtuous agents? And if we are, are we therefore able to solve moral dilemmas, and know for ourselves what to do? Although I will say something about the first of these questions, my focus here is on the latter.

Some problems

Set some evident difficulties aside, and suppose we have correctly identified a virtuous person from whom we hope, in time, to learn how appropriately to behave within a complex and testing world. And it will be in time, rather than right now, for, as I have noted, the virtue approach is alive to nuance. If the virtuous person keeps a promise on one or a number of occasions, we won't be able to conclude that promise-keeping is always the right thing to do. Suppose that in a given situation the virtuous person is confident about what should be done. Presumably following their example is appropriate only in so far as they are guided, on this particular occasion, by virtue, and only in so far as they are both well informed and acting rationally with respect to the situation. Someone may think that these worries are not real, for it is sometimes suggested that a virtuous person is virtuous through and through, and cannot be virtuous in certain respects, or only on certain days. Further, if being reasonable is itself a virtue, then emotion will not cloud the issue, and steps will be taken to acquire the relevant information on which to base a decision. Moreover, even if in this last respect the virtuous person is not entirely successful, and so acts differently from how they would were they better informed, still their action will stem from the right motives, and to that extent is worth copying.

A difficulty here is that virtuous people can disagree. Virtue, and confidence in virtue, can and does take different sides on issues such as abortion, hunting, animal experiments, patriotism and many others. Depending on which virtuous person one chooses to emulate, different lessons will be learned. A larger difficulty is that confidence is not always present. The virtuous person may just be uncertain as to how to respond to a particular moral dilemma, say about nuclear waste, or whether to permit the reintroduction of whaling. Acting virtuously may be always a good thing, but there are many situations in which it is unclear what this amounts to.

I say here that it may be a good thing because, of course, there is opposition to the virtue approach. It won't do to think that being virtuous is obviously a good thing, just as being good is obviously a good thing, for such a thought glosses over the distinctiveness of the virtue approach. Whereas consequentialism can be accused of putting too little emphasis on personal integrity, the virtue approach may give this too much weight. Even without going all the way down the consequentialist road, it isn't obviously wrong to think that there are times when one ought to set aside a concern with character and being true to oneself, and act instead, even if in some ways disreputably, in the service of some greater good.[35] If it is objected here that to speak of a concern with character is to picture the virtuous person as unduly narcissistic, too consciously looking after self at the expense of the world, then let the claim simply be that there are times when habit can get in the way. But my point here is not simply about those cases where the virtuous person is well aware that a rival theory recommends a different course of action from the one they are inclined to follow, but about the cases also where they have no strong inclination either way. Consequentialists can, of course, find themselves in this situation, but they know, in principle, how the dilemma should be solved. A worry about the virtue approach is that it lacks the theoretical apparatus to say even what a solution would look like. Solutions, though, are needed.

Virtues and the environment

Again, as with previous accounts, it seems reasonable to suppose that were more people virtuous, the environment would benefit.[36] Many of its perceived problems are attributable in large part to what can be described as defects of character. Because people are greedy, because they lack generosity and sympathy towards others, because they are dishonest, shifty or economical with the truth when it comes to offering proper assessments of risk and damage, so the environment suffers, as indeed people suffer, in unaccountably many ways. Yet, as I note, the virtue approach is perhaps less effective than rival accounts when we are faced, as often we are, with genuine dilemmas about what to do. Should we impose apparently small risks of serious environmental damage for considerable gains in human welfare, or are no such risks worth taking? Should we allow nature to run its course when the result will be widespread animal suffering, or should we hope to intervene? Should we, for environmental benefits, limit growth in developing countries even while standards of living there are way behind ours? And so on. Whereas consequentialism offers, at least in principle, a means whereby such questions can be answered, the approach through virtue is less forthcoming.

There are two related limitations on virtue's efficacy where many environmental problems are concerned, both of which stem from the need to find, and fairly soon, workable solutions to large-scale problems. Virtue theory, unlike consequentialism, which is initially framed and best equipped to help shape matters of law and politics, is mostly centred on what individual human

beings do. This is no accident, for while certain of the theory's concerns –
dispositions, agency, even integrity – can be predicated of various kinds of
things, the central notion, that of character, applies clearly and unequivocally
only to human beings. Only they can have character, and only they can be or
fail to be, in the deeper sense, genuinely happy. But an individual's ability to
shape the environment is limited, with most of the important and large-scale
decisions being taken by governments, government agencies or international
bodies representing, often, the voice of several governments. So first, whereas
there is room among individuals for personal decisions that are not imposed
on others – I might believe that eating meat is wrong but have no wish to
proselytize – governments typically need the consent at least of their own
citizens in what they choose to do. So the demand for justification is greater.
Acting virtuously often leaves room for subtlety, hesitation, a reluctance to
public pronouncement, which is inappropriate for bodies that have no private
face. And secondly, it isn't clear that we should or even can want such bodies
to act virtuously. It isn't clear that we should, for it can seem that at times hard
decisions have to be taken and a government that was habitually honest, loyal
or generous might be seriously ineffective. And it isn't clear that we can, just
because a government is not the kind of thing that can have character, and so
not the kind of thing that can be benefited or harmed, made happy or
unhappy, as can a human being, by being disposed to act one way rather than
the other.[37] There is an obvious rejoinder, of course, and that is to point out
that governments and similar bodies are made up of human beings, who are
just as capable of virtuous or vicious action as the rest of us. This is right. But
is it equally right to suggest that one should not do collectively what one
would not do as an individual, such that a government whose members are all
virtuous will be incapable of acting in a way that a virtuous person could not
act? This isn't, I think, immediately clear, though the issues are not ones that
can be pursued here. Suffice it to say only that there at least appear to be
difficulties in applying the virtue model to many of the larger environmental
problems that the world presently faces.

Intuition and theory

Go back a little. I suggested that the virtue approach, unlike consequentialism, will simply fail to offer answers to a wide range of substantial moral
dilemmas. Is this a shortcoming? I want to suggest that in certain respects it is
not. One way of looking at the situation as it has unfolded so far is to think
that we have three competing moral theories,[38] two of which offer firm and
unequivocal answers to a range of moral dilemmas while the third is often
vague and indecisive. If we assume that straight answers are what we want,
then this third account will be found wanting. But of course consequentialist

and rights theories notoriously offer different straight answers to the same moral dilemmas, and so how, unless there is a way of choosing between them, can it be clear that their alleged benefits are genuine?

There are, in general, various considerations relevant to selecting one theory over another. One concerns internal consistency. A theory needs to fit together in such a way that it can always be consistently applied, or appealed to. A second consideration relates to a theory's economy and elegance. It is usually considered a virtue of a theory that it makes use of minimum number of terms and concepts, that it isn't awkward or clumsy. It counts in favour of the Copernican system that it explains planetary motion in a more straight-forward manner than does the epicycle-heavy Ptolemaic account. A third concerns the theory's relationship to the facts with which it purports to deal. Earlier accounts, which put the earth at the centre of the universe, were elegant enough, but unfortunately they didn't fit with observations of heavenly bodies. A closely related issue is that of explanatory power. A theory needs some punch, and it only gets this if predictions made in accordance with the theory, while it is hoped they come true, might in principle turn out to be false. In short, and somewhat obviously, what theories want to be are appropriately generalized accounts of what are in the world appropriately structured sets of phenomena.

However, now it seems that moral theories have certain important obstacles to overcome. While they might well enough meet the first two criteria – consequentialism, for example, is both internally consistent and surprisingly elegant, and there is something undeniably attractive about the way in which seemingly disparate virtues are supposed in the end to fit together – there are pronounced difficulties where matching the theory to the facts is concerned. For there is just very little agreement about what sorts of things, if anything at all, moral facts are, and about what particular things are the facts in a given case. The first worry here might be thought of as uncomfortably abstract, and the ontological status of purported moral facts something we might for practical purposes set aside. But it spills over into the second, into our heated disputes as to just what is true and what is false, just what we ought to do and what not, where morality is concerned. I don't want to be unduly sceptical here, or to exaggerate the differences between scientific theories on the one hand, and so-called moral theories on the other. It might be said that there are disputes, too, in science, and that when active disagreement is over, still we fall short of complete certainty. It might be said also that conversely, where morality is concerned, not everything is up for grabs. As there is broad agreement that the earth goes round the sun, so there is similarly broad agreement that torturing the innocent is wrong. And as there is protracted debate about the morality of abortion, or animal rights, or how principle and pragmatism should be weighed, so in science, too, disagreement can be prolonged. But there are differences nevertheless. First, there is just much more agreement about science than morality. Secondly, and more important, we have a fairly clear notion of what agreement in science depends on. We have a good enough grasp of what scientific facts are like, and understand, often, what sorts of facts are relevant to, and would help settle a particular contentious case. And it is this that is lacking in the moral situation. We might agree about all the scientific facts that have a bearing on a case, and agree too that no further facts will make any material difference, and yet still disagree about what should be done. It isn't clear, then, even in principle, how moral disputes are to be resolved.

This gives science the edge. For the predictions that its theories makes might, even if we are at first disinclined to believe them, be later established beyond all reasonable doubt. And the more this happens, the more we will be obliged to accept the theory, and to buy into its further implications. But it is much harder to see how a moral theory can in any similar way compel assent. Take consequentialism, and suppose that you are in general sympathetic to the idea that it is right to produce the best outcomes overall. But then a situation arises in which it becomes clear that to produce the best outcome you are required (as is alleged of a number of politicians) to sell your own grandmother. Should you do this? Yes, in so far as you subscribe to the theory, but your intuitions may well tell you that this is a best outcome too far. And it is stubbornly unclear how the theory takes priority over intuition here. Similarly for rights. Although disposed to acknowledge that there is a right to life, you might believe that in extreme situations this right is overridden by benefits available elsewhere. You might even kill your grandmother, or at least someone else's grandmother, in order to save a city from annihilation. Again, the theory's dictates conflict with intuition. Yet it isn't clear, and I think it can't be clear, that such conflicts ought to be resolved one way rather than the other. As some will believe theory has to give, so others will insist that we dump these particular intuitions. But however in the end the argument is supposed to go, it is hard to see how on either side there can be the sort of reasoned confidence or conviction that so often figures in disagreement in science. And so it is hard to see how moral theory, in particular, can acquire the status of its non-moral counterpart. How could there be in morality, as opposed to beliefs others may have about it, any great surprise?

This isn't at all to suggest, however, that moral theory has no proper role, or that intuitions here are sacrosanct. For as consistency is a virtue where theory is concerned, so it is more generally, and one problem for raw intuitions is that they often don't mesh well together. Thus someone might deplore the felling of trees and yet happily eat steak in a restaurant. Or they might fight for more access to the countryside and yet worry about many of the effects of tourism. There is no gross inconsistency between such pairs of positions, but there are degrees of tension, which many feel ought to be re-solved. And when intuitions are at odds in this way, what often happens is either that considerations are appealed to that dispel the tension, or that in the end one or the other is amended or abandoned. I am against killing plants, but for killing animals. This looks odd. I might see that my objection in the case of trees is that they are rare, ancient or beautiful, while the cow is none of these. Or I might come to think of my concerns as sentimental. Or I might change my diet. And then I am on the way to theory. None of this is really news, and the inability of moral theories simply to swamp our intuitions, and the consequent need for readiness to adjust these theories in the light of such intuitions, is central to John Rawls's well-known account of reflective equilibrium,[39] a two-way process in which theory sometimes provides reasons (and persuasive power) to jettison our first and intuitive thoughts, while at other times is itself adjusted in order to take intuition into account. But while it is clear that there is a need for give and take, it is perhaps less clear what the final upshot will be. One the one hand is the belief that at the end of the day some stable, coherent and consistent position will be found, and that there is, even if markedly complex, some systematic procedure for settling the puzzles of morality. But on the other is the suspicion that even when we have given, and taken, and done in every way our best, morality will remain something of a haphazard thing, resistant even to sophisticated theorizing, and incapable of generating answers to every problem.

So go back to the virtue approach. If this is presented, as it not infrequently is,[40] as a third, competing theory, then it will labour under as many if not more difficulties than its rivals. There is no powerful argument showing that this is the approach to take. Its pronouncements will clash with intuition at many places, and, at least arguably, it will fail to deliver verdicts about a large number of difficult cases. But if instead it is offered as a critique of the very idea of an all-embracing moral theory, and a reminder of the enormous complexity of our moral lives, then the virtue approach has much to recommend it.

Summary

It is time to step back. I have wanted, so far, to focus on one issue: to what extent does a concern to promote human well-being give benefit to the environment? And I have suggested that the linkage here is considerable. A concern for our long-term futures will encourage a more cautious approach to new and dangerous technologies, and a much more careful attitude to limited resources. An aspiration to at least a roughly equal distribution of goods will work against the exploitation and degradation of parts of the world for the sake of alleged benefits elsewhere. And a broader perspective on what our well-being consists in encourages a concern for spiritual and aesthetic goods, which, again, are often well served by caring for and encounters with the natural environment.

I have wanted to suggest also that while an appeal to voting and pricing mechanisms might go some way towards furthering this well-being, it is more effectively and directly advanced via a commitment to some general theory of morality. Quite unsurprisingly, the best known moral theories have a concern with human well-being pretty much at their core. So I have been concerned, in this chapter, to consider how far consequentialist and rights-based or deontological theories in particular might, via their concern for our welfare, bring benefit to the environment. Again, the results here will be impressive. Commitment to such theories will, I have argued, require us to take greater care of the environment, putting it into the sort of shape many of us would like it to have, reducing the number and extent of its more evident problems, and making the natural world a fitter and longer lasting place than it at present looks like being. But such theories can take us only so far. None of them demands our allegiance, so none of them can offer convincing solutions through the range of moral dilemmas. There is no panacea, but even limited benefits are real. What underlies the approaches considered so far is a commitment to the broad shape of the philosophical method, a belief that through reason, reflection, discussion and argument lies our best hope of making any sort of progress in discovering what to do. Even if they offer no overarching and final solution, there are various local, provisional and piecemeal solutions to be had along the way, and we do better with them than without.

There will be a worry, however, that we are taken only so far in a further way. I have suggested that our well-being, unlike, say, having money in the bank, is something we should care about for its own sake. It is of direct moral concern. No one will argue with that, but the implication may well seem to have been that this alone is of direct concern. Just as money in the bank is valuable as a means to promoting our well-being, so, too, are clean air, preserving the rainforest and saving the whale. If we are concerned for ourselves, we must be concerned for the world about us. But what this overlooks, or so the worry has it, is the thought that the environment, or certain non-human elements within the environment, are also of direct concern, things we should care about for their own sake.

CHAPTER 5
Animals

We can justify a concern with the environment. Our getting pleasure depends on it. And, more important, our well-being depends on it. In so far as we are concerned with the long-term good of human beings, we have reason to care about the world around us, both instrumentally, in that it offers resources or commodities that we can use to further our good, and non-instrumentally, in that we can and should value certain of its aspects for their immediate relation to our well-being. The environment matters. Many environmental problems could be solved and its overall quality much improved if, for short-term and local concerns with pleasure, profit and material goods, we substituted a broader and longer-term perspective, focusing not on ourselves and our immediate wants, but on people in general, and their deeper needs. Perhaps we can have videos, cars and food, but human beings cannot flourish in a denatured and impoverished world.

So far, some good. But what is still missing, and some would say is obviously missing, is any direct concern for the well-being of anything other than human beings. We may be able to explain why we should care about the health of lapwings, or the conservation of fish or forests, or the preservation of national parks, or the state of the ozone layer, or the diversity of insect and plant life, all from a human point of view. Our well-being will suffer if we don't. These things, in various ways, matter to us. But do none of them matter in themselves? It is not enough to say that some things have non-instrumental value; for a beautiful sunset, seen not as a means but an end, still appears to get its value from human beings. For something to matter in itself, as I am using that phrase, its value is wholly independent of human concerns. Are there are any such things? Or is a world without human beings one completely without value, a world in which things exist, and changes occur, but in which none of these things are good or bad, and none of the changes for better or worse?

Some modest claims

Begin with animals. Isn't it obvious that the well-being of animals matters in itself, that their welfare is of concern even when it doesn't affect human well-being?[1] Or at least, isn't this obvious in so far as it is obvious that animals, like us, are capable of feeling, and do often feel, pleasure and pain? Like many others, I will focus here on pain. Pain is a bad thing and, other things being equal, the less of it the better. And isn't it also obvious that at least some animals do feel pain? So there is animal suffering. And a world in which animals suffer is, other things being equal, a worse world than one in which those same animals live a life free of pain. As they can suffer, so we cannot do with them just as we will. Wanton cruelty, and at least some forms of non-wanton cruelty,[2] are just impermissible, not because of their effects on us, but because of their effects on the animals concerned. These are modest claims, and most people, I think, will accept them as true.

Objections are of two sorts. There are those, first, who while agreeing with what is suggested here, think significantly more powerful claims can be advanced. Unless we give consideration to these further claims, we will unduly neglect the cause of animal welfare. And then there are those, secondly, who in different ways disagree with these suggestions, believing that even such apparently modest and, as I maintain, obviously true, claims are untenable. Both sorts of objection need to be addressed.

Advances

If there are already suspicions about my claims, it may be that they have been misunderstood. I say only that we cannot do with animals what we will, in so far as it is obvious that they feel pain. Now maybe there is room for doubt as to whether some animals do feel pain. I don't know much about oysters or their nervous systems except that they are rudimentary, and I have no qualms about eating them alive; I doubt if this hurts. But the claim is not that all animals can feel pain, and not that the well-being of all animals matters in itself. Although I don't want to deny flatly either of these claims, they don't figure in the modest position that I want to defend here. That position needs only that some among the animals can suffer pain.

The first kind of misunderstanding conflates *some* with *all*. A second conflates *some* with *equal*. But I make no claim here that animals deserve equal consideration with human beings, or that any of them have any kinds of rights, the force of which is equal to that of similar rights as applied to us, and a result of which is that certain actions are subject to an absolute prohibition. And so I make no overarching theoretical claim about the morality of our treatment of animals, and offer no formula for deciding, in every case, whether what we do is right or wrong. All that I am suggesting is obvious is that in so far as animals can suffer, we cannot treat them just as we like. If what we propose to do will cause them pain, then there is some reason to refrain, and we will need to be able to justify going ahead. But although there will be some reason to refrain, there may be a stronger reason to act, and I so far leave it open as to what will count as a reason, and what will make a reason strong. Perhaps it is easy to justify causing animals pain; perhaps it is difficult. Either way, though, the justification is called for.

There could also be a further misunderstanding. My thought is that because pain is obviously a bad thing we need to be able to justify increasing the amount of it in the world. Perhaps we propose to increase it directly by, say, killing some animals for food. Or perhaps we plan to increase it indirectly by, say, any of various developments that reduce the extent of animal habitats. But what about decreasing the amount? It may seem that if we are not permitted to cause animals to suffer, then, equally, we are not permitted simply to allow suffering to occur. We are under some obligation (although again one that might easily be over-ridden) to reduce animal suffering whenever possible. This may be so, and this latter obligation might be equal, or it might be somewhat less strong than the former, but I haven't so far suggested that it is obviously so. And all I want to focus on for the time being are claims about what we might or might not do, rather than corresponding claims about what we might or might not allow.

Go back to the second misunderstanding. My claim is that the well-being of animals requires some consideration, but perhaps not equal consideration with that of human beings. Although there is some obligation not to cause suffering in animals, it may be that this can be justified as a means to relieving equal or even lesser amounts of human suffering, or even that it can be justified as a means to producing modest amounts of human pleasure. I am not here arguing against foie gras. Against this, others claim that animals deserve or have a right to equal consideration with human beings. Not only are they in the same ball park, but the playing field is level. The modest claims are, I suggest, obviously correct, whereas the more ambitious claims are not obviously correct. Are these ambitious claims correct nevertheless? It is often held that they are, and much of the recent discussion of our treatment of animals has centred around arguments for and against them. I need now to consider aspects of those discussions. My intention, though, is not to give a comprehensive account of the animal welfare or animal rights debate, but simply to mark the differences between the modest and ambitious claims, and to suggest that the former still stand, although the latter may fall.

Singer: utility

Much of the shape of this debate is attributable to Peter Singer, who, almost certainly more than anyone, has forced on us a wholesale reappraisal of our treatment of and interactions with animals. Singer has a genuine concern for animal welfare, and is clearly prepared, as is often made evident in his lectures and writings, to further his cause by pulling at his audience's emotions, with graphic descriptions and illustrations of various forms of maltreatment[3] that animals too frequently undergo. But he writes always as a committed utilitarian, and insists that his prescriptions and proscriptions alike have a firm theoretical underpinning that (at least by reasonable people) cannot be denied. Radical change in our dealings with animals is called for, and the need for such change is argumentatively justified.

How does the argument go? Singer takes as evident the fact that animals can suffer, adds to it the moderately uncontroversial claim that they have an interest in not suffering and adjoins this with the moral claim, now more controversial, that equal interests be given equal consideration. His conclusion, then, is that much of our treatment of animals is morally indefensible.

This is utilitarianism, but not of a straightforwardly hedonistic variety. The emphasis is on interests and preferences, with, on Singer's account, the capacity for suffering forming a necessary and sufficient condition for a thing's having any interests at all. The point here is to generate an understanding of animal well-being that can be directly compared with that of human beings. Our good is only implausibly seen in the narrow terms of pleasure and pain, for our interests are wide ranging. Make clear that animals have interests too, and they fall within the same proto-moral frame. But do they have interests? It is unreasonable to suppose that animals consciously desire for themselves a better life, or even in rudimentary form ever think that such and such would be of interest to them, or in their interest. But Singer, quite correctly, understands having an interest in a different manner. Just as human interests are not always aligned with desires or conscious thought, as when it is observed that it is not in my interests to drive while drunk, though I would like to, or that it is in my interests to take more vitamin B2, though I have no beliefs in vitamins or their effects either way, so, too, animal interests are connected more with longer-term well-being than any immediate satisfaction of desire. So if an animal is in pain it is normally[4] in its interests that the pain should cease. And we may be happier about saying that, than saying that it wants the pain to cease. A worry here is that the capacity to feel may not be so obviously necessary to a thing's having interests as Singer supposes – if a chicken has interests, why not also a tree? – but that can be taken up elsewhere. The essential claim here is that animals do have interests, and not that plants don't, and I see no reason to deny that this is true.

What now follows, however? Singer's critical claim is that it simply doesn't matter, morally speaking, which creature's interests (and so which creature's suffering) we are considering. Just as within the human sphere utilitarianism requires that we give equal consideration to friends and strangers alike, so, Singer insists, we are similarly required to give equal consideration to the interests of both human beings and animals. Any discrimination, any favouring of creatures in some or other way closer to us just because they are closer, is, for the utilitarian, unwarranted and unjustifiable. And just as the blanket biases picked out by racism and sexism are morally wrong, so, too, is the comparable bias that leads us to the systematic downplaying of animals' interests in favour of our own. Singer makes much use of the term *speciesism*[5] to drive this point home. Unequal treatment of other human beings is something that many of us have come to see as manifestly unfair; this familiar moral insight needs now to be extended to members of other species.

Singer makes no obvious mistake. Speciesism names unwarranted discrimination between species, not the identification of and appropriate response to genuine distinctions. Given that genuine distinctions do exist, some differences in treatment may well be legitimate. So the claim is not, for example, that animals have just the range of interests we do – as Singer notes, pigs simply cannot vote, and so we do them no wrong in failing to include them on the electoral roll – nor that in the case where their interests do correspond to ours, these interests are satisfied or thwarted in exactly the same way. Slapping a small child may be morally wrong while slapping an elephant with the same degree of force is something to which we, like the elephant, may well be indifferent. The abiding thought is that, relative to species, a certain degree of pain, no matter how caused, is as much against the elephant's interest as is a corresponding amount of pain, again no matter how caused, against the interests of the child.[6]

Utilitarianism enters the argument at this stage. What, having given equal consideration to the interests of people and animals, are we now to do? For Singer it is plain that we should act impartially in order to maximize overall welfare, reducing suffering and promoting pleasure and happiness to best effect.[7] And it is equally plain that this will be very much to animals' benefit. Factory farming, certain alleged sports, product testing, vivisection and breeding for fur or for pets will all be severely curtailed. Your very moderate satisfaction in eating chicken nuggets is well outweighed by the miserable life and distressing end the hen has to undergo. The dubious pleasures of coursing can hardly justify the agony the hare will suffer. And the vast array of products in any chemist or supermarket undermines any case for squirting even more shampoo into rabbits' eyes. But, of course, utilitarianism issues in no general proscriptions, and so rules out no particular treatment *tout court*. We have to calculate the overall benefits and burdens involved in a range of options. So although it will be hard to justify the use of animals for seemingly frivolous purposes, still, in principle at least, such justification might be available. And they might continue to be used for medical research relating to both human and animal diseases, even if they are fewer in number, and better cared for.[8] Further, there can be no blanket proscription on the use of animals for food; although certain practices are sure to disappear, it is, in the end, a matter of weighing the various pains and pleasures involved. The benefits for animals may then not be quite so straightforward or universal as Singer seems to believe,[9] but they will be substantial nevertheless.

Assume we accept the argument. But there are difficulties. The first relates to the perfectly general one, already encountered, of giving any defence of the utilitarian bedrock. Why is it wrong to favour friends over strangers? And why is it wrong to favour human beings over rats or pigeons? The answer, in so far as one is available, is that we are required to exercise impartial benevolence. But that is an injunction for which there can be no effective sound argument. So if this underlying principle of utilitarianism doesn't fairly swiftly strike you as correct, the chances are it never will. And the problem here is that the greater the clash between a theory's basic principles and our own intuitions, the more reason there is to reject the theory. It is always uphill in this way with consequentialist or utilitarian accounts, but the incline is steeper when it is made clear that we are to consider not only human beings, but animals as well. Equal consideration, when applied to our kind, has a certain appeal. When directed elsewhere this appeal is considerably weakened.[10]

The second difficulty is more particularly relevant here, and worries at the analogy between racism and sexism on the one hand, and speciesism on the other. Although it may now seem naive to deny that there are any race-based differences (as it now seems more thoroughly naive to deny that there are sex-based differences – men and women differ physiologically, so it would be a strange evolution if there were not attendant psychological differences)[.11] the points remains, first, that we can well enough understand what and how great these differences are, and secondly, that men and women, blacks and whites, are still sufficiently alike for talk of equal interests, and the plausible measuring and assessing of those interests, to get a pretty firm foothold. We can, in short, make the reasonable assumption that, in general, one person's pain might be very much like another's, and so that, in principle at least, information about these pains can be entered into our calculations about what to do. But can we make any corresponding assumption where vastly different species are concerned? Even while not wanting to deny that fish feel pain, do we know how to begin comparing the pain of fish with that of birds? How is ten minutes of pain for a rabbit, which has a relatively short life, to be weighed against an equal pain of the same duration for a parrot or tortoise? What sorts of pleasures do swallows get from their low-level aeronautics? And so on.[12]

So even if we agree that the capacity for suffering is always morally relevant, and agree that animals have this capacity, it is still unclear how in practical terms we are, as utilitarians, to proceed. Animals are so very different from us as to make any deep or detailed understanding of their mental lives quite impossible. Singer might allow that there are genuine difficulties here, but urge that we err on the side of caution, assuming that animal suffering is often considerable. But how, and why, should we do that? All that is secure in this utilitarian thinking is the claim that a great deal of what we do to animals is morally indefensible. But the calculations required to issue in many verdicts about what we may or may not do will remain elusive.

Regan: rights

Although a concern for animal welfare is often couched in terms of animal rights, and although Singer himself often refers to such rights, the term is best reserved for the particular claim that attributes to animals, as it attributes to people, certain characteristics that are such as to generate absolute, and not merely conditional, prohibitions on the sorts of treatment they may be given. So while utilitarians and rights theorists agree that animals deserve equal consideration, this is quite compatible, for utilitarians, with using animals for food, experiment, sport and the like whenever the benefits outweigh the losses. Not so for rights theorists, who insist that just as it is wrong to treat people as a means, or resource, so too for animals. Certain actions are categorically, unconditionally wrong, and not wrong only when compensating benefits cannot be found.

The case for animal rights is most thoroughly articulated by Tom Regan in a number of books and articles[13] which rival Singer's work in bringing philosophical arguments to a wider audience. The focus, unsurprisingly, is on moral rather than legal rights, and then on those of a negative rather than positive kind. Regan's thought seems to be that we more clearly do wrong in killing or harming animals than in permitting death or injury to befall them. Further, the claim is not that animals have the full quota of rights that accrue to human beings, but that they have rights appropriate to their status, in the same way that we have rights appropriate to ours. Certain basic rights – to life, to freedom, to not being subject to torture – are at the core of the discussion. And just as human beings cannot be killed or tortured for the sake of benefits elsewhere, so, too, for animals. They, like us, cannot be treated merely as a means, no matter how valuable the resulting end. An important upshot of such restrictions is that, more comprehensively than under utilitarianism, animal experimentation is disallowed.[14]

Yet although Regan's position may be superficially attractive, not least because talk of rights, most noticeably in America but with Britain not very far behind, is becoming increasingly pervasive and entrenched, objections to it are several. First, there is space for a reiteration of a general scepticism about moral rights, to do with the allegedly unnecessary and metaphysically dubious multiplying of entities. Although that scepticism is sometimes inappropriate, it may, where Regan is concerned, become especially pertinent. A second objection, this time focusing on the extension of rights to animals, is perhaps more clearly insubstantial. Take seriously the contractarian basis of rights talk, match rights with correlative responsibilities or duties, and the attribution of rights to animals cannot get off the ground.[15] A third objection fastens on the absolutism, and the seriously counterintuitive consequences, of such deontological positions. Even while agreeing that the torture of animals is *prima facie* wrong, many people would allow such treatment if vast benefits to the human, or indeed to the animal, population would otherwise be lost. An argument that flatly rules this out is not one that we can be obliged to accept. The objections here are in some ways connected. Thus, for example, the more extravagant Regan's views about the status of rights, the more easily might he avoid the implications of the contractarian account. And the more he favours such an account, the easier it is to avoid the counterintuitive absolutism with which he is otherwise saddled. But although they are connected, it is more convenient to deal with them separately.

What does Regan think rights are, and where does he think they come from? A concern about the overall structure of his account will begin to take shape if we consider the particular nature of animals, and Regan's claims about them. For these claims depend on a network of related ideas, the connections between which are often less than perspicuous. There is, first, and critically, the notion of inherent worth. One of Regan's major objections to utilitarianism is that it emphasizes the satisfaction of an individual's interest, rather than the individual themselves. He refers in an analogy to a cup containing sweeter and less sweet liquids: whereas utilitarians allegedly find value in the liquids, he locates value in the container itself. Where both people and animals are concerned, Regan's idea is that lives have inherent worth, or value, which doesn't at all depend on various contingent facts about how a life is going at a certain time, or how an individual life is related to the lives of others, or about the uses to which this life might be put.

Then what does it depend on? A cup has value in so far as it functions as a possible container for various liquids. By analogy, the inherent value of people and animals will surely seem to depend on some further facts about them, and will accrue in virtue of the kinds of lives they might lead. Just as some cups might be more valuable than others, so, analogously, one might expect some people, and some animals, to be more valuable than others. The alternative here, that these facts about value are just a given, and equally given, does seem to suggest that there is indeed some wholly independent moral realm having no discernible connection with the more mundane physical facts with which we are more familiar. Lives are valuable, and equally valuable, and there is just no more to be said. That is unpalatable, but it isn't quite Regan's position. Just as Kant attributes moral worth only to rational agents, so Regan, who very willingly acknowledges this Kantian background, holds that only the animals that are subjects-of-a-life (and I explain this in more detail below) have this inherent worth, and have, as a consequence, moral rights. But animals either are or are not in this way of moral value: where being subject-of-a-life is concerned there are no half measures. Rights are not utterly mysterious, utterly ungrounded, therefore, but there surely is something of a puzzle as to what this wholly invariant inherent worth is to come to.

Regan is not similarly bedevilled in answering the second objection. One option here is to resist heroically, claiming that some animals do have something like a sense of duty, and behave eminently responsibly in relation to family or herd members. And so there are not grounds for denying them rights.[16] But all this is contentious, and will be effective in only handfuls of cases at best. This is unsatisfactory enough, but looking to the details of animal behaviour won't even get the rights argument off the ground where the basic contractarian move is concerned. It is just implausible to suppose that animals have either the intellectual abilities or the degree of kinship with us to make plausible our giving them rights under the contract model.[17] But Regan rejects this whole approach, arguing that it is independently unsatisfactory, and cannot explain our attitudes to babies, young children and adults suffering from various forms of mental illness. We allow that they have rights, even though they uphold no contract, and carry out no duties. So why not the same for animals? There is something in this. Certainly it seems implausible to hinge the idea of an unconditional prohibition on, say, torture to the claim that a creature has either responsibilities or duties, or has agreed not to torture us. Surely, not everything has to be bargained for. Perhaps we can quite reasonably link some sorts of freedoms to responsibilities, but others might just as reasonably be decoupled, and allowed to stand on their own. So there is scope for two senses in which we might speak of rights. But then it cannot be clear, once the space for different notions is uncovered, that one of them rather than the other better captures the true nature or real essence of rights talk. Dispute in this area is merely verbal, and the case for animal rights, thus far, continues to stand.

More problematic, though, is the notion of absolute prohibitions. Suppose I agree that I always do something wrong in torturing a cat. Suppose I also agree that all cats have equal inherent worth, and that their worth is neither more nor less than that of human beings. None of this rules out there being circumstances in which torturing the cat is either permitted or required. This might, for example, be the only way of preventing many other cats from being tortured. There may be reasons to reject the utilitarian contention that one should seek always to maximize overall benefit, while yet a puzzle as to why major benefits cannot justify a minor harm. And this puzzle is hardly solved merely by insisting that animals like cats should always be treated as ends, and never as means. This Kantian dictum is really at the heart of Regan's account, displacing what might have seemed to be a more comprehensible concern with suffering. Certainly suffering matters but it isn't the "fundamental wrong".[18] If it were, then the puzzle about why we shouldn't simply minimize its amounts would be vexing. What is fundamentally wrong, and what blocks all variants of the consequentialist approach, is treating as a mere means, a thing to be eaten, used for tests, or tormented for sport, those animals that ought to be treated as ends. But this doesn't solve the puzzle, for the question then is, where does that ruling come from?[19] Why believe the very idea of using an animal, not frivolously, but in the pursuit of some significant and substantial good, is simply to be vetoed? I don't mean to suggest here that the absolutist prohibition is wholly indefensible, but only that uncovering the defence isn't simple, and in particular that it connects at best in unobvious ways with the idea of inherent value. And nor do I mean to suggest anything against cats – if they can be tortured for the sake of huge benefits, so, too, can human beings. The difficulty Regan has to face here doesn't surface only in the endeavour to bestow rights on animals, but infects similar accounts even when restricted to human beings. Nevertheless, it has more bite in the animals context: we do, particularly in medicine, want to use animals for human benefit, while a similar institutionalized utilization of human beings is, reasonably or not, considered outrageous.[20] So what Regan preaches will, if heeded, seriously affect our practice.

Death and subjects-of-a-life

Some light is thrown on certain of the puzzles in Regan's account and, at the same time, some further clarification is provided of key differences between that account and its utilitarian rivals, by considering the badness, or other-wise, of death. What I have claimed to be obvious is that pain and suffering matter. The problem here is that being dead does not and dying might not involve either. So is it wrong to kill a pheasant or a rabbit with a clean shot? And would the slaughter of sheep and cows be wrong if the abattoir were a less forbidding, and more deceiving place in which to end their days? Consider these questions from the point of view of both theories.

Utilitarians often waver here, with what seems to be an instinctive feeling that killing is a bad thing grasping hard for some theoretical underpinning. Thus Singer maintains that the suffering we cause animals gives "an even clearer indication"[21] of speciesism than the fact that we kill them. This suggests that the wrongness of killing, even if less clear, has somewhere been discussed. But the discussion is hard to uncover, and it is hard to see what form it might take. It doesn't appear evidently to follow, from a creature's having an interest in not feeling pain, that it therefore has an interest in staying alive. For while pain seems to be obviously bad, the same cannot be said of non-existence. And while we may think it clear that an animal would prefer not to be in pain, it isn't similarly clear that an animal would prefer not to be dead. Nor, further, is the importance of such a preference evident within the utilitarian framework. In most cases unsatisfied preferences lead to feelings of frustration and pain, but the preference for life is here notoriously an exception. It can be objected that killing involves not only the death, but, typically, the premature death of a thing. But it isn't clear how this makes for a difference here. We won't want to suggest that animals can, in general, anticipate their impending death. Were they to do this, and then to worry about it, the wrongness of killing would be plainer to see. But death can take them, as it can take us, completely by surprise. The suggestion is not that consequentialism is wholly incapable of accounting for the wrongness of animal killing, for we can at least imagine a version of the theory that sees the good in terms of the fulfilment of natural processes, and then views killing as an interference with such processes. The difficulty is one for utilitarians of Singer's hue, where sentience and interests deriving from sentience play the dominant role. Suffering is one thing; death another.

Rights theorists are in a somewhat different position, in that their belief in the value of life is given a central place in their accounts, with their confidence in the wrongness of killing no less great than in the wrongness of torture. But confidence is one thing, and cogency another, and a wholly satisfactory account of why there should be a right to life, and who should have it, is not altogether easy to provide. Regan's notion of a subject-of-a-life, to which I promised to return, plays a critical role here, but with mixed results. As he explains it:

> To be the subject-of-a-life . . . involves more than being merely alive and more than being merely conscious. To be the subject-of-a-life is to . . . have beliefs and desires, perception, memory, and a sense of the future, including their own future; an emotional life together with feelings of pleasure and pain; preference and welfare-interests; the ability to initiate action in pursuit of desires and goals; a psychophysical identity over time; and an individual welfare in the sense that their experiential life fares well or ill for them, independently of their utility for others.[22]

It is in virtue of this evidently complex and highly developed mental life that animals have inherent worth, and in virtue of this in turn that absolutist prohibitions regarding their treatment allegedly arise. And now this helps explain the puzzle about death. Certain sorts of creatures have a complexity and coherence to their lives that means that their interests can be thwarted or harmed in ways that go beyond pleasure and pain. Consider human beings. The best answer to why a sudden, painless and unanticipated death is bad for the one who dies, as opposed to those left behind, is that death puts an end to a worthwhile life that would otherwise have continued to be lived. And the best answer to why killing human beings, against their will, is wrong is that such killing terminates their selecting for themselves a certain route through life. I need to gloss over many details and objections here, but at heart of this suggestion are the ideas that we have plans and projects for the future, and that these plans and projects involve us, and so can only be realized if we, each of us a distinct psychophysical entity, persist into the future. This is the best, and not a perfect, answer.[23] The task here, however, is not to explore its general shortcomings but to consider how it might square with a concern for animal welfare.

Not too well. At best, Regan's subject-of-a-life approach will afford rights only to certain mammals.[24] It seems wholly implausible to suppose that

103

oysters, or hens, or fish have a sense of their own future, or an emotional life. And even within mammals it may seem that distinctions have to be drawn. Consider the sheep of the field. They can certainly seem to be distressed when their lambs are taken away. But nothing seems clearly to suggest that they have a sense of the future, memories of the past, or much that we might describe as an emotional life.[25] We may give the benefit of the doubt to higher apes, dogs, and perhaps elephants, dolphins and pigs, but the danger is that a rights-based approach in which the notion of a subject-of-a-life is central will very likely founder on genuine, deep and intractable problems concerning the nature of the animal mind.[26]

Admittedly, in other places Regan paints the view with broader strokes, suggesting that a creature is a subject-of-a-life if it is (a) conscious and (b) has an individual welfare.[27] Sheep, chickens and frogs will all count. But the victory is hollow. Either we single out those few animals the sophistication of whose mental lives resembles ours, in which case it is somewhat plausible to suppose that killing them is wrong. Or we widen the net, taking in more animals, but thereby losing hope of explaining just what is bad about their deaths. Either way, the "right to life" as something that all animals enjoy is a chimera.

Retreat

Because animals can suffer, and because suffering is bad, we ought not to hurt them without good reason. This is a modest claim, but is it true? While Singer and Regan both agree that it is, and then seek to advance beyond it in different but (or so I have suggested) equally unsatisfactory directions, others contend that even this modest claim is suspect. One kind of objection fastens on to the moral component, while another denies that suffering ever occurs. The first objection takes several forms that, in the order I present them here, become increasingly plausible.

Moral scepticism

Suppose that it is agreed that suffering occurs, and is bad. Does it then follow that it is *prima facie* wrong to cause animals to suffer? It can be insisted that this doesn't, strictly, follow. Any deductively valid argument for this conclusion will contain premises that are at least as contentious as the conclusion itself. But equally there is no available proof of the claim "if a claim cannot be proven to be true, there is reason to doubt it", and so no general defence of the sceptical stance. Argument has to start somewhere, and about several basic claims genuine doubt is not, for most of us, a live option.

Give up on proof, but it still has to be settled whether in the present case anything is as firm as I have suggested. Is it obviously wrong to torture animals for fun? Could there be a genuine doubt about this? Consider what our attitude might be to torture elsewhere, of the old or the infirm, or of innocent children. Some of us may think that even in such cases torture might be justified, but almost all of us think that at the very least substantial benefits will need to be involved. Almost none of us believe that we can torture people willy-nilly, or on a whim, or to make some minor improvement to our own lives. Wanton or near-wanton torture is as clearly wrong as anything can be. Anyone who claims to doubt the wrongness here is either affecting a philosophical stance or is in some way disturbed. And now I want to make just this, and as yet no stronger, claim where animals are concerned. It isn't easy to see how, if the wrongness is allowed in the former case, it can be denied in the latter. Admittedly, there are perhaps those who find that they can accommodate the wrongness of torturing children within some structured account of morality, but find the claim for animals harder to locate. Theirs is then a restricted scepticism, but it is the philosophical stance again. And it shows, I think, too great a respect for theory, and too deep a distrust for intuition.

Pain and nature

A somewhat related objection focuses not so much on the particular pains that we might cause, as on the more general and diffuse phenomenon as it occurs, and always has occurred, within animals in the natural world. Pain is a part of nature. Can it be a bad thing? It has been denied:

> There are desires, pleasure in the satisfaction of desires, acute agony attending injury, frustration, and chronic dread of death. But these experiences are the psychological substance of living. To live is to be anxious about life, to feel pain and pleasure in a fitting mixture, and sooner or later to die. That is the way the system works. If nature as a whole is good, then pain and death are also good.[28]

That is from the body of a text. But Callicott is even more firm in a footnote, declaring that "in all soberness . . . I see nothing wrong with pain. It is a marvellous method, honed by the evolutionary process, of conveying important organic information".[29] But it is one thing to refer, as Callicott does, to the function of pain within the biological process and another to hold that this is enough to demolish our belief in its badness. An argument that depends on the contention that whatever is natural is good will deliver the conclusion here, yet fail to be evidently sound, while the concluding argument of the passage above commits, blatantly, the fallacy of division. Good wholes can have bad parts. Nor is the position advanced by the running together, in much of Callicott's discussion, of remarks about pain and about death, or comments about the badness on the one hand, and about the wrongness on the other, of pain. My claim is that there is something bad about pain, such that, other things being equal, it would be better if it didn't occur. And I have no idea how in various respects we would go on if we didn't think this were true. This is a quite general point, relating to human and animal pains alike. The Panglossian attitude adopted by Callicott here, if taken seriously, would have us acquiescing in suffering wherever and to whomever it occurs, and muttering all the time about best worlds. And there is something obscene in this.

This is not, though, to deny that there are important issues lurking just beneath the surface. Callicott is right, I think, to suspect that a blanket desire to be rid of all pain is one we should avoid, and right also to suggest we have no conception of a good world in which pain does not figure large. Without pain much that we value, much that gives life its seriousness, would be lost. And he is right, further, to worry that we may seem committed to such a desire, if we believe that in all of its occurrences pain is bad. But although the worry is real, it is misplaced. We can hold that for each pain it would, other things being equal, be better if it didn't occur, without thereby holding that there might be a better world in which pain is wholly absent.[30] For we cannot conceive of a pain free world in which other things are equal.

Animals and the moral community

One of the problems with Callicott's position, as I have suggested, is that it seems to require us to hold that human suffering is also good. A response here is to deny that human beings are a part of the natural world. That is one, perhaps extreme, way of justifying different views about the human and non-human realms. But perhaps there are other, more modest ways of showing how we might worry less about animals, while still preserving most of our intuitions about ourselves. For there are long-established theological and philosophical traditions, not wholly separate, and far from disreputable, both of which have promoted certain doubts about the exact nature and importance of animal suffering.

I have discussed already the alleged importance of Christianity in giving to us the view of the non-human world as resource for our convenience and use. Nature is to be subdued and governed by us, with both plants and animals serving essentially human ends. There is not so much a gradual increase in value and importance here as a firm and threefold distinction – God, human beings and then all the rest. And the second division, between us and the rest of nature, has been thought by many to connect with rationality. Thus Aquinas:

> [T]he very condition of the rational creature, in that it has dominion over its actions, requires that the care of providence should be

106

bestowed on it for its own sake; whereas the dominion of other things that have no dominion over their actions shows that they are cared for, not for their own sake, but as being directed to other things . . . Hence it is not wrong for man to make use of them, either by killing them or in any other way whatever . . . And if any passages of Holy Writ seem to forbid us to be cruel to dumb animals, . . . this is either to remove man's thoughts from being cruel to other men and lest through being cruel to animals one becomes cruel to human beings: or because injury to an animal leads to the temporal hurt of man.[31]

There are difficulties in this to which I will shortly return, but the thrust is perfectly clear. We have no *carte blanche* to do with animals as we choose, but the restrictions on our dealings with them derive from human concerns, and not directly from any consideration of what is good or otherwise for the animals themselves. The upshot may in several (although far from all) respects correspond to what the animal welfarist wants, but the rationale is importantly different. And nor is it different only in a medieval, hocus-pocus sort of way, for a very similar position is put forward a half millennium later by Kant, in writings often referred to in recent debates. In opposition to a contemporary's insistence that we have duties to creatures both above and below us, Kant argues that our direct duties to animals (what we ought or ought not to do with them not in reference to human beings, but simply for their own sakes) are non-existent:

If a man shoots his dog because the animal is no longer capable of service, he does not fail in his duty to the dog, for the dog cannot judge, but his act is inhuman, and damages in himself that humanity which it is his duty to show to mankind. If he is not to stifle his human feelings he must practise kindness towards animals, for he who is cruel to animals becomes hard also in his dealings with men. We can judge the heart of a man by his treatment of animals.[32]

Were it not for its effects on human character and motivation, then, our treatment of animals, no matter what its form, would deserve no recrimination. And, as with Aquinas, it is Kant's view that rationality marks the significant difference between ourselves and other animals, and thus the grounds on which direct duties are absent. There are odd things here, not only about the views themselves, but also about some claims made as to their typicality, for it is often said that this profoundly anthropocentric position somehow exemplifies Enlightenment and post-Enlightenment thinking, with its undue emphasis on reason, and corresponding inattention to feeling. As Mary Midgley put it:

Since the Renaissance . . . there has been a deliberate effort to exclude from concern everything non-human, and many supposedly non-rational aspects of human life as well. Though this campaign was aimed chiefly at the dominance of the churches . . . it has usually taken the form of a "humanism" that excludes non-human nature too. This is still the unquestioned creed expressed in the ministries and offices from which our society is run.[33]

However, one has to be way too enamoured of certain parts of the philosophical tradition to think these views so pernicious. Hume and Bentham held to contrary positions, as did Mary Wollstonecraft (although some will place her more on philosophy's margins). These are well-known figures, whose views might be thought eccentric, but Keith Thomas, in his history of our relationship with them, has documented the variety and complexity of perspectives on the animals issue, and shown clearly the paucity of any unnuanced account. So the idea that post-Renaissance, or even post-Enlightenment, thinking should best be seen as this highly focused celebration of rationalism is not one that can be long sustained. Of course we know more about the psychology and physiology of pain than did our predecessors, and so a denial of animal suffering has today more theoretical obstacles to overcome. Even so, there is reason to think that in general those in the past exposed to and still indifferent to animal suffering were more inclined to be cruel than in the grip of a theory.[34]

What of the theory, however? Even if we allow that people are rational and animals are not, it is still hard to see how the rest of the argument should go. The prevailing thought in both Aquinas and Kant seems to be that cruelty to animals is indicative of a character failing in those who inflict it, and disposes those responsible to be similarly cruel to people. And only the latter cruelty is wrong in itself. Such an approach, in which aspects of a virtue approach colour arguments that have their underlying rationale elsewhere, is not without recent support,[35] but it is strange. There is a problem with cruelty, to begin with. And then, following from that, there is a problem in reconciling what appear to be central components within Aquinas's and Kant's views.

What is it to be cruel? A relatively straightforward view might be that to act cruelly involves inflicting pain for the sake of pain, and that to be cruel is to be disposed so to act. So intention matters, and one is not cruel, for example, in causing unavoidable pain during an operation.[36] But what about success? Although intending to inflict suffering for suffering's sake is a defect of character, and one who so acts may be intending to be cruel, one is not being cruel, it seems to me, unless one does succeed.[37] I may come to believe that my rather rudimentary computer feels pain and, hating it for losing yet more work, seek to punish it by switching it repeatedly on and off, but I am not being cruel to it. One puzzle about Aquinas and Kant, then, is whether they think, as they appear to think, that genuinely cruel treatment of animals is possible, but not forbidden, or whether they think it flatly impossible. Does Aquinas think that animals have an "own sake" that we can justifiably ignore, or is the idea that in lacking reason they lack all capacity to be benefited or harmed? Does Kant think that a dog's inability to judge means that not only do we have no direct duties towards it, but also that we can do it, directly, no wrong?[38] What both writers appear to put forward is not the robust and serviceable – albeit false – view that animals simply don't suffer, but a position both more modest and more puzzling: that although they suffer, this is not in itself of any direct concern. But this is strange. If something bad happens when sheep or cows fall over a cliff, if it is to any extent regrettable that before dying they suffer, then surely we do something wrong if we herd them over a cliff. There seems to be a fundamental instability, then, in allowing that animal pain can occur, while yet denying that we have any straightforward obligation not to promote it.

These sorts of views, in which an animal's lack of reason, or language, or self-consciousness is somehow supposed to license our doing with it as we will, have often been puzzled over, and sometimes ridiculed.[39] Why think that morality is so intimately tied to these higher features of the mental life? Why think that mere sentience or mere consciousness is not enough? But even if there is not, in the end, a compelling defence, there is nevertheless a partial explanation that can be given by those having sympathy (as Kant has at least some sympathy) for contractarian accounts.

Suppose that we grant connections between duty, morality and self-consciousness. Animals, we might agree, are not themselves capable of self-consciousness, moral thought, or of doing or neglecting their duty. Now if the moral community, or those creatures having moral status, or independent worth, is defined as consisting of all and only creatures capable of moral thought, then it uncontroversially follows that animals stand outside the moral community. But nothing else follows. In particular, it doesn't at all follow that they cannot be treated cruelly, wrongly or immorally by creatures that are part of that community. To put this somewhat archaically, if we define the moral community as comprising all and only moral agents, it won't at all follow that there are not, without that community, moral patients. But now we might go further. If we insist on mutuality – patients are agents, at least potentially, and vice versa – then animals will stand wholly outside the moral sphere. Still, it won't at all follow that we do them no wrong. For we can, if somehow it suits us, cordon off morality. But this is as far as the partial explanation goes. Consider a further step. If, finally, we agree that doing right and doing wrong have no application at all beyond the moral domain, then, indeed, animals cannot be wronged. We bring about a bad state of affairs, but do no wrong, in herding them over a cliff. But this is one agreement too many. We can give some words away, but not all of them.

Animals and pain

One of the points that I said is obvious is that if animals can suffer, then there are some direct constraints on what we may do to them. I want to stick to this.

And perhaps it is no accident that Aquinas and Kant, in arguing to the contrary, appear to waver on the critical question of whether genuine cruelty to, and genuine suffering in, animals is possible. For of course, if one were firmly negative here, denying the very possibility of animal suffering, then the case for permissions is immediately the stronger. So what about this second point? I also said that it is obvious that animals can suffer. But is it?

Some of the claims that they don't are mendacious and self-serving. Thus the chicken farmer who insists that his hens quite naturally peck at one another, the abattoir worker who cuts corners to increase production or the hunter who leaves wounded animals to die are, in their marginally different ways, all bad witnesses to animals' not suffering. In other cases we might very charitably suppose that people have to deceive not so much others as themselves about the degree of suffering involved, so that they may continue with their work. But cases of both kinds, where the claimants are not impartial, can, I think, fairly readily be identified. Animal suffering seems often painfully evident to the dispassionate observer.

Are there, though, considerations to show that what appears evident is not in fact the case? Descartes, notoriously, argued that animals are mere automata, possessed of neither language nor souls nor feeling.[40] They may act and sound as if they are pain, but there is nothing within to correspond to this outward show. Except for behaviourists, to be persuaded of this is to be persuaded that animals are strangers to pain, and so to be persuaded, in turn, that the suggestion that we might wrong them is seriously undermined. And again, it is the very same package – language, reason, self-consciousness, the capacity for doing right or wrong – appeal to which was claimed to place animals outside morality, that is now used to deny them sentience. But is the argument any good?

One response is to question these several claims. It can be argued that animals do have language, are capable of moral distinctions and so on.[41] Much of the argument here is dubious, both philosophically and scientifically, but there is little need to get into details, as it seems evident that these endeavours will bring only limited rewards, and like Regan's subject-of-a-life view, will be plausibly attributed, at best, to very few animals. And our belief in animal pain is wide-ranging. A second, and better, response is simply to deny the relevance of such characteristics to the question of suffering. Speaking can't have anything to do with pain, as the dumb are as capable of being tortured as the most vociferous. Nor can rationality, as babies, on the one hand, and the severely demented, on the other, evidently suffer as much as the rest of us. Pain, sentience and consciousness are one thing, while the allegedly higher rational faculties are another.

This may, however, be too hasty. We might think we see that neither language nor reason can make a difference to the subjective character of pain, but what about self-consciousness? I know both what toothache feels like, and what it feels like to me. But these are not evidently two distinct thoughts, and although I can imagine how it feels to you (namely much as it feels to me), it isn't altogether clear how far even my imaginings can extend. I can't, to begin with, at all imagine what unattached, free-floating pain – a pain somewhere in the room – would feel like. Nor can I imagine a pain in a tomato or (as in a fairy story) a pain not so much in my foot as in my shoe, without imagining that the tomato or the shoe is, in important respects, like a human being, and aware of, and minding the pain and wishing it would end. This may seem irrelevant in so far as the issue is about pain in animals, and not wafting either through space or fantasy land. Doesn't toothache in a horse feel to it something like my tooth-ache feels to me? But the critical question is, can we imagine what pain feels like to a creature that cannot know what it feels like to itself? Can we imagine pain in creatures that are not self-conscious? What can it feel like if it doesn't feel like something for someone? And without that complex thought, what can it feel like? There are complex issues here that, even if they are not easily articulated, could well (although elsewhere) be much further explored.[42]

What, meanwhile, can we do with such thoughts? One response, in so far as we find some substance within them, is to suggest they do, after all, put the reality of animal suffering in doubt. If we are unable to show the fallacy in the reasoning that suggests that animals cannot feel pain, then we ought no longer claim with any confidence that they can. An alternative, however, is to insist that their feeling pain is possible, but agree that an explanation as to how this is possible, or, indeed, a fully articulated account of just what it is that is allegedly possible, is so far missing. There are, again, useful analogies. Most of us continue to believe in the existence of the external world, in the reasona-bleness of induction and in the reality of freedom, even while we are unable to defeat the sceptical arguments intended to eat away at such beliefs. The point is essentially Humean: certain beliefs are irresistible, and cannot be jettisoned in the face of philosophical difficulties.[43] It may be objected that belief in animal suffering is not on a par with belief in physical objects; it isn't one that we are simply unable to set aside. And as we have the option we should here follow the argument, and agree that in spite of intuitions to the contrary, animal suffering is an illusion. But although our common-sense belief is not wholly basic, and does depend for substance on further beliefs about animals – that they are made of similar biological stuff to ourselves, that they are born, develop and die, evolve naturally, have nervous systems, and so on – the same is true of beliefs in induction, freedom and other human minds. Given this background in science, a background that most of us now share, a belief in animal suffering is irresistible enough.

Liberation, welfare and the environment

So far in this chapter there has been no explicit discussion of any overtly environmental issues. I will remedy that, and explore the relationship between some apparently different concerns, but first a reminder of the point so far. I have wanted to begin exploring the question of whether all our moral thinking should be human centred by first looking at an area where that narrow claim most clearly breaks down. And I have wanted to maintain that the case for including animals cannot be denied. They can be harmed, and they can be wronged. Although they are not clearly moral agents, they are, nevertheless, a part of the moral community. So that community has other than human members, and creatures other than human beings can be subject to moral or immoral treatment. I have wanted, on the other hand, to disagree that either a utilitarianism or a rights-based theory can be highly persuasive in offering a coherent and comprehensive account of where our treatment of animals goes wrong. These theories are not especially good at dealing with human beings. With animals they encounter further problems. But difficulties here ought not to deflect us from what is nevertheless achieved: a, thus far, modest extension of the moral domain.

How does this result connect with the environment? It might be suggested that any concern for animals straightforwardly embraces that larger concern. Animals are part of the world, after all, and their faring well or badly cannot fail to impinge on situations elsewhere. But, as has been explained, there are reasons not to construe environmental matters too widely, and so reasons to hold that it is in principle possible for the two areas of concern not to overlap. And what is possible in principle has often been held to be the case in practice: it is frequently claimed that not only are there concerns beyond animals, but that the sorts of concerns for animals discussed so far are too focused and too few to show for the animal kingdom as a whole appropriate respect and care. Standard environmentalism and the sorts of welfare considerations discussed so far are at odds with one another, exemplifying quite different, and conflicting concerns.[44] How are these differences to be characterized? I will mention three ways in which, allegedly, the welfarist is unjustifiably restricted in her concerns. There is something in each, but not enough, even in all, to sustain the view that the opposition here is profound.

Domestic or wild

Those concerned with well-being – and I will refer variously both to welfarists and, acknowledging a broad and influential movement that takes animal well-being as its major concern, liberationists – focus mainly on the fortunes of domestic animals. Its apostles, Singer and Regan prominent among them, are concerned with the miserable conditions that prevail on the factory farm, with the intensive rearing of certain animals either as pets or as products, or for use in laboratories, or with the experimentation that those laboratory animals are eventually subjected to. Environmentalists, in contrast, are concerned with the situation confronting animals in the wild, tending moreover to view domestic breeds as human artefacts almost as much as the fridge or the car, and often generating environmental hazards in their own right.[45] The two groups are concerned, then, with different kinds of animals, living in vastly different conditions.

There is little hope of sustaining this distinction, however. For welfarists are far from blind to the situation of wild animals. They are as much concerned about experiments on monkeys as on beagles; they are concerned about the fate of wild animals in zoos; and they are concerned also to defend foxes, badgers, deer, pike, seals and elephants not only from hunters and poachers, but also from those conservationists who, in the interests of some allegedly larger good – either the health of the species concerned, or the overall "balance of nature" – organize and authorize culls of various of such animals.[46] This is, of course, as it should be. A focus on domestic animals is appropriate, often, in countries like ours, as these are the creatures whose fortunes we can more easily and in greater numbers affect: simple legislation can bring benefits to millions of farm animals, or tens of thousands of laboratory rats. But for utilitarians animal suffering is a bad thing wherever it occurs, and while rights theorists may be more concerned with wrongs than pains, they want no principled distinction between domestic and wild.

Many environmentalists, in contrast, do give by far their greater attention to animals in the wild, even if they sometimes consider domestic animals when, for example, a rare and valued breed is at risk of becoming extinct.[47] But it isn't easy to justify firm distinctions here. First, to sideline cats and dogs, sheep and cows, because they are in part human productions is, by implication, to suggest that human beings, and all that they do, somehow represent a threat to an otherwise valuable world. And, as will emerge, there are many reasons to resist this. Secondly, it is unclear anyway whether any clear division between two sorts of animals can be sustained. There are several difficulties. Many kinds of animals simply straddle the divide, belonging to what Mary Midgely has referred to as a "mixed" community,[48] and are themselves both semi-domesticated, and semi-wild: deer, pigeons and, at least on the margins of cities, foxes and racoons. Animals that are members of wild species can be bred in captivity, for laboratories or zoos or for pets, and so lose many of their former characteristics. Domestic animals can escape and interbreed with wild animals, creating hybrid types. Many populations of wild animals are introduced into new habitats, either by accident or design, as a result of human intervention. And this vagueness as to boundaries in the field derives, I think, from an underlying conceptual confusion. Are wild animals all members of species that have evolved without human intervention, or are they the individuals, of whatever species, who live at a distance from human beings?[49] Are domestic animals identified by species, breed or habitat? There is, of course, a serviceable distinction to be drawn between the domestic and the wild, but it isn't precise, and it doesn't altogether line up with the concerns pursued by two distinct bodies of people.

Individuals or species

It is sometimes suggested that liberationists and welfarists are concerned for the well-being of individual animals – a single cat, whale or falcon – while environmentalists are concerned not for individuals, but for species as a whole. The liberationist has thus piecemeal, often local and short-term concerns, while the environmentalist looks to the bigger picture, wanting to do what is necessary to ensure, at least for the foreseeable future, viable populations of endangered species, within their natural habitats.

Again, qualifications are needed. Although it might be allowed that liberationists are thinking in terms of individuals, the environmentalist's attitude is somewhat harder to characterize. The oil spillage from the *Exxon Valdez* in Alaska was rightly seen as an environmental issue, even though none of the species of birds, razorbills, gannets or gulls was in danger of extinction, and similarly for elephants in Africa, or the tuna fishing that snares dolphins in its nets. So it should simply be admitted that the environmentalist can display a range of concerns, even if, among them, that for species predominates.

There is something in this distinction, however. Unlike the contrast between domestic and wild animals, the line between individuals and species seems to be clear. Although I explain this in more detail later, it can be said now that they are different kinds of things. But though the distinction clearly has substance, the same cannot be said for the environmentalist's complaint that welfare considerations are unreasonably narrow. True, liberationists typically do not, and probably could not, show a concern for species considered in themselves. A species is not sentient, can feel neither pleasure nor pain, and so cannot fit, at least in any obvious way,[50] into utilitarian calculations. Nor is it clear how it can have any Reganite rights. A species is not, after all, alive. But in wanting a different perspective there are difficulties for the environmentalist, for while a concern for the welfare of individual creatures is relatively unproblematic, there is a puzzle about how anyone can be concerned for species as such. One response suggests itself: the continued existence of the species is a necessary condition for the existence of further members of the species, further individual animals: no species tiger means no tigers. But then a worry about that response is that it appears to put the boot back on the liberationist's foot: what we really care about is welfare, and the condition of individual sentient creatures. Concern for the preservation of species is a means to an end. What many environmentalists appear to want, a subordination of the individual to the species, is a thing that makes no obvious sense.

Some or all

Liberationists are sometimes accused of being speciesist. This can come as a surprise, for it is just this charge that they level at those of us who appear to give animals a secondary (if that) place in the moral hierarchy. Redressing this, and insisting on either an equal consideration of equal interests, or equal rights for all subjects-of-a-life, seems to be the broad goal of liberation and welfare concerns. So how is the charge to be made out?

Environmentalists often complain that while Singer and Regan have admittedly gone far, they haven't gone far enough. Rather than mount any serious opposition to this hierarchy, they merely tinker with its internal boundaries. For they allow, in effect, all creatures to apply for membership of the moral community, but then set, or, perhaps better, borrow from elsewhere, standards that ensure that only a minority of these applications are successful. Singer gives equal consideration to all animals in so far as they can experience pleasure and pain. This works well for dogs and cats, less well for toads, and not at all for oysters. Regan posits rights for those animals that are subjects-of-a-life. On his account, too, toads and oysters will fail to qualify. Liberationists, then, whatever their colour, are concerned for animals in so far as they approximate to human beings. This, for many critics, is just woefully anthropocentric, and the net result is that only handfuls of animals are considered to have moral standing. Serious environmentalism, in contrast, wants to extend the area of concern far beyond creatures like us, and to attribute to all animals some measure of inherent worth.

Welfarists endeavour to defend themselves. Speciesism occurs when we draw unwarranted distinctions, but the distinctions between animals that do and do not feel pain, or that are and are not self-conscious, are, first, real distinctions,[51] and, secondly, of evident moral relevance. Sentience counts, but it is not ubiquitous. So although we have no justification for any blanket exclusion of animals from the moral community, we have, equally, no case for an open door.

The environmentalist who wants the wider net has to explain. It is easy enough to say that all animals count, but harder to explain on what that counting depends. It is, similarly, easy enough to accuse liberationists of fastening on to characteristics that are valuable among human beings, but harder to explain why some further characteristics – just being an animal? just being alive? – should give us grounds for concern. Again, one immediate response is ultimately unsatisfactory. All animals, all species, matter in that they figure in the whole and impinge in various ways on the lives of other creatures, ourselves included. They probably all, uncontroversially, have instrumental value. But what is sought here is some explanation of their having value in themselves, some argument for our showing a direct concern. And this argument, as will emerge, is not easy to provide.

What substance is there, then, in the case against welfarist concerns? There are two respects in which those concerns are undeniably restricted, but these restrictions are, at least on the surface, justifiable. It isn't at all clear why we should be concerned with species as such, or that we go wrong in emphasizing sentience. A further charge against welfarists cannot be sustained. They don't restrict their attentions to the fate of domestic animals, even if many environmentalists do incline to the opposite restriction, but there they go wrong; there are no good grounds for bracketing out the situations of the non-wild. So, in so far as there is disagreement between welfarists on the one hand, and environmentalists on the other, it is the former group who appear to have the upper hand.

The predator problem

The case for widening the scope of animal concern beyond the admittedly rough boundaries that the welfarist wants to draw has, then, still to be made. Perhaps there are reasons to be concerned with species as much as, or more than, with individuals. And perhaps the premium we put on sentience can be shown to be irrational. These are large issues to be taken up in later chapters. For the moment we might consider one area where, even though we are involved with sentient individuals, welfarist and environmental concerns can conflict.

Many animals are carnivores, and get their food by killing other creatures, often in ways that involve some considerable pain. Watch a stoat with a rabbit, or a hawk with a vole, or, perhaps on television, a leopard with a deer. There are mixed blessings here for animal welfare. In some cases these can be unmixed. We might be persuaded to give up our meat. We might try to make our cats vegetarian, or keep fish instead. But as long as wild nature survives in anything like its present state, the killing will go on.

How ought we to think about this? And what ought we to do about it? For the environmentalist this killing is a part of nature, and should be accepted as such. It isn't necessary to think, along with Callicott, that the pain itself is good, but still it might be tolerated, as an unavoidable component within the whole. Killing, and in a painful way, is what these creatures do. But for the utilitarian it isn't so easy. In some cases it seems clear that the pain suffered by the prey outweighs the pleasure enjoyed by the predator, and, further, might outweigh the pain that would be felt were the predator to starve to death. Think of a snake and its supply of mice. What it seems the utilitarian ought to think is that in many cases it would be better overall if predators didn't exist, or were to die out. Of course, there are complications here: it may be that too many mice will in the end somehow lead to an increase in overall pain, or it may be that some of this killing turns out to be good, when our own pleasure is factored in.[52] But in so far as the focus is on pleasure and pain, it seems unreasonable to believe that every killing that occurs within the animal world is somehow for the best. And, as the way we ought to think should help to shape the way we act, perhaps we ought to try to prevent at least some of this killing from taking place. We could exterminate owls, or wolves, or polar bears.

Singer acknowledges the difficulty, but counsels inaction:

116

It must be admitted that the existence of carnivorous animals does pose a problem for the ethics of Animal Liberation . . . Assuming that humans could eliminate carnivorous species from the earth, and that the total amount of suffering among animals in the world were thereby reduced should we do it? We cannot and should not try to police all of nature. We do enough if we eliminate our own unnecessary killing and cruelty to other animals.[53]

This argument for inaction doesn't hang on the difficulty in foreseeing the consequences of what we might do. Singer is explicitly assuming that there would be overall net benefits from a carnivore reduction. Still, although presumably we might wish for it, this is not a situation we should try to bring about. But why not? Perhaps, indeed, we cannot police the whole of nature, but we can, on a small scale, attempt to reduce animal suffering. I could come between the stoat and the rabbit, or shoo the neighbour's cat, or the circling hawk, before it gets the wren. I could even shoot a fox. Nor will it do to suggest that such localized and piecemeal intervention will only swap one victim for another, and so will achieve nothing. Cats don't kill to survive, and a dead fox will eat no more chickens. Our intuitions are often confused about what we ought to do in such cases, but the problem for utilitarianism is that this confusion is not mirrored within the theory. It tends to issue straightforward directives, even when we are disinclined to follow them through.

The approach of rights theorist is, if anything, more problematic. Animals are not moral agents, they cannot be selfish, heartless or cruel and cannot be blamed or held responsible for the suffering they cause. We might agree, then, that in killing each other no wrong occurs. But does anything bad happen? For the utilitarian, it is reasonably clear that it does, and that it would be overall better if at least some of these killings didn't occur. For many environmentalists, the situation overall isn't bad, even if, *contra* the likes of Callicott, it is agreed that the existence of some elements within it (the pain, say) are bad. But what view does the animal rights advocate take here?

Something like a consistent position can be put together, but it is one, I think, that reveals something of the paucity of the rights view. The consistent position emphasizes the connection between rights and duties, and draws on the predominant concern in all animal rights discussion, which is not so much on animals as on human beings. Animals have a right to life, or not to be tortured, or to freedom just in so far as we have duties not to kill, torture or confine them. The emphasis is on morality, and on what we, as creatures who can act freely, decide, and so do right or wrong, are prohibited from doing. And that is as far as it goes. An animal's right to life, like yours or mine, is not infringed by the natural processes of death and decay, whether they occur within their time, or prematurely, as a result of drought or disease. No animal is wronged, then, if it is killed in a flood or a storm, and equally it is not wronged if killed for food by another animal.

117

So we either focus on just wrongs, and pass no comment on situations that would be deemed intolerable if we were to bring them about – for it isn't clear that an animal suffers any more by being hunted by men and hounds than by wolves alone – or we try, within a rights account, to extend the range of concern. But it isn't clear how we might do that. If one animal's right to life means that it ought not to be hunted and killed, then doesn't another's right to life mean that it is permitted to get food in the only way available to it?[54] Utilitarianism offers a means of resolving conflict here, while rights theory, as far as I can tell, is silent.

There is an irony here, in that a rights theorist like Regan is not slow to accuse utilitarian welfarists of speciesism: they will look out for animals, Regan suggests, only so long as this is not seriously inconvenient for human beings.[55] Not only is this unfair – welfarists like Singer just don't construe the greater good in exclusively human terms – but it overlooks the way in which rights theory, unless it can find the wherewithal to extend its concern, betrays an indifference to all that naturally happens within the world. Nor is this simply regrettable. What I find hard to understand is how there can be any consistent rationale for caring about morality, about what human beings do, that doesn't depend on a prior concern for value, the states of affairs that might or might not obtain and how we might think about them.

Summary

There is a genuine difficulty in understanding how we should think about predators and their prey. Utilitarianism offers an easy but unconvincing solution. So unconvincing is it, in fact, that major utilitarians are unwilling to adopt it. Rights theorists see the activity here as beyond their purview. Environmentalists are accepting of this naturally inflicted pain, holding that it would be wrong of us to interfere. It is difficult to find any of these responses wholly satisfactory. Our natural abhorrence of pain, suffering and distress is neither accommodated within, nor overturned by, any decisive theoretical considerations.

Some may see this as deeply problematic, while others, as I suggested in Chapter 4, will find hope of a comprehensive match between intuition and theory to be built on illusion. There are certainly difficulties here, but these ought not to deflect attention from what has, I hope, been satisfactorily argued: there are good reasons for believing that much of what we do to animals is wrong, not because of its effects on us, or for what it says about our character, but simply because of how it feels to the animals involved. We ought not to think that animal pain stands outside the moral domain, something that matters, if at all, only because of its effects on human beings. That such pain occurs, that its occurrence is, other things being equal, a bad thing and that it is therefore, on the face of it, wrong of us to inflict such pain, are all, I have insisted, claims that are both modest and secure. Venturing beyond this modest position is hardly straightforward, with consequentialist and deontological accounts disagreeing both with each other and with the often imprecise but nevertheless frequently robust deliverances of our every-day intuitions as to what may and may not be done. It is still unclear, then, exactly how far animals count. But that isn't a reason for thinking they don't count at all, and so isn't a reason for rejecting what is established here: an extension of our moral responsibilities beyond the range of purely human concerns.

CHAPTER 6
Life

Many people are concerned about our treatment of animals. And many people are concerned, too, about our treatment of other living things, most notably and most often plants, and particularly trees, but also embryos, cells, bacteria and viruses.[1] Perhaps this second concern is less widespread. And, more important, perhaps it has, for most people, a different character. Other living things matter, but perhaps they matter in a different way.

Plants

A large part of our concern for animals is a concern for creatures very many of which, like us, can enjoy pleasures and suffer pain. Because of this, what happens to them, and what we do to them, is of direct moral concern. Other living things cannot feel pain. Even so, it seems that much of what we do to them is wrong. Objections are often raised to felling trees, either on the purely local or on the massive scale; there are widespread concerns about genetic modification of foods and crops; and, although less widespread, there are concerns, too, about the dwindling numbers of rare orchids, snake fritillaries in an Oxford meadow, or the handfuls of alpines living within delicate microclimates in northern Canada. The bog plants and grasses in the Scottish Highlands hold subtler charms, but even here considerable numbers agitate on their behalf.

In certain respects this concern for plants is unproblematic. Most of the reservations about GM foods centre on their effects on us. Perhaps the so-called improvements will, in the long run, turn out to be harmful. Similarly, at least some of the worry about the extinction of plant species is motivated by the thought that medicinal uses are still to be discovered. And a concern for rainforests is, in part, connected with anxieties about the planet's atmosphere, and the long-term sustainability of human life. Anthropocentrism, and a concern for our own well-being, will, then, readily justify a fairly wide-ranging concern with the state of plant life.

This concern can be wider ranging. If we believe that the well-being of animals can matter in itself, and not simply because of their relationship with us, then a concern for plants is required. Animals need their food, medicines and shelter very much as we do. If we care about pandas we should care about bamboo. Even tigers and wolves have an indirect need for plants, for otherwise their prey would starve. And if we allow that human beings, if not also other animals, have other than material needs, then our concern with plants can be further explained. In a recent case, at Rusland in the English Lake District, local residents fought hard and in the end successfully to prevent the felling of an avenue of beeches. Various arguments were made, but it seemed clear that the major concerns were aesthetic; not unreasonably people wanted to preserve the beauty of these ancient and magnificent things. There are similar concerns about the giant sequoias in California, concerns that are often voiced even before a tree's life is threatened. Can the concern be wider ranging still? Many people argue that it is not simply because of their usefulness that plants matter, not simply because and when we like the look of them that their destruction is wrong. We ought to be concerned for plants just for their own sake, and to see that as living things they, as well as, even if not as much as, animals, have a claim to our consideration.

Others insist that a direct concern for plants is irrational. They will agree that such trees as sequoias can impress us in various ways, and will sympathize with the sadness, anger and disgust many feel when, as occurs too often, they seem to be cut down unnecessarily. But none of this suggests that we can do them any genuine and direct wrong. Trees know nothing of their situation. They don't even know that they're alive. They can feel no pain. We can, in destroying them, harm ourselves, but it is we who matter. Trees, considered in themselves, don't. That animals can feel pain gives an immediate plausibility to the suggestion that they make direct claims upon us. We can hurt, injure, cause suffering in and do wrong to animals. But nothing about trees suggests that they too should be considered to fall within the moral domain.

Suppose that there is dissatisfaction with this sceptical view. How, if at all, can we make plausible the idea that, considered in themselves, plants count? How can ethics be extended this far? Several suggestions are made. Some can be rejected early on as either implausible or ineffective. Others require a more extended discussion.

Pain

Some people believe that plants can feel pain. They think that we are simply wrong to suppose otherwise. We used not to think that new-born babies and fetuses could feel pain, but modern science has established that they do, and science's findings here have gained widespread acceptance, albeit only after some time. Similarly for plants. Evidence for their feeling pain has already been discovered, and, in time, resistance to facing the facts will be broken down.

However, this isn't so. Science can establish that certain biochemical reactions occur in the face of certain stimuli, linking microscopic and macroscopic aspects of the response, but cannot in the same way establish that a creature feels pain. Scientists have discovered a wealth of information about the life of plants, and have shown that there is a complexity to the electrochemical processes working within them that far exceeds our earlier understanding, but they haven't shown that they feel pain. To be in pain is to feel a certain way, inside. Scientists cannot show that plants have feelings.

This is not to make a merely sceptical point. Even if pain can never be proved to have occurred, there are, of course, many circumstances in which it is wholly unreasonable to doubt that it has. People feel pain, and so, I claim, do animals. But our confidence in animal pain has a twofold foundation. First, it is natural to think that pain occurs. As many animals are significantly like us on the outside, both in the ways that they look and the ways they behave, so we cannot but assume they are like us on the inside. Secondly, this assumption is justified, for other human beings are like us on the inside, and at least the higher mammals are substantially similar. If we assume that the universe fits together, and that psychological feelings have a physical cause, then the consonances here make pain attribution, over a range of cases, perfectly reasonable. But imagine a difference in the facts. Suppose that there are aliens among us. We think the people next door are human beings, and we think that scalding water hurts them, as it hurts us. But then we discover that inside they are just wires and chips. Although their simulation of pain behaviour is undeniable, it is no longer reasonable to suppose that they feel pain, and in light of this information the natural tendency to sympathize will be reduced.

Plants are closer to us than these imaginary beings in some ways, and more distant in others. Plants, like us, are made of organic material. But they don't exhibit any of the obvious signs of feeling pain. Even the biggest trees put up no fight, make no fuss, when we chop them down. And their inner structures are markedly different from those found in both human beings and other animals. Again, the consonance between inner and outer differences makes it reasonable to suppose that there are unobservable differences as well, and that plants lack sentience. And there is a further point. Because animals can adapt fairly readily to changing situations, pain serves an evolutionary purpose. It stops us putting our hands in fires, jumping off cliffs, and doing other things that would be bad for us. But plants are not adaptable in these ways. Only a sadistic god would bring it about that trees suffer when they are cut down. So although it remains conceivable that plants feel pain, there is no good reason to believe that they do.

Rights

Do plants have rights? Some people insist that they do. Just as human beings and animals have, most importantly, a right to life, so, too, for at least some plants. This thought about the rights of plants is most often advanced in favour of trees, and in particular of trees of some age in what is thought of as a natural setting. An argument that trees have rights was famously put forward by the legal theorist Christopher Stone in response to a proposal by the Walt Disney company to build yet another ski resort in America's Sierra Nevada. An initial attempt to prevent this, in an action brought against Disney by the Sierra Club, was unsuccessful as the California courts decided that the club's members, although clearly opposed to the development, would suffer no recognizable harm if it went ahead. In response to this Stone argued that natural objects within the environment ought to be seen as things that might themselves be harmed, and so themselves have rights not to be harmed, and so themselves deserve legal protection.[2] Fight the case on behalf of the environment, rather than aggrieved environmentalists, and there might be more hope of success.

The argument is, in one respect, about giving legal rights to natural objects. This is not obviously hopeless. As Stone points out, whether and to what extent something has legal rights is for courts to decide. And, as is evident, the range and variety of objects enjoying such rights is continually being extended, with states, businesses, women, foreigners, former slaves, children and fetuses now afforded the protection of the law, whereas previously this was denied. Legal rights are not, then, simply a given, but a matter over which reasoned decisions have to be made. At the time of writing Stone readily acknowledged that trees and other natural objects were not viewed as themselves having any rights but, he argued, it would be to the environment's benefit if rights were extended towards them.

This can appear uncontroversial. Surely it is up to us to hand out legal rights wherever it suits us. And to give, in this way, rights to trees is just a convenient way to reflect our complex, wide-ranging and hard to quantify interests in the condition of the environment. Take into account only those of our interests currently recognized by law and, as in the Walt Disney case, we will be ill served. But use the fiction of rights in relation to the environment, and more of our interests will be protected. So giving trees rights does not, in and of itself, show that they are of direct moral concern.

This is to betray a certain confusion, however, and to ignore the critical elements within Stone's argument. We can't give rights to things senselessly, and can't give trees a right not to be harmed unless harming them is possible. And Stone's contention that legal rights ought to be extended to cover natural objects, that "the rightlessness of the natural environment can and should change",[3] derives, not from a concern for human good, but from a concern for what is, independently of us, good for the objects themselves. That trees are not yet afforded rights is an indication that we have failed correctly to see what trees are like, what needs and interests they have and how they can themselves be benefited and harmed. In certain respects, according to Stone, natural objects should be viewed in a way analogous to infants, incompetents, states or universities, which are similarly unable to speak on their own behalf, and whose interests have to be represented where necessary by others, but which have interests nevertheless. Nor does this analogy fall down, he insists, because natural objects, unlike states, infants or incompetents, don't genuinely have interests or needs. On the contrary:

> Natural objects *can* communicate their wants (needs) to us, and in ways that are not terribly ambiguous. I am sure I can judge with more certainty and meaningfulness whether and when my lawn wants (needs) water, than the Attorney General can judge whether and when the United States wants (needs) to take an appeal from an adverse judgment by a lower court. The lawn tells me that it wants water by a certain dryness of the blades and soil – immediately obvious to the touch – the appearance of bald spots, yellowing, and a lack of springiness after being walked on; how does the "United States" communicate to the Attorney General? For similar reasons the guardian-attorney for a smog-endangered stand of pines could venture with more confidence that his client wants the smog stopped, than the directors of a corporation can assert that "the corporation" wants dividends declared. We make decisions on behalf of, and in the purported interests of others every day; these "others" are often creatures whose wants are far less verifiable, and even far more metaphysical in conception, than the wants of rivers, trees and land.[4]

This is mostly right, but there is room for reservation about certain details. First, the wants, needs and interests that a state, corporation or university might be said to possess derive, if not always in obvious ways, from those of the human beings who are its members. A corporation wants to reinvest its profits when the majority of the board votes for it. What a lawn wants or what a tree needs is not in this way derivative from human concerns. And so the question arises as to how we can tell what the wants, needs and interests of a tree might be. Secondly, a tree wants things, I will suggest, only in a metaphorical sense, while it might more literally have interests and needs.[5] And, thirdly, these wants, needs and interests may be more straightforwardly attributed to some natural objects than to others. Stone discusses various things, including streams and mountainsides, as well as lawns and trees, and it seems to me that whatever difficulties there might be in supposing that trees have interests or needs, these difficulties are seriously compounded when we focus instead on streams, deserts, mountains or swamps. This is obviously an issue to which we will need to return; for the moment I want to focus on more secure ground. Stone aims to base the legal rights, the standing, of trees and other living things on their having needs and interests. More secure, but how secure is that?

Interests

Should we agree that trees, like children, have interests that might be deserving of the law's protection? Many have argued that they do, but others have insisted that this is patent nonsense:

> The capacity for suffering and enjoying things is a prerequisite for having interests at all, a condition that must be satisfied before we can speak of interests in a meaningful way. It would be nonsense to say that it was not in the interests of a stone to be kicked along the road by a schoolboy. A stone does not have interests because it cannot suffer. Nothing that we can do to it could possibly make a difference to its welfare.[6]

Moral consideration extends as far as sentience, but no further, on Singer's account. A very similar point has been made more recently by Ronald Dworkin:

> Not everything that can be destroyed has an interest in not being destroyed, of course ... Nor is it enough, for something to have interests, that it be alive and in the process of developing into something more mature – it is not against the interests of a baby carrot that it be picked early and brought to the table as a delicacy – nor even that something that will naturally develop into something different and more marvellous: a butterfly is much more beautiful than a caterpillar, but it is not better for the *caterpillar* to become one ... It makes no sense to suppose that something has interests *of its own* – as distinct from its being important what happens to it – unless it has, or had, some form of consciousness: some mental as well as physical life.[7]

Consciousness, a mental life, and so a capacity for suffering and enjoyment are not only sufficient, but also necessary for a creature to have any interests at all. Trees and carrots, rocks and stones, will not count.

The arguments are problematic on two counts. One is minor. We might concede the point about stones – they are not even alive – and also about caterpillars – they might be said not to have an interest, as nothing can have an interest in turning into a different kind of thing[8] – but stick to our guns about carrots and trees. And then it might appear that these arguments are ineffective. It has already been observed that "interest", even when applied to human beings, is a somewhat complex term, admitting a range of meanings: I have interests, take an interest in certain things and find this and that interesting. All of this depends on my having a mental life. But it is also true that some things are, while other things are not, in my interest, irrespective of whether or not I desire them, or am even aware of their existence. To draw on an example much employed in another context, and that will be used again below, it is against my interests that I be slandered or betrayed, even if this is never discovered, and makes no difference whatsoever to my pleasures and pains.[9] So although sentience may be a sufficient condition of a creature's having interests, it is not immediately clear why it should also be considered necessary. What I want, and what is good for me, don't always coincide, and talk of interests can be properly introduced in relation to both notions. And in so far as the attempt is made to consider interests in connection with non-sentient life forms, it is plainly in this latter sense. Plants find nothing interesting, but certain things are in their interest. If it is claimed that it is in the lawn's interest to be watered, and not in a tree's interest that cable companies cut through its roots, all that might be meant by this is, first, that water will contribute to, while hacking at the roots will detract from, these plants' chances of survival, and, secondly, that survival is the state to which the plant naturally tends. Both conditions are needed, for otherwise Singer's stone, kicked eventually into non-existence, may, counterintuitively, be granted interests. But neither condition is particularly problematic: things can cease to exist, and living things are disposed, at least for a time, to resist non-existence, having built-in mechanisms for searching out the conditions of survival, for fighting against invasion by predators or disease and for self-repair.[10] In claiming, then, that it is against a tree's interests that we cut through its roots, or surround it with unadulterated fumes from exhausts, all that we can reasonably mean by such claims is, surely, true.

It is hard, then, to see any space for genuine disagreement here. There is some sense of interest in which, clearly, plants don't have interests. But there is another sense in which, just as clearly, they do. Nevertheless, the likes of Singer and Dworkin may yet resist, for, they may claim, while human beings literally have interests, trees and plants have interests in, at best, a metaphorical sense. Indeed, all the terms that I might employ in supporting this interest claim – needing water, resisting destruction, fighting disease, wanting to survive – are themselves used metaphorically; a tree cannot literally fight anything, need anything and so on. I might resist this strongly, and argue that such terms are in such contexts clearly used non-metaphorically. Or I might resist more temperately, and suggest that the literal/metaphorical distinction is itself not altogether clear. This temperate resistance will do.[11]

Well-being

Even if we set aside claims about interests, and allow that this term is better or more appropriately used in connection with sentient creatures, grounds for thinking that plants are morally considerable may still seem to remain. For surely we should think that things can go well or badly, to their benefit or detriment, for better or for worse, as far as living things are concerned. Things go well for a tree when it inhabits the sort of environment that is conducive to its health, in which it is close enough to other trees for cross-pollination to occur, and in which it can live the sort of life-span normal for trees of this type. Things go badly when it is affected by smog or acid rain, when honey fungus eats at its insides, when is is too severely pruned or trained,[12] or when felled and turned into bedroom furniture, pencils or bedding for hamsters. A tree, shrub, potato plant or fly agaric can be in a good condition, or its condition can be poor. It can flourish, or it can decline. Just as we can speak of the well-being of human beings and other animals, so, too, for plants. And just as we can benefit or harm sentient creatures, so, too, can we do this when, although life is present, sentience is not.

This idea, that there is such a thing as the well-being of plants, ought, I think, to be seen as uncontroversial. And various objections that can be raised here will all fail. It is no objection to point out that disease, destruction and death are a part of nature, and so will inevitably come each living thing's way. A part of nature they are, and all things must pass, but, setting causal determinism apart, there is nothing inevitable about premature death, or the onset of a particular disease in a particular individual. And even if there were, this would do nothing to counter the suggestion that what befalls the individual is still bad for it. Suppose that it is inevitable that I die in agony aged 42. This is bad for me, and still bad for me even if I am anaesthetized beforehand. Nor is it an objection to note that what is good for one thing is bad for another. Indeed this is so. As the honey fungus thrives, so the tree withers and dies. The suggestion here is not that we have some idea of what is good for the whole of nature, but only for living individuals that fall within it. What is good for honey fungus is not good for an oak. What is good for roses is bad for blackspot and greenfly, and so on. Nor, again, is it an objection to complain that all of this is seen from a human point of view, that we are somehow imposing our own values on the natural world. Certainly it is we who speak of and think about what is good or bad for this or that living thing; it is we who come to conclusions about their well-being, and it is we who, as Stone suggests, will argue the case as necessary with lawmakers or in courts. But the conclusions we reach and the cases we make need not mesh at all comfortably with what will serve our needs. We can allow that what is good for smallpox is bad for us. Nor, finally (and this is to revisit a point made above), can it be well objected that although we might properly give a wholly neutral and scientific account of what happens in nature, once value terms are introduced we just muddy the waters. It is difficult to see how, if we are permitted to describe one thing as killing another, we are prohibited from speaking of harm. And then the thought that what harms a tree is bad for it is surely innocuous. We can entertain such thoughts without mistakenly supposing that trees feel pain, and without using "bad for" in a metaphorical sense. That smog is bad for trees is as much and as firmly a fact about the universe as that the earth is bigger than the moon.

These claims about the interests, the well-being, the good of plants should not, I have claimed, be seen as controversial. Nor should they be thought new, for this is a broadly Aristotelian picture of the workings of nature, one in which the idea of certain things' having a nature is taken seriously, taken to imply that there are internal mechanisms or principles of governance that determine the proper development of those things over time. These mechanisms or principles might in various ways be impeded. And it isn't good for the things concerned when they are. But even if there is agreement, and there are firm facts here, this is only part of the picture. What remains to be considered is how and to what extent these claims about the well-being of plants can issue in prescriptions as to what we ought and ought not to do.

Reverence and respect

A concern for people, coupled with a concern for animals, added to a concern for plants and then spilling over into a concern for micro-organisms amounts to a concern for life itself. The idea that all living things, or that life itself, is of value is not one that has played a prominent part in recent thinking in the West, but it is hardly unfamiliar. It is a view that is encountered most frequently in the thought of many non-Western cultures, including those of Native Americans and Australian Aborigines, as well as certain peoples in Africa and, in India, the Jains. It has, by various means and for various reasons, been disseminated more widely in recent decades, but, although other influences are many, the emergence of the view within mainstream Western thinking is in some major part due to experiences in Africa of the doctor, musician and theologian Albert Schweitzer, whose exemplary life and wide-ranging writings made him a figure of considerable influence during the first half of the twentieth century.

Schweitzer came to believe that life itself was of fundamental value and sat at the basis of morality, for our ordinary thinking about moral questions, about the relationship between what we do and its consequences for our material and spiritual satisfactions derives, or so Schweitzer believed, first from an underlying concern for human life, and then at a deeper level, for the entirety of living things. As he succinctly put it, "It is *good* to maintain and cherish life: it is *evil* to destroy and check life".[13] And thus:

> A man is really ethical only when he obeys the constraint laid on him to help all life which he is able to succour, and when he goes out of his way to avoid injuring anything living. He does not ask how far this or that life deserves sympathy as valuable in itself, nor how far it is capable of feeling. To him life as such is sacred. He shatters no ice crystal that sparkles in the sun, tears no leaf from its tree, breaks off no flower, and is careful not to crush any insect as he walks. If he works by lamplight on a summer evening, he prefers to keep the window shut and breathe stifling air, rather than to see insect after insect fall on his table with singed and sinking wings.[14]

Schweitzer insists we should have reverence for life. There are undisguised religious overtones in that, and, in his many claims about the power and scope of the will to live, scarcely disguised allusions to Schopenhauer. He has, too, as is evident in the reference above to ice crystals, a fairly generous interpretation of what the sacredness of life implies. But setting aside its explanation and its extent, what seems clear in Schweitzer's injunction that we show reverence or respect for life itself is that we make no exclusions on the basis of rationality, sentience, usefulness to us or the inherent beauty of living things. At least thus far, the view appears profoundly anti-hierarchical, and so firmly opposed both to the robustly anthropocentric views that see human beings as the only creatures that matter in themselves, and to the range of related views that afford moral worth to other things in so far as they manage to approach the human condition.

In spite of the seriousness of his ethical concerns, on the one hand, and the evident breadth of his learning on the other, Schweitzer is not in the prevalent scholarly sense a philosopher, and his work does not aspire to the kind of perspicuity, nor the argument to the levels of rigour, that are commonly thought desirable in serious academic writing. Indeed, there are times when he simply seems to dismiss as wholly inappropriate any analytical or critical approach to his position, and to reject, too, any rule-based procedures for adjudicating between conflicting claims. In this, and also in thrusting the responsibility for making decisions back on the individual – his ethic "forces him to decide for himself in each case how far he can remain ethical and how far he must submit himself to the necessity of destroying and harming life and thus become guilty"[15] – there are similarities with a virtue-based approach to moral dilemmas. It isn't enough simply to put emphasis on good character, however, for even if there are fine judgements as to the detail of its application, the underlying contention, that living things, simply because they are alive, are deserving of both reverence and respect, very much looks to be the sort of claim for which justification is appropriate.

Yet although the natural world is such as to demand of us a certain response, it remains unclear just what reverence and respect amount to. And it comes as either a disappointment (for the would-be radical) or relief (for those wanting to avoid too much constraint) to find that Schweitzer appears to envisage rather less change to our customary practices than might be expected. Consciously intending to injure and kill is permitted as and when necessary. And so, while there are profound objections to causing animals avoidable pain, to "roughness in slaughterhouses", to "horrible deaths from unskilled hands", to experiments without anaesthetics and to the use of large numbers of animals for demonstrations in schools and universities, there is no objection to killing plants to feed cattle, and no objection, provided it is humanely done, to killing cattle to feed us. This, for many, will appear to give a rather generous reading of necessity.[16] Unconscious and unintended killing is also permitted, as Schweitzer holds that we should take all reasonable steps, but again not all possible steps, to avoid causing death to plants, insects and bugs wherever we go. This isn't meant to suggest that any alternative procedures are more viable, and isn't meant so much as a criticism of Schweitzer's view as an attempt to indicate its somewhat fluid nature. I can claim reverence for life even while going on much as before.

While Schweitzer is probably the best known advocate of a life-centred account, this approach to ethical thinking has been most fully developed and precisely articulated in a series of writings by the American philosopher Paul Taylor, the most substantial of which is his influential book *Respect for Nature*.[17] The account there, and elsewhere, is essentially threefold, as Taylor advances first what is effectively a non-moral thesis about the character of and relationships between all living things, moves on to a contentious and somewhat confusing claim about value, and then draws from this (in ways that he acknowledges are not in all respects logically compelling) a wide-ranging and allegedly radical ethical programme centring on the respect that we owe to nature. The programme as a whole constitutes what is often referred to as a biocentric account, but the appropriateness of that title isn't altogether clear, even if the pointed contrast with anthropocentrism is evident enough. Centring on life is one thing, while working through the full implications of this centring is yet another. And although there are, as will emerge, reasons for thinking that there is something of substance in Taylor's position, there is, in respect of at least two of its three strands, considerably less than he believes. Although it doesn't altogether mirror Taylor's exposition, and although there are unavoidable overlaps, I will start with the first and second of these strands here. These, in Taylor's own summary, essentially involve:

(a) The belief that humans are members of Earth's Community of Life in the same sense and on the same terms in which other living things are members of that Community

(b) the belief that the human species, along with all other species, are integral elements in a system of interdependence such that the survival of each living thing, as well as its chances of faring well or poorly, is determined not only by the physical conditions of its environment but also by its relations to other living things

(c) The belief that all organisms are teleological centers of life in the sense that each is a unique individual pursuing its own good in its own way

(d) The belief that humans are not inherently superior to other living things.[18]

Is any of this contentious? There is a danger that biocentrism may appear unremarkable, involving precepts that any decent person should be prepared to follow. But the account offered here, in its details, does advance a number of questionable claims, and Taylor recognizes that there needs to be some argument for several key aspects of his position. And although, of course, he expands on what he means, there are already some difficulties within the four points given above.

What does it mean to say that human beings are members of the Earth's community *in the same sense* and *on the same terms* as other living things? What sense and what terms does he have in mind? And with reference to creatures that are often considered to be struggling for survival, how seriously are we to take the idea of community? How does our survival or chance of faring well depend on other living things? Does Taylor mean *all* living things, or just some? If all trees died we would indeed be deeply and seriously affected, but what if all tigers died? How much difference would that make? Perhaps we can agree that all organisms are "teleological centers of life", but what about "pursuing its own good"? Suppose we agree that there is a good for trees. Isn't it a further step to think that trees are *pursuing* this good? This seems to be, if anything is, fairly clearly the metaphorical use of a term. Think of human beings. Some of us are, while others are simply not, pursuing our own good. Pursuing the good seems to be an option, and not something that all organisms do in their own way. And what about inherent superiority? Does Taylor think that we are not superior to any living thing, or not superior to all of them? Or does he think that although we might be superior, we are not *inherently* superior? Suppose that we are not superior. Is this a contingent fact about us, such that we might have been superior to this or that other living thing? Or is it somehow a necessary truth? And would this truth then be that we are somehow inferior, or that all living things are somehow equal, or that the whole notion of superior, inferior or equal worth somehow makes no sense?

I will make no attempt to answer all of these questions directly. I raise them in part to indicate how biocentrism can seem to involve claims that veer between the innocuous and the controversial, but I raise them also in order to point the way to some issues that do need to be further explored, if a life-centred ethics is properly to be understood. Of these four claims, the last demands the closest attention. The other claims here are, in their major respects, non-moral theses to which, broadly at least, we might give assent. Living things do depend on other living things, and, as I have argued, it makes good sense to speak of things going well or badly for them. But with the fourth claim Taylor shifts to more controversial ground, putting forward a thesis about value on which the rest of his argument critically depends. From bringing together the rejection of human superiority along with the insistence that living things have a good of their own, Taylor develops the full substance of his respect for nature account.

How does this argument go? There is some complexity to it, for Taylor acknowledges that any conclusion about what we ought to do will not readily fall out of non-moral premises. And there is going to be some bite to this conclusion: unpack what the claim about human superiority leads to, and:

> We would have to face the possibility that our true relation to other forms of life, even to those that might do us harm, is a relation among beings of *equal* inherent worth, and not a relation between superior, higher beings, and inferior, lower ones. We could then no longer rightly look down on animals or plants, or think of a human individual as naturally having a greater claim-to-existence than any "mere" animal or plant. We would see ourselves and our place in the natural world in a new light. Our whole ethical orientation would undergo a deep and far-reaching transformation, entailing revisions in our treatment of the Earth and its biotic communities. A total reordering of our moral universe would take place. Our duties with respect to the "world" of nature would be seen as making claims upon us to be balanced against our duties with respect to the "world" of human culture and civilization. We would no longer simply assume the human point of view and consider the effects of our conduct regarding other living things exclusively or primarily from the perspective of what will promote our own good.[19]

This is what the argument promises.[20] But there are important questions, or so I will suggest, as to whether it can deliver.

Superiority and inherent worth

At the centre of Taylor's argument are the closely connected claims, first, negatively, that we are not superior beings and secondly, positively, that all living creatures (or at least, when normal) are of equal inherent value. The target of the first claim is the suggestion that human beings are, in some respects, superior to other creatures, and thus, in virtue of their superiority, are warranted in putting their own interests first, and assigning all other creatures a subsidiary place. And the point of the second claim is to establish that all living things are equally deserving of moral consideration, and so, in turn, to establish the radical biocentric view. The denial of superiority was, of course, the fourth of the claims listed above, and the one that, I suggested, needed the closest attention. I can start with it.

Taylor's strategy here is straightforward: to consider and reject various claims as to our alleged superiority, beginning with the suggestion that this rests on certain of our capacities, and move on to the contention that we are inherently superior beings. It doesn't take him long to dismiss the first type of claim. We are better at mathematics than monkeys and more creative than birds, but we're not much good at climbing trees and can't fly at all. Only by a prior high ranking to those capacities in which we excel do we come out as superior on approaches such as these. But this is a little fast, and there are two ways in which a believer in human superiority might attempt a reply.

First, there is a move resembling the utilitarian's distinction between higher and lower pleasures. Mill argued that poetry can be shown to be better than pushpin just because those who have experienced both prefer the former.[21] The more limited one's range of pleasures, the less those pleasures count. This favours intellectual types like Mill, who allegedly have tried the life of the body as well as that of the mind, and puts libraries above restaurants, opera above football and the J. Paul Getty Museum above Disneyland. There are well-known problems with this, but, nevertheless, something to be said for variety. Perhaps someone who likes opera and football is superior to those who are rather more focused, whatever their bent. And perhaps human beings are superior to other creatures not because our individual skills are of more worth, but because there is a greater range. We can climb trees a bit, eat bananas and ride bicycles, swim underwater, play the violin and more. This isn't obviously *ad hoc*, cooked up to give us first place, for it allow that aliens from other galaxies might, in virtue of having an even greater range, count as superior to us. Secondly, we might think further about one particular characteristic that Taylor considers and rejects as offering us overall superiority. Suppose it is agreed that only human beings have a sense of right and wrong, are able to distinguish between what they want and what they ought to do, and are able willingly to sacrifice themselves for the sake of others. Might it be said that we are morally superior to other creatures? Taylor rejects this, questioning the coherence of a comparison with creatures that are simply not moral agents.[22] This is just a little odd: it allows that monkeys are superior where getting into trees is concerned, but denies that birds are superior aeronautically, for we climb a little, but fly not at all. More important, it misses the point. A claim as to our superiority that makes reference to morals is best interpreted, surely, not as contending that we are better at morality than other creatures but simply that we are better because of morality. That may be false but it is certainly neither incoherent nor wholly implausible.

The second claim, that we are not inherently superior, takes Taylor rather more time. For some version of the contrary claim has figured, or so he argues, within a number of important religious and philosophical traditions; it is well entrenched, crucial to our self-image, and so correspondingly harder to dislodge:

> According to this interpretation, humans are superior to nonhumans not as regards their merits, but as regards their *inherent worth*. Thus the claim of human superiority is to be understood as asserting that all human beings, simply in virtue of their humanity, have a greater inherent worth than animals and plants.[23]

The idea here is that our superiority doesn't depend, precariously, on this or that property, which presumably we may come to lose, but is somehow much more deeply embedded. This is indeed a familiar view, but it is open to two interpretations only one of which is hopeless, and only one of which Taylor is easily able to reject. His problem, as will emerge, is that it is just a variant of this hopeless view that he depends on for his biocentric account to go through.

What I think of as a hopeless view connects with belief in the sanctity of life. This belief, typically, turns out to be concerned only with human life and, again typically, insists that these lives are of significant value even when all signs of rationality, even of consciousness, are absent. Some people insist that such lives ought to be preserved for as long as possible, and some hold that they are more valuable than any animal life, or even any number of animal lives.[24] It is hard to see even the beginnings of a justification for such views, unless appeal is made to certain religious beliefs, themselves not rationally defensible, about the existence and value of the immaterial soul. Otherwise all that can be said, unhelpfully even if true, is that all of these people are equally people. But there is an alternative to hopelessness, and an equally familiar view construes our humanity in terms of a complex of properties, intellectual and moral in particular, by which at least normal members of our species are distinguished from all others. And our value rests on this. So there are here two accounts of inherent worth. On one account our value has simply no explanation (or at least no natural explanation – I can grant that an appeal to souls does some work), while on the other it is explained by reference, not to contingent properties, but to properties that are inherent or essential or defining of the kinds of things we are. Our value is either wholly free-floating or it depends on the particular features that are constitutive of our humanity. This second account, I suggest, is both the more defensible, and the more deeply embedded in the traditions to which Taylor is opposed.

Things now begin to go adrift for Taylor, for he seems to have need of both the hopeless and the more plausible accounts of inherent worth. Begin with the latter. Like Regan, and in a similarly neo-Kantian vein, Taylor is concerned to lay out and defend some notions of non-instrumental value, and in particular to squash the idea that things other than human beings have value only in so far as they satisfy the desires, serve the interests or promote the well-being of human beings. Given sentience, it isn't too difficult to see some notion of inherent worth as relevant to animals: "To say that it possesses inherent worth is to say that its good is deserving of the concern and consideration of all moral agents, and that the realization of its good has intrinsic value, to be pursued as an end in itself and for the sake of the entity whose good it is".[25] So if animals have some measure of inherent worth, then we have some obligation to consider and promote their well-being. But what a biocentric ethic requires is that we need to consider other living things as well. This is more difficult. And as Taylor allows, the insistence that plants can be said to have a well-being, or a good of their own, is not enough to ground any such obligation: "we do not contradict ourselves by asserting that an entity that has a good of its own lacks inherent worth".[26] There is work to be done here, then, but the aim of that work should be tolerably clear: it is to show how we are similarly obligated to consider the welfare of non-sentient life.

However this, so far, is compatible with holding, first, that value depends on properties, and, secondly, that as properties differ, so, too, does value. It is compatible, in short, with holding both that we have some moral duties towards plants, and that we can always put people first.[27] Or, shorter, biocentrism and anthropocentrism are not at odds. Yet this isn't what Taylor wants, and is, rather, what he proposes to avoid by claiming that living things not only have inherent worth, but have it to an equal degree. This, though, is where the hopeless view re-emerges, for how can vastly different things – people, finches, carrots – be equally valuable? Their value either depends on their having some property or properties, or it is free-floating. The latter option is no good, and the only property these various things have in common is that of being alive. This, like the earlier appeal to our being equally human, is unhelpful even if true. We would need to know just how being alive, and being, as we might concede, equally alive, gives us inherent worth to an equal degree. (Someone might object that if it is allowed that we are equally alive, and that life provides worth, then equal worth follows more or less straightforwardly. But it doesn't. We would also need to show that no further properties can add to or detract from this worth. And if it is objected that given inherence, properties are irrelevant, then we have to abandon the grounding in life, and revert to free-floatingness. And this isn't much good.) Until answers are provided it ought surely to be allowed that this doctrine of equal inherent worth has little to recommend it.

Taylor, though, will have little time for all this, believing that there is a quick route to his desired conclusion:

Rejecting the notion of human superiority entails its positive counter-part: the doctrine of species impartiality. One who accepts that doctrine regards all living things as possessing inherent worth – the *same* inherent worth, since no one species has been shown to be either "higher" or "lower" than any other.[28]

But this is too quick. I might hold another species to be superior: lions for their nobility, or ants for persistence. Or, more plausibly, I might hold that the whole notion of superior and inferior species makes no sense. Either way, nothing about equality will follow.

I could leave it there, but want instead to offer a suggestion as to one source of Taylor's mistake. On several occasions he indicates a considerable degree of sympathy for Singer's insistence on equal consideration. My suspicion is that Taylor runs together, quite without justification, this aspect of Singer's position with key elements of his own. Thus in a note[29] he describes Singer's anti-speciesism as providing a different argument against the doctrine of human superiority. A little later he expressly connects the claim that living things deserve equal consideration with his own claim about equal inherent worth. But this is to misunderstand Singer. Speciesism involves making unwarranted discriminations between members of different species, and equal considera-tion is perfectly compatible with holding that different creatures are at the end of the day unequal. (And, of course, Singer has to hold some such view, in order to emphasize sentience as a criterion of moral relevance. It isn't on his account a prejudice or bias against plants that excludes them from any direct role in our moral deliberations, but a just assessment of the kinds of things they are.) The slide from equal consideration to equal worth is, perhaps, one that might easily be made, but it is nevertheless illegitimate.

Is superiority the issue?

Taylor devotes a lot of time and energy to the denial of human superiority, arguing, first, that there are no good reasons to believe that human beings are superior to other life forms, and secondly, that there are in fact good reasons to believe that we are not superior.[30] But it isn't clear that biocentric ethics has any real need of this. In at least two respects our ranking, on the one hand, and our obligations, on the other, are distinct. We could put people first even if we are not superior to other living things, and we could be superior even while having serious moral obligations to consider the welfare of other creatures.

Our putting people first may be morally defensible, even if human beings are not superior to other life forms. First, it may turn out that members of any given species are justified in putting members of their species first, even if, from a wholly neutral point of view, the species in question reveals no particular merits. Each of us knows and understands more about things of our own kind than about creatures that are, to varying degrees, alien to us. We are likely to be better judges of our own needs than those of others, and so it may overall be more efficient and effective if we devote rather more of our energies to looking after ourselves. Of course, this point will apply as much to cats, dolphins and Martians as it does to human beings. All are better able to look after their own. Secondly, and more importantly, it may well be that certain individuals, or members of certain species, betray characteristics that require that certain of their interests be prioritized within the moral calculus, but there is no clear need to consider the species to be superior in virtue of such characteristics. Again, I go back to sentience. It is surely possible to think that one has a greater obligation to aid a goat, rather than a sycamore, when both are dying of thirst, just because the goat's thirst is accompanied by pain. I am not claiming here that the goat must come first, but only that one can coherently believe that sentience puts it first, without thereby needing to think it is in any way superior to the tree. Rather the reverse: one may as well think that sentience, as it allows for pain, is a defect that, from the moral point of view, can place a number of inconvenient demands on us.[31] And now just as the animal may come before the tree, it may turn out that people come before animals. Their receptivity to pain may be straightforwardly greater and, because of their psychological complexity, importantly multi-dimensional. This, again, is not to renege on any commitment to equal consideration. We might consider the chaffinch and the child equally, and find ourselves obligated to save the child.

Even if we are superior there may well be a range of obligations elsewhere. In effect I have already made this point, both immediately above, and earlier in the discussion. We ought to consider animal pain. And this obligation will remain, even if we are, and know ourselves to be, superior creatures. It will in that case be more quickly overridden by obligations to fellow human beings, but it will in no way simply disappear. And if there are obligations to consider the well-being of plants, they, too, will remain in place even if they are lower in status. There is no reason to suppose that things need to be of equal value in order to be of value at all, and there is no reason to suppose that allowing a hierarchy of value gives those better placed *carte blanche* with respect to creatures below them.

A life-centred ethic, one that attributes to all living things some degree of inherent value (allowing now, as I have argued we must allow, that this value is not wholly independent of the character and capacities of that living thing) has, then, no pressing need of equal value, and consequently no pressing need to reject the claim that we are the superior beings. All it needs, in place of the radicalism implied by Taylor's equality claims, is some sort of account of how we can have direct obligations to consider the good of non-sentient forms of life. Construed non-radically, such that this obligation might be slight, and easily overridden by claims elsewhere, it may seem that this account should be easy to provide. That, however, would be a mistake.[32]

From well-being to considerable

Important elements within Taylor's argument are so far untouched. I have adopted a sceptical stance towards several of his claims about superiority and equal inherent worth, while allowing that if there is any such worth we are obligated to consider it. But is there inherent worth in living things, even to some small degree? I tried earlier to show that we can appropriately refer to the well-being of plants and agreed, more or less, with Taylor that we might think of them as pursuing their own good. But, as he and I also agree, this doesn't immediately issue in any obligation on us to consider or promote this well-being. One question, then, is as to how this obligation might arise, and another concerns its limits, for biocentrism wants to go beyond animals, but to stop short of stones, claiming that it is precisely life that demands our reverence or respect. But this is not adequately explained unless it is made clear why we need feel no corresponding concern for the fortunes of inanimate things. What I will suggest is that although there may be some reasons to extend our concern beyond sentience, there are no further reasons to end it just where life itself gives out.

An untenable position?

One difficulty has probably already been noted. We can, if we choose, respond to the perceived value in the life of animals by refraining from killing or eating them, by not using their skins or fur and by ceasing to experiment upon them. But what are we to do if we want similarly to show respect for all life? Vegetarianism is a genuine option, but there is an evident difficulty if plants join them in the moral domain. We eat them, or we starve. The problem with biocentrism, then, is that it takes on too much. We cannot eat, move or breathe without destroying life. Morality here threatens to reduce us to impotence, and to guarantee our extinction. And as it is hard to believe that morality demands so much, so might it be tempting to dismiss this life-centred view out of hand.

The worry here is in the end unjustified, and an ethic centred on life is not so readily dismissed. Neither Schweitzer nor Taylor holds that reverence or respect demands that we simply refrain from killing. What Schweitzer wants is that we acknowledge that all destruction, all injury, is evil, and that we kill only when it is necessary. But, as I noted, here he is generous, and seems to think that testing drugs on animals, cutting meadows to feed cows and eating meat are all, broadly speaking, necessary evils. Taylor, similarly, avoids the suggestion that even equal inherent worth confers an inalienable right to life on all those things that possess it. We do not signal a lack of respect merely by killing some other creature or by allowing it to die when we could, without serious inconvenience, give it assistance. It might be thought that fudging by well-known proponents of a position is one thing, and genuine scope for compromise another. Is reverence or respect really possible as long as we continue, more or less, to put ourselves first? Certainly much more work might be done, both within environmental philosophy and without, on unpacking notions of respect in particular, but I am inclined to think that some compromise position is defensible. It is not, after all, simply a desire to sustain human existence that motivates Schweitzer and Taylor. The idea of necessary evils, which underlies some of the tensions within their accounts, is, as I have suggested earlier, one that any persuasive morality cannot easily do without. Although Taylor does offer fairly detailed suggestions as to how competing claims might be settled,[33] neither he nor Schweitzer pretends that this will be easy, both acknowledging, as it surely should be acknowledged, that there is considerable complexity to living the good life. So even if there is some difficulty in reconciling the seeming radicalism of their initial claims with the eventual moderation of their views, it ought not to be thought that the sorts of views outlined here are ones that cannot in the end be sustained.

An unjustifiable position?

How might we justify eating plants once we allow that their existence is inherently valuable? There are at least two ways. One is to abandon equality claims, and allow that this value is lower in plants than it is in people.[34] Another is to hold on to such claims, but then allow that this value is one among many, between some of which there will be significant differentials. Having made the fuss about equality, the latter is more likely to appeal to Taylor. Yet either way, there seems room for a modest biocentric view, under which we show concern for life in general while still putting human life first. Even if biocentrism is flexible in this way, and can be advanced without threatening human existence, it may still not yet be clear that the view is one we ought to adopt. Interpret "respect for life" as minimally disruptive, yet it remains as a moral injunction. The question remains as to why we should obey it.

The difficulty here is in going from a position that I have argued we ought to adopt, that of holding that living things have their well-being, which we might promote or impede, to one that claims that we ought to promote or at least not impede this well-being. Some things are good for trees. We can think about the good of trees, but why should we do them any good? Even if this "ought" is one that can fairly readily be overridden, and so one that we can accept at little or no cost, the move still needs explanation. Although he acknowledges the importance and the non-obviousness of this move, perhaps Taylor glides over it:

> [Once we separate the objective value concept of a being's good from subjective value concepts] there is no problem about what it means to

140

benefit or harm a plant, to be concerned about its good, and to act benevolently towards it. We can intentionally act with the aim of helping a plant to grow and thrive, and we can do this because we have genuine concern for its well-being. As moral agents we might think of ourselves as under an obligation not to destroy or injure a plant. We can take the standpoint of a plant and judge what happens to it as being good or bad from its standpoint. To do this would involve our using as the standard of evaluation the preservation or promotion of the plant's own good. Anyone who has ever taken care of flowers, shrubs or tress will know what these things mean.[35]

Indeed, we might think of ourselves as having certain obligations here, but the question is of whether we would be right to do so. Taylor thinks we would, but the major problem for biocentrism is in accounting for this shift. How do we progress from agreeing that plants can be benefited or harmed to further agreeing that we have some sort of duty to benefit, and not to harm, them? I don't want to adopt a merely sceptical stance here, and question the general legitimacy of such a move. Consider animals. Imagine someone who says, "I agree that if I beat this animal, it will feel great pain. But why does this give me any sort of reason not to beat it?" This person sounds like a psychopath or a monster. The question seems perverse. With plants the issue looks to be less clear. Imagine someone who says, "I agree that if I cut down this tree it will be harmed. But why does what give me a reason not to cut it down?" This person doesn't sound like a monster, the question seems fair, and the biocentrist needs to furnish a reply. Otherwise we haven't yet been persuaded that there are any direct moral duties to plants. And the boundary between objects that are, in themselves, of moral concern, and those that are not, will remain where many have supposed it to be located, with sentience.

It is, then, one thing to maintain that some notions of well-being and interests are applicable to plants, and another to suppose that we have some sort of responsibility, albeit minimal, to promote this well-being. I have suggested that many of the advocates of a biocentric ethic are other than perspicacious here, either, like Kenneth Goodpaster in a well-known piece,[36] seeming to suppose that moral considerability falls right on the heels of interests or, like Taylor, acknowledging the gap but then doing too little to plug it. What are needed, and are so far elusive, are good grounds for thinking that the mere fact of a thing's being alive provides some reason for us try to do well by it.

Life and beyond

There is one further avenue that might be explored here. Consider whether there might be obligations to sentient creatures which, whether they are fulfilled or not, make no difference to how a thing feels. If there are, then perhaps there is scope for uncovering some roughly similar obligations involving non-sentient life. And arguably, there are such obligations.

First, go back to an issue raised in Chapter 5. It will be said that even a painless, sudden and unanticipated death is bad for a person. Such a death is not at any time something that the person can anticipate with dread, feel as it occurs, or look back on with regret. And as such a death is bad for a person, so it is wrong (other things being equal) to kill someone, even in this manner. So if my going out of existence, even when I am completely unaware of it, can be bad for me, why cannot a similarly unfelt going out of existence be bad for plants? And if where people are concerned even this sort of killing is *prima facie* wrong, why is it not similarly *prima facie* wrong to kill plants? In both cases, it can seem, moral obligations make no reference to sentience.

There is a confusion here, however. Even if a person's unanticipated death is in no way an object of experience, it still impinges massively on experience: it ends it. We might think that it is here that the badness lies. But in that case, although death is bad for animals, it still isn't bad for plants. Their deaths do not put an end to a life they would otherwise continue to enjoy. And this explanation of death's badness might still not be right, for, as I have suggested, a further, and I think more plausible, suggestion is that human death is bad in so far as it curtails a future that we had planned to enjoy. So neither animal nor plant deaths are bad. Still, it may be too soon to dismiss completely this line of thought. For such discussion of death's badness is linked, perhaps now irrevocably, with a similar discussion of betrayal. Nagel has argued that a person is wronged by even undiscovered betrayal,[37] and that the wrong here is to be explained neither by the possibility of later discovery, nor by betrayal's general tendency to bring about feelings of unhappiness. For even if the innocent party is on a one-way mission to Jupiter and, because of a malfunction, destined to die within hours, still they may be wronged by activity back home. And even if it causes pain in most cases, the more plausible thought, according to Nagel, is that betrayal causes this pain because it is wrong, rather than the other way round. Undiscovered betrayal is importantly different from death. For, *ex hypothesi*, it makes no difference to the person's experience. It leaves the person not only oblivious of this particular wrong, but with just the same hopes, beliefs, feelings and states of mind as they would have had otherwise. But this does not remove the wrong. It is against someone's interests to be betrayed, even if this betrayal makes no difference to their beliefs or feelings about those interests.

So can we use our intuitions about such a case to support the view that a plant can similarly be wronged by some activity of ours that runs counter to a plant's interests? In one respect this might seem easy. Where betrayal is concerned there is room for doubt as to whether any real harm has occurred, but with the alleged wrong to a plant this doubt is misplaced. If we cut down the plant, we harm it. The only question here, then, is whether we therefore do wrong to the plant; whether we do something we have some obligation not to do. The thought that we do is impeded by the further thought that wrongdoing must affect feeling, but the intuition about betrayal shows this further thought to be confused. As wrongdoing need not affect feeling, so nothing stands in the way of agreeing that we have wronged the plant, and done to it something that we ought, for its sake, not to have done.

This is still too fast, for there remains one clearly important respect in which undiscovered betrayal does affect the victim's mental life. Beliefs that would otherwise have been true, about whom to trust, what a partner is doing, and so on, are by the act of betrayal rendered false. The character, if not the content, of these beliefs is therefore changed. This is a relational rather than an intrinsic change in the nature of these beliefs, to be sure, but it isn't therefore obviously unimportant. But if the wrong of betrayal rests on its having this kind of effect on someone's beliefs, then, on the assumption that beliefs about the world depend on awareness of the world, it is not, after all, a case where wrongness is independent of sentience, and so it doesn't offer the desired support for an account of wrongs to plants.

One remark in the above discussion needs further thought. I said there that we certainly harm plants in cutting them down, even if there is then a question as to whether we wrong them, but this can seem mistaken. To do something harm is, surely, at least on the face of it, to do wrong. Even if we agree that there are some cases where harm is justified, say where a doctor breaks a leg in order to reset it, still justification is called for. Harm seems not to be something we are at liberty simply to inflict on other things. And so to agree that we can harm plants is in itself to agree that they figure within the moral domain.

There are several responses. One is to think again, and deny that we can, after all, harm plants. Another is to insist that the relationship between harm and wrong is less strong than it may at first appear. A third, which I am inclined to favour, is to concede the link here but then to reinterpret the nature of the wrong committed. These responses all need further discussion.

The denial of harm is unconvincing. Certainly plants can die, and we can kill them. Just as certainly, they can decline, and we can bring about such a decline. It doesn't seem inappropriate to speak of harming plants in such circumstances, when, for example, we so severely prune a shrub that it neither flowers nor fruits for several years, or when we introduce pollutants that curtail the lives of trees. Nor does it seem appropriate severely to limit our language where plants are concerned, such that we forbid ourselves to talk of injury, disease, poor health, weakness and the like. "Harm" figures within this language, and there is no good reason for denying its applicability to plants.

Might we, then, instead construe harm as a wholly value-neutral term, such that there remains always a question as to whether one does anything at all wrong in harming or injuring a plant? This question won't so readily arise with animals, just because most harm to at least many animals impinges adversely on feeling, and the connection between pain and wrongness is hard to break.[38] But with plants, where pain isn't at issue, it may seem that there is a clear distinction to be drawn, and that wrongness doesn't follow on the heels of harm. I am inclined, though, to think this mistaken, and that in this case, too, there is some sort of conceptual connection between the terms. Even if we want to agree that often the harm is justified, so that no wrong occurs, still the justification is called for.

Does this, then, amount to a vindication of the life ethic? Granted that our duty to plants can be overridden, and might be minimally demanding, the biocentrist may suggest that his demand that we justify our harms can fairly easily be satisfied. All that is required is that we refrain from harm unless we can offer some reason for proceeding. And this is surely not too much to ask. It is wrong, then, to cut down trees, unless one has a reason for doing so. On a generous account, the pursuit of self-interest might be enough – we cut down the tree to win a bet, or impress someone – while a more cautious view will require that we should thereby do some good. We cut down trees for firewood, or to improve the view. But even if justification is easily provided, still thoughtless harms and wanton destruction will be wrong. Isn't this already enough to locate trees within the moral domain, to view them as things with respect to which certain of our actions are proscribed? I think that in the end there is some sort of vindication here, but it needs to be tempered in two highly important ways. I will merely sketch these ways here, as both are more appropriately developed and explored in later chapters.

First, it isn't at all clear why there is anything special about life. Only living things can be killed, but not only living things can be destroyed. Perhaps only living things can be injured, but non-living things can quite easily be damaged. And surely thoughtless harm and wanton destruction are bad whenever they occur, whether to animals, plants, sculptures or greenhouses. There remains the case for setting animals to one side, as creatures who, when harmed, will often suffer pain as a result. But is it any more wrong, or in any different manner wrong, to uproot a young sapling than it is to break the icicles from a waterfall in winter? I find it very hard to see here what difference life makes.[39] Nor can this simply be dismissed by pointing out (what may in any event be contested) that non-living things, whether they be natural – streams, dunes, mountains – or artefactual – tractors, chairs, car parks – have neither interests nor well-being to take into account. That won't put trees above icicles. Nor, too, I think, will it prove easy to maintain that the wrong in all such cases is done to others. I can do wrong in destroying statues even if no one cares. And so a central plank in the biocentric view, that the moral domain extends as far as, but no further than, individual centres of life, may in the end prove difficult to sustain.

Secondly, it isn't clear that the emphasis should be, as it has so far been, so much on what we do, as opposed to what happens. Moral questions do indeed connect with questions about our actions, but there are several prior issues about events, and states of affairs, that at some point need to be explored. Thus the wrongness of killing depends on intuitions about the badness of death, and the wrongness of injury typically presupposes the badness of pain. So one question is, does anything bad occur when, independently of human activity, a wall falls down, or a mountain is eroded, or a tree dies? The answer to these questions is, I think, not immediately clear. But there isn't a similar lack of clarity where many of the questions in relation to animals are concerned. Does anything bad occur when an animal, in the course of nature, suffers pain? I am inclined to think it does. The upshot here, of course, is that the concession to the life ethic may need to be modified. Even assuming that we do something wrong in destroying a tree, if it isn't straightforwardly bad for a tree to be destroyed, then this wrongness will have to be explained in some other way. The way in which plants enter the moral domain may, in the end, have more affinity with the moral status of rocks and chairs than it does with animals.

Summary

There is, perhaps, a natural tendency to want to extend the sphere of moral concern to cover trees, plants and other living things as well as human beings and other animals. What is often seen as an important component within the argument for this extension, the claim that non-sentient forms of life also have interests, well-being and a good of their own, is, I have suggested, less controversial than it has sometimes appeared to be. We should allow such claims, but the progression from here to the further claim that living things are all of them objects of moral concern is not straightforward. Although several writers have attempted to make this argument, none of them can be judged entirely successful.

Some of their attempts suffer from overambition. Taylor tries to show that all living things are of equal value, and that respect for nature involves our demonstrating equal concern for sentient and non-sentient creatures. Were he successful, this might, I suggested, put impossible demands on us, but the arguments for equality are not well made. In particular, it looks as if this argument needs but is unable to demolish the view that value depends on properties. Yet even if a radically egalitarian position cannot be established, a more modest biocentrism, in which plants count but people count for more, still needs to be considered. Even if we are persuaded that there is little practical cost to adopting such a view, the theoretical obstacles remain, and the gap between there being good plants, things that are good for plants and plants having a good of their own, all on the one hand, and our having some obligation to promote or further that good, on the other, needs somehow to be bridged. Can it be? I have suggested that there is in the end some sense in which we can do right or wrong by plants, and some sense in which they enter the moral domain, but, I have argued, that sense doesn't draw lines just where biocentrism would have them. The distinction between sentience and non-sentience still seems to have greater significance than that between life and non-life.

CHAPTER 7

Rivers, Species, Land

I have wanted to argue that there are no compelling grounds for supposing that plants, like animals, are of direct moral concern. If there were no grounds at all, and sentience were a condition of something's being directly morally considerable, then it would follow that other non-sentient things were similarly not of such concern. But what I wanted to suggest towards the close of Chapter 6 is that there might still be some reasons, even if these be less than irresistible, for thinking that certain sorts of wrongs, under certain sorts of conditions, can be delivered to a wide range of entities. And so, although there is, I believe, an important line at sentience, it is still too early to conclude that beyond sentience we can do simply as we will. In this chapter, then, I want to consider several of the claims made for extending the area of moral concern some way beyond the boundary of life, to include non-living entities of various different kinds. I will begin with one seemingly obvious extension, towards certain particular things which, although themselves not alive, are just as much a part of the natural world as living things.[1]

Rivers

A river, provided it is not too seriously polluted, will typically contain many living things. Even so it mainly comprises water, which although supportive of life is not itself alive. A river here is in many ways like a mountain, a lake or a desert. Such things are similarly not themselves alive and their connections with life, although often intimate, are in the end similarly merely contingent. There are mountains on the moon, and there could have been rivers, as well as canals, on Mars. There is a contrast here with, for example, a forest. Even if a forest is not itself a living thing, its connection with life is not contingent. There are no forests without trees. Rivers, mountains and lakes are objects that occur in nature and that will be of interest or concern in so far as the natural world is of interest or concern. A contrast here is with canals and reservoirs, and this contrast survives even if it is conceded that there are man-made lakes and could be, were we so minded, man-made mountains: even if not precisely mirrored by differences in terminology, the nature/artifice distinction is here tolerably firm.

Are rivers, mountains and the like objects of direct moral concern? Are they things that, for their own sake, we ought to treat one way rather than another? It is often suggested that they are, and that our interests in preserving such things are not all of them reducible to a concern for the living things whose existence might otherwise be compromised. But perhaps the thinking here is confused. Rivers and streams will look to be poorer candidates for eliciting such concern than will animals and plants, for not only are they not sentient, but in not being alive they cannot in any particularly informative way be said to have a good of their own. Or so many will want to claim. But others will insist that rivers, waterfalls, deserts and canyons can be in a better or worse condition just as surely as can a fox or an oak, that something can be good or bad for a river, and that the distinction here between living and non-living things is of little significance from the moral point of view. These others will also insist that as something can be good or bad for a river, so we are under some obligation to promote this good, and ameliorate this bad. Who, then, is right? The position of life-theorists may appear to be weak. Their difficulty is in pointing to some relevant facts that justify the claim that moral considerability falls precisely at the boundary of life, such that without life things can have no good of their own. Some avenues hold only the illusion of promise. It makes little sense to ascribe to non-living things any purposive activity, to suppose that a mountain is pursuing its own good, or that a stream wants to find the quickest way downhill. This sort of language, I have suggested, is surely used only metaphorically in connection with plants: a stream is presented with no choices, and makes no decisions as to where it runs, just as a sunflower has no option but to grow and turn towards the light. So, having allowed non-sentient things into the moral domain, there is little in the way of including non-living things as well.

Still, there is something in this appeal to teleology. The underlying, more defensible thought here is that rivers and the like are not subject to the sorts of developmental processes that are of the essence where living things are concerned. Although rivers and mountains are at some time formed, undergo change and then eventually cease to exist, and although these changes, even if affected by human activity, are often brought about by natural forces, still it is not in the nature of a river, as it is in the nature of an oak, to develop in certain ways rather than others. A living thing is acted on from within, as well as from without, but there is no within, no internal mechanism or principle of governance, where non-living things are concerned. To put this another way, the sorts of entities considered here do not fall into natural kinds. And, surely, it is some such thought as this that justifies, if indeed anything does, the drawing of a firm and morally weighty line between living and non-living things. As there is no pre-determined order where the non-living is concerned, so nothing that happens can disrupt that order, introduce abnormalities and render such a thing's condition other than it was supposed to be.

Against this, however, there remains the stubborn thought, or series of thoughts, that non-living things can be damaged or destroyed, can exist in better or worse conditions and can be benefited or harmed by what occurs. A rock face can be shattered by blasting or earth tremors; a lake can silt up and disappear; rivers can be spoiled near irreparably by pollution. Various evils can occur. Dwell on the last of these examples. Although pollution may be a fact, the occurrence of damage, in many cases, is harder to pin down. Is it always good for a river if pollution is reduced? Recent endeavours to clean up the Trent, in the English Midlands, have perhaps been too successful. There are now fewer fish, as the purer waters have not favoured plant life, and so, in turn, have reduced both the amounts of food and the degree of protection from predators. The water may be pristine, but there is less going on. Yet even supposing the relationship between pollution and the river's contents to be more straightforward – the greater the pollution, the greater the levels of sickness and death – it is not obviously to the detriment of the river that it should in this way prove inhospitable to life. Although it is, of course, true that rivers can be made safer, more beautiful, better for fish, and so on, it isn't at all clear that any of these changes will really benefit the river, as opposed to sailors, aesthetes or ducks. This is not to deny, of course, that we speak as if the river itself can be benefited or harmed, but so to speak may be either shorthand, or a mistake. Given a certain desideratum, then certain actions or activities can be considered good or bad relative to that desideratum. But whereas greenfly are bad for roses *simpliciter*, nothing is, in this way, bad for a river.

Much of this, though, is to consider only changes in the character of a robustly existing thing. Clean or dirty, meandering or canalized, the river, I am assuming, continues to flow. Other sorts of change may threaten this, and when a thing's existence is challenged or undermined, harm more unequivocally occurs. Thus drought is bad for a river. It is as bad for a river to cease to exist as it is for a plant, and this is what will happen if the water refuses to flow. So it is bad for the Owens River in California that almost all of its water is extracted to feed the lawns, wash the hair and grow the strawberries of the citizens of Los Angeles. Similarly, it was bad for the River Lowther in the English Lake District that it was dammed, in the 1930s, to form Haweswater reservoir, offering comparable luxuries to the people of Bradford. Similarly again for the Italian mountains near Lucca, which visibly shrink under the demand for marble. Diminish or destroy a thing, and you do something that is bad for it. Nor is the point here restricted to human activity. The diminution or destruction of a thing, however it should occur, is bad for that thing.[2]

The presumption of existence

In this important respect, then, it may seem that there is no crucial distinction between living and non-living things. What is bad for a plant is whatever threatens its existence, and precisely the same is bad for a river, mountain or lake. But now a second arguably unimportant distinction is that between the natural and the artificial. As it is bad for a river if its feeding streams are diverted or dammed, so it is bad for a garden if it is covered in cement, bad for a table if worm or rot eats it away and bad for a tractor simply to be left out in the wind and rain. However a thing starts to exist, it is bad in the same way if its existence is terminated. This may appear to be a contentious claim, extending the range of value too far, but, as long as an important reservation is noted, it can, I think, be defended. The reservation is about the substantiality of the claim, and, as I intend it, this is not at all great. We don't say anything particularly important, weighty or profound in insisting that ceasing to exist is bad for a thing. Nevertheless, I think that what we say is true. But now a pair of objections needs to be considered. One derives from confusing two different claims about badness. The other results from wanting to separate off a distinctive area for environmental concern. The objections are connected, but I can start with the latter, and the argument that this is an extension too far:

> A tractor may disintegrate from rust. The relevant difference between a living being with a good of its own and a tractor is that a tractor has no self-identity. A tractor has a function, an identity as a tractor, only insomuch as someone considers it as a tractor, assigning it that function. It has needs only with respect to its externally assigned identity. By itself, it is only a lump without needs. In contrast, a living being has a self-identity that, within a broad range, entails its own requirements. Whereas cancer is bad for an organism, rust on a tractor is bad only for the farmer. Were there no tractor-user, rust would only be change. Were there no other being to care about or have use for a cancer-stricken worm, cancer would still be bad for it.[3]

There are, though, several curiosities in this passage. First, the contrast is extreme. Much of what Johnson says about the tractor could as well be said about the non-artefactual river or stone. And although a worm is a lowly thing, it is still an animal and, as seems here to be implied, perhaps able to feel pain. Vegetative and non-living nature, both of which raise serious difficulties for views about value and morality, are ignored. Secondly, it perhaps isn't clear enough what is meant by self-identity. There are issues here that need exploring, but, in brief, that a tractor's needs, function and identity should all depend on people might appear to be three separate points, the differences between which could usefully be unpicked. And thirdly, there seems to be a running together of two issues that ought, for as long and as far as possible, be kept separate: what is good or bad for a thing; and what we ought or ought not to do or to care about. Focus for now on this third point.

Johnson presumably agrees that a tractor can be damaged or destroyed. He presumably agrees, too, that in so far as something can be bad for a tractor, then damage, destruction and creeping disintegration from rust will be bad for it. But "in so far as" is not good enough, and he evidently believes that we would speak inappropriately in claiming that rust is bad for the tractor itself, as opposed to the tractor owner. I cannot agree. Even if the owner gets a new tractor, and ceases to care, even if he sells his tractor at a vast profit to an artist whose work explores corrosion, the tractor is damaged and not merely changed; it becomes less of a tractor in virtue of the rust. Why not say, simply, that rust is bad for it? And why not allow that in this respect there are no lines to be drawn within natural things, either living or non-living, and no lines either among all the things there are, either natural or artificial? It is bad for a thing to cease to exist, whatever the thing, and however its non-existence comes about.

At least a part of the reason for Johnson's reluctance to concede what I think of as an uncontentious claim is, surely, to avoid what may seem to be an inevitable consequence: the thought that we do wrong in doing, or allowing to occur, that which is bad for something or other. But there is no inevitability here. The farmer may do nothing at all wrong in allowing his tractor to rust, and may, in selling it to the artist, do substantial good. He deserves not even minor condemnation in allowing or encouraging what is bad for the tractor to occur. Yet even if there is no straightforward and intimate connection between bads and wrongs, still there are connections here that need to be teased out. And it should first be noted that I haven't said that it is bad that the tractor should disintegrate through rust. There may be no sense in which ceasing to exist is from a neutral or objective view a bad thing, even while it is bad for the thing itself. Again, though, there are no grounds here for distinguishing between the tractor and the river or, in turn, between the river and the tree. In none of these cases can we infer from its being bad for the thing in question to be destroyed that it is a bad thing that it is destroyed. And now, if the difference here is clear, a corresponding distinction between the ways in which destroying a thing might be wrong can also be made. If it is, for some reason, bad that a thing is destroyed, then we do wrong in knowingly destroying it. But it doesn't at all follow, from its being bad for a thing to be destroyed, that we similarly do wrong in knowingly destroying it.

There are further distinctions that need to be made here. First, it might in some respect be bad that a thing is destroyed, but nevertheless not a bad thing overall. The death of her guinea pig distresses my daughter, but he was old, and in pain. Death was for the best. Should we then say that when, in such cases, we destroy a thing, what we do is wrong in some respect, but not wrong over-all? I don't think we need to say this. It isn't at all wrong to put an animal out of its misery. Secondly, should we think that destruction of a non-sentient thing, when this has no bad consequences, is in no respect a matter of moral concern? Not at all. We can, while agreeing that the tractor's ceasing to exist isn't a bad thing, still think that we might do wrong in destroying it. We might, first, be asked to justify what we do. A justification will often be easily provided, but sometimes it won't, and there are good reasons for thinking that wanton acts of destruction – microwaving the cat, trampling bluebells, smashing icicles, slashing paintings – are wrong in all cases. It isn't always bad that these things cease to exist, but it is bad that their ceasing to exist results from gratuitous acts of violence. Once again, however, although we can set the cat to one side, there aren't significant distinctions to be made between the other sorts of case.[4]

Creation and death

Destruction, and ceasing to exist, is always bad for the thing destroyed, and acts of destruction have always to be justified. I am not, however, claiming that there is any correspondingly general badness in permanent non-existence, or that we need typically to justify the failure to create. It isn't a bad thing, then, that dragons are merely mythical, or that there are no pyramids bigger than the Pyramids. Nor, to make a second, and now related, contrast, is there a corresponding presumption against creation. The "last man" example is salient here. Post-nuclear holocaust, the sole human survivor, who will in any event soon die, sets about destroying residual cats, bluebells, icicles and paintings with a flame-thrower, just for kicks.[5] It is the intuition of many, and a position that I have been arguing towards, that the survivor does wrong in all these cases, and not simply to the cat because it feels, or to the cat and the flowers because they live, or to the cat, the flowers and the icicles because they're natural. But there are not, I think, parallel intuitions, and nor shall I argue that he would do wrong in wantonly creating (he bulldozes the ruins, mindlessly, into a rough and ready ziggurat, or carelessly tosses handfuls of seeds on to the last remaining fertile plain). Both creating and failing to create may be instrumentally bad, of course, but, or so I want to claim, they are not intrinsically bad in the way that destroying is. Nor, thirdly (to repeat an earlier claim), should mere changes in existence be included in this general category of bads. The vegetation on a mountain is washed away in a storm, leaving only fragile soil and bare rock. This is bad for the vegetation, but not for the mountain. And our changing the character of a thing does not, in all cases, have to be justified. The last man, again mindlessly, diverts the path of a river so that it runs north rather than south of a bombed-out town. The river, I claim, is unharmed, and he does nothing wrong with respect to it.

There is one important qualification that might be introduced. Death is often premature. In all such cases death is, to some degree, bad for the thing that dies. For premature death is against a thing's interests, and puts an end to its well-being, even if it is unfelt and even if it makes no difference to feeling. Bad things happen to young trees when we cut them down, even if neither the tree, nor the birds, nor tree preservationists know or care what is happening. And such a death is bad whether or not it is brought about by human or non-human agency. But is it similarly bad for something to die, of natural causes, at the end of its natural life? Of human beings it has been argued that death is bad whenever it occurs,[6] but this, if so, is presumably because we can form projects for, and have an interest in and knowledge of, the future, which death thwarts. Where animals are concerned dying is bad, whenever it occurs, in so far as it is marked by pain. But is it bad for trees? Many will think not, for given that the only plausible account of a tree's interests or well-being depends entirely on what is in the tree's nature, and given that eventual death is as much a part of that nature as are growth and reproduction, then even minimally regretting the death of plants, at the end their natural life, can appear sentimental or bizarre.[7] Suppose this is so. Then there is a relevant distinction between living and non-living things. Whether natural or artificial, non-living things have, except in rare cases, no inevitable point of termination. A river could flow forever, and a sculpture, properly cared for, might never crumble into dust. But if we grant this distinction, the case for the badness of non-existence is firmer in one respect, where such things are concerned. Destruction is always bad for non-living things, whereas death isn't always bad for living things.

I make one final point. I have used "bad for" and "bad that" to refer to two grounds on which a situation might be regretted. The terminological distinction here is useful, but I am not claiming, of course, that it is or should be rigorously applied. Yet the underlying difference is real. The former bad is, in a way, local, and the latter global. For on the face of it, to allow that it is bad for the river if it dries up is not in itself to say anything about the world at large. Should we say anything? What we say may be quite minimal, for even if ceasing to exist is always a bad thing, bad in itself, it may be a minor bad, and it may easily be outweighed by the benefits it brings. Consider a distant star. It may cost us nothing to agree that it is bad thing that this star should explode, but, even so, I see nothing driving us to agreement. If we think that ceasing to exist is bad in itself we presumably think that it would be a bad thing if the universe were to become a little bit smaller, a little bit emptier, than it actually is. And why think that?[8]

Species

The extension of the moral community beyond human beings proceeds inevitably in the direction of animals, but thereafter the exploration of two avenues is perhaps equally natural, and equally tempting. The first, and the one I have so far followed, moves from sentient to non-sentient living things, and thereafter to natural and then (with reservations for many) artificial individuals of a non-living kind. The second, to be pursued now, moves from the particular to the general and sees, after a discussion of individual animals, a consideration of species as the more obviously pressing. There is no final setting of priorities here. What matters is that in some order or other all the ground is covered. Even so, there is some advantage to having postponed this particular discussion, deriving from the problematic character of just what a species is. I will begin with some facts.

Extinction

Concern with environmental issues often focuses on species loss. Whether it be with well-known and undeniably attractive examples, such as tigers or pandas, with cases like the snail darter or the barn owl that give rise mostly to a local concern, or with the seemingly inexorable disappearance of unknown and often unnamed species as a result of development, industrialization, hi-tech agriculture and the like, extinction is an issue of undeniable importance on a world-wide scale.

How serious is it? Along with growing concern about particular extinctions there goes an increasing familiarity with some of the data relating to varieties of plant and animal life. Some of the figures might be rehearsed. More things, and kinds of things, exist than are known about. Described living species number around 1.8 million, more than 50 per cent of which are insects, and more than 75 per cent of which are animals of some or other kind. From this base, estimates of a total figure vary markedly from 3 million to 30 million. There is an equally marked variation in estimates as to species loss. While some believe that the closing twenty years of the last century saw roughly half of all species becoming extinct, others put this at a very much lower 4 per cent. This is still undeniably significant. Assuming the lower figures both for existence and loss, it nevertheless appears that 120,000 species became extinct during this period. Most of these losses involve undocumented insects in areas of rainforest, but there are equally inexorable threats, even if fewer species are involved, to plant and animal life much closer to home. Since 1949 Britain has lost virtually all of its lowland meadows, over half the lowland heath, and well over a quarter of upland heath and grassland. These massive alterations to habitats have put considerable pressure on hundreds of species populations.[9]

Sceptics about the environmental crisis, while acknowledging that all this amounts to extinction on a giant scale, point out that mass extinctions have occurred before, most notably around 65 million years ago, between the Cretaceous and Tertiary periods, when about half of all marine genera vanished.

Yet life on earth clearly recovered. There are two difficulties with such comparisons. They are beside the point. Unless it is claimed, implausibly and infrequently, that we are on the verge of extinction of all life, then no solace can be gained from the current situation's having been visited earlier. And they are misleading. Although very large numbers of species have on different occasions become extinct, a compression into such a short time period is not known to have occurred previously. Not only is the current rate of change unprecedented but, and most significantly, responsibility for it rests almost entirely with members of one species in particular, namely ours. Human activity, sometimes unwittingly, often in full knowledge, has hunted, poisoned, uprooted, burned, felled uncounted millions of plants and animals, and removed at least hundreds of thousands of species from the face of the earth. This is new, and it cannot be welcome.

What can appear to be an unutterably dark picture does, however, need to be tempered in several respects. First, high profile extinctions are relatively rare, and their rate of occurrence may be showing some signs of decline. Secondly, most of the species that do become extinct are, and always have been, rarities, and so have in one way always been on the verge of extinction. This isn't to make light of their loss, but it should be noted that relatively small changes are needed, in most cases, to bring about particular extinctions. Thirdly, human activity can also, and often does, prevent extinction, and lead to an increase, at least in certain areas, of biodiversity. There are two kinds of case. In the first, there is a conscious attempt to save a particular species from extinction, and to restore breeding populations to a viable size, either back in the wild, or in some approximation of the wild, in better zoos or parks. This is the less important case, and one in which the accusation might be levelled that we are simply attempting, belatedly, and often with indifferent results, to undo harm we ourselves have brought about. In the second, the benefits are to some extent accidental, as aesthetic or economic interests, both more easily pursued as a result of globalization on the one hand, and technological developments on the other, encourage the introduction of alien species into habitats where many of them are able to thrive. Consider trees again. While something approaching three hundred different species have been discovered in a single hectare of Amazon rainforest, the native species of Great Britain number only around seventy. By far the majority of trees and plants we see about us have only recently been introduced. Take a particularly hard line, and biodiversity brought about by such means will be deplored, but as it is only a historical accident, rather than some grand design, that is responsible for this limited variety to begin with, and as some introduction of alien species is itself a natural phenomenon, it seems again to be a symptom of an unreasonable hostility to human activity of every kind that blanket reservations should be expressed here. Detailed and particular reservations can more readily be seen as appropriate, however, as there are, in many cases, reasons for thinking that the benefits are not even mixed. Exotic species will typically compete with indigenous types, often to the detriment of the latter. Thus with grey squirrels, giant hogsweed and muntjac deer in Britain, and so-called "killer bees" in the USA. When such competition leads to the extinction of the less robust indigenous species, then alien introductions can appear to be unambiguously calamitous. But when the several species continue to exist, albeit in different proportions and different locations, then the precise focus of reservations and regret becomes less clear.

Reconsider the figures for extinction. It might be thought surprising that estimates vary so widely, but there are explanations for this. As with crowds at political demonstrations, figures will be higher or lower depending on which axe you want to grind. And there are genuine and substantial technical difficulties in working with tiny undiscovered creatures in inhospitable locations. But there are further factors to be taken into account, of the more abstract and philosophical kind. For suppose it isn't clear just when a particular species is extinct. Is it when all its members are dead, when none survive in other than artificial conditions, when there is no longer even one breeding pair or when there is no viable breeding population? If there is dispute about the answer here, then there will be disagreement about the number of extinctions. And even if we agree on the last of these suggestions, then, as viability is a matter of judgement, there will still be disagreement about the number of extinctions. And suppose it isn't clear, for theoretical rather than practical reasons, how many species there are. Then again there will be disagreement about the number of extinctions. Both the extinction question and the species question need to be considered in more detail. I will begin with the second.

Individuals and species

A starting point is the belief that every individual living thing is a member of one and only one species. That starting point cannot long survive, however, as it is standardly held that certain infertile products of inter-species breeding are not themselves members of either, both, or a different species. Thus it is for asses and mules, and thus for very many domestic and garden plants. So modify the point: most living things are members of one and only one species. Even while accepting this, some biologists have adopted a conventionalist account, holding that any species grouping is, in principle, as legitimate as any other, while others have advocated a realist interpretation, insisting that species boundaries are pre-theoretically given, and targeted with varying degrees of success by the accounts we provide. The first group, then, will claim that we are able ourselves to decide on the number of species in existence, while their opponents insist that the figure here is one that, at best, we can hope to discover. Others hold a middle position: there are facts about the relationships between individuals that make certain groupings – subspecies, species, family, order, and so on – more plausible or viable than others. An analogy might be made with mountains. One view is that there is already a precise number of mountains in the world, while its opposite is that we can decide, if we wish, that any hill – the Great Orme at Llandudno, the grassy knoll in Dallas – is a mountain if we so choose. The intermediate position is that we can't decide on just anything, but we can decide on some things: perhaps whether a high ridge walk links separate mountains, or whether just one mountain is involved. The intermediate position is the best view of mountains, and it is the best view of species. There are pre-theoretical facts as to how certain animals relate to one another, and these facts in part, but not in whole, determine whether or not we are faced with one species or many.[10] So what is left to us? Just as there are questions as to the relevance of height and shape with mountains, so there are questions as to the sorts of properties that warrant our classifying an individual as belonging to one species rather than another species. And various suggestions are made.

One seemingly plausible account copies our classificatory practices for chemicals, where a substance is described as neon, benzene, an acid or whatever in virtue of its having certain internal properties that are considered to be essential to things of that kind. Thus there are available in this area definitions of the sort "For any substance X, X is water if and only if X is H_2O". This definition identifies the essence of water, and stipulates the necessary and sufficient conditions for anything's being a member of that particular kind. Biology is messier than this, but the question is, can species membership be construed in broadly similar terms? Can we, even in principle, pick out the properties that an animal must have if it is to be a member of the species tiger? It has been argued that we cannot:

> To see why essentialism is a mistaken view of biological species, we must examine the practice of systematists themselves. With the exception of pheneticists . . . biologists do not think that species are defined in terms of phenotypic or genetic similarities. Tigers are striped and carnivorous, but a mutant tiger that lacked these traits would still be a tiger. Barring the occurrence of a speciation event, the descendants of tigers are tigers, regardless of the degree to which they resemble their parents. Symmetrically, if we discovered that other planets possess life forms that arose independently of life on earth, those alien organisms would be placed into new species, regardless of how closely they resembled terrestrial forms. Martian tigers would not be tigers, even if they were striped and carnivorous. Similarities and differences among organisms are *evidence* about whether they are conspecific, but a species is not *defined* by a set of traits. In short, biologists treat species as *historical entities*. They do not conceptualize species as natural kinds.[11]

There is a fair amount here that needs to be unpicked. Consider first the Martian tigers. Part of Sober's comment is ineffective as it stands. Just as we realize that Martian gold would not count as real gold in virtue simply of being yellow and shiny – we all know there's more to gold than that – so we similarly know that there's more to tigers than being striped and carnivorous. A plausible essentialist account of species membership will surely appeal to some deeper properties, having greater explanatory power, than those relating to the superficial appearance of a thing. And Sober points the way here, with his mention of genetic similarities. What needs to be asked, then, is why that more plausible version of essentialism is wrong. Why should we not hold that genetic constitution picks out species membership just as surely as molecular constitution identifies membership of chemical kinds? Part of the answer here is that where species are concerned there are competing accounts to consider. Sober claims that species membership is to be construed historically, via the parent–offspring relationship. So whatever its internal constitution, the Martian tiger is no tiger unless it has the right sort of causal connections with tigers on earth. How this is to be explicated isn't immediately clear. Being a descendant of two members of a certain species might be a necessary condition of being a member of that species, but it cannot be a sufficient condition, or there would be, at best, a handful of species in existence at the present time. The difficulty here is what Sober is getting at in referring to a speciation event. What is clearly a part of our understanding of species differences is that situations can occur in which it becomes appropriate, in spite of unbroken historical relationships, to speak of a further and distinct species having been formed. There are complexities here, and it is, perhaps, unsurprising that Sober doesn't go into details. What is more surprising, however, is that he doesn't in this context mention what is arguably (arguably just because the ideas here might be said to be included under the notion of a speciation event) a third account of same species membership, that of interbreeding:

> Biologically, the species is the only taxonomic unit that nature recognises . . . because it is the largest group that is held together, and indeed defined, by a biological process: namely mating among its members. So a species is a group of organisms that are able to interbreed in nature.[12]

It might be useful to make explicit the further condition that offspring are themselves fertile; otherwise mules show that horses and donkeys are, after all, of one species. The point being made here is neither unfamiliar nor unpersuasive: being able to breed together is well taken as indicating that two individuals are members of the same species.

The suspicion that there are three competing accounts of same species membership – that this notion is defined in terms of intrinsic similarities, parent–offspring relationships or breeding possibilities – and that we need to choose between them, is one that should be resisted, however. In practice the accounts will often converge on the same results. Similar looking individuals, traceable to the same ancestors, will usually, when appropriately aged and sexed, be able to breed together. But note "usually"; this is not always the case. Palaeontologists systematically determine species membership on the basis of phenotypic similarities alone, having no further evidence available; and there is a raft of particular problem cases that in part undermines the coherence of this tri-partite account. Even so, the thought that these three accounts are in many respects complementary, and that collectively they usefully inform our understanding of what species membership consists in, is one that survives difficulties of these kinds.

There is a difficulty of a further kind. It is one thing to allow that the three accounts are all of undeniable practical use, and that where actual cases are concerned the results will tend to converge, and another to claim that any of them constitutes, in a philosophical sense, a definition of what a species is. Sober will insist that a definition is what he is after, and that here we are obliged to stick with the historical account. But are we?

The remarks about tigers invite consideration of a range not only of actual, or physically possible situations, but also of what is merely conceivable. But very much is merely conceivable, and what to make of it is often problematic. So suppose that we come across tiger-like creatures on Mars, and discover that they resemble earth tigers not only superficially, but on a deeper level as well. Suppose that the average biologist cannot tell them apart. Suppose, however, that we know that these creatures developed quite independently of earth tigers. Would they be tigers? Sober insists that they wouldn't, their independent development overruling considerations of similarity, no matter how profound. But it is hard to see any warrant for this. Suppose now, what is clearly conceivable, that these Martian creatures can interbreed with earth tigers. (This would be possible even if there were some differences between the two groups – qualitative identity is not a condition of interbreeding even in the actual world.) The offspring resemble tigers and will breed, in turn, with the tiger-like creatures from either planet. It is even harder to justify denying that there are tigers on Mars.[13] And so it is hard to see why we should hold to the historical account.

This isn't a difficulty with Sober's suggestion alone, however, but infects any attempt to shift from a practically useful to a theoretically impeccable account. Suppose, what is again conceivable, that although the historical lines are separate and there are massive dissimilarities between us – they're green, for a start – we find that we are able to interbreed with Martians, giving rise to fertile offspring.[14] This wouldn't, surely, demonstrate that we are of the same species. And as possibilities for interbreeding are not sufficient, neither, too, are they necessary for species membership. Suppose that radiation from the sun makes us all sterile. As I suggested earlier, the absence of a viable breeding population does not altogether plausibly render a species extinct. And suppose that cloning means that life can continue, pretty much as before. There would be no good reasons for denying that these cloned creatures are human beings, and so members of the species *Homo sapiens*. Or suppose that a human population gives birth to a number of offspring who, perhaps because of nuclear or biological warfare, bear very little resemblance either on the surface or in depth to their parents, and they are unable to breed with members of the parent generation. It cannot be clear that they and we are members of the same species.

What these various science fiction cases all show, then, is that there is some considerable distance between allowing that for day-to-day purposes a certain condition may well be taken as a mark of species membership, and holding that this condition is necessary and sufficient for such species membership, through all possible worlds. Hopes for this are, I think, vain. Again, consider mountains. We can dogmatically insist that mountains are all land points of 3,000ft or more, but this definition is unlikely to fit with our interests. Nor have we need of possible worlds here, as there are many plateaux in this world that, on the definition, are mountains but that are, frankly, just not mountainous. Conversely, there are many impressive, precipitous and snow covered hills under 3,000ft that we are, quite properly, inclined to think of as mountains. The definition can make certain things easier, but it hardly squares with what we want. Our interest in mountains suggests that we might best explicate the notion, even if this cannot be precise, by making some reference to shape.

It is the same for species. In outlining objections to purported definitions above I was intentionally cagey about the shortcomings of the similarity account, but now I want to suggest that while we are unlikely to uncover a tight definition either way, emphasis on similarities does fit reasonably well, and better than history or breeding, with the kinds of interests we typically have in species preservation. Would radically modified children be members of our species? We might think of them as forming a subspecies but, as often observed, the species/subspecies distinction is hardly clear. What motivates even this halfway house is an undeniable and legitimate concern with the looks of things. Would Martian tigers be tigers? We can, of course, consistently maintain that they are not, but only, I think, at some cost in terms of plausibility, for, given that resemblance is not merely superficial, these alien creatures will seem as tigers seem, do what they do and satisfy most of our tiger interests in the very same way.[15] So why not call them tigers? There are, then, weighty reasons for prioritizing the similarity account, at least as theoretical considerations go. In practice there are complications, and an interest in lineage on the one hand, and interbreeding on the other, are both appropriately viewed as serving the cause of similarity, and are actually better indicators of deep similarity than is mere sameness of appearance. Setting these practical considerations aside, there are, in the end, powerful analogues between our approaches to biological stuffs on the one hand, and chemical substances on the other. In both cases, some version of essentialism is the better path to follow.

All this is not of merely theoretical interest. The environmentalist's concern with species in general, and extinction in particular, needs to be picked out and explained. What I am suggesting here is that a concern with, say, the extinction of tigers is best or most plausibly seen as a concern that creatures of a certain kind, understood here as implying a certain characteristic appearance, with certain characteristic ways of going on, be not forever lost. Given current methods of tiger production, this generates a derivative concern that present tiger populations do not die out. But methods may change, and new ones may be discovered, and the derivative concern may, in some circumstances and for some people, be primary. There may be something to be regretted when a line, long intact, is broken, even if it can be taken up again. Consider, for example, the Olympic torch. But it can still be said with some confidence that concerns about extinction would be much reduced if the phenomenon were reversible.

Species and populations

There are further questions to be considered, and these might best be approached by returning to certain of the environmentalist's typical concerns. A distinction is often, and at first blush quite legitimately, made between a concern for individual animals on the one hand, and a concern for the species as such on the other. It is often denied that what is good for the individual is good for the species. The attempt, usually vain, to clean oil from gulls caught in a spill is an attempt to better the well-being of an individual bird, but will do nothing for the species. Things might be made worse. Foxhunters often argue that welfarists may save individual foxes, but as the hunt targets the weak it, rather than they, best preserves the health of the species as a whole. It is the same for plants. Lopping, pruning, feeding, weeding and propping up may extend the life of an old tree, but if it were to die, seedlings would more readily take ground in its place.[16] It is often claimed that what the environment needs is greater attention to species as a whole, and rather less to individual members.

Yet there are difficulties here. One concerns the suspicion that, in the end, it is always individuals that are of concern. Take the tree. It can certainly appear that the choice is between preserving the life of one individual, or promoting the life of a half dozen or so more. Or take foxes. What the hunter's claim surely amounts to is that his or her policy will result in a greater number of healthy foxes than that of the welfarist. A closely related difficulty concerns the well-being of a species as such. It is easy enough to give substance to the idea of individual well-being, whether this relates to an animal or a plant, but what is it for the species itself to be in a better or worse condition? The highly tempting answer here holds that a species fares well when there are appropriately large numbers of healthy individual members of the species and, because of both internal and external factors (their health, age, reproductive capacity on the one hand, their location within, and the overall condition of, the external environment on the other), good prospects for more. It is easy enough to see, then, how looking after particular individuals can be to the detriment of the species, but not at all easy to see how looking after the species can do other than benefit individuals. Admittedly, many of these individuals will not yet be born, but that doesn't yet suggest that there is some independent good of the species that we are able to consider and promote.[17]

What all this suggests, then, is that the real contrast is not between individuals and species but, less striking, even if ultimately more defensible, between single individuals on the one hand and entire species populations on the other. There is a lesser contrast here, but the suggestion that we should sometimes sink our concern for this or that individual creature (whose life, and the significant consequences of whose life, will in any event be short term) into one for whole groups or populations, ranging over the present and the future, is one that has some considerable bite.

This distinction between a species and a species population is so far only half made, for the upshot of bringing the latter notion to the fore is to render the former somewhat more obscure. Just what is a species, if it isn't a group or collection or population of individuals? What sort of entity is said to be of direct moral concern, the kind of thing we should to some degree care about, when it is said that species are of such concern? What kind of existence does a species have when, depending apparently on the existence of individual members, the species itself can be extant or extinct? There is here an issue for environmentalism, no longer in explaining what is involved in membership of this as opposed to that species, but, rather more abstractly, in elucidating the concept of species as a whole.

Focus on the last of the above questions. Does, as might appear, the existence of a species depend on the existence of its members? Suppose that there is a substantial number of frozen tiger embryos stored in laboratories around the world, and there is jungle, with food, waiting. There are currently no tigers, but there is the wherewithal to re-establish a viable community of tigers, which will then breed, reproduce and sustain the population in the normal way. Should we believe that the species tigers is or is not extinct? There are two quick ways with this question, neither of them wholly satisfactory. The first is dismissal. It might be said that as we have enough information to say how it was, is now and will be for tigers, then we can simply ignore this extinction question; nothing hangs on it. But this is, in one way, to miss the point. It is commonly believed that preserving species, and so avoiding extinction, is an important concern. Given that belief, it is worthwhile trying to see what such notions involve. The second is to insist that the question is easy. As extinction is final and irreversible, then that there will soon once again be tigers shows that extinction has not occurred. There may currently be no tigers, but there is still the species tiger. The assumptions here are, first, that the future creatures will be tigers, and, secondly, that extinction is irreversible. While the first may seem innocuous, the second might be considered further.[18] In practice there is overlap between the situations where we have no current members of a given species, and those where we have no future members. The coincidence here could break down, and then we would need decisions as to what to say. I don't offer to settle these questions, but can make a few observations towards clarification.

The distinction between a species and a species population is undoubtedly useful, and it encourages us, in what is surely the right direction, to think of a species as an abstract thing, and so possessing only the sorts of properties that an abstract thing might possess. Unlike a tiger, then, or a population of tigers, the species tiger displays no stripes, eats no meat, has no size, weight or location in space and time. Consequently, and this is now a surprising result, a species, like the value of pi, can neither begin nor cease to exist. So the whole question about extinction is thoroughly wrongheaded. But there is a flurry of thoughts here, and things go wrong, surely, in so severely limiting the properties of abstract things. Consider other examples. A nation, government and team are abstract things, as too is a thought, promise or desire. None of these things has or can have stripes or weight or, in any non-metaphorical sense, a shape, but they can certainly have temporal and, arguably, spatial location. Thoughts can plausibly be said to be in the heads of thinkers, and governments somewhere within the country whose nation they govern. The underlying point here is that certain abstract entities depend for their existence on the existence of certain concrete individuals. The concept "horse" is not a horse, and neither is the species, but whereas the concept might survive even if horses do not, the same, it is beginning to appear, is not true of the species.

However, appearances are deceptive. Given the distinction between a species and a species population, there is surely no powerful objection to holding that in the case of frozen embryos the species is not extinct. The existence of the species depends, we might agree, on the existence of some further stuff, but this stuff might be embryos rather than full-blooded species members. If embryos will suffice, then, arguably, so will zygotes, or separate gametes, or any bits of material from which further individuals might be cloned. The species survives, I want to suggest, as long as there remains the material from which further individual members of the species can be derived. Given modern technologies, then, extinction may more easily be avoided.

An assumption here is that we are looking to appropriate organic material to provide the means to generate new individuals, and so to keep a species going, but we could conceivably make do with less. Conceivably, at least, all the genetic information necessary for the production of further individuals of a given kind could be stored in digital or computerized form. As long as this information survives, then so does the species. What is beginning to emerge, then, is a notion of a species as some kind of blueprint or recipe for the construction of individuals of one or the other kind. The instructions are standardly encoded in organic form, and standardly realized by natural reproductive processes, but there is no necessity to this, of either the logical or, increasingly, the practical kind, such that we are able to claim that extinction is avoided as long as the information survives. This notion is not excessively abstract. It might be argued that all blueprints, recipes and formulae already exist in some Platonic heaven, and can be neither created nor destroyed, so that a species, understood in this way, can never become extinct. But more attractive views are, first, that this picture still allows for the discovery (or rediscovery, or recollection) of information, such that extinction can be said to have occurred when the information is, albeit temporarily, lost; and, secondly, that a better picture opts simply for creation and destruction, so that new species can come into being, and with the loss of information the species straightforwardly ceases to exist. There will be grey areas, but they remain tolerable.

One outstanding issue can be taken up here. Those Martian tigers, on Sober's account, were not, in spite of appearances, true tigers just because they were causally disconnected from the tigers of earth. And that, I suggested, was unconvincing. But if so, then the blueprint picture I have wanted to sketch out here might be amended. All the suggestions so far assume that new information rests on the old. Just as the test-tube embryo is developed from standard source material, so digitalized data, I have implied, will have been drawn from information first realized in its normal, organic form. But need that be so? Mere random twiddling in some post-apocalyptic laboratory produces a simulacrum of the common toad, but is it then really a toad? If we are interested in internal properties along with, as structural replication implies, the ability to interbreed, then here is all we need, but if history and genesis is of concern, something is missing. It might seem that this latter concern is spurious, but in an important sense the desire for continuities has its rationale. As long as we have the requisite information, then even if there are currently no instantiations of the species, we will have reason to believe that there could be more. Waiting on utterly fortuitous replication could well be waiting in vain.

Certain further questions concerning what might be thought of as the metaphysical status of species can be postponed until Chapter 8. These interim conclusions, that a species is an abstract thing closely connected to but not identical with the existence of individual concrete things, can be augmented, but will not need to be rescinded. More pressing questions need to be addressed here.

Species and value

The larger programme, remember, is to consider the various claimed extensions to the area of moral concern. The current question, then, is as to why anyone should think that species matter. Many species have been, and many more will be, lost. The responsibility for most of the losses that have occurred in the time that human beings have existed lies with those same human beings. Still we can ask, but why should we care?

What is quite a good answer is irrelevant here. It is often argued that the continued existence of species is of serious instrumental value. This argument has several strands. It is claimed of some species that they are of direct and determinable value to human beings: the loss of wild salmon is the loss of a food only palely shadowed by the farmed varieties. Others are similarly of direct value to still other species as, for example, owls and falcons have a need greater than ours for mice and voles. Of very many species it is argued that their loss will upset the balance of nature, bringing in the end as yet inestimable consequences for human beings. There are good instances of this. During the so-called Cultural Revolution, Mao Zedong ordered the elimination of all sparrows, on the grounds that they were eating into (human) food supplies. So they were, but things turned out to be considerably worse for the Chinese without the sparrows than with them. Of yet more species the argument has it that they offer the potential to be of direct value, typically to human beings. About a third of modern medicines and drugs are derived from moulds and plants,[19] and it is claimed that each lost species represents the loss of potentially vast benefits in terms of health, foods, dyes, textiles and so on.[20]

This is only quite a good answer. It is true of very many species that they are valuable in one or other of these ways, but there are millions of species and it is far from demonstrably true of them all. Every loss has some consequences, as does every gain, but if "balance of nature" is to be used in any meaningful way it is just not true to suppose that every loss of a species upsets that balance. Some populations are and always have been small, and the consequences of extinction are limited and local. Further, some losses that arguably do upset the balance are only with difficulty presented as regrettable. Certain disease bearing insects, bacteria and viruses might be eliminated with considerable benefit to human beings, and little or no disbenefit elsewhere. Nor is the potentiality argument very powerful. That there is some incalculable possibility that a species might hold benefits is just not a good reason for preserving that species. It might be that the certain benefits of its extinction, either because it presents some direct threat, or because its continued existence stands in the way of some planned development, are rightly judged to outweigh the possible benefits of its survival. Right judgement here doesn't preclude our being mistaken about the outcomes, but simply involves our making the best of the available information. And we make the best of such information when, in mirror image of the claim that everything should be saved for the good it might bring, we choose not to exterminate virtually all of earth's species on the grounds that we cannot entirely rule out the possibility that each of them presents an enormous threat to the rest.

Yet even if several of the shortcomings in the answer can be addressed, it remains irrelevant. The concern here is with enlargement to the sphere of direct moral concern: just as animals, plants, rivers and so on all uncontroversially have instrumental value, so too do species. But what we want to know now is whether there are reasons to preserve species for their own sake, whether it is bad in itself that so many become extinct, or whether, as many suspect, there is no direct or intrinsic value in species preservation. So write out extraneous considerations. Imagine a South Pacific island, perhaps something like the Galapagos, inhabited by members of three dozen species unknown elsewhere in the world. Spillage from an oil tanker wipes out all members of one species of beetle, such that it is now extinct. These beetles are of no value to human beings, and although birds eat them they are just as happy with different beetles. As a result of the extinction, the other beetle populations increase in size. The "balance of nature" on the island is altered slightly, but there is still a balance. Does the extinction matter?

Some will claim that it does. There is, again, a religious answer. It might be held that as each species is created by God, so each species is of value. For the theist such a claim may be weighty, affording reasons to show concern about extinction in every case. For the agnostic or atheist it offers little help. There is the unelaborated intrinsicness answer. The continued existence of each and every species is of value in and of itself. Therefore extinction is, properly and directly, of concern. But elaboration is needed. Assume that in this case extinction is final. Beetles of this kind will never again crawl anywhere on the surface of the earth. It just isn't enough to say that this is a bad thing. If we agree that it is bad for the beetles, we still need to be persuaded that the world is somehow, in itself, any worse off. Another answer confuses the bad and the wrong. It might be thought that we do wrong in taking such a careless attitude to dangerous substances like oil, with the result that these beetles go extinct. Perhaps we do do wrong. But the question is not, do we do wrong in causing extinctions, but, is it bad when extinctions occur? And it is hard to see, at least thus far, that it is.

Two further answers need to be considered. They touch on highly important issues for environmental concern, but as these issues will be met with again, my dealings with them here will be less than complete.

Concern about extinction often focuses on particular species. We care about pandas, tigers, curlews, polar bears and whales; and less about slugs, voles and the more nondescript beetles. There are species that we think of as more beautiful, graceful or dignified than others. There are three observations to make here. First, a concern for extinction that fastens on to the aesthetic properties of animals or plants will inevitably be highly selective, showing concern for a rather narrower field than extinction in general. Secondly, there are questions to be asked about the nature of beauty. If we think that beauty is a genuine property of objects, then, even though selective, the claim will be that those species the members of which exemplify these (positive) aesthetic properties will be valuable in themselves. If, on the other hand, we think of beauty as in the mind of the beholder, the claim, in contrast, will be that these species are in some way of instrumental value in contributing to human satisfactions. A fuller discussion of how we might most properly think of beauty is a major concern of Chapter 10, so I say no more about this here. Thirdly, it should be noted that a species, as opposed to its members, can hardly be beautiful, graceful, dignified or whatever. Of course, it isn't just this or that tiger, as it is merely this or that human being, that is beautiful; they all look much the same, and it can with a certain propriety be said that this beauty is embedded in the species itself. Nevertheless, just as a recipe may aid in the production of nutritious food without itself being nutritious, so, where beauty is concerned, a species might best be seen as of instrumental value, and not in itself of direct moral concern.

The second of the further answers concerns diversity. The more species there are, the greater the biodiversity. Assume that diversity is good. Then, as every extinction reduces diversity, so every extinction is a bad thing. The first question here is about this assumption. Why should we think that the more species there are the better? One answer will give to diversity an instrumental value, holding, not unreasonably, that a greater mix of life is more resilient to environmental damage, and more likely to help secure some further good. This may well relate principally to our continued existence, but it is perfectly possible to hold, say, that a greater variety of plant forms will better serve the animal population. If we care for pandas we may think that the more bamboos there are the better. Yet, as with beauty, some people think that biodiversity is good in itself, that it is just an excellent thing that there is a wide array of life forms living together on and near the surface of this small planet. While a species member might itself be beautiful, neither a member of a species nor the species itself can be diverse. Ought we to say, then, that a concern for diversity implies that the extinction of particular species is instrumentally, rather than intrinsically, bad, such that we are again unable to hold that species themselves are of direct moral concern? Not quite. When we think of something as instrumentally valuable, as a means to an end, our thought is that if we might in some other manner secure a desired end, then the particular means under consideration loses its value. Fossil fuels are of value only as long as better energy sources are unavailable. But the relationship between species preservation and biodiversity is not like this. We couldn't have this diversity without having a range of species. The relationship here is conceptual, rather than causal. Given the extent of our concern to maintain biodiversity, are there good reasons for thinking that species are of direct moral concern? Hardly. We still need to show that valuing diversity in itself is reasonable.

Creation

Concerns for beauty and diversity are not in the end intimately linked to species preservation. Consider beauty. Suppose that tigers are valued for their distinctive striped appearance. Sober's Martian tigers have this, even if, as the resemblances are after all superficial, we agree that they are not of the species tiger. Similarly for other kinds of replicant tigers. Or suppose that tigers lose, or are caused to lose, their stripes. We might preserve the species without preserving what is allegedly valuable within it.[21] This particular example suggests a more general point, of considerable practical concern, and that is that an interest in beauty fits only very loosely with a concern for species as such. Not only are the members of very many species lacking in any particular aesthetic merits, but probably most of the living things we consider beautiful are so because they are members of subspecies, or are hybrids, or particular breeds, rather than members of the species as such. So although we may do no harm in preserving entire species, we will, if looking after beauty is the concern, still fail to do much good.

There is a closely corresponding worry about diversity. It can be aided by the preservation of species but it can be aided in other ways as well. To lose all examples of a certain hybrid rose is to lose forever a particular kind of thing.[22] Concern that there should continue to be Gloucester Old Spots, Herdwicks, Rhode Island Reds or Texas Longhorns is a concern that there be particular breeds of pig, sheep, hen and cattle, and not just that the species be preserved. An interest that there should be many different kinds of thing, then, does not always mesh closely with a concern for species. Of course, it might be claimed that diversity below the level of species is not something with which we are or should be concerned, but again it is hard to see how such a claim might be made out.

Not only might we further the goods of beauty and diversity by protecting things other than species as such, but we might further these goods by creating more. It is not too difficult to develop new varieties of clematis or rose, and nor is it too difficult to breed a distinctive line in pigs. Even if the pigs are not particularly beautiful, they will be a further kind of thing. It is more difficult, but not impossible, to develop new species. Ought we to do this? New species might be artificially created in one of two ways, either as a chance by-product of some man-made procedures, as in the folkloric examples of new kinds of fish in radioactive seas, or, as seems increasingly likely, as a result of planned forays into molecular or genetic engineering. Beauty and diversity achieved by such means are rarely welcomed, as what appears to many people to be of value is that nature has its way, neither aided nor impeded by human activity. Suppose it does have its way, and new species are introduced as a result of natural evolutionary processes. Ought we to welcome this? Just as I think that species loss is not clearly of direct moral concern, so, symmetrically, for species gain. But our actual attitudes seem to be skewed, with distress at extinction far outweighing our pleasure at creation.

A related matter concerns preservation. In many cases species are threatened with extinction as a result of human activity. In such cases the prevalent thought is that we should, if we can, preserve the species. But in other cases even current losses are attributable to natural processes. And then questions are raised as to whether these processes might legitimately be resisted, or whether we ought to let nature have its way.[23] I know of no good arguments on either side here.

What are in the end probably rather inchoate views about the importance of nature's following its own course probably best explain a further attitude to species loss, now concerning restoration. There are currently no living mammoths. It has long seemed obvious that mammoths are extinct, but this may recently have become less clear, for there has been a deal of excited talk about cloning new animals from bits of frozen mammoth material found in northern Siberia. Suppose that this can be done. One issue raised here, and discussed earlier, is what bearing this would have on whether mammoths were ever extinct. Another is the moral issue. Although many would be interested, few think we positively ought to reintroduce mammoths. Suppose the technology could be perfected. There would be no further practical objections, as they would presumably be kept in zoos as safe, well-looked-after, tourist attractions. The objection, once again, is that we would be interfering with nature.

Land

Behind much of the recent expansion in environmental awareness, particularly in so far as this awareness is not piecemeal, but attempts a systematic and coherent approach to what can at first appear a series of disparate problems, lies the work of Aldo Leopold, who, with respect to attitudes to land in particular, is often seen as the godfather of modern environmentalism.

His major work, *A Sand County Almanac*,[24] is a highly allusive, consciously literary and sometimes autobiographical collection, which, while often sidelining the conventional norms of both scientific and philosophical rigour, nevertheless wants to articulate and refine a case for a robustly holistic approach to environmental issues. The power of Leopold's writing stems in part from the felt nature of his own conversion – long after establishing a conventional career within the US Forest Service, where he worked to maintain and develop species such as deer, quail and salmon for sporting and food purposes, Leopold began to see the practical and philosophical inadequacies in his endeavours – and in part from his belief that he is writing at a historically important time, that he is of the moment.

The guiding principle behind Leopold's critique is one of value that transcends that of purely material and economic worth. At the occasion of writing, in early twentieth-century America, the prevailing ethos was figured by what today seems a naive and simplistic belief in the possibility of progress, unsubtly defined in terms of material well-being, and crudely effected by the application of science, or parts of science, to nature. Leopold is able to chart many instances where this optimistic and unnuanced approach to land and resource management goes wrong, situations in which an earlier *modus vivendi* between man and nature is replaced by a wholly one-sided relationship, in which a desire to make the most profitable use of the land leads to massive overgrazing, the development of fragile and inflexible monocultures and, eventually, the degradation and decay of soil itself. The fault here, on Leopold's diagnosis, is not occasional misfortune, local ignorance or individual greed; it is rather the systematically maladjusted perspective of farmers, politicians, lawyers, conservationists and, behind them, the public at large, who, on Leopold's account, are collectively responsible for this near-disastrous situation.

What is needed, then, is not some minor tweaking of the present scheme, but something more radical, a wholesale development in our moral attitudes, and an extension of the area of our concern from that with other individuals, or with whole societies, to embrace our relationship with the land. But the need is for development, rather than a complete volte-face, for Leopold insists that we stand already on the brink of maturity in our relationships with nature; and as this expansion of the range of concern is unavoidable, the land ethic "simply enlarges the boundaries of the community to include soils, waters, plants, and animals, or collectively: the land".[25] Even if he is a prophet, then, Leopold claims for himself a relatively modest role: that of warning against an impending environmental calamity, the remedy for which is already within our grasp.

The critical questions to put to Leopold are, somewhat obviously, what has this land ethic to do with the land? And what has it do with ethics? The first is the easier.

It is, as his comment above itself indicates, quite wrong to see Leopold as simply adding a further object of moral concern to that already extended list, for although he talks often enough, and in detail, of the character and characteristics of the soil itself, Leopold sees and understands land very much as a collective: it is both with land in particular and with the generality of things that live upon and within it that we should be concerned. His account goes further. Informed by what was then the relatively new science of ecology, Leopold's emphasis is rather more focused on the processes and procedures with which land is essentially involved than with the various stuffs, or collections of stuffs, themselves. And so he takes some objection to the phrase "the balance of nature" as implying stasis among several discrete components, and neglecting the essential dynamism of natural processes and progressions. Leopold prefers instead to speak of the land pyramid, as better capturing an active and hierarchical structure of which soil is the foundation, various plant and animal kingdoms the intervening levels, and higher carnivores, including the species of which we are members, the apex. Crucially, there are complex relationships throughout the several layers of this hierarchy as energy, initially supplied by the sun and later converted into food, flows within it. So although he begins with the base matter of land, Leopold's eventual focus is on power, light, energy and its transmutations:

> The pyramid is a tangle of chains so complex as to seem disorderly, yet the stability of the system proves it to be a highly organized structure. Its functioning depends on the cooperation and competition of its diverse parts . . . Food chains are the living channels which conduct energy upwards; death and decay return it to the soil. The circuit is not closed; some energy is dissipated in decay, some is added by absorption from the air, some is stored in soils, peats and long lived forests; but it is a sustained circuit, like a slowly augmented revolving fund of life.[26]

Although approving of stability, Leopold is not opposed to change. The land pyramid is a network of shifting procedures, and these in turn, via the workings of evolution, alter the character of the pyramid as a whole: "Evolution is a long series of self-induced changes, the net result of which has been to elaborate the flow mechanism and to lengthen the circuit".[27] But not all change is good, and Leopold argues that human development, in particular of tools first and agriculture later, has upset the stability of the system as a whole, introducing changes of "unprecedented violence, rapidity and scope".[28] Thus, in redeploying members of the animal kingdom, in overuse of soils, in redirecting, canalizing and polluting rivers, we bring about alterations within energy chains that have incalculable consequences elsewhere. Leopold provides his own summary of the argument so far, insisting:

(1) That land is not merely soil
(2) That the native plants and animals kept the energy circuit open; others may or may not.
(3) That man-made changes are of a different order than evolutionary changes, and have effects more comprehensive than is intended or foreseen.[29]

So although life is important, the land ethic is not centred on any living thing or group of such things, or even on life itself, so much as on the systems that give rise to and support life in its various forms. This eco-centric perspective requires an interplay of attention, with human beings, other animals and plants all playing important but none of them decisive roles in sustaining the system as a whole.

171

Land and morality

If there are questions about Leopold's construal of land, there are further and rather more difficult questions about his understanding of ethics. We ought to do things differently, that much is clear, but it is much less clear as to why these differences are called for. Although there is no denying Leopold's uncompromising holism, there are deep ambiguities as to whether this is married to a similarly radical rejection of anthropocentrism, or whether, in the end, our place at the top of the pyramid, though adequately justified in ecological terms,[30] coincidentally reflects the measure of our moral worth. And this difficulty in fathoming Leopold's ultimate position has a twofold explanation. First is the inherent elusiveness and ambiguity in the writing itself, and secondly, and sustained in part by this, is the undeniable tendency, in several of Leopold's followers and critics alike, to emphasize, perhaps unduly, the radical elements within his account. I focus here on Leopold's own writing. It is given, at times, to sloganeering. Thus, and famously: "A thing is right when it tends to preserve the integrity, stability and beauty of the biotic community. It is wrong otherwise."[31] This is just as pithy as any conventional utilitarian manifesto and, in the end, just as frustrating. It appears to invite judgement on all our actions from the point of view solely of whether they further, or tend to further, in these particular ways, the lot of nature as a whole. But, of course, the apparent simplicity here must be considered deceptive, and there are questions of several kinds. Unlike utilitarianism, with its emphasis on the single and apparently straightforward end of happiness, Leopold here posits a variety of less familiar aims. We might ask what these various desiderata amount to, and what we are to do when pursuit of one falls foul of another. We might ask, further, just what is so good about these characteristics in particular, and why they, as opposed to certain rivals, are singled out for promotion. And we might ask, finally, for reasons why our endeavours, if they are to be morally acceptable, should be so severely circumscribed. A thorough exploration of these questions will take time. All I will do here is uncover some of their ramifications, but then, as there is another way to approach Leopold, and as these questions will in any event re-emerge, leave it at that.

Integrity, to begin with, is a notion not easily unpicked. It might be taken to refer to the interplay between a system's component parts. To put it crudely, we might think that an environment loses some integrity when wood is replaced by plastic, but Leopold doesn't appear to have this meaning in mind. He often speaks of disorganization, as when soil loses most of its nutrients, or water becomes polluted, and perhaps intends that integrity, or its absence, should figure in here. Disorganization might also be linked to stability, but there are difficulties in teasing this out. Leopold, as mentioned, is in many respects welcoming of change and seems, not unreasonably, to think that a wholly stable system would be inert or dead. Some measure of instability, some kind of disorganization and perhaps also some lack of integrity might then all be welcome. Beauty is problematic in a different way – the difficulty here is in giving any account that is not founded on human tastes and preferences. If to claim that a thing is beautiful is not simply to claim that we like the look of it, and so not in the end to license putting pandas before worms, or sequoia or oak before some indifferent sedge, then it is somewhat hard to see just what it is. But whatever, in detail, the three things individually mean, there are further difficulties about their interrelationship. Much that is stable – massed concrete, for example – would to most eyes be lacking in beauty. Similarly, beauty and integrity may conflict if, as might appear, integrity concerns the inner workings of a system while beauty attends to its surface appearance. Such conflict is only increased if we add, as some will think we should, additional desiderata. It is often suggested that diversity is a further environmental good, and although Leopold gives it less than star billing, he does seem to think that the pyramid is in certain ways degraded if either the number or breadth of its various layers is diminished. But perhaps only in certain ways, for while acknowledging that human intervention can radically increase diversity, Leopold suggests that this typically offers a short-term benefit at best, leading to overuse of the underlying energy systems, and an eventual deterioration of the pyramid as a whole. Diversity will need careful handling, then.

Perhaps the critical question, however, for this emerging picture of Leopold's eco-centric ethics, is one of its claim upon us. For even supposing that there is available some coherent account of the biotic community's health or well-being, there is still the question as to why this is something we should care about. There is an issue, first, as to why we should care about it at all, and then a further issue as to why we should care about it to the exclusion of all else. Suppose that we could understand what it would be for things to go well on Jupiter. It wouldn't, I think, be at all obvious why Jupiter's good should detain us for a moment. Now the biotic community as construed under the land ethic is hardly like this, of course, as this community is one to which we belong, but it isn't really clear why being a member of a community should give one any obligation to promote that community's good, unless one's own welfare otherwise hangs in the balance. It might, of course, be natural to extend sympathy to the familiar and local, but a question will remain as to whether this is rational. It might, for example, be good to be generous, even though generosity is not rationally required. But even supposing we were to accept not only that there would be something good about, but also some reason actively to promote, the community's flourishing, this is still a long way from acknowledging that all meritorious action will further this one end. Could it not be good to celebrate Christmas with one's family, or help little old ladies across the road, or work to alleviate world poverty, even if such activities to some degree count against the biotic community as a whole? This is, of course, to rehearse one of the major difficulties for utilitarianism, with here the added complication that the distance between a conventional and pre-theoretical notion of moral activity and a postulated ideal is widened when we shift from maximizing for people to maximizing for the biosphere as a whole. Some aspects of a plurality of values is attractive, and not readily sacrificed on the altar of elegance and coherence.

Many of the questions here will, as I say, need to be revisited, but the issue that is more immediately pressing is whether they are fairly levelled at Leopold. There are reasons for thinking they are not. Lurking behind the radical vision that certain of his pronouncements seem to imply is a rather more conventional account of ethics' requirements, and one that does leave human beings at centre stage.

Morality and moderation

Reconsider the initial account of morality's development. Human-centred ethics involves a compromise between the individual and the community: a man's "instincts prompt him to compete for a place in the community, but his ethics prompt him also to co-operate (perhaps in order that there may be a place to compete for)".[32] The suggestion here, then, is that societal cooperation is in part a means to individual well-being rather than simply an end in itself. There are mixed motives, then, and it is, I think, a very similar compromise position that is aimed at even when ethics is, as Leopold insists it must be, further extended. We shift from conqueror to plain member and citizen of the land, yet this is at least partly because the "conqueror role is eventually self-defeating". The land ethic demands that we respect non-human members of the biotic community, and affirms their right to continued existence in a natural state, but this may well be limited to "spots", while elsewhere "alteration, management and use"[33] of natural resources will continue. So there is an acknowledgement of rights but, importantly, no insistence that they are all equal. And not only is Leopold able to side-step those difficulties generated when rights conflict, but now this implicit ranking of the parts permits rather more old-style environmental thinking to resurface. The prime target seems at bottom to be abuse or mismanagement of land, which will in the end lead to human misery, rather than a predominant concern for human beings as such.

This is not at all to deny that there are real advances in Leopold's account. The old style of conservation, working with its narrowly economic calculus, is deficient not simply in that even in its own terms costs will in time outweigh benefits, but also in that it gives little or no weight to the profounder elements of the human spirit. Even if multinational mining and construction companies, along with technology-hungry agribusinesses, could house, feed and clothe the world, Leopold would remain dissatisfied. There would continue to be neglect of both the (admittedly limited) right of non-human creatures to exist simply for their own sake, and that breadth to human experience and well-being that cannot easily be captured in strictly economic terms. The break between the old and the new is hardly clean, and there are various subtleties within the argument:

> When one of these non-economic categories is threatened, and if we happen to love it, we invent subterfuges to give it economic importance. At the beginning of the century songbirds were supposed to be disappearing. Ornithologists jumped to the rescue with some shaky evidence that insects would eat us up if birds failed to control them. The evidence had to be economic in order to be valid.
>
> ... A parallel situation exists in respect of predatory mammals, raptorial birds and fish eating birds. Time was when biologists somewhat overworked the evidence that these creatures preserve the health of game by killing weaklings, or that they control rodents for farmers, or that they prey only on "worthless" species. Here again the evidence had to be economic in order to be valid. It is only in more recent years that we hear the more honest argument that predators are members of the community, and that no special interest has the right to exterminate them for the sake of a benefit, real or fancied, to itself.[34]

Leopold is not claiming to be alone, then, in believing that there is a wider range of values. This is acknowledged elsewhere, even if advancing those values, so far, has had to be wrapped up, disingenuously, in the trappings of cost. That is one subtlety. Another is in Leopold's comment here, which might appear to give greater credence to a non-human perspective than he wants, in the end, to sustain. Three observations might be made. First, the shaky evidence might not be that shaky. Leopold has already argued that interventions in one place have typically incalculable effects elsewhere. Secondly, although extermination might be proscribed, "control" will apparently be allowed. Thirdly, beauty is muddying the waters. Leopold's discussion begins with wildflowers and songbirds, refers to things we "happen to love" and moves on to further animals and birds, which, for most of us, have undeniable aesthetic merit. There isn't here any unequivocal assertion of the right for dull and uninteresting things to exist untrammelled, while there is indication that the economic model most obviously goes wrong in overlooking the deep importance (although again, importance to us) of the aesthetic sense.

This offers some help with the sloganeering. One of the problems was in seeing how beauty might be understood in non-human terms, but for Leopold this problem is unreal. His holism is undeniable, and in that respect his views are more advanced than those of, say, Taylor. In other respects he is a more cautious and conservative thinker. Anthropocentrism remains, and even if his vision of the good is complex, generous and, as he would say himself, enlightened, it remains, for all that, the good construed in human terms.

Reading Leopold

If Leopold is himself a prophet, J. Baird Callicott is his most fervent and loyal disciple. In "The conceptual foundations of the land ethic", a patient and painstaking commentary on his master's considerably lighter prose, Callicott puts a quite distinctive spin on the land ethic story. I have suggested that Leopold is neither an extremist nor particularly concerned with the niceties of philosophical rigour. Callicott agrees with the first claim but thinks, where the second is concerned, that Leopold elects to present in a somewhat elliptical manner what is nevertheless "a serious intellectual challenge to business-as-usual moral philosophy".[35] He spells this out in some detail, and while some may find it persuasive, others will detect signs of overinterpretation, suspecting that Callicott's own philosophical background begins to infect his reading. A further concern is that, however it relates to Leopold, this allegedly challenging account is far from unflawed.

Callicott's reading takes as its starting point a divergence within the philosophical tradition. Whereas much of our moral thinking is dominated by an approach that puts a heavy premium on reason, Callicott sees in Leopold implicit support of an alternative sentimentalist view, traceable to Hume, Adam Smith and Darwin, which construes us very much as creatures of nature, given to and motivated by habit, instinct and feeling. Why care about other people? An answer, on this account, is that we simply have no choice. Even if it is not rational, still it is perfectly natural to manifest concern. Why care about non-human animals, plants or the biosphere? The same answer might be suggested. One of the questions I put in the direction of Leopold concerned the ethical import of his observations about the land: how do we come by our obligation to preserve, or work alongside, the natural order of things? And now Callicott suggests there may be no need for rational justification here:

> A land ethic, furthermore, is not only "an ecological necessity" but an "evolutionary possibility" because a moral response to the natural environment – Darwin's social sympathies, sentiments, and instincts translated into a body of principles and precepts – would be automatically triggered in human beings by ecology's social representation of nature.[36]

The same emphasis on our natural sentiments allows Callicott to dispose of another difficulty in Leopold's account: that of its relationship to anthropocentrism. Radical egalitarianism between species is avoided, not because there are external or impersonal justifications for promoting distinctively human concerns, but simply because our bias in favour of ourselves is perfectly natural. There is a double inevitability about morality's development, therefore. Not only are we unable to avoid the expansion of outlook that the land ethic advocates, but we are similarly unable to relinquish our privileged position within it. So just as, at least on the sentimentalist account, newfangled ties to nation or superstate do not overrule earlier loyalties to neighbourhood or home, so too for more recent ties to the biotic community at large. We have no choice but to put people first.

Radicalism is avoided, and so, too, is quietism. Callicott is at pains to unpick the interventionist thinking in Leopold's account, insisting that our duties to the good of the whole can make for hard choices with respect to individuals:

> it is not only morally permissible, from the point of view of the land ethic, but morally required, that members of certain species be abandoned to predation and other vicissitudes of wildlife, or even deliberately culled (as in the case of alert and sentient whitetail deer) for the sake of the integrity, stability, and beauty of the biotic community.[37]

But these duties of care to the world as a whole, thanks again to the force of natural instincts within us, will lose their force some time before human culling is required.

I think there are doubts as to whether the picture Callicott aims at can, in the end, be consistently presented. There are well-known difficulties in giving a fully articulated account of a broadly Humean moral philosophy, and there are further difficulties in extending that way beyond the human sphere. There are doubts, too, as to how far this picture can be attributed to Leopold. Consider the following argument, which begins by quoting Leopold:

> "The trend of evolution [not its "goal," since evolution is ateleo-logical] is to elaborate and diversify the biota". Hence, among our cardinal duties is the duty to preserve what species we can, especially those at the apex of the pyramid – the top carnivores.[38]

There's a gross *non sequitur* here, and it is Callicott's. There are difficulties in seeing how reason can sustain this inference, but it is clear that in speaking in just this way of the duties we might have, something more is needed than an appeal to feeling. Perhaps, because he rarely attempts anything as crisp, Leopold avoids this sort of difficulty. Callicott better sees the problems that have to be faced, but he offers no solution. Suppose, though, that the details can be filled in here, and we are able to see what is so important about the top of the pyramid, and our place in the scheme of things. The worry will be that in spite of his claims to the contrary, Callicott may have presented a softer, less challenging Leopold than he intended. The holism makes for some difference, but even if the business isn't run in quite the usual way, it remains the same business. And this may be no bad thing.

Summary

I have needed to follow through, in this lengthy and disparate chapter, on a number of issues that have already been aired. The central question still asks what sorts of things are of direct moral concern, and I still want to maintain that the critical line is at sentience: human and non-human animals are of concern just because they can feel pain. But of course it is in various ways wrong-headed to suppose that beyond sentience anything goes. Not only are there various instrumental reasons for evincing a concern with non-sentient things, but there is a spread of further considerations that suggests that they get a foothold on the moral terrain.

Living things, as I argued earlier, get this foothold just because they can plausibly be said to have a good of their own. A broadly Aristotelian account, under which such things possess an inner nature, have purposes, aims and ends, is defensible, I suggest, against the critique of Darwinism. But this account is defensible, at least in part, just because it has no weighty implications for what we might or might not do. There is no quick story about how, from this, duties fall on us.

It can hardly be any better, even if it isn't in the end much worse, where non-living things are concerned. Although we may with good reason prefer a river, mountain or sand dune to be in one condition rather than another, this is not, I have claimed, because this preferred condition would be better for the thing in question. Non-living things have no interests, needs or well-being. Nevertheless, I allowed that we can hold, innocuously enough, that it might be bad even for rivers to cease to exist. But this is moral minimalism, and cannot provide us with reasons to care. Moreover, artefacts are in the same boat here. It is bad for tractors, chairs and fences to be destroyed, and although it may well be wrong for us gratuitously to destroy such things, we can often easily enough justify doing what is bad for a thing.

Where species are concerned I first needed to explore just what sort of thing a species is, and to consider how its existence relates to the existence and the well-being of the creatures that are its members. The relationships here, I suggested, are neither uninteresting nor unsubtle. Thereafter I settled on what is by now becoming a familiar conclusion: it isn't easy to see why the existence or non-existence of species as such should for long detain us.

The same goes for land, energy, systems, or whatever it is that Leopold and other land ethicists are concerned with. There are many reasons to take note of and then to care for the complex interrelationships between living things. But here, though, the direction of the argument begins to shift. Although it might at first seem that Leopold is advancing a challenging and untenable position, it turns out, after a closer look, to be considerably more moderate. The tensions here – on the one hand apparent radicalism and on the other a subtly conservative stance – are evident, too, in the thinking of certain of Leopold's successors, as I hope to show in Chapter 8.

CHAPTER 8

Deep Ecology

My major concern has been with thinking straight. But for many, when faced with our current range of environmental problems, this is hardly enough. And deep ecologists, in particular, are committed not only to reflecting on what ought to be done, but to going ahead and doing it. They aim to change the world. While many are philosophers,[1] others[2] bring a range of different and sometimes competing influences. Diverging views are not unwelcome, with deep ecologists insisting not on a rigid programme but rather on an attitude or approach, which then expresses itself in various writings and in various ways. Some of those ways are obscure. Deep ecologists quite correctly believe that the traditional voice of academic philosophy is ill suited both in manner and substance to the active promotion of social and political change. The manner is wrong for obvious reasons – it is cautious, elitist and detached – but the substance is wrong as well, and much of this philosophy, it is claimed, is both a symptom and a cause of the attitudes that so much need revision. Deep ecology thus takes on a different, less familiar voice and with it puts forward what to many are unexpected and unwelcome views. In what follows I try to bring out some of what is central to that voice. Even if some deep ecologists will distance themselves from the characterization that follows, several others, or so I believe, will identify themselves with it.

Ecologies and ideologies

What is ecology? And when is it deep? The term itself was put together in the 1860s by the German biologist Ernst Haeckel from the Greek words *oikos*, meaning home or household, and *logos*, variously translated as word, order or systematic understanding. Thus, it is the study of homes, or environments. So, rather than an investigation of, say, the mating habits of the tawny owl, or fungal decay in timber, or weather patterns in northern Europe, the ecologist is concerned with relationships between these and similar things: investigating how weather affects vegetation, which affects small mammal life, which affects in turn the habits of the owl, which in turn has effects elsewhere. These relationships might be explored on a relatively small scale, as when an ecologist studies the activities and life cycles in a copse, a limestone fissure, or particular pond, or they might be much wider ranging, taking in rainforests, tundra or wetlands.

Systems, of course, are many, and although the term itself doesn't proscribe a wider use, ecologists are in practice concerned (as these examples suggest) with living things. And just as, in studying human systems, economists are concerned with the flow of money through those systems (through businesses, communities, countries or groups of countries), so the ecologist's approach to living systems is similarly focused. The concern here, however, is with the flow of energy throughout a biological system, with photosynthesis, the production of food and the various ways in which animals and plants feed on each other all playing a role.

Although, in studying whole systems, ecology is an activity of some considerable generality, there are two important respects in which its interests are circumscribed. First, while acknowledging the inevitable consequences for human beings, ecologists are in the main concerned with what might be called the natural world. They will investigate birds and insects in a wetland, or the interplay between sheep and plant life on high mountain pasture, rather than the doings of students in a university, or political activity as it unfolds in parliament, the media and the business world. Secondly, ecology is principally a science. As such, it isn't concerned with values. A tough-minded ecologist could watch a living system collapse and decay, a bog dry out and its life forms expire, or a sheltered microclimate succumb to atmospheric pollution. A particularly tough-minded ecologist could watch the whole of life on earth come to an end, drink coffee, take notes and waggle his finger.

Deep ecology (and the term was coined in the 1970s by the movement's founding father, the Scandinavian philosopher Arne Naess[3]) wants, in contrast, to be restricted in neither of these ways. Although their concerns are noticeably focused on systems within the natural world, deep ecologists take the influence of human beings on those systems very seriously. This is not simply to make the obvious point that we can wreck the environment. It is, further, to make a point about the influences, often undetected, of our political, religious, cultural and philosophical beliefs on our attitudes to and thus dealings with those natural systems. And they are concerned with values. Deep ecologists, unlike the typical scientist, evaluate as well as describe the systems that they choose to study, claiming that this or that change is for the better, or for the worse, or that this activity contributes to overall well-being, while that one inflicts damage or harm.[4]

It is in following through on the combination of these two characteristics that deep ecology is most sharply distinguished from various of its predecessor environmental philosophies. Our problems are system wide, but earlier approaches consider only detail, merely tinker at the edges and offer little more than piecemeal change and the quick fix.[5] Such approaches are embedded, in ways that their proponents quite fail to recognize, within a network of political and philosophical assumptions and values that, in various ways, determine that our response to these problems is half-hearted at best. Taking systematic interconnectedness very seriously, then, deep ecology insists that attention to the parts demands attention to the whole: we cannot hope to address a discrete and finite number of "environmental problems" without looking more generally and deeply into everything that impinges on those problems, including, in particular, our own attitudes and beliefs, which typically help create them and give them shape. And in so giving attention to the whole, deep ecology identifies two contrasting ideologies or "world views", one of them long established and familiar, the other in many ways at odds with our prevailing cultural outlook.[6] The former still has the upper hand, but its weaknesses are becoming evident, for it

> regards humans as isolated and fundamentally separate from the rest of Nature, as superior to, and in charge of, the rest of creation. But the view of humans as separate and superior to the rest of Nature is only part of larger cultural patterns. For thousands of years, Western culture has become increasingly obsessed with the idea of *dominance*: with dominance of humans over nonhuman Nature, masculine over feminine, wealthy and powerful over the poor, with dominance of the West over non-Western cultures. Deep ecological consciousness allows us to see through these erroneous and dangerous illusions.[7]

This fundamentally wrong-headed attitude or "world view", deeply infected by anthropocentric, crudely materialistic and hierarchical thinking, accounts both for many of the environmental problems we now face, and for our limited and feeble response to them. The rival view, in contrast, wants harmony with nature and recognition of its intrinsic value, limits on both consumption and the technologies that encourage consumption, and a rediscovery of local, community and human-scale concerns. And with all that, the claim goes, there will be benefits not only for the environment, but also for the quality of human life.

Is this rival view the one advocated by deep ecologists? There is fudging here. Often they unambiguously want to bring to the fore the oppositional character of debate. Naess, in further exploring the implications of the deep approach, described as "shallow" the beliefs and attitudes sustained by the supposedly dominant view.[8] This term has stuck, but whereas shallow ecology opts wholeheartedly and unthinkingly for one side of the divide, its deep rival supposedly questions both. Even so, its "tentative conclusions" favour low growth, decentralization, and view of nature as other than a resource.

Tentativity is less evident elsewhere. In 1984, after camping together in California's Death Valley, Naess and Sessions brought back – and the Mosaic resonances here are undeniable – the eight basic principles of deep ecology that, even though their authors have expressed reservations about their status, have long had something of the authority of sacred texts for many followers.[9] These principles are explicit in their insistence, first, that there are significant non-human intrinsic values, and, secondly, on the need for political activity in order to realize those values. If we buy into the theory, we need to make changes to practice. What deep ecology offers, then, is not merely a solution to certain self-standing environmental problems, but a thoroughgoing and wide-ranging critique of our contemporary culture as a whole.

Two worries

Deep ecology is ambitious. It sets itself in firm opposition to what it sees as the basic underlying attitudes that have dominated Western thinking, at least from the time of the Renaissance, and offers a different and a differently rooted approach. It has an overt religious dimension; Buddhism, Taoism and American Indian beliefs, as well as some aspects of Christianity, have all influenced its writings. So, too, have parts of Western academic philosophy, including works by Spinoza, Whitehead, Heidegger and Kuhn.[10] It has connections with the anarchism of the late nineteenth and early twentieth centuries, and it acknowledges a debt to a tradition of conservationist and wilderness thinking, including, in particular, that of Thoreau, John Muir and Leopold. Finally, it has, importantly, a good part of its roots in the 1960s, with the radical political consciousness, the New Age thinking, most clearly seen in California.

Not only is its pedigree impressive, but its range of influences is broad. Although indirectly, it has succeeded in changing both government policy and the wider public consciousness on a range of environmental issues, influenc- ing, in its early days, attitudes to the biochemicals industry, nuclear weapons and nuclear power, and more recently helping to shape resistance to such allegedly anti-environmental institutions as the General Agreement on Tariffs and Trade (GATT), the International Monetary Fund (IMF) and the World Bank. Greenpeace International is the best known example of a pressure group that is marked by deep ecological thinking, but similarly successful activism characterizes many animal liberation protests, massed opposition to road-building schemes and, more recently, the media-friendly destruction of GM crops.

Viewed in general terms, then, deep ecology finds considerable support. Being at one with nature, rejecting materialism, capitalism and imperialism, and showing respect for the whole earth are themes that speak to a great many people. So, too, on a less elevated level, do the merits of recycling, eating organic food, limiting consumption and thinking green. It may be tempting, therefore, to suppose that deep ecological views are now very close to mainstream, and in that respect are hardly controversial. Yet even if there is much here with which to sympathize, there are still several broad areas of concern. One attaches to its insistently oppositional nature. Another, feeding into that, derives from the special character of its geographical provenance. I will say something about both.

It is no accident, surely, that deep ecological thinking is most prevalent in those parts of the world – the American West, Australia, Scandinavia – where, either because the land is inhospitable, or because the influx of European or post-European settlers is recent, the contrast between "nature" and "civilization" is pronounced. Cities are mostly recent, built and maintained with highly sophisticated technologies that allow for materials, water and power to be brought in from afar, and inhabited by people who have no long-standing relationship to the area in which they now live. Agriculture is similarly often indifferent to local conditions, with complex irrigation systems, high use of fertilizers and pesticides allowing for the quasi-mechanical generation of large crops, most of which are then destined for national or global markets. The distinctions between town, farmland and country are typically pronounced, highlighted by both the inflexibility of these technologies and the demands for the convenience of urban and suburban living. Large areas of the countryside are virtually uninhabited, viewed sometimes as barren waste, and at others either as dedicated recreation areas, or as natural wilderness. Very different conditions prevail in much of western Europe, where the landscapes and townscapes have together been fashioned over centuries by patient cooperation between human beings and nature, and where tradition even today demands that the distinctions between the two remain blurred. So subsidies are given to "traditional" methods of farming, to a system of national parks that, on the whole, eschews the wilderness idea, and to a heritage industry that actively promotes nostalgia for a pastoral and village idyll.

There are profound cultural differences here, with New World attitudes markedly more disposed to see an inherent opposition between civil society and nature, the former, at least for hundreds of years, viewed typically as an interloper, trespassing, usually to ill effect, on the non-human world. Given this background, it is unsurprising that many deep ecologists see, or at least often appear to see, the choice between human beings and the environment as stark. It is hard to resist the suspicion that deep ecological views and arguments may be coloured, perhaps unwittingly, by these background beliefs and attitudes. This doesn't warrant their dismissal, but does invite a degree of circumspection.

There may be too much polarity here, then, and there is certainly too much in the self-selecting description of the views under consideration as deep, in contrast to the shallowness of their rivals. This ought not to go unchallenged, as it ought not to be overlooked that non-deep environmentalists can hardly be lumped together as equally shallow. Their views are not all equally anthropocentric, for a start, as recollecting the positions of Singer, Regan, Schweitzer, Taylor, and many others will make evident. Nor are they equally enamoured of science, technology, reason, capital or indeed any of deep ecology's *bêtes noires*. So it has been suggested by some that the deep/shallow distinction, with its undertones both of evaluation and of a fairly firm distinction between divergent views, be replaced by a nomenclature of light and deep green, depending on the extent of one's commitment to environmental friendliness. Colours shade into one another, and to so describe the outside positions allows for intermediate accounts to emerge.[11] But to amend the terminology in these ways is perhaps still not enough, as there remains the suggestion, first, that the various different positions can be given an overall ranking against one scale, and, secondly, that deep ecology occupies one extreme. Yet, as will emerge, there are reasons for thinking that this isn't really so. Ambiguities in the deep ecologists' position at least allow for the suspicion that when all is said and done, their views are in critical respects less radical, less demanding of a change in attitude, than those of apparently moderate reformers such as Regan or Singer.

Ecology and philosophy

The second worry, about opposition, is relevant here. Although central figures within the deep ecology movement have suggested very much an us–them perspective, there are several fellow-travellers. I discussed Leopold's land ethic earlier, and will need briefly to consider Lovelock's Gaia hypothesis below. What these, and certain others, share with deep ecology is, first, a profound concern with ecological systems, and, secondly, a commitment to exploring the philosophical implications of those systems. The term "eco-philosophy"[12] has been used as a way of bringing these various positions under one umbrella, and I will make use of that term here and below.

Many eco-philosophers insist that we need to think about much more than ethics. They argue that environmental concerns force us to ask questions about knowledge, and often take a critical stance towards many of the assumptions underlying conventional epistemology. They present us with problems of metaphysics, in particular about the various kinds of things that exist, and about how these kinds of things, and the relationships between these things, are best to be classified and understood. Where ethics is concerned they demand that we come face to face with some of the deeper questions, not simply of what we should do, or what we should value, but questions about the principles of obligation, and the very nature of value. Having raised these questions they go on to answer them in ways that, it is claimed, sit uncomfortably on the shoulders of much in traditional philosophy. Some of these questions, and their answers, need to be considered here.

Metaphysical holism

What is real? Philosophical thinking often attempts to draw distinctions between what, on the face of it, might appear to be a rich and varied array of objects, claiming that some are real, while others are not, or that some are more or less real than others. Thus Platonism has it that ordinary physical objects – human beings, horses, tables, caves – are less real than are their ideal forms to which they only approximately correspond. Materialism, in contrast, holds that reality is coextensive with physical or material stuff. So either numbers, thoughts or concepts are not real, or they have to be understood in material terms, such that a thought, for example, is identified with the brain state that obtains just when we are thinking the thought in question. A third distinction, and the one relevant here, is that between individuals and wholes. Metaphysical holism is, in some form or other, a view about the nature and importance of the whole, in contrast to the individuals that figure within it. As far as deep ecology goes, holism here amounts to the claim that the kinds of things that are supposedly underrepresented in earlier and shallower accounts – species, ponds, deserts, particular ecosystems – are in some way as significant as or more significant than the individual animals and plants that together comprise these wholes, and are thus highly legitimate objects of concern.

This is merely to sketch a position, yet certain problems may already be evident within it. First, the distinction. Even allowing that we can distinguish between such particulars as animals, plants, microbes and bacteria on the one hand, and the environments or systems in which they live on the other, there is still a question as to how this maps onto any more general distinction between individuals and wholes. For, as is evident, living things equally have their parts and so can equally make the claim to be considered as wholes. At the same time they might be considered parts of larger wholes that then figure in yet larger wholes, and so on. Thus a fish is not a mere jumble of bits and pieces but is itself an integrated system of bones, organs, muscles and skin, and it contains various living things – bacteria, parasitical worms, smaller fish eaten yet so far unexpired – within it. Moreover, fish are hardly known for their individualism, and many will spend the whole of life in a shoal, feeding, resting, and moving as one with hundreds of others. Is a fish then an individual, a whole, a part of a bigger whole, or what? Similarly for trees, where coppicing and suckering can make the answers to part/whole questions thoroughly arbitrary. As I have suggested earlier, it isn't always clear whether we should think of a species as a mere collection of individuals, as a coherent whole, or as itself a particular individual thing. With non-living things, where boundaries are often inherently fuzzy – rivers, valleys, mountains, deserts, landscapes – there are obvious difficulties in making any perspicuous distinctions of the individual/part/whole kind.[13]

Secondly, the rival views. Deep ecologists often see shallow consciousness and the dominant world view as all too ready to divide things up in certain ways, and then to prioritize among these divisions. Human/animal, reason/ nature, sentient/non-sentient, individual/species, male/female, intellect/ emotion and self/other figure among the contested distinctions. That between individuals and wholes is, therefore, part of a general trend. But even if there is a dominant world view, and even if it does in some way erect polarities of such a kind, it is far from clear that it is open to the detailed charges levelled against it, and that it insists on firm lines between individuals and wholes. As almost everyone will agree, there are lots of players in the football league, lots of fish in the sea and lots of words in a book as long as this. But equally, there are lots of cells in a football player, lots of leagues, a fair number of letters in the longer words and so on. What is looked on as an individual in one context is viewed as a whole in another. Even allowing some such distinction, it surely isn't true that run-of-the-mill environmentalists systematically focus on the individual to the neglect of the whole. They have, even if for various reasons, been much concerned with species, forests, global warming, seas, atmospheres and various other putative wholes. Indeed, it is hard to see how anyone might claim that individual human beings are important but the whole world is not, even if we can see why many might think that the world gets its importance from having human beings, and perhaps also animals, within it. So even if it might be charged that conventional thinking does in the end come down in favour of individual animals as opposed to their habitats, this is still some way from showing that this betrays a larger and more general metaphysical confusion.

Some deep ecologists take a different approach. They readily acknowledge the absence of firm lines, maintaining that it is a characteristic of, and indeed a defect in, their opponents' account to insist on boundaries between one thing and another. One version of holism is not, then, a view that there are both various individuals and various wholes, the latter of which are more real, but rather that there is just the one whole, within which no clear distinctions can be drawn. And the movement has been said to be committed to

> the idea that we can make no firm ontological divide in the field of existence: that there is no bifurcation in reality between the human and the non-human realms . . . to the extent that we perceive boundaries, we fall short of deep ecological consciousness.[14]

This is open to two interpretations. One, which is fairly innocuous, will greatly stress "firm" and "boundaries". Very many people, of all environmental persuasions, will agree that the universe consists of microparticles in various combinations, all of which are capable of interacting with one another. In that sense there are no firm boundaries. Very many people will also agree (as is already implied) that there is no abrupt human/non-human distinction – they will accept evolution, that we share very many genes with pigs, and that scientists could create half-human monsters with very little trouble. The second interpretation is more contentious, holding that distinctions as they are ordinarily made, between me and you, cats and dogs, Venus and Mars, are all of them symptomatic of a shallow view. But why think this? Even if these distinctions do not hold of necessity – we can imagine blended people, colliding planets and the like – they hold of certainty. There are boundaries, even if in some sense there might not have been. So the difficulty, for the apostle of deep ecology, is in coming up with a reading that is both distinctive and plausible. To put it bluntly, "everything is connected" is true, while "everything is one" is false.

What about reality? Suppose, tentatively, that we accept some version of the individual/whole distinction, and suppose that we accept that traditional accounts have emphasized individual animals, rather than the ecosystems in which they tend to be located. There is a further objection to holism. It is often suggested that the wholes are more important, or more basic, or even more real than the individuals located within them, but the meaning of such claims is often unclear, and the arguments used to support them are often unconvincing.

The claim that such and such is unreal is often well enough understood. Dragons are not real, as there are no dragons. Nor are witches, for although there have certainly been real women who are said to be witches, they have been quite unable to perform genuinely witchly activities. Some might even think that they can understand Margaret Thatcher's notorious claim of the 1980s, that there is no such thing as society. Perhaps her thought was that society, as opposed to the individual human beings who (allegedly) figure within it, is not a robustly physical thing, and doesn't in that way measure up. But none of this is of much help with environmentalists' holism. Take the kindest spin on the Thatcherite dictum. The deep ecologist's position is quite the opposite, as he wants to prioritize the diffuse, large-scale, abstract thing at the expense of the concrete individual. But then, as the reality of these individuals – human beings, whales, oaks – is not easily denied, what appears to be a sort of compromise position is advanced: that such individuals are less real than the wholes in which they are located. The problem here, as the following passage unwittingly shows, is that this idea of there being different degrees of reality is not easily fleshed out:

> Consider what it means to say that an individual organism is alive. Minimally, an individual organism is alive only if certain chemical

and biological processes are occurring. When these processes cease to occur, the organism ceases to live, thus the processes are necessary for the existence of the organism. When the processes are present life exists, thus the processes are sufficient for life. Because chemical and biological processes are both necessary and sufficient for the existence of life, we have some reason for saying that the processes are at least as, if not more real, than individual living organisms.[15]

Suppose that these processes are necessary and sufficient for life. That is indeed a reason for thinking that the processes are real. (How could unreal, imaginary or illusory processes play a part in generating life?) But is it any reason for thinking that these processes are *more* real? It is just not easy to see what "more real" could mean here. And nor does this offer much help:

> the ontological primacy of objects and the ontological subordination of relationships characteristic of classical western science is, in fact, reversed in ecology. Ecological relationships determine the nature of organisms rather than the other way around. A species is what it is because it has adapted to a niche in the ecosystem. The whole, the system itself, thus, literally and quite straightforwardly shapes and forms its component parts.[16]

Callicott seems to want to support the belief that systems are in some sense of greater reality than their component parts. That, at least, is one interpretation of "ontological primacy". The reason for thinking this is that systems "literally and quite straightforwardly" shape their parts. But this is unpersuasive. Consider mountains. Perhaps they are shaped by weather systems, systems of movement in the earth's crust and the like. Does this suggest that mountains are less real than those systems? It is hard to see how something could be more real than the Matterhorn, or Mount Everest. A different and more modest conclusion might be supported here, for if mountains are literally shaped by weather and earth movements, then, indeed, you could conclude that those systems exist prior to the mountain. If the systems cause the mountain to exist, then, apparently, the systems must come first. But this doesn't at all show that the system is more real than the mountain. Parents are not more real than their children. Moreover, what causes something to exist may itself be destroyed while the thing itself continues. The ecosystem in a pond may bring it about that there are frogs, but I might capture and keep the frogs while draining the pond. Again, "ontological primacy" is unestablished. A still more modest conclusion is that even if the system doesn't come first (as, say, the material of the mountain, if not its current shape, coexists along with the processes), still the processes shape the thing, rather than vice versa. But even this conclusion will often be unsupportable. Consider society again. Against Thatcher, many will agree that society deeply influences its individual members, but does it literally and straightforwardly shape them? Many will say both that there are certain limits on societal influence, and that the process is in any event two-way, with individuals influencing and helping change the shape of society. And consider, say, a Canadian polar bear. Is it literally and straightforwardly shaped by the Canadian ecosystem in which it finds itself? If that were so, it would be curious as to why it retains so much of its shape when born, not in Canada but the rather different environment of the San Diego Zoo. The truth, again, seems to be slightly more complex, and slightly less captivating. Animals are shaped very much by the genetic material of which they are made, and are further shaped by the environment or ecosystem in which they live, which system they help shape in return.[17] It is hard to see how any traditional environmental ethic could quarrel with this.

A similar argument follows:

> Viewed from the point of view of modern [ecology] each living thing is a dissipative structure, that is, it does not endure in and of itself but only as a result of the continual flow of energy in the system . . . From this point of view, the reality of individuals is problematic because they do not exist *per se* but only as local perturbations in this universal energy flow . . . An example might be instructive. Consider a vortex in a stream of flowing water. The vortex is a structure made of an ever-changing group of water molecules. It does not exist as an entity in the classic Western sense; it exists only because of the flow of water through the stream. If the flow ceases the vortex disappears. In the same sense the structures out of which the biological entities are made are transient, unstable entities with constantly changing molecules dependent on a constant flow of energy to maintain form and structure.[18]

Again, the problem is that while certain of the claims here are wholly uncontentious, others, which are supposed readily to follow, are simply obscure. Of course, biological entities consist of constantly changing molecules, and depend in some ways on energy flows, but does this means that fish, trees and human beings don't exist *per se*, don't endure in and of themselves? My claim that Bill Clinton exists, is an entity, is real, is not to be understood in any way that challenges the laws of physics.

I will mention briefly one further, general and often encountered argument for holism. It is frequently said that the whole is greater than the sum of its parts. This might suggest that the whole is somehow more real, but there is an innocuous interpretation. It is true that one will not have a human being in virtue of having a collection of human being parts, just as one will not possess a bicycle simply in virtue of having a set of bicycle parts. The parts need to be arranged in a certain way. With the bicycle this is straightforward;

with a human being less so. In that sense, the whole is greater than the parts. But this is a sense with which few will argue, while alternative and rather more contentious senses are hard to find.

Other holisms

Different versions of holism are advanced, either by different writers or by one writer on different occasions. Even if these different versions can shade one into another, such that it can be unclear where the boundaries are supposed to lie, it is worthwhile trying to draw certain distinctions. Rather than the nature of reality, epistemological holism is concerned with knowledge. It claims that, "we would have an inadequate and incomplete understanding of an ecosystem even if we knew everything about its constituent parts, if that is *all* we knew".[19] So knowledge of the whole system requires more than a knowledge of its parts. This much is surely right – I might know about wood, hammers, wires and bits of ivory, but still not know what a piano is, or how it works. Perhaps the epistemological point can be put more strongly. It has been argued that not only are we unable to understand a whole merely by understanding its parts, but that we cannot have a complete understanding of those parts, unless we understand the whole. Consider the human body. It could be said that we cannot fully understand one organ, say the liver, unless we understand the whole system, the whole body, in which the liver plays a role. Or consider a single theme in a Beethoven symphony. Again, someone could well argue that the complete character of the theme is not grasped unless one sees how it fits into, contributes to and is in turn informed by, the whole work. Epistemological holism, then, seems to be a defensible position.

Yet is this really so? Or is this no more than a truism? The question, once again, is about what weight to put on words like "full" and "complete". The danger is best seen if we try to take this holism to what might at first appear to be extremes. Everything that exists can be seen as a part of a circle of increasingly large and extended systems. The liver is situated within the human body. The body exists within a certain space, and at a certain time, and has relationships to other things existing in that space, and at that time. Further, it has relationships to things existing in different spaces and at different times; if things had gone differently in the course of evolutionary history, there would be no spleens today, and if things go differently on the sun, or in the asteroid belt, there will be no livers tomorrow. But should we agree that we cannot really or fully understand the liver unless we understand the whole cosmos? Perhaps it is tempting to say that a full understanding of anything is impossible, unless one fully understands everything. But perhaps it is tempting instead to allow that what counts as a full understanding depends on context – in normal situations it is proper to claim a full understanding of how a bicycle works without any knowledge of nuclear physics. We can know what we need to know about the liver, without knowing everything.[20]

A further variant on holism addresses itself to values, and the moral considerability of wholes. Where the environment is concerned, this ethical holism will have it that ecosystems in particular are deserving of moral consideration. Holism here opposes, evidently, the claim that only individuals count, that only they are proper candidates for moral concern. But there are several ways in which the holist's view can be fleshed out. It might be claimed, first, that individuals and wholes both count for something. Or, more radically, it might be claimed that although both count, wholes count for more. Or, more radically still, the claim might be made that wholes alone count.[21] Deep ecologists, in opposition to what they see as the ethical stance of more traditional views, typically advance ethical holism in some or other form. But the details of their claims need to be explored further.

Consider the first reading. That wholes deserve moral consideration is, as it stands, an uncontroversial claim. Even the meanest anthropocentrist will agree that what happens in the biosphere is important, for what happens to it will have a bearing on what happens to him or her. Similarly the condition of marshes, deserts, glaciers and seas will be of importance to those concerned, for whatever reason, with the welfare of creatures that live in such places. What needs to be brought out is the distinctive character of the deep ecologist's view, namely that wholes are of direct moral concern, that what happens to at least some of them is important in itself, and independently of its effects on human beings, other sentient creatures or even on living organisms more generally. But although giving direct moral considerability to wholes is what sets deep ecology apart,[22] the difficulties here are not new, and have surfaced in earlier chapters, in discussing intermediate ethical positions. There are problems in explaining how what happens to non-sentient things is of direct concern, and these problems are neither more nor less pressing when, among non-sentient things, systems or wholes are given particular consideration. These rather general difficulties in explicating the key notion of direct concern, of intrinsic or inherent value, are not a particular feature of holism as such, and are best set aside until later.

Even if this major stumbling block impinges on deep ecology's ethical holism in any guise, certain of the differences between those guises might still be explored. Consider the claim that what happens to systems or wholes is of more consequence than what happens to individuals. One suggestion, that a given whole is more important than any of the individuals that figure within it, is uncontroversial. It is surely worse to obliterate Madagascar than to chop down any of its trees, or kill any of its human inhabitants. Another, that any whole is more important than any individual is, in contrast, too controversial. Or at least this is so if an array of wholes is allowed; if there is but the one then controversy falls away. An intermediate position, that a whole is more important than the sum of its separate parts, does, in contrast, appear to have both substance and plausibility. The claim here will be that there is added value in arranging things in one way rather than another.

Consider the claim that only wholes count. This might appear to be included just for completeness, for surely no one could deny that micro-waving a cat is straightforwardly and directly wrong; even if measured against, say, harm to the ozone layer, one is reluctant to say just how wrong it is. Indeed, I know of no deep ecologist who wants to hold explicitly to any such position. However, something like it might seem to be implied by what I have suggested above is a rather dubious metaphysics. If cats are not really real, it isn't easy to see how we might do them any harm. Moreover, such a position does seem to be implied by Leopold's quasi-utilitarian dictum. Microwaving a cat, like helping old ladies across the road, is likely to make no difference either way to the integrity, beauty and stability of the biosphere. Yet surely it doesn't for that reason simply drop out of the moral sphere.

Holisms compared

These different varieties of holism will have relevance often to the same things. Think of species. Metaphysical holism will say that species are as real as, or more real than, individuals. Epistemological holism will say that a member of a species (say, your own cat) can only be understood if we under-stand the working of the species as a whole. Ethical holism will say that the health and well-being of the species matters quite independently of, and perhaps more than, the health and well-being of individual members of that species. But if it is agreed that the various holisms can settle on the same things, should we agree that they must so settle? Hardly. Consider the relationships between epistemology and metaphysics. Must we think that if knowledge of parts is impossible without knowledge of wholes, then wholes are more real? There is simply no reason to think this. If we consider the reverse relationship, the connections are arguably more profound. It may not seem implausible to suppose that if wholes are more real than their parts, knowledge of the parts will require knowledge of the wholes, but the plausi-bility here is undermined by the difficulty in getting a handle on this idea of greater reality. And it is, in any event, slight unless we further suppose that the fleeting reality of parts somehow depends on the firmer reality of wholes.

Nor does ethical holism require its metaphysical counterpart. Ethical holism is a view about differences in value, and there is no need to think that this must map onto differences in reality. I can think one thing more valuable than another, without thinking it more real. And I can maintain that a complex system is more valuable than its simple component parts, again without thinking that this is because it is more real. Finally, ethical and epistemological holisms are also distinct. The valuation of a whole has no immediate bearing on our knowledge of it, or vice versa.

Why spend so much time in considering these various holisms? Deep ecologists, along with other non-shallow environmentalists, systematically emphasize such notions in drawing attention to the virtues of their positions and, in contrast, to the vices of their rivals. Such holism is central to their claims. If the claims are to be taken seriously, so must the substance in and arguments for their philosophical underpinnings.

Human beings, nature and the wild

Deep ecology contends that rival accounts, shallow and anthropocentric, posit a strong contrast between human beings and nature, and then insist that while human beings matter in themselves, nature has only instrumental value as a resource for furthering the interests of those beings. The opposition to this account, although there is some hedging, is not full-blooded, for while rejecting the evaluations given here, deep ecologists can sometimes appear to accept the bifurcation on which they are based. Devall and Sessions, for example, suggest that nature is something we might live with in harmony, rather than seek to dominate, still implying here that it is a thing apart.[23] It would be uncharitable to take this as indicating any deep confusion, however. Although it lacks the rationale it once had, this familiar way of couching a distinction knowingly sacrifices accuracy for convenience. I have done it countless times in this book. But again, there is a spread of positions, and deep ecologists do at times give voice to a contrary view and, while referring often to the human and non-human worlds, accept that these are both a part of the whole, just as we are ourselves a part of nature. And it may be that in this respect deep ecologists show greater acuity than some mid-green environmentalists, who more occasionally suggest that the human and non-human worlds occupy distinct realms.

Yet even if there is wavering on the separation question, there is a marked consistency on a related matter: that of the value attaching to the two worlds. Deep ecologists appear to believe that while human beings are often careless, self-serving, destructive, hostile to and undermining of non-human nature, this nature is overall a good thing, every part of which is intrinsically valuable, and all of which we should respect and hope to conserve. This sharply contrasting view of human beings and nature is widespread, surfacing in both deep ecology and several of its predecessor accounts, making appearances in certain mid-green views, and, more broadly, characterizing much of Romantic thinking in both Europe and America. It is riddled with obscurity and confusion, however, most of which it is not too difficult to sort out.

What many people believe is that human beings are a part of nature, at least in the sense that we are biophysical creatures who have taken shape within the natural world, and are subject, just as much as ants, trees and mountains, to its laws. Everything we do, everything we can do, is natural. And as this part-of-nature view is widespread, so too is a further view, which holds that the realm of nature is the only realm there is, and thus that all that happens in the universe happens naturally. So the supernatural – the world of gods, demons, wizards – is no more than a fiction. Here there are, of course, variant views. Many other people believe that the supernatural world is not empty, and that there is at least one God who, although the creator of nature, is not himself a natural creature, nor himself subject to the laws of nature which figure as a part of his creation. Ancillary to this is the view that human beings have immortal souls, created by God, which are also not subject to natural law. These more or less explicit beliefs in the supernatural may, in Europe if not in North America, by now be minority views, but they connect with two further views, both of which are mainstream, yet only one of which is uncontroversial. The first is that human beings have free will in a sense that implies that we are able to start causal sequences *ab initio*. So determinism is false, and our choosings, decidings and actings are in part free of natural law. This view may be false, and may even be ultimately incoherent, but it is, or appears to be, widely held, and is, importantly, a view that denies that we are in all respects a part of nature. The second is that human beings have ratiocinative faculties by which they are distinguished from the rest of nature. There are two versions. On the first this is the essential or defining property of human beings, while on the second, defining or not, it is nevertheless a property that most of us, and arguably none but us, enjoy. Either way, belief in the distinctiveness and the importance of human reason is perfectly compatible, in a way that belief in libertarian free will is not perfectly compatible, with the part-of-nature view. Most people, whether of a religious persuasion or not, hold that reason is as much a product of evolution and biology as are tentacles or feathers.

This part-of-nature view is perfectly compatible with another view: that there is a distinction to be drawn between what occurs as a consequence of human activity on the one hand, and what results from non-human activity on the other. There are reasons, deriving in part from customary usage, to gloss this distinction in terms of nature and artifice, even though, given what is implied by the part-of-nature view, this is potentially misleading. To avoid confusion, it has been suggested that we might here speak of wild nature in contradistinction to the artful and artificial manifestations of human activity, many of which involve nature tamed and domesticated or, as with certain parks and zoos, with its wildness artificially preserved. The distinction here has considerable substance – only human beings wear clothes, build chariots, cities, motorways – even if, as some animals engage in rudimentary thinking while others fashion buildings, or decorate nests, we might resist supposing that everything artificial or artefactual can be laid at our door.

Nature and value

The difficulty for deep ecology is that nothing pertaining to value or morality is implicated in any of this. Suppose we are, as many people believe,
thoroughly a part of nature. That doesn't count for or against the claim that
there is good or bad in any of what we do.[24] Suppose, as some believe, that
there is also a supernatural world to which we, as opposed to animals and
plants, rivers and deserts, in some way belong. That, too, as it stands, has no
implications for where value lies. Similarly, a distinction between the natural
and the artificial, between what we don't and what we do have a hand in,
doesn't at all suggest that one is any better or any worse than the other.
Introducing evaluations here might begin to seem plausible, however, on
attending to a third distinction: that between the natural and the unnatural.

The undoubtedly widespread tendency to think of the natural as good and
the unnatural as bad is perhaps in large measure defensible. It certainly gets
off the ground, for while the supernatural might be an empty category, that
of the unnatural is not. This might for a moment appear not to be true,
however, and in clear conflict with the view that I have described as highly
plausible, that everything is a part of nature, and governed by nature's laws.
But to reason in this way is simply to be deaf to some fairly evident nuances
of language: "nature" and "natural" don't sit as comfortably together as might
at first be expected, with the latter's more familiar contrast picking out a
subset of all that is included in the former.[25] The non-natural might be
vacuous while the unnatural is rather too full. It will include such things as
freak storms and weather conditions, certain products of random mutations,
deformities resulting from disease or distress, and aberrant behaviour
patterns stemming from these or further causes. What is unnatural might be
identified on a purely statistical basis, or it might, where reproductive
processes among living things are concerned, make reference to adaptations
that counter the viability of the species, and that are then only fortuitously
sustained. In the latter case it is possible, at least in principle, for a clear
majority of instances of a certain kind to be appropriately described as
unnatural. Having got off the ground, the connection between what is
unnatural and what is bad will then begin to take shape. Unnatural weather
conditions are not bad for the weather, but they are often bad for the many
forms of life that have adapted to, and now depend on, the weather's following certain patterns. A plant that develops unnaturally, perhaps bolting under
stress, or attempting to adapt to an erratic water supply, is unlikely to survive.
So far these are examples drawn from nature's working without human intervention, but our activities can supply many more. Bulldogs are highly unnatural in that their very wide ribcages, selectively bred for who knows what
reason, cause them to breathe only with difficulty. Bonsai trees are unnatural,
obviously, as are many of the results of grafting, pollarding and topiary. And
there are more than enough examples of unnatural behaviour and practices

195

among human beings: matricide, self-mutilation, washing too little or too often. None of the objects, activities or situations referred to here are contrary to nature in the sense of depending on outside intervention, or the random suspension of nature's laws, but that doesn't preclude their being unnatural in the ordinary sense of the term. And this is so even if in origin the unnatural and the supernatural were more closely intertwined.

Still, this doesn't yet square with deep ecology's claims about nature and goodness for at least two important reasons. First, there are no grounds for thinking that all that human beings do is unnatural. Even if there are several bizarre, repellent and dangerous practices that spring to mind, most of these are minority pursuits, and hardly undermine the prevalent view that much of what we get up to – pairing up, having children, telling jokes, fearing death – is perfectly natural, susceptible to an adequate evolutionary explanation, and contributing to species preservation. Secondly, the connection between values and nature might easily be exaggerated. Certainly what is unnatural is often harmful, but there are many random mutations that offer benefits to the individuals concerned, and many unnatural occurrences – frosts, hailstorms, calms – that do no harm. Moreover, in many cases where harm is done there are often compensating benefits elsewhere, as a drought, for example, in killing many plants will give others the opportunity to thrive. And even more certainly, what is natural is often bad. Earthquakes are relatively rare, but are in no way unnatural. Nor are illness, disease and a painful death. So what surely cannot be maintained, then, is the quasi-Romantic view that non-human nature (even excepting its unnatural parts) is a benevolent, kindly force, well disposed to its inhabitants, and something with which we might live in harmony, or as friends.[26] If this perspective is untenable, so, too, is its converse, the older view to which deep ecology is opposed. Nature shouldn't, surely, be treated always with suspicion as something malign, wholly alien and needing to be conquered and tamed. Both views are in strong danger of anthropomorphism, seeing nature as having certain plans or intentions, possessed of a certain character, and bearing certain relationships, either sympathetic or hostile, to human ends.

An objection sometimes raised here is that if certain evaluations are made too much from the human standpoint, so too is criticism of these evaluations. We need a broader perspective. So when it is claimed, with Barry Commoner, that "Nature knows best",[27] the thought is not that nature conforms to some particular human notions of value, but that nature, as a whole, looks after itself perfectly well. On this reading every alleged evil, as long as it occurs naturally, and doesn't result from human interventions, is a part of the whole unfolding of the natural order, and cannot be properly assessed independently of its contribution to that whole. When it is so assessed, the belief is that the appearance of evil will dissipate. Nature knows best for nature, even if this at times isn't especially accommodating to human interests and concerns. This may well be to underestimate the difficulty we have in refraining from these particular evaluations – it is, after all, perfectly natural deeply to regret a forest fire that wipes out thousands of animals and thousands of plants and lays waste to vast tracts of land – and seems to want it both ways. Does nature know best? All that is certain is that the universe has existed for as long as it has existed, and that within that universe, life has so far, for a short period, trundled along in one corner. What is best about this, what was best about ice ages, or swapping dinosaurs for mammals, or creating the species *Homo sapiens*, is deeply mysterious. Better, perhaps, if so large or distant a perspective is urged, to keep quiet about it.

It is difficult in a further way to get any useful purchase on this Commoner dictum. It appears at first to advocate quietism: as nature knows best so we cannot improve on it, and all our endeavours here, to rescue seabirds, save species from extinction, alleviate the effects of flood or drought, are wrong-headed. We should just let things be. A twist here is that such endeavours are certainly wrong-headed only on the assumption that the alleged evils have non-human rather than human causes. Considerable effort might need to be expended in ascertaining just how an apparent evil – global warming, the depletion of the ozone layer, the disappearance of sparrows – is brought about. If we find that we are the cause, we might attempt a cure, and the reaction of many is that this is effort wasted. What matters is the predictable consequences of some situation, and not the nature of its origins. On closer consideration it becomes clear that this message of quietism is sustainable only as long as we revert to what I have insisted is an untenable position, that human beings are radically distanced from nature. For otherwise our efforts at remedy are as much a part of nature, and as much a part of nature's knowing best, as the ill to which they are addressed. Swans attempt to salvage something of their nests if water levels rise; we build sea defences along the East Coast. So be it. And so be it, equally, if we destroy rainforests, empty the seas of fish or concrete Berkshire. If we are outside nature we should do nothing, whereas if we are within it we may do anything. Neither position is really tenable.

Losing Eden?

Should we then abandon all efforts to generalize about the relationships between nature and value, holding instead that the non-human world is morally neutral, while human beings are capable of good or ill to roughly equal degree? There is a rejoinder that deep ecologists might now make, and with considerable effectiveness, for it might be argued that rather more than I have so far suggested of what we do is unnatural, and so contrary not only to nature but to our own good. It might be argued that we as a species have somehow lost our way: language, reason, families and community may be natural but motorways, mass cities, an insatiable craving for newness, new goods and new experiences are not. Human life as it is currently lived in many parts of the world, and as it is aspired to in many further parts, is a perversion of nature, good for neither us nor the planet. There is scope here for serious, detailed and widespread criticism of much contemporary and global culture, and at the same time a description of an alternative but still human way of living, in which resonances with and responses to the non-human world are more deeply embedded within us. Living closer to nature than we currently do, becoming more accustomed to its ways, but at the same time altering nature, allowing that its good and ours may not always coincide, is a model for human existence that is often recommended, not only in the present day by those increasingly disaffected with a homogenized world, but throughout history. Witness Virgil, Montaigne, Voltaire, Goethe, Wordsworth and Chekhov, to name a handful critical of the unthinking drive to urban life. Is this unabashed sentimentalism? I think not. Although it will be impossible to prove any of what is suggested here, there is a nevertheless plausible story that can be told. As we are natural creatures, and products of evolution, it is not unreasonable to suppose that our well-being might depend on retaining some reasonably intimate connection with the kind of environment to which we have adapted, and might require that we accept ourselves as creations of nature, unable to transcend many of its limitations. No absolutist claim is being made here, that nature is good in itself, something that quite independently of its relationship to us we should want to sustain, and nor is it suggested that deviations from nature, even when genuine human benefits are thereby offered, ought not to be made. The point is only that it may be in our best interests to maintain some closeness of fit.

Yet this isn't quite deep ecology's story. The picture I am sketching here gives rather more space to culture, and urges a rather more discriminating attitude to non-human doings, than does the typical deep ecological account. Even if more or less the same ills are identified, the remedy, as sketched here, is less extreme. At the centre of the difference, once again, are attitudes to the wild. It is hard not to see deep ecology's reverence for pristine nature, virgin territory and untouched wilderness as very much an admission of defeat for most familiar notions of culture and society, and so for those correspondingly familiar notions of human life. I have hinted already at the residues of religion that everywhere penetrate deep ecological views, and they surface again here. For what seems to be a picture of human beings as irredeemably and long ago fallen, and the prelapsarian paradise as a place to recollect, occasionally still to wander in, but never again really to afford us a home, connects with Old Testament theology in explaining, first, this deeply ambivalent attitude to human beings – good in principle but not in practice – and, secondly, this respect for the wild, as a place we were made by God to dwell within.

There appear to be extremes here: arguably we are more jumbled than polarized, and wild nature can quite often present itself as a frightening, unfriendly or simply dull place in which to find oneself. So in spite of the calls to change attitudes, to reinvent and reinvigorate our relationships with the natural world, it is hard not to see in this a deeply pessimistic vision, in which the possibility of salvation, even if an article of faith, is not something in which one can any longer reasonably believe, and in which hopes for reconciliation between nature and culture are in effect abandoned. This is a blinkered vision. Deep ecologists may prefer the desert to Palm Springs, but in Europe one of our choices has been to replace parts of a marshy lagoon with the city of Venice. That is surely to put wilderness to good use. They may see, apart from food, little of value in the intensive farming of California's Central Valley, but it would be difficult to make the same point about the man-made landscapes of much of the north of Ireland, or the grass and heather uplands of the Yorkshire Moors, or the terraced olive groves of Corsica or Greece. In its reluctance to allow that we can, working with nature, do marvellous things, deep ecology betrays itself as victim to a puritanism of the most miserable kind.

Environmental fascism, or business as usual

Suppose we try to take deep ecology seriously. What difference will it make to our lives? It is often argued that it will change too much, insisting on substantial and ultimately unmotivated sacrifices of both human and animal well-being in the somewhat nebulous cause of abstract principle. Another concern is that deep ecology is, in the end, relatively undemanding and, because of its flexible and diverse approach, will allow most of us to carry on much as before. Either way, there are challenges to the deep ecological programme.

Take the former concern. Tom Regan was the first to make the suggestion, since then often repeated, that deep ecology, along with certain sister environmentalisms, is in some sense a fascistic movement.[28] This is presumably intended to offend, but, as there are two respects in which the accusation could be made, it might be unclear which offence should be taken. Fascists habitually put the community, the state and the fatherland first, and are prepared to sacrifice individuals to this supposedly greater good. Individual rights and individual lives hardly count. And they evince a deep distrust of reason, seeing in the Enlightenment ideal of rational man shallowness, superficiality and a mistaken rejection of the deeper, sometimes darker and often inchoate side of human nature.

With respect to the first component, it may not be easy to see why deep ecology should be singled out for attack. Regan's terse comment "Environmental fascism and the rights view are like oil and water: they don't mix" may come as no surprise, but of course a respect for rights will, in principle at least, generate opposition to a range of views. Fascists, communists and utilitarians will set individual well-being aside in pursuit of some greater good. But there are important differences here. Both communists and unreconstructed utilitarians are interested in the welfare of humankind. The sacrifice of the one, when it occurs, is made in the interests of a familiar many. But fascists have interests elsewhere, in more abstract ideas of the spirit of the people, or the nation's soul, or the tide of history. And they might sacrifice not only an individual, but also the collective good of humankind, in pursuit of this more abstract ideal. This difference helps explain, I think, why Regan sees parallels between fascism and holistic environmental philosophies in particular. There is an alleged good for systems of things, only some components of which are living, or sentient, which we are supposed to put before our own good, or even the good of human beings in general. This might seem to be getting priorities wrong. And now whereas some holists might attempt to explain and justify this hierarchy of values, deep ecology in particular often seems antithetical to familiar notions of reason and argument, seeing them as part and parcel of the dominant world view that it wants to reject.[29] Thus this important further respect in which the fascism charge might be levelled.

It is, however, resisted. Callicott allows that Leopold's land ethic appears "richly to deserve" Regan's hostile characterization. For it

> would seem to imply a draconian policy towards the human population, since almost all ecologists and environmentalists agree that, from the perspective of the integrity, diversity and stability of the biotic community, there are simply too many people and too few redwoods, white pines, wolves, bears, tigers, elephants, whales and so on . . . It would also seem to imply a merciless attitude towards non-human individual members of the biotic community. Sentient members of overabundant species, like rabbits and deer, may be (as actually presently they are) routinely culled, for the sake of the ecosystems of which they are a part . . . From the perspective of both humanism and its humane extension, the land ethic appears nightmarish in its own peculiar way.[30]

If the community comes first, individuals may suffer. And if the biotic community comes first, then millions of human beings may suffer. We, too, may be culled. But just as many utilitarians, when the going gets rough, temper the apparent excesses of their theory, so the land ethic might be rendered similarly hospitable. And, on Callicott's account:

> An ecosystemic environmental ethic does not prohibit human use of the environment, it requires, rather, that that use be subject to two ethical limitations . . .
>
> The first requires that human use of the environment, as nearly as possible, should enhance the diversity, integrity, stability and beauty of the biotic community . . .

The second . . . requires that trees cut for shelter or to make fields, animals slain for food or fur, and so on should be thoughtfully selected, skilfully and humanely dispatched, and carefully used so as not to waste or degrade them. The *individual* plant, animal or even rock or river consumed or transformed by human use deserves to be used respectfully.[31]

Several questions might be asked here, about "as nearly as possible", "thoughtfully", "respectfully" and the like, but the thrust is clear: we can continue to look after ourselves. Johnson, similarly, insists that the fascism charge depends on a too stodgy reading of holists' claims, arguing that to suppose, as Regan seems to suppose, that we must choose between individuals and wholes is not, wrongly, to have it both ways, when having it both ways is both possible and in the end necessary.[32]

It isn't, however, merely the moderate and moderating land ethicists who want to turn their acceptable face here, for deep ecologists, too, on a closer reading, emerge as rather less than extreme. There may well be tension between certain of the movement's principles, but these are resolved, in much of the further comment, in favour of less challenging views. So, for example, biocentric equality, and the insistence that "all things in the biosphere have an equal right to live and blossom",[33] will not only appear to put impossible demands on us, but will be in some sort of conflict with the third of the movement's basic principles, which allows that we might reduce richness and diversity when our vital needs are at stake. So, what do we do about this conflict? And what is covered under vital needs?

On both counts deep ecology turns out to be a paler thing than it seems at first glance. Egalitarianism holds only "in principle" because, as Naess immediately adds, "any realistic praxis necessitates some killing, exploitation, and suppression".[34] Treating everything equally is just not something we can be expected to do. Elsewhere he insists that "no right to" doesn't for him imply "ought not to",[35] so that although we have no right to kill for non-vital needs, such killing isn't immediately proscribed. Even if we stick with vital needs, it seems that a fairly generous interpretation is allowed, referring not only to what is necessary to sustain life, but also to certain styles of life. Devall and Sessions discuss the Alaskan Eskimos' relationship with the bowhead whale. Although it has always been hunted, in the 1970s the International Whaling Commission wanted to introduce a ban, on the grounds that these whales were members of an endangered species. The Eskimos resisted, insisting that their "myths and lifestyle were dependent on it".[36] Many environmentalists were in favour of the ban. Others, including Friends of the Earth, supported the Eskimos, as long as the number of whales taken was regulated, and only traditional methods of killing were used.[37]

Is killing whales, for Eskimos, a vital need? This is, as the authors readily allow, "left deliberately vague to allow for considerable latitude in judgement".[38]

Just as not only killing whales, but owning snowmobiles is, for some Eskimos, a vital need, so also no overnight change in the lifestyles of Westernized consumer society is envisaged. There is certainly realism here, and deep ecology, in line with its avowed political aims, cannot be dismissed as an ivory tower philosophy; but it might be suspected that there may in the end be too little firm principle, and too much room for compromise. The more generous our interpretation of such needs, the more environmental damage deep ecology allows. Perhaps fudging is inevitable here. Precisely because what holism appears to demand is so evidently unattainable, there is always the need for a considerably flexible approach. One of the dangers, though, is that while there is no denying the call for serious and wide-ranging changes, it may be that many of them are directed elsewhere. Leopold was able, within the land ethic, to justify the continuation of his hunting, shooting and fishing lifestyle, and deep ecologists similarly appear to find living in accord with their principles not particularly burdensome or onerous. Contrast this with the more unambiguous and stringent demands of utilitarian or rights-based approaches. Singer, by all accounts, found putting principle into practice not particularly easy.

Summary

Deep ecology characterizes its position on the environment as radical, wide-ranging and coherent. I have suggested, though, that there are many respects in which its claims, both about itself and about contrasting positions, might be met with justifiable reservation.

There is its strident and oppositional tone, for a start. The characterization of its own stance as deep – hardly an unloaded term – and its rejection of all alternatives, all criticism, as shallow is both wearing and, on at least two counts, unwarranted. Contrary views cannot all be lumped together, and not all of them are shallow.

There is, related to this, its ambition to restyle philosophy. This isn't a success. The endeavour to deconstruct much of "standard"[39] metaphysics and to replace it with something allegedly more accurate and more profound first misidentifies its target, and then fails to articulate and defend a rival account. This is not to say that all is well within the so-called standard approach, for, of course, there are many philosophical views, theories and positions that can well be criticized, and even rejected. What is unsatisfactory about the deep ecological approach is the implication that these supposedly non-deep views are of a piece, and that it is relatively easy to subject them to blanket dismissal.

There is, too, its apparent hostility to things human. Something approaching hostility is perhaps suggested by its claims, none of them fully worked out, about intrinsic value and biocentric equality. These claims alone require that we seriously downsize our position within the natural world, but deep ecology seems to believe further that there is something irredeemably spoiled within human nature, so that almost all of our substantial interventions within the non-human world – cities, large-scale agriculture, cutting and planting forests – are to be regretted. These sorts of attitudes can be explained, I suggested, by looking to deep ecology's geographical centres, on the one hand, and its susceptibility to puritan elements within the Christian tradition, on the other. Its belief in its reasoned and dispassionate approach to environmental, political and social concerns might, then, be queried.

There isn't, however, a surfeit of idealism. Deep ecology isn't, as it rightly insists, fascistic, thoroughly anti-human and impossible to follow. It is, in contrast, curiously flexible, suspicious of principle and accommodating. Take its rejection of things human. This, as I have suggested, is not in the end as thoroughgoing as it at first appears. The misinterpretations here may well be deep ecology's own fault, for it has chosen to advertise itself as radical, new, and quite at odds with the otherwise all-pervasive shallowness. Only on a closer reading does its more moderate, less forceful and less exciting side appear. New clothes, but the same emperor.

These criticisms of deep ecology are, as is evident, marked. Yet I don't at all want to insist that it has nothing to recommend it. As suggested in Chapter 1, an abiding concern for truth may well stand in the way of effective action. The concern in this book is with truth, but there is a world beyond. Deep ecologists fully recognize this, sit in no tower and end up with dirty hands. That is to be commended.

CHAPTER 9
Value

Even if thought about the environment does involve various areas of philosophical inquiry, moral questions remain in many ways central. But answers to such questions can only be given, and decisions about what we ought to do only be made, against a wider and more general background concerning the relative values of certain situations or states of affairs as against others. Even if morality is not simply about producing the best outcomes, any plausible view will at least take those outcomes into account. So there is a need to engage with ethical matters more widely construed, deciding what sorts of situations are in any way valuable or worthwhile, and then, of course, which are more valuable or worthwhile than others. This isn't straightforward. As well as measurement problems, encountered when two admittedly valuable situations compete for attention, there are further and prior difficulties in deciding what sorts of values are relevant, what sorts of things, events or situations might possess these values, and what to do, how to adjudicate, if it turns out that different sorts of values are on the table. So the philosophical perspective will remain broad: the normative questions have need of various metaethical and axiological inquiries.

All this, of course, has surfaced already. The several attempts to extend our moral responsibilities further and further beyond the range of human concerns have each raised questions, first, as to the legitimacy of such extensions, and, secondly, as to how, assuming legitimacy, the ensuing moral dilemmas might best be tackled. And at least tentative answers to various of these questions have been offered in passing. What I need to do here, though, is give deeper and more focused attention to the more important of these questions. Several claims, some contentious, will emerge. Central among them will be the claim, levelled against deep ecologists but not them alone, that there is no defensible notion of intrinsic value that involves our having substantial obligations towards the natural world.

Instrumental/non-instrumental

Start with some familiar territory. In a world containing living things, all of which can be said to have a good of their own, almost everything is in some measure valuable in so far as it contributes to the good, the well-being of something or other. Exercise, vegetables and a glass of wine contribute to our well-being, just as mice, voles and dark nights further the good of owls, and water, sunlight and fertilizers aid the flourishing of plants. There is no evident tension between the examples here, but clearly what is of value or benefit to one thing may be of disvalue to, dangerous for, another. The manure that helps my roses will not do me, or my cat, or my fish any good at all. So as there are very many things that have a good of their own, and which might or might not flourish, so very many things, as they help further this good, therefore have *instrumental value*.

Where human beings are concerned instrumental value can be understood in a different way. As we have a range of interests and concerns, not all of which are connected with our well-being or good, so the things that help further those interests or concerns can be said to be of instrumental value to us. Because I want a good bike, developments in suspension technology, promising to improve the ride, are of value to me. And drugs, and then in turn the means to acquire drugs, are of value to those seeking particular psychological states. Thus something is of instrumental value when it serves to promote some end, whether that end is given by nature, and thus a part of a thing's flourishing, or whether it is self-selected, in which case the connection with flourishing may be strained.

I mention nature here, and began by speaking of living things. Should we extend this, and claim, for example, that oil is of value to a car, in that it enables it to do what a car is supposed to do? We might, and if we allow (as I have suggested we should) that oil is good for a car, and then connect "good for" with "of value to", then we should. But the connection here is one that many will want to deny, on the grounds that a car has neither desires of its own, nor ends given by nature. So oil is valuable to us, the objection will go, in so far as we want cars to perform well. Yet I still have reservations about making this distinction between the natural and non-natural worlds. Suppose that creation stories are true, and natural things are designed by God. As that doesn't in itself imply that trees don't have a good of their own, so our making cars doesn't rule out their having a good of their own, and doesn't rule out, in turn, the things that further that good – oil, balanced wheels, a well-tuned engine – being of value to cars. And what gaps there are between nature and artifice might be plugged in two further ways. We might build self-replicating, self-repairing machines. And we might in time build machines – computers, robots, cybermen – that choose their own ends.[1] Then, certainly, there will be instrumental values whether or not there are living things.

Are there *non-instrumental values* as well? It is often said that not all values can be of the instrumental kind, whereby a thing is valuable as a means to some good, and that some things must be valuable as ends, or have value in themselves. This, though, has been criticized on the grounds that it is in principle possible for one instrumental value to lead to another, *ad infinitum,* valuing exercise for the sake of health, health for the sake of procreation, that for the sake of children, and from there to someone to take over the family business, to keeping faith with grandparents, and so on.[2] The criticism here might seem laboured, but it remains the case that the argument for non-instrumental values is not straightforward. There is no logical need for a point of termination. Moreover, even when there is such a point, it won't follow that some non-instrumental value is therefore uncovered. So even granting that fertilizer is of instrumental value to, or is good for, trees, and even supposing that the good of trees serves no further purpose, and promotes no good elsewhere, there is still the question of whether it is a good thing, valuable in itself, that trees should flourish, and have their good, or well-being. Similarly, exercise may be good for human beings, and the good of human beings may serve no further good, but whether it is good, or valuable, that there are human beings is, some will think, moot.

Yet even if instrumental value doesn't straightforwardly issue in values of a non-instrumental kind, that there are such values is beyond dispute. Consider human beings again. Often, of course, we want things for the sake of something else, valuing them instrumentally, but often too we want things just for their own sake. And so there are non-instrumental values. Hedonists insist that the only thing we can value for its own sake is pleasure, and that everything else is valued as a means to pleasure, but that must be wrong, as we value, first, other mental states and, secondly, and more importantly, many objects, events, states of affairs that lie out there, beyond us, as parts of the world. Although not averse to pleasure, it is not as a means to cultivating pleasant states of mind that I value Mahler, or peace in Northern Ireland, or my bicycle, or certain shades of grey. And it has been proposed[3] that we might refer here to *personal values*, a term that seems doubly apt, alluding both to the dependence of this kind of value on persons who do the valuing, and also to the variation from person to person of the things so valued: I value a walk in the hills while you value an afternoon on the beach; Uncle Tom values military marches while Aunt Hetty values Liberace; and so on. "Person" might, however, be interpreted liberally – all that is required is some quasi-personal mind – and so we might speak as well of a club or committee's valuing, say, success in the league, of a dog's valuing some well-chewed toy, or a robot's valuing the company of other robots.

Yet the range of things that we value for their own sake is very wide, as already indicated in the examples above, and there are reasons for wanting to make further distinctions within the category of non-instrumental values found here. First, then, some of our preferences are idiosyncratic or quirky, such that we might say they exhibit *merely* personal values. Marches, Liberace, film stars' dresses and old corkscrews are like this. Perhaps nothing is valued by just one person, but the examples here are all, and I think uncontroversially, very much minority pursuits. Elsewhere our values coincide, as when, for a while, millions value the Spice Girls, or hula hoops or, for a longer while, the fortunes of Manchester United, or performances of Handel's *Messiah*. Secondly, although some of the things we want for their own sake are things we want for ourselves – mountain bikes, corkscrews, to see Venice, to stroke a cat – others we want on behalf of other people or (though the distinction here will often be blurred) just for themselves. Thirdly, although there is of course the thought that while some of the things we value are, whether quirky or widespread, merely matters of taste, opinion or subjective preference, others may seem to be such that we *ought* to value them, and have in some way or other objective value.

If, as here, our concern is with things that people value, then of course talk of personal values is not wholly inappropriate. But there are reasons for wanting a richer vocabulary when something is valued by many, or when what is valued is not to the person's benefit, or, and especially, when what is valued is, arguably, something that ought to be valued. These different reservations about personal values can overlap: peace in Ireland is something I want for others, rather than myself; the survival of Venice I may want for its own sake; while the continued existence of wilderness areas, on this increasingly crowded planet, is widely believed to be something we all ought to value, but neither for our sakes nor for the sakes of any creatures that happen to live there.

How far, though, can the claims about objectivity, about there being things that we ought to value, be defended? "Ought" has different uses. Two uses, to do with consistency, can soon be set aside. I cite my aunt's fondness for Liberace as an instance of a merely personal value, and in so doing suggest that hers is a taste no one ought to have. But in so far as this is her taste, then she ought, first, to value what aids its satisfaction. If she wants his records she ought to care that junk shops stay in business. Generally, if someone values something as an end, then they ought to value the means to that end. Secondly, given her taste, she ought to care that my Liberace records, stashed away in the garage, are not accidentally destroyed. Given an end, one ought to value the several manifestations of that end. The "oughts" here are relatively weak, and relatively unimportant. They get going only after some end is first established, and have need of persons, with values, for their cogency.

A further use of "ought" is more important. Many people value health. Yet it is hard to believe that this is just a widespread quirk among us. Rather, the thought is, health is something that it is normal and natural to want and to value. Good health is a component in human flourishing. And so it seems plausible to claim that health is something we ought to value, not because it is a means to some further end that we happen to value but because there is something unnatural, or at odds with our being human, in not valuing it. It is a part of, rather than a route to, our living good lives.

It will be objected, however, that the explanation here isn't good enough. Even allowing that it is unnatural to disregard health, this alone cannot issue in any recognizable notion of obligation. We might say of the stunted tree, the wall-eyed cat or the purple lemon that these are similarly unnatural, and that it would be better for them if they were, but not that they ought to be, different from the way they are. If we ought to value our health, that must be because it is, independently of our actual desires, desirable, good, valuable that what is natural for human beings should obtain. And given the connection here, then if it is, similarly, desirable, good, valuable that trees should live and die according to nature, valuable that deserts should continue to exist, and valuable that there should be considerable diversity among life on earth, then we have reason to, ought to, promote trees, deserts and bio-diversity.

I might now pull some of this together and make, at the same time, one or two additional points. Many things, I have suggested, are instrumentally valuable in that they further the well-being of different kinds of creatures. Other things help further, not this, but the satisfaction of human or quasi-human desires. The connection with well-being may, in such cases, be tenuous. There are non-instrumental values as well, as human beings, at least, do want various things to exist, or situations to obtain, not as a means to some further end, but as an end in themselves. At least some of this may be usefully described in terms of personal values, but there are questions about how widely that term should be deployed. It is, for example, perhaps inappropriate to think of a concern for our general well-being as among our personal values. But then how should we think of such a concern? There is a question of whether that well-being itself is (non-instrumentally) of value, whether it is good in itself that creatures like us should flourish. Similarly for other creatures, and other things.

There are questions still to pursue, then, but others, which might be asked, can already be answered. While it is correct, if not particularly helpful, to say that something is valuable if it is of value to something or other, it is incorrect, surely, to suppose that if something is valuable then it is valued. Something is valued only if there is some person or quasi-person, some valuer, who actually values that thing. Valuing requires an attitude of mind. And yet were there no people, and no minds, valuable things might still exist. Uncontroversially, there would still be instrumental values; water would still be of value to, good for, trees. More controversially there would be still be non-instrumental values; it might still be valuable, good, that there are trees. It is incorrect too, to think that "valuable" means, as taking the look of the word too seriously might suggest,[4] "able to be valued". That covers too much, as various valuers are both possible and able, given the right circumstances, to value anything at all. Nor, of course, does it mean "ought to be valued". That covers too little.

Intrinsic value

How should we describe the sort of non-instrumental value that, according to some, health, for example, can be seen to possess? A familiar suggestion is that it has *intrinsic value*. But can this right? It depends, of course, on what "intrinsic" is taken to mean.

On one reading, where "intrinsic" simply means "non-instrumental", the existence of intrinsic value is already established. But we impoverish ourselves in using the term in this way. Pokémon may be valued as an end, not as a means, may be valued for its own sake, for itself, but it is surely not valuable in itself. Similarly for Havana cigars, flavoured vodka, Milan fashions and so on, through a range of contemporary and adult tastes. It is implausible to suppose that these things should exist for their own sake, irrespective of human desire, or that we who don't value them are somehow failing to get to grips with what is truly valuable. Given, on the one hand, the offer of "personal value" as a term to pick out what is valuable in so far as we happen to value it, and given, on the other, the claim that the value of certain things may not depend at all on our valuings, it is at the very least confusing to equate "intrinsic" with "non-instrumental".

A second and narrower reading, picking out only a subset of non-instrumental values, may fare better. It can, as I have suggested, be argued that health is something we ought to value for its own sake, and that to fail to want and to value health is to fail to promote our own good, to fail to realize our potential as human beings. And a similar argument can be used in relation to further alleged goods. Enjoying the company of friends, behaving morally, having and caring for children, or pursuing some medium- to long-term interests or goals can all be urged as genuinely constitutive of, and not simply as a means to, a fully fledged human life. Add these to the appreciations of art and nature, and an impressive list of candidates for intrinsic value begins to emerge. Nor need the items on this list be so resolutely focused on states of the human mind, for if appreciation of art is intrinsically valuable, so, too, is art itself, with, surely, certain works being more valuable than others. If there is value in understanding, living with or respecting nature, then there is value in nature itself, as the thing we understand, live with or respect. And nor is there good reason to retreat here to claiming that these things are either of merely personal value, things we merely happen to care for, or that they are of instrumental value, productive of valuable states of mind.[5]

Nevertheless, there are reasons to doubt that this gets us very far. And both where human beings, on the one hand, and the larger environment, on the other, are concerned, it will be claimed that there is space for a richer, more solid account of intrinsic value than the one being canvassed here. Such a claim, I'll suggest, is more clearly and fully defensible in the former case than in the latter.

Consider the value that might be alleged to reside in Beethoven's piano sonatas. This depends, presumably, on their subtle and complex contribution to human well-being, and also on their various ways of reflecting something of what that well-being involves. Nothing so far suggests that Beethoven has value wholly independently of human concerns. So although we may be tempted to think that human beings ought to value Beethoven, we wouldn't want to succumb to this temptation where Martians are concerned. Perhaps, more controversially, Martians wouldn't do anything wrong, were we to die out first, in neglecting to care for Beethoven's scores. But now if the value in art is in this way human centred, so, too, on the account presented so far, is the value in nature. We have evolved in a world where the sky is blue and the grass is green, and arguably we ought to want to continue in such a world, but there is no obvious reason why Martians should value earth's nature in the way or to the extent that we do. There is not yet, then, the suggestion that nature is valuable just in itself, quite independently of human interests and concerns.

Focusing on human beings like this is not, as I have already hinted, the only way in which the account given so far falls short of what believers in intrinsic value tend to want. What I have suggested is that certain components in human flourishing are things that we ought to want or value, in so far as it might be considered unnatural not to want these things, and not care about our own flourishing or well-being. What I haven't said is that it is good in itself that human beings should flourish, or that their lives should go well. Some of the gap here might be filled in. Remember my harping on about sentience? Pain is bad, and bad, surely, just in itself, independently of further considerations, intrinsically. So if there are human beings it would be bad in itself were their lives to go badly, just in so far as these bad lives would cause them pain. And if there are human beings who, supposing they do not flourish, then their lives are full of pain, then flourishing is good.

The environmentalist might exploit this in two respects. First, there is now room for claims to intrinsic value beyond the human domain, for a parallel case can be put on behalf of other sentient creatures. Given that they exist, it is better that their lives go well, and that they avoid the intrinsic badness of pain. Secondly, where human beings and other animals are concerned it can be argued that just as pain is bad, so pleasure is good. So where flourishing brings pleasure, it is good in itself that flourishing should occur. The life of sentient creatures, when it goes well, is intrinsically valuable.

Of course, I allow the first point here, even if I have reservations about the second, but it evidently doesn't get environmentalists very far. Their concern is predominantly with nature, and what they are after, where intrinsic value is concerned, is a non-instrumental value that is wholly independent of human concerns, and that depends, as it has been recently and usefully said, "entirely on the nature of its bearer".[6] It is possible in some ways to get close to this. The value of mice for owls, like that of manure for roses, has nothing at all to do with what we think or believe, with what will do us good, or what will chime in any way with our condition. But though the values here are appropriately distanced, they are resolutely instrumental. The value of mice depends on the digestion of owls. Instrumentality, in turn, can be avoided if we are prepared to recognize, as I have insisted we should, that there is such a thing as the well-being, the flourishing, the good of turtles, aphids or ferns. What falls between the fingers here is any robustness to value. We can allow that there are these goods, that they have nothing to do with us, and yet still wonder why we should care, or in any way bother ourselves to preserve or promote them. Perhaps turtles feel pain. Then they are of direct concern and, if promoting pleasure is also good, we might want there to be more turtles. But this has no bearing on the status either of non-sentient creatures, or of the non-living but natural things with which the environmentalist is so often concerned. What is so far profoundly unclear is that there are good reasons to believe, as many environmentalists would have us believe, that certain natural things have a value that derives neither from the things' being sentient, nor from life, nor from their having any instrumental value either to human beings or to other things, nor again from subtler human evaluations, and yet which nevertheless imposes some sorts of obligations upon us. It is easy enough to *say* there are such values – to say, for example, that a desert ought to continue to exist, irrespective of its relationships to living things, human and non-human – but it is somewhat less easy to explain and justify such claims. Make do, though, with something less, and we are so far without intrinsic value in its richest and most often invoked sense.

Other views

The taxonomy of value is, therefore, complex. Further complexities, inessential to present concerns, can be ignored here, but the picture that I have tried to sketch might become a little clearer by plotting against it some of the accounts offered elsewhere. Many writers have commented on the scheme of values, not always persuasively, but often in ways that can usefully be explored. In particular, there are accounts that make use of a term I noted earlier, but have so far overlooked in this chapter: inherent value. Paul Taylor finds much use for this, and for intrinsic value as well, describing both at some length in a survey of value terms:

(5) *The intrinsically valued.* An entity is intrinsically valued . . . only in relation to its being valued in a certain way by some human valuer. The entity may be a person, animal, plant, a physical object, a place, or even a social practice. Any such entity is intrinsically valued insofar as some person cherishes it, holds it dear or

precious, loves, admires or appreciates it for what it is in itself, and so places intrinsic value on its existence. This value is independent of whatever instrumental or commercial value it might have. When something is intrinsically valued by someone, it is deemed by that person to be worthy of being preserved and protected because it is the particular thing it is. Thus, the people of a society may place intrinsic value on a ceremonial occasion (the coronation of a king), on historically significant objects (the original Declaration of Independence) and places (the battlefield at Gettysburg) on ruins of ancient cultures (Stonehenge), on natural wonders (the Grand Canyon) and of course on works of art. Intrinsic value may also be placed on living things, which then are intrinsically valuable to (have intrinsic value for) human valuers. A pet dog or cat, an endangered population of rare plants, or a whole wilderness area can be considered worth preserving for just what they are. Finally, anyone we love and care about has this kind of intrinsic value for us. From a moral point of view, correlative with intrinsically valuing something is the recognition of a negative duty not to destroy, harm, damage, vandalize, or misuse the thing and a positive duty to protect it from being destroyed, harmed, damaged, vandalized or misused by others.

(6) *Inherent worth.* This is value something has simply in virtue of the fact that it has a good of its own. To say that an entity has inherent worth is to say that its good (welfare) is deserving of the concern and consideration of all moral agents and that the realization of its good is something to be promoted and protected as an end in itself and for the sake of the being whose good it is. Since it is only with reference to living things, (humans, animals, or plants) that it makes sense to speak of promoting or protecting their well-being and of doing this for their sake, having inherent worth is extensionally equivalent to the class of living beings.[7]

Several things here are worthy of comment. First, Taylor's account of intrinsic value is not that most often advanced either within environmental philosophy, or elsewhere; his *inherent worth* is closer. Although a contrast is clearly intended, the detail of the contrast is less clear. His position on intrinsic value resembles, in several respects, that which I have characterized as personal value – value that derives from the attitude of some human valuer. But whereas I took pains to point out that values here could be quirky, Taylor's examples are all of things about which it might be said that valuing is appropriate, such that someone who fails to see value in Stonehenge, the Grand Canyon, works of art and so on is making some sort of mistake. So what the examples, in contrast to the initial description, suggest is that Taylor has in view here that subset of personal values about which I said that their relationship to human well-being might well make positive valuations appropriate. This is borne out by the otherwise puzzling comment on duties. To say that my aunt has any duties with respect to her Liberace collection is surely wrong.

As far as inherent worth is concerned, there is some lack of clarity about exactly when any contentious claim is made. I have agreed that a rabbit has a good of its own. Have I therefore agreed with Taylor that the rabbit has inherent worth, or do I agree with that only if I further agree that the rabbit's well-being should be of any concern to me? Inherent worth is uncontroversial if it needs only the first claim, while it will be strongly resisted if it requires the second as well. In obfuscating just when and how this value begins to emerge, Taylor might find more agreement than he deserves.

The account as a whole bears a complex relationship, then, to more standard views on intrinsic value. Inherent worth is clearly and intentionally restricted to living things, for as Taylor points out, only there does it make sense to talk of promoting well-being, but that restriction might seem arbitrary. Why shouldn't the Grand Canyon equally be "deserving of the concern and consideration of all moral agents" and, if it is, then why the premium on life? Perhaps Taylor's view is that desert here depends on a thing's having a good of its own, and cannot otherwise be sustained. Then his examples of intrinsic value, all of them in one way or another worthy, are once again puzzling.

Tom Regan, similarly, stands to one side of the standard terminology in referring to inherent value as that possessed by those animals (human beings included) that are subjects-of-a-life. But his position is simpler than Taylor's, as no contrasting reference to intrinsic value is made, and Regan appears to construe the former term just as the latter is standardly understood, even though giving it a much narrower application.[8] So subjects-of-a-life have value in themselves and for themselves, and have this value quite independently of human concerns or evaluations. The narrower application may, though, be tentative: "Inherent value, then, belongs equally to those who are the experiencing subjects of a life. Whether it belongs to others – to rocks and rivers, trees and glaciers, for example – we do not know. And may never know".[9] This is surely disingenuous. Inherent value accrues to subjects-of-a-life, as explained earlier, in virtue of consciousness, purpose and so on. Regan presumably does know that rivers and trees have no mental life at all, so he is presumably affecting to believe that there may turn out to be some quite different basis on which such value might be assigned. "Turn out", however, is odd. What might we never know, either about rivers or about value, on which such evaluations might hinge?

While Regan's circumscribed account of a quasi-intrinsic value might be thought defensible, a further account, wider ranging, is not. In "Intrinsic value, environmental obligation and naturalness",[10] Robert Elliott advances what he calls an "indexical theory of intrinsic value", which can crudely be represented as "the claim that a thing has intrinsic value if it is approved of by a valuer in virtue of its properties".[11] The crudity here is on Elliott's own admission, and the account is in certain respects refined, but the first steps towards this refinement are not particularly illuminating:

> when George says "X has intrinsic value", his assertion will be true only if George approves of X. Whether Georgina or anyone else approves of X is beside the point. Similarly when Georgina says "X has intrinsic value" her assertion will be true only if Georgina approves of X. Whether George or anyone else approves of X is irrelevant.[12]

Yet on the face of it, if "X has intrinsic value" is true, it would seem, contrary to this, that in uttering that sentence I make a true assertion whether or not I approve of X. So there are puzzles here, and strong hints of both relativism and subjectivism, both of which Elliott acknowledges to be implicated in his account, and the latter at least of which he sees as among its virtues. I will need to discuss that in more general terms below, but for the moment I want only to look at a prior difficulty. In what I have quoted here, Elliott claims, consistently with the subjectivism he is after, that approval is necessary for intrinsic value. But the earlier representation, "value if it is approved of", is couched in terms of sufficient conditions. This isn't a mere slip, as the surrounding discussion makes clear, and it seems reasonable to think the intention is that both conditions are operative. But there are difficulties with sufficiency, whether or not it stands alone. First, there is no attempt here to distinguish between intrinsic value as it is commonly understood, and what I have called personal value, as when I approve (unlike George, Georgina and very many others) of the way in which paint seems to change in both colour and texture as it dries. Again, to say that there is intrinsic value here is at best simply to miss an opportunity to make some worthwhile distinctions. Secondly, however, Elliott appears not even adequately to distinguish between intrinsic and instrumental value. That is, although nothing he says rules out there being instrumental values that are not approved of, his account does seem to imply that if I approve (as well I might) of dentistry, bleach or anti-virus software, then such things are intrinsically valuable.[13] Elliott grants that his theory might be seen as offering only "a deflated, deficient or truncated notion of intrinsic value". In some important respects it might offer too little, but in other important respects it offers too much.

Finally, I will mention briefly a view that is, in several respects, congenial, and which encourages reflection on a pair of terms that have so far been given scant attention here: *anthropocentric* and *non-anthropocentric*. Eugene Hargrove sees the way forward as involving, as he puts it, weak anthropocentric intrinsic value.[14] I am not concerned with the details, but just with highlighting certain of the difficulties with these somewhat slippery terms. Hargrove characterizes Taylor's account, discussed above, as one that (via inherent worth) proposes an uncontroversial non-anthropocentric account of intrinsic value – uncontroversial, at least, "if all that is claimed is that these entities have sakes or goods of their own".[15] He goes on:

> It is only anthropocentric intrinsic value assignments – judgements made by humans that such and such living and nonliving entities are non-instrumentally (intrinsically) valuable – that fully and truly depend upon human judgement, rather than mere discovery, and are not ever reducible to facts or scientific hypotheses.[16]

Yet something seems to be missing here. Taylor's non-anthropocentric account is uncontroversial, in Hargrove's view, because it deals in "disguised facts". No genuine values are involved in understanding what it takes for monkeys, aphids or kelp to thrive. Surely, though, if the account dealt in more, it wouldn't thereby forfeit non-anthropocentrism. Of course, judgements are made by and depend on human beings, but anthropocentrism is usually taken to involve more than that, and to involve, in particular, the idea that the truth of what is judged also depends on human beings. So the claim that it is good in itself that there are tigers, good that they flourish, is a claim to non-anthropocentric intrinsic value of a controversial kind. It isn't reducible to facts, it is made by human beings, but its truth depends on how it is with tigers, and not at all on how it is with us. Hargrove may well be right that, in the end, such claims cannot be sustained, but there is no need to throw in the towel at this very early stage.

Intrinsic value and the environment

It ought by now to be tolerably clear just how claims about intrinsic value are best understood. If tigers are intrinsically valuable, then it is good in itself that there are tigers, irrespective of their larger environmental role, irrespective of our feelings for tigers and irrespective of how any threat to tigers should come about. Among environmentalists the making of such claims is widespread, but are they essential? It has been said that they are, and that "To hold an environmental ethic is to hold that non-human beings and states of affairs in the natural world have intrinsic value".[17] As Robin Attfield has more recently pointed out, this (assuming a plausible account of what intrinsic value is[18]) flies in the face of the activities of many seeming environmental ethicists, and projects an unnecessarily narrow construal of their field. Better, then, to allow questions relating to such value to be raised, and then answered either way, within the framework of the subject as a whole.

One question asks just what sorts of things are supposed to have this value, and for what sorts of reasons. At least partial answers have already been encountered here. Thus it is claimed that wild animals, indigenous plants, certain natural features, ecosystems, species and the biosphere as a whole are intrinsically valuable.[19] It is claimed also (as this list might already suggest) that it is at least in part in virtue of displaying certain characteristics that such things are in this way valuable, and among these characteristics being alive, naturalness, diversity, beauty and rarity are often singled out as of particular importance. I will focus on such characteristics here. They are central for many environmentalists, and in considering them further light is thrown on value issues more generally.

A first concern is with the relation between the things said to have intrinsic value and the properties in virtue of which this value accrues. These properties might be either essential or accidental to the things in question. A particular ecosystem will be only contingently diverse, or beautiful, whereas the naturalness, and perhaps also the beauty, of tigers is essential to their being tigers. Might these properties similarly be either intrinsic or relational in respect of their bearers? Following certain famous observations of G. E. Moore,[20] it has often been suggested that intrinsic value is a function of a thing's intrinsic properties; that the value it has in itself is because of how it is in itself. Yet that, in turn, is seen as in tension with certain key claims about the location of such value, to which relational properties are evidently important. Rarity, most notably, is often seen as conferring a special value on certain natural objects – tigers, snails, orchids and so on. But it is certainly not an intrinsic property of tigers that they are rare. As John O'Neill has insisted, rarity is "irreducibly relational".[21] So if tigers are intrinsically valuable even in part because they are rare, the Moorean suggestion has to go. Yet there is an alternative, for it is surely just a mistake to think that rarity contributes to intrinsic value. Suppose it is allowed that tigers, the individual animals, each have intrinsic value. The more tigers, the larger the population, the greater the amount of such value there is. Conversely, as tigers become rarer, their total value diminishes. But, of course, as they become rarer, so each remaining tiger gains considerably in instrumental value, as a means of keeping the species, and hence substantial tiger populations, in existence. O'Neill is surely right to hold that rarity is often seen as intrinsically valuable, but wrong to suppose that confused thinking here provides any reason to deny that intrinsic value derives from intrinsic properties. And he is wrong in a different way in holding that diversity, too, is irreducibly relational. Suppose that there is considerable species diversity in a square mile of rainforest. That is an intrinsic, although contingent, property of that area of forest. Again, there is no reason to dump Moore's claim. This doesn't show that Moore is right, of course, but so far the dependence of intrinsic value on intrinsic properties appears to stand.

There may be more of a difficulty with a further favoured candidate, that of naturalness. It might be argued that such and such a feature – a pond, a tree, a desert – is natural or otherwise, in part in virtue of its history, and that we might fabricate, say, a pond, suitably locating it, refashioning the land, introducing apposite life forms, in such a way that no internal inspection can discover that it is the product of artifice. But, many environmentalists will want to say, a pond produced by human endeavours is less intrinsically valuable than an indistinguishable pond that results wholly from natural processes. A similar point can be made about tigers. The thing having intrinsic value has both a certain internal structure and a certain origin; it is the natural offspring of a pair of tigers. Martian tigers, cloned tigers or synthesized tigers are arguably less valuable. But having one origin, rather than the other, is evidently not an internal, or intrinsic, property of a thing.[22] And so, given that naturalness is intrinsically valuable, Moore's claim does now have to go.

I will mention, in brief, two ways in which the difficulty here might be tackled. First, one might read Attfield's suggestion, that intrinsic value depends "entirely on the nature of its bearer",[23] somewhat generously, such that the natural and artificial ponds, like the standard and the synthesized tigers, are said to have different natures. Secondly, one might posit some sort of role for essentiality after all, suggesting that a difference between naturalness and rarity here is that the relational properties implicated in the former alone are essential to a thing's being of a certain kind. Change the origin, and you no longer have tigers at all, but simulacra, whereas change the rarity, and genuine tigers remain.

What, though, of the candidates themselves? Many environmentalists do believe that diversity is intrinsically valuable, that it is good in itself that there is a wide range of natural phenomena and forms of life still in existence on the surface of the earth. Yet it is very hard to see why anyone should think this. What is emphatically discounted is that the value of diversity should be construed in instrumental terms, even though it is undeniable that there is such value. It is to our advantage, and to the advantage of many other species, that there is variation in habitats, foods, raw materials and so on. What is also emphatically discounted is that this value should be construed in non-instrumental but nevertheless anthropocentric terms. That we like there to be different plants in a wood, different birds in the garden and different sorts of places in which to holiday does not give diversity its intrinsic value. But having made the discounts, it is not clear what is left to support the value claim or give it any advantages over a rival candidate, uniformity. That might seem just as good, or better, and a wholly undifferentiated Parmenidean sphere just as, or more, valuable in itself than a blistered and pitted planet teeming with life.

This sphere would, of course, exhibit to a quite marked degree another candidate for value, stability. But again, setting instrumental and anthropocentric considerations to one side, it is not clear why this should be thought valuable. Stability can be dull, and although it might gratify certain types, the

Parmenidean model is not obviously better than a universe of imploding galaxies, exploding stars and wobbly solar systems. (Although, of course, it may just be unclear what is meant by stability here. This planet has undergone many upheavals and radical changes in personnel. Are we to think that it would, in a way, be better in itself were dinosaurs and cycads still to dominate, or are we, as often seems to be suggested, to construe these changes as consistent with stability?)

Beauty is problematic in a different way, and one that might be thought to cast serious doubt on the entire intrinsic value programme. The difficulty here, I think, is in arriving at any conception of beauty that is suitably distanced from anthropocentric concerns. I think tigers are beautiful and toads less so, but might it be said that in viewing matters in this way I am thinking of beauty, not instrumentally, but still in human terms, in terms of what pleases me, or, more generously, of what tends to a much wider appeal, but an appeal still to those partaking of human nature? Toads, after all, might think differently. So what we need to do, the defender of intrinsic value might claim, is to consider how beautiful things are in themselves, and not in so far as they square with any of our tastes, interests or concerns. Yet it is not at all clear what this radically non-anthropocentric notion of beauty is supposed to come to. There seem to be two possibilities: either everything is equally beautiful, or there are differentials in beauty, which are detectable from some non-anthropocentric and neutral standpoint. But it isn't clear, first, how we could select between these alternatives, or, secondly, how either could allow us in any coherent way to promote or protect the intrinsic beauty of the natural world. Either what we do, other than altering the number of things, makes no difference, or, although we do make a difference, we cannot tell whether it is for better or for worse.

The larger doubt that is uncovered here concerns the broader tension between our having any knowledge of what is truly valuable on the one hand, and the demand for full-blooded non-anthropocentrism on the other. The difficulty is particularly pronounced with beauty, where, having dropped anthropocentrism, we cannot be expected even to identify the property at all, but it is no less pressing elsewhere. We know what diversity is, but cannot really be expected to know, I have suggested, whether it, or its opposite, is valuable. And what of other properties? Suppose it is suggested that size matters, and the bigger the universe the better; or that angles are better or worse than curves; or that noise or haze or stickiness are good; or that reds and greens are preferable to blues and yellows. The problem here is not the very general one of our being unable to occupy any other than the human perspective. If that is true, it is nevertheless innocuous with respect to many properties, and we can, I am happy to allow, form a perfectly adequate conception of what, say, squareness, expansion or diversity are in themselves. The problem is in giving up perspectives, and then doing anything worthwhile where value is concerned. Either we can form no conception whatsoever of what is valuable just in itself or, having formed such a conception, we can still do nothing about seeing where and where not such value lies. Either way, our hands are tied.

Biocentric egalitarianism

A further difficulty, where intrinsic value is concerned, is in the oft-encountered suggestion that such value obtains, where it obtains at all, to equal degrees. The difficulty is acute wherever it occurs, but even so is more acute in some areas than in others.

I said that value derives from properties, and now certain properties may be more amenable to stories about equal value than others. The advantages here are held by middling approaches. Consider again the life-centred theories of Schweitzer and Taylor. It is, first, not implausible to hold that all living things, assuming perhaps that they are not very close to either birth or death, are equally alive. So if being alive is the property in virtue of which things are intrinsically valuable, it would not seem implausible, secondly, to hold that living things are equally valuable. As I have suggested earlier, however, the attractiveness of such a view is superficial, for there are several difficulties in working out its implications. Why think either that an elephant is just as valuable as a beetle or, assuming that it has more parasites on and within it, that it is more valuable?

Even this limited and temporary appeal of a life-centred account is wanting, however, if intrinsic value is connected with other properties. Regan insists, as I noted above, that the various subjects-of-a-life have equal inherent value. In the background here, as I noted earlier, is Kant, whose views on the equal worth of and respect for all human beings many have found uncompelling. In Kant's favour, it might at least be urged, even if not altogether convincingly, that people are in some way essentially the same, that we are equal in the sight of God, and that differences between us are accidental, and temporary. No such claim can be made about the various different kinds of animal. Although consciousness remains deeply mysterious, and although it is often denied that it can come in degrees, still the consciousness, the imagination, the hopes and fears of a human being are immeasurably richer than those of a rabbit or a mouse. Even if we grant that their lives have inherent or intrinsic value, it is hard to see the basis for claiming they are of exactly equal value to ours.[24]

Regan, like Taylor, wants to found a number of substantial moral principles on these claims about equal value. The considerable practical difficulties that need to be faced here are not shared by the biocentric accounts put forward by Leopold, Naess and their followers. Naess, it will be recalled, is explicit in his insistence that egalitarianism is only a theoretical ideal; what happens in the field will be messier. Even so, it is worth asking what, even in principle, biocentric egalitarianism is supposed to come to, and in virtue of just what, exactly which things are supposed to have equal intrinsic value.

Again, a difficulty is that the properties that are supposedly relevant to intrinsic value can well hold to different degrees. Systems can be more or less stable, exhibit greater or lesser diversity, and on any plausible account can be more or less beautiful. Naturalness (in what seems to be the biocentricist's favoured sense, implying a contrast with artifice) might seem to be an exception here, with the thought that if two things are natural, neither can be more natural than the other. But pristine nature is rarely encountered, and the scope for value will be massively depleted if an admixture of human activity is disallowed. The biosphere, for one, is not wholly natural. One view would be that something that manifests any of these properties to any degree will, in virtue of that, be intrinsically valuable to exactly the same degree, while another would be that variations in value will track variations in the exemplification of such properties. Why the latter view should not be the more appealing is deeply mysterious. Further, biocentricists face Regan's equality problem in spades, just because they countenance intrinsic value all over the place. Naess insists that "To the ecological field worker, *the equal right to live and blossom* is an intuitively clear and obvious value axiom",[25] but when it is remembered that for deep ecologists "life" has to be interpreted generously, referring to the whole of nature, it is tempting to think that what is clear and obvious is a mere illusion. The intrinsic value of the Mojave Desert is just the same as that of one of its Joshua trees on the one hand, and just the same as that of the biosphere as a whole on the other. Even if action is not to be based solely on such claims, still they should not be made.

Claims to equality might well be dropped. It seems perfectly possible to hold that there is intrinsic value in nature without holding to any attendant egalitarian thesis. So we might say, not implausibly, that the whole of Yosemite has more intrinsic value than Half Dome alone, that the English Lake District loses value the more it is ring-fenced with wind generators, and littered with antennae for mobile phones, or that sequoias are more valuable than sycamores. The notion of differentials here, even if there is disagreement about these examples, has some appeal in itself, and gets some support from corresponding differentials in other areas where claims to intrinsic value are often made. Thus it is highly tempting not only to claim that pain is bad in itself, but that more pain is worse. And where art is concerned there is a similarly entrenched view that even if values cannot be fully determined, it is nevertheless the case that among valuable works some are more valuable than others. Blanket equality claims, going beyond the thought that equal pains are equally bad, or that works are equally valuable if there is no discernible difference between them, would be very odd.[26] To allow that within nature there might also be differences in value is to do more both for immediate plausibility and for consistency overall.

Subjective and objective

To do more might still not be to do enough, however, for what I have suggested is that even if we jettison these unnecessarily troubling equality claims, there are still major difficulties for intrinsic value. In brief, though it is clear enough that many things can have a good of their own, it is far less clear why we should have other than a minimal obligation to preserve or promote that good. And though there are many things that we might value for their own sake (including, of course, that certain things should pursue their own good), it isn't clear that this valuing of ours can have a strong enough connection with a value that exists independently of our valuing, or even what it means to suppose there should be such value. So there might still seem to be two quite distinct spheres: one of the many relationships holding between things outside us; the other of our own inclinations, tastes and preferences. Or, to be blunt about this and to employ again a pair of terms I introduced earlier, objective, real, but instrumental values on the one hand, and subjective, less than fully real, non-instrumental values on the other.[27]

This, though, is too blunt, and the despairing picture already compromised in several ways. There is, first, the abiding thought, reiterated above, that pain is fairly clearly a bad thing in itself, and would remain so in a world without people. Secondly, there is need to remember what was earlier said about those things, constitutive of our well-being, that arguably we ought to value, whether or not we currently do. Thirdly, it has already been hinted that we might look more closely into the allegations and criticisms of anthropocentrism, around which much of the discussion tends to revolve. Taken together, all this might open the way to an account of value that straddles a subjective/objective divide. There can be such an account, and, I will argue, it is the best the supporter of intrinsic value can hope for.

The way into this, as might be anticipated, is to attempt a distinction between the location and status of the valuation on the one hand, and the thing valued on the other. So even if subjectivism puts value wholly within the mind, the objects of value might lie elsewhere. Although someone may value only the mind and its states, a more common position is to value widely, seeing as valuable a range of objects, events and situations. And as we can value things outside our minds, outside ourselves, so we can value things beyond our particular regions of space and time. I can value, think good, approve of, the Colossus of Rhodes, dinosaurs, future peace in Northern Ireland and so on. And I can also value merely possible states of affairs, thinking it would have been good if mammoths had not been wiped out, or if nuclear power, wheels, or America had never been discovered. And I can disvalue my own existence, thinking it would have been better if I had never been born.

The slogan "values are just subjective" is thus misleading on two counts. First, even if there are no valuations with valuers, there can be objects of value without valuers, both in that these objects stand outside human minds, and in that they can exist independently of those minds, as, clearly, the mammoths and dinosaurs didn't depend on us. Secondly, as already noted, valuations often go beyond the quirky, are frequently shared, and are not infrequently such as to warrant support. So there are important ways in which we might agree that values are subjective, and still want to claim that there are things out there in the world – Beethoven, Venice, the Yosemite Valley – that are themselves valuable, and valuable for what they are, rather than what they do.

Nothing here is new, and similar themes have been explored by several writers. I have mentioned Elliott already, and Callicott offers a further example:

> I concede that, from the point of view of scientific naturalism, the *source* of all value is human consciousness, but it by no means follows that the *locus* of all value is consciousness itself, or a mode of consciousness like reason, pleasure or knowledge. In other words, something may be valuable only because someone values it, but it may also be valued for itself, not for the sake of any subjective experience (pleasure, knowledge, aesthetic satisfaction, and so forth) it may afford the valuers . . . An intrinsically valuable thing on this reading is valuable *for* its own sake, *for* itself, but it is not valuable in itself, that is, completely independently of any consciousness since no value can, in principle, from the point of view of classical normal science, be altogether independent of a valuing consciousness.[28]

Perhaps there isn't quite as much here as there might be, for Callicott seems to elide intrinsic and personal value, making the case that not all values are instrumental, but insisting that when a thing is valued for its own sake, it has that value only in so far as someone actually values it. Value depends on consciousness, even while the things that are valued exist independently of the mind. Opponents will find this unsatisfactory, and while conceding that valuing, finding value and so on depend on consciousness, think that there is still space for value itself to have more life of its own. Callicott's account, from this perspective, will appear compromised, asking that we accept much less than we might demand where intrinsic value is concerned. But his reply, insisted on at the end of the above passage, is that we might not after all demand this, that what is here on offer is all there could intelligibly be, as far as value is concerned. There is a looseness in that reply, however, which might encourage the opponent to pursue his case. One thought, that a thing might be in itself valuable, just as it is, say, spherical, alive or powered by electricity, is one that Callicott rightly rejects. Non-instrumental values will not be objective in that full-blooded sense. But a closely related thought might offer more promise, and ought not to be too hastily dismissed, and that is that as we value things in virtue of their properties, so the properties that a thing possesses might be such as to require that we value it. The properties will be in the object and the valuing in the mind, while the value itself, on this account, is more difficult to locate. It might not be "altogether independent" of the mind, while yet its dependence is less than entire.

There are complex issues here, relating not just to value but to the relationship between the world and the mind more generally. Callicott, like Leopold before him, is considerably indebted to certain of Hume's views on these issues, but whereas one account of those views gives support to a robust subjectivism, another,[29] arguably subtler, will have that subjectivism tempered.

Hume, following the empiricist tradition, wants to distinguish between the primary and secondary qualities, holding that while the former, most notably here shape and size, exist independently of observers, the latter, including colour, sound and taste, are not genuine properties of objects, but rather are located in the minds of observers, and then as it were spread back on things the observation of which excites the ideas of such qualities. We first seem to believe that redness is out there in the world, but, after a little science and a little philosophy, come to see that it exists only in the mind. Nevertheless, we cannot but help see objects as if they are themselves coloured. And, Hume insists, just the same phenomenon occurs where aesthetics and ethics are concerned. We think that a certain thing is beautiful, or a certain action good, when in fact what happens is that we react to some admittedly objective properties of things or situations, are pleased or approving, and then transfer that reaction back on to the objects themselves. Like colour, beauty and goodness exist only in the mind. Or, as Hume puts it, speaking of the alleged beauty of a circle, "It is only the effect which that figure produces upon the mind, whose peculiar fabric or structure renders it susceptible of such sentiments".[30] Several things are right in this. We might agree that not only do human beings and insects see things as differently coloured, but at the end of the day there are no grounds for describing one of these as the true, or real, colour of things, and the other false or illusory. We might agree that colour does not figure in a purely physical description of the world, and that scientists can restrict themselves to discussion of wavelengths, refraction, the structure of the eye and so on in giving an account of colour perception. And we might agree that moral and aesthetic properties are similarly not among the furniture of the world in the way that shape and size are. Paintings are not beautiful in the way that they are flat, nor torture evil in the way that it is too often protracted. But in agreeing thus far, we are not therefore obliged to agree that beauty, colour and value exist only in the mind. Certain intermediate positions are still to be explored. Perhaps this is Callicott's point, with his source/locus distinction offering a somewhat more complex picture than any which is uncompromising in its siting of value. But the account is still close to Hume, implying as it does that in the absence of consciousness, nothing has any value at all. Perhaps, on this account, value resides within the valuable thing, but unless it is being valued, the value simply disappears.[31] Describing this as a subjectivist account remains apt.

It is possible, however, to get further from this Humean or subjectivist view, without thereby ending back in the objectivist fold, claiming that values, colours and the like have no need of minds but exist in themselves as part of the world. We need only appeal to dispositions, in order to sketch out a position well able to avoid extremes. One account of colour, for example, holds that an object is, say, red, if it is such as to excite sensations of redness in normal observers under normal conditions. Or, to put it slightly differently, an object is red if it would appear red to normal observers under normal conditions. What this allows, evidently, is that things have colour in the dark, when not observed, even if never observed, and even if they exist in a world where, as there are no observers, they never could be observed. And it allows too that the true colour of a thing may be other than the one it appears to have; both individuals and groups, when there is abnormality about, can get things wrong.[32] These common-sense beliefs about colour's independence and location are reinstated even if they are here given a new twist. Something is red if it emits or reflects such and such light waves, but to say it is red is to say more than this. So although blind people might well know just which objects are red, and might, with the appropriate instruments, accurately sort objects by colour, in lacking the requisite sensations they cannot really know what redness is. This dispositional account manages to have it both ways, then. It has colour back in the objects, where it seems to belong, but it makes essential reference to the minds of observers, in accounting for the colours that things have. And here, with such dispositional accounts, the simple subjective/objective dichotomy breaks down.[33]

This dispositional account can similarly be deployed in connection with beauty and goodness, and to similar advantage. Objects are beautiful if they are such as to appear beautiful to normal observers under normal conditions. As with colour, there is something akin to sensations in the mind, while beauty remains in the object.[34] Again, someone with underdeveloped aesthetic tastes might be able to know which objects are beautiful, which are not, while in lacking the appropriate internal response is unable fully to understand what it really is to be beautiful. Similarly, things are good if they are such as to be judged good by normal observers under normal conditions; the approval, the judgement, is in the mind, but the goodness is elsewhere. Here, too, the dispositional account leaves space for poor judgement: morality is not merely a matter of taste, and an individual's verdicts as to what is good or bad, right or wrong, might be revised either by further knowledge of the objects or events under scrutiny, or by cultivation or refinement of his or her sensibilities.

There is both opportunity and need for considerable detailing in these accounts and, as things stand, room for several reservations, both as to the overall plausibility with respect to colour, and then with the extensions into matters of value. There isn't space for such detailing here. Having now sketched a way in which the insistence – subjective or objective? – may be simply too crude, I want first to suggest that this may be the best bet for intrinsic value, and then secondly to allow that it may still not be good enough. It is the best bet in part because it is a reasonably good bet to begin with. To construe colour or beauty in these quasi-objective, quasi-realist[35] terms is not in general found unsatisfying, and proffering a parallel account with respect to value leaves the believer in value with at least much of what he or she was after. And it is the best bet because it wins out over the alternatives.

O'Neill disagrees. For even if we allow both that Hume believes that colour and value are together in the mind, and that the dispositional account, in a seeming advance, locates them back in the objects, nevertheless

> it is not clear to me that any point of substance about the nature of values divides the Humean and his opponent. The debate is one about preferred modes of speech, specifically about how the term "real property" is to be read. For the Humean such as Mackie, the term "real property" is understood in its strong sense . . . The opponent of the Humean . . . merely substitutes a weak interpretation of "real property" for the strong interpretation.[36]

Against this it might be countered that in the end most philosophical questions are about preferred modes of speech; one reason that they are worth pursuing is that this is for a long time disguised. That the debate here shows that the seemingly straightforward question – subjective or objective, in the mind or in the objects? – cannot in the end always be straightforwardly answered, is to offer progress of the philosophical kind. O'Neill is unhappy with such attempts to salvage something of the intrinsic value view, and sets up his own rescue mission along quasi-Aristotelian lines, making what he can of the idea that living things have a good of their own. But what can be made is, I think, not nearly enough. Allow that it is an objective fact, quite independent of human concerns, that mice are good for owls. Allow, too, that there is such a thing as the good, well-being or flourishing of owls. O'Neill insists that none of this issues directly in obligations for human beings. But I think there are two complications. First, given owls, it is better that they flourish than not, such that we do acquire some sorts of obligations to care. But, secondly, neither the claim that it is good that living things exist, nor that, where non-sentient life is concerned, flourishing is good, can be sustained. There is really very little remaining of objective intrinsic value in this, and I suspect that it will be too little to please anyone. The dispositional account offers more.

A difficulty remains. The dispositional account of colour, even while offering to explicate true colour in ways that go beyond mere appearance, has nevertheless to concede that important elements in a realist account are inevitably missing. Suppose that there are Martians, and that they see things

differently. There is no neutral or objective position from which colour
questions can be adjudicated; relativization to species is the best that we will
do. It is similar for beauty, where their developed and defensible tastes might
yet be at odds with ours.[37] Where morality is concerned there are further
complications, for although we might allow, as with beauty, some sort of
species relativity,[38] with Martian goodness being a substantially different
animal, there are likely to be core areas where our firm view is that to do
things differently is to do them worse. Parts of morality, then, may lay claim
to strict universality. Even so, what morality teaches has, surely, to be
graspable by us, when we are at our best. Most claims as to intrinsic value
aspire to more, wanting a complete divorce between our concerns on the one
hand, and the good of the environment on the other. The difficulty is not
simply that of saying why this non-human good should be of any concern to
us; it is, as I noted earlier, in having the faintest conception of just what this
thoroughgoing objectivity would be like, or of how the survival of, say, the
desert might be good just in itself, or from the point of view of the universe as
a whole, or whatever.[39] There is one last straw. A theist might say that intrinsic goodness falls where God will have it, and that human beings can then
recognize or fail to recognize that which, quite independently of their
concerns, is good, or otherwise. There are well-known difficulties even
here,[40] but this is, in any case, presumably not a straw at which the deep
ecologist, or indeed many other defenders of intrinsic value, will be eager to
grasp.

Summary

Much of what motivates the belief in intrinsic value, I have suggested, is
wrong-headed. If we take pains to query many of the simplistic accounts that
are offered as starting points, a more complex picture, covering plenty of
ground but allowing none for deep intrinsicness, begins to emerge. Thus it is
a mistake to think that if some values are non-instrumental, some must be
intrinsic. We can value things for their own sake. It is similarly, even if less
obviously, a mistake to think that if any of these non-instrumental values go
beyond the realm of individual tastes and preferences, they must now be
intrinsic. We can agree that certain values are not only widespread, but
arguably bound up with the good of human beings. So we might say to someone, "You ought to value nature", believing not that nature is good in itself,
but that it is better for us if we do. Although these non-instrumental values
might be wide-ranging, and touch on many of the environmentalist's
concerns, they don't mesh with intrinsicness as it is normally construed.
 Different kinds of mistakes can surface elsewhere. One temptation is to
divide all values into the subjective or objective, and then identify what is

objectively with what is intrinsically valuable. It should be resisted. Seeds are of value to finches and the value here is not generated by, dependent on or in any important way connected with human beings, even if there is some sense in which only human beings can recognize this value. Even allowing that there is objectivity and non-anthropocentricity here, there is, as yet, no candidate for intrinsic value. The seeds are of instrumental value, after all, and unless the end that they serve, the well-being of finches, is something that we take to heart, it isn't clear that any moral demands are made on us. Thus the attempt to find intrinsic value hereabouts carries a double burden. A concern with flourishing or well-being, in its restriction to living things, limits the scope for such value. Even so, it is unclear how the non-instrumental value claims – well-being is good, and should be promoted – can be supported.

If finches not only starve, but also hurt for want of food, then arguably we ought to get involved. Perhaps, then, pain is bad in itself, something that we should regret and want to reduce whenever and wherever it occurs. Perhaps, conversely, pleasure is good and should be promoted or sustained. The scope for intrinsic value is thus restricted again, and now covers only sentient things. Here, though, it does begin to seem as if this limited scope is nevertheless real, and that there are certain states or situations that are genuinely good, or not good, in themselves. But to locate intrinsic value and disvalue here, in the existence of certain states of minds, although defensible, is to offer immeasurably less than many environmentalists would like.

If there are different ways of missing the target it may be a matter of judgement as to what comes closest, but my suggestion has been that the quasi-objective, quasi-realist dispositional account offers the environmentalist's best bet. Even if it is not true (and not in the end even intelligible) that all of nature has value in itself, it may still be true that much of nature is such that we ought, for non-instrumental reasons, to value it.[41]

CHAPTER 10
Beauty

There are several reasons to consider beauty in more detail. First, it surfaces often in connection with intrinsic value, and relates to that notion, I have suggested, in ways importantly different from other of the environmentalist's concerns. Secondly, beauty in nature ties in, evidently, with beauty in art, and reflection on the one both illuminates and is illuminated by reflection on the other. Here, then, thinking about the environment ties up with other areas of philosophical inquiry. Thirdly, and most obviously, it figures large in our reactions to the environment. We think of nature, or of parts of nature, as beautiful, care deeply for that beauty and urge its preservation. A concern for the beauty of nature is probably as strong a motivation to environmental activism as an interest in either animal or human welfare, and so has practical as well as theoretical implications.

It can be considered in more detail because it is important, but it can be considered, also, because it is not straightforward. Some people will want to deny this, claiming that beauty is in the eye of the beholder, that tastes vary from person to person and from time to time, and that room for philosophical engagement with questions of beauty is slight. And not only this, for on such a view, although we may need to take these fluctuating tastes into account, appeals to beauty will not afford any firm or important basis for dealing with the natural world; we need better reason for saving pandas than that some people think them cuddly.[1] I have already indicated that this is an unsatisfactory position, and that as with morality, so, too, with aesthetics: there are better and worse, more and less reasonable responses to the way that things look, sound, smell, taste or feel. There is little point, then, in giving space to extreme subjectivism, and in denying that some of our responses to the alleged beauty of nature can be better grounded, better informed than others. Perhaps the key question, where the aesthetics of nature is concerned, is just what sorts of considerations are relevant to our judgement that this or that animal, landscape or rock formation is beautiful. This question has two aspects: there are issues concerning what, to a beautiful thing, is an appropriate response; and issues as well about in virtue of what a thing is or is not beautiful. But if extreme subjectivism is to be avoided, so, too, is its opposite, and in what follows I want to suggest that the arguments designed to show that precisely this or that consideration is relevant, and that exactly this or that response is appropriate, are rarely as powerful as their proponents claim. As the arguments about goodness are seldom clear-cut, so too for those involving beauty.

Art and nature

The key question here is central to aesthetics more generally. In looking at and reacting to a painting there are issues as to how far art-historical information – about subject matters, intentions, relationships to other works – should help to shape our response. In looking at and reacting to nature, similarly, there are questions of whether our response should be affected by how and when the thing came to be formed, whether it is young or old, healthy or diseased, the extent of human involvement and so on.

Even though a similar question is posed, there are so many important dissimilarities between art and nature that one might expect substantial differences in the answers provided. First, nature, unlike art, is not intended to look a certain way. Some theists might disagree, but it is generally accepted that even if parts of nature unfold systematically, the system as a whole is not planned or designed. Secondly, unlike much of art, nature doesn't represent anything beyond itself, and isn't about anything beyond itself. Many of Constable's works are pictures, representations, of landscapes, but the landscapes are not in turn representations of other things. With non-representational art, be it certain sorts of painting, architecture or music, it is still often claimed that a work is about something other than itself, that it deals with memory, nostalgia and loss, or explores the ambiguities of the picture plane, or says something about our relationships with the natural world.[2] But nature doesn't point elsewhere in any of these ways. Again, some theists might disagree, thinking that not only is nature designed by God, but that it is designed in order to represent to us the workings of God's mind, or to illustrate some moral, or is in some other way inscribed with religious doctrine.[3] Thirdly, nature is typically not parcelled or packaged in the way that art typically is. Constable's landscapes end, usually, where the frame begins, yet a real-life landscape, prospect or view has no firm boundaries, but changes as our eyes move, and fades as peripheral vision becomes less and less distinct.[4] Art's bounded works want, moreover, in turn to bind their audience, and are usually supposed to be seen from a certain distance, under certain lighting conditions, or heard at certain volumes, or read in a certain order.[5] The works of nature, in contrast, don't ask to be experienced in any particular fashion. Further, we can fairly easily tell how many landscapes Constable painted, or how many are housed in any gallery or museum, but there is no way of determining how many landscapes or views exist in nature. As boundaries are indistinct, so the boundaries of one overlap with those of countless others. Fourthly, there are differences of scale. Although there is variation within art – compare a lute prelude with a Mahler symphony, or Hilliard's miniatures with the roughly contemporary Sistine Chapel – no art works are as large as the Cuillins, or the open sea, or the moon half revealed through broken cloud, and none are so small as to reveal their beauties only under a microscope.

There are substantial dissimilarities, then, and a concern with the aesthetics of nature gives rise to issues not normally encountered when considering art. But are these differences perhaps so severe as to suggest not only that the two fields will not altogether coincide, but that there is a more radical division between them? It has been suggested that this is so, and that there is not, in the end, even such a thing as an aesthetics of nature, for, allegedly, "The conceptual structure of an aesthetic judgement . . . includes a reference to a creator, i.e. an artist", such that "Nature cannot be the object of aesthetic appreciation".[6] But even if it is agreed, as I think it should be, that nature isn't art, this account of aesthetic judgement is unacceptable. We can take delight in, be pleased by and respond emotionally to, a sensuous engagement with nature precisely as we can with art, and it is with just such employment of the senses that aesthetics is principally concerned. Even if this is denied, and it is insisted that "aesthetic" is now a term of art, whose application should in this way be restricted, the point becomes merely verbal: no one will deny, surely, that parts of nature are beautiful. A more moderate suggestion is that although both nature and art can sustain an aesthetic response, the differences between them are still great enough to warrant our talking of not one admittedly extended aesthetic, but two.[7] Again, this may seem to be merely a matter of words, but, as will emerge below, there are in this case issues as to the particular characters of art and nature that bear closer scrutiny. In the end the better position, or so I will argue, is one that emphasizes similarity above difference, even while the several differences are fully acknowledged.

Terms and history

Have people always been affected by natural beauty? It is tempting to think so. If we look at painting, read poetry or study landscaping and the siting of buildings from any past cultures, then evidence of an aesthetic response to nature seems undeniable. Think of wall paintings from Pompeii or early

Islamic gardens. There may seem also to be *a priori* considerations in favour of such a conclusion, for if, as I have suggested, an aesthetic response to nature is in part determined by our own natures, then in so far as human nature is unchanged the response, too, will continue. There are various reasons for not giving wholehearted assent here. First, the evidence in art for an aesthetic appreciation of nature is limited, in the main, to relatively sophisticated cultures – Greece, Rome, China, Japan – and even there it is hard to disentangle from the sorts of religious concerns that suggest that nature may be anthropomorphized before it is valued. Secondly, the *a priori* argument is hardly strong. My earlier suggestion, in fact, was only that an appreciation of familiar nature – the pastoral for shepherds, the steppes for nomads, the sea for islanders – might be to some extent natural. So even if there is a causal story that connects us with nature as a whole, there is no reason for that to seep into consciousness, and no reason for large expanses of nature not to strike many of us as alien and hostile. And, as is well known, the evidence bears this out. Wild mountains, even if as a backdrop they might be admired, were objects of fear and dread until the late eighteenth century, not at all places that people were willing to encounter at close quarters. Fondness for wild animals is also a relatively recent phenomenon, encouraged by their less frequently appearing either as food or as rivals for food. There are several reasons for thinking, then, that only in a fairly limited way is the aesthetic appreciation of nature itself natural.

Just as the late eighteenth century saw an expansion in the range of things that might be admired, so also did it give rise to an expansion in the terminology by which to account for that admiration. Burke's distinction between the beautiful and the sublime[8] was well articulated, and construed beauty in much narrower terms than it might be understood today. This twofold distinction was soon augmented by increasing reference to the picturesque, a notion that again has somewhat shifted in meaning between its original and its current use. The upshot of these expansions is that there is now a very wide range of natural objects, events and features that are not only possible candidates for, but actual recipients of, aesthetic appreciation, and a correspondingly wide range of terms in which that appreciation may be couched: thus animals, birds, fish, jellyfish, trees, ferns, lichens, deserts, marshes, seas, skies, mists, fogs, smogs,[9] glaciers and the like; and parts of things, feathers, scales, petals, branches, bones, viscera, wounds; and thus beautiful, sublime, awful, pretty, delicate, exciting, peaceful, inviting and so on.

For the most part I will stick with conventional, even trite examples. They will serve my main purposes well enough. Similarly, I will continue to refer most often to beauty and the beautiful, even while recognizing that positive aesthetic appreciation can easily be such that to cast it in terms of beauty alone might be thought misleading, inaccurate or simply lazy. But it is worth noting here how one important distinction might be blurred by this tactic. The Romantics' distinction between the beautiful and the sublime corresponded in large part to differences in scale. Aspects of nature, mountain gorges, cascades and glaciers were considered sublime in part because of their overwhelming size, humbling us and giving a sense of human unimportance. There is some danger, in thus emphasizing beauty, of paying too little attention to this uncompromising otherness within the natural world, not in denying that it can be unfathomable and unfriendly, but in denying that it can be in certain respects thus, and at the same time moving and attractive to us. The danger here is in fabricating a psychic wholeness, coherence and simplicity to our being, wherein our relationship to the larger world seems in the end to be quite unproblematic. Where words go, thoughts will follow.

What these shifting responses to the natural world suggest, as do similar shifts where art is concerned, is that beauty is not straightforwardly an objective property of things but, as was contended in Chapter 9, is in some part constituted by our reactions to such properties. As cultural change affects the reactions, so there will be differences in just where beauty is to be found. The non-objectivity of beauty is merely suggested, and not at all established, by these variations in response, for variation of this kind is perfectly compatible with realism in what is responded to. All that is needed is some sort of account about why the real, objective properties of a thing might escape our attention, and appeal to familiar perceptual and ratiocinative limitations can fuel such an account well enough. A better argument for beauty's not being thoroughly objective was sketched earlier. We find, on reflection, that it is not the sort of property we can conceive of as part of the wholly mind-independent furniture of the world. Now the anti-realist position so understood is, in principle, perfectly compatible with universal agreement as to what things are beautiful. In short, although certain parallels might well be expected, the status of beauty is one thing, and the consonance, or otherwise, of our response another.

Having said that, then, the full thrust of some recent comments on natural beauty turns out to be not altogether clear. Terry Diffey has written:

> we can all think readily enough of examples of natural beauty: a prospect, say, of the Sussex Downs as viewed along its line from the top of one of its hills is *undoubtedly* beautiful. This is literally true; I have never heard it doubted nor would I understand anybody who did deny it any more than G. E. Moore would understand a person's denying that a person's hand held in front of his face was his hand.[10]

What Diffey has wanted to reject, in the preceding section of his paper, is the kind of extreme subjectivism, associated rightly or wrongly with Hume, that I summarily dismissed above. Too much is lost on the eye of the beholder view. But that rejection, I have argued, is compatible with something less than fully fledged realism, where beauty is concerned. Perhaps Diffey would agree. The Sussex Downs, we might allow, are truly, literally beautiful even if beauty isn't an objective property of things. But are they *undoubtedly* beautiful? Surely not. Beauty in nature connects with familiarity and acculturation. It is easy enough to imagine people who would find such landscapes petty, constraining or simply too green. So just as there is nothing that is beautiful in itself, so, too, is there nothing of which we can say that it will appear beautiful to all decent and reasonable people, wherever they are, and whenever they live.[11]

Formalism and against

Much of this will be challenged by those adopting a formalist position where the aesthetics of nature are concerned. Formalism holds that what we ought to do, in considering the aesthetic value of an object, is concern ourselves only with its intrinsic and surface properties. Thus where painting is concerned, formalism obliges us to respond only to the arrangements of paint on the surface of the canvas, and not to be influenced by, or interested in, questions as to authorship, influences, purposes, representations and so on. Suppose that we are looking at David's *The Oath of the Horatii*. That it is by David, a central work in French Neo-Classicism, about political activity and allegiances within ancient Rome, and intended and viewed as making comment on the political situation in pre-Revolutionary France are matters of art-historical interest but not, on the formalist account, of relevance in judging the painting as a work of art. And the same with natural beauty. My aesthetic response to Tarn Howes, in the English Lake District, is not to be influenced by facts concerning the history of the place, the intersections of natural woodland and Victorian plantings, whether the perimeters of the lake are artificially maintained and so on. It is beautiful, or otherwise, depending just on how it looks, or more particularly here on how it looks, sounds and smells.

To adopt this formalism is not to go back on an earlier point. There is still space for a distinction between how a thing appears and how it appears to me, so the formalist can still insist that some things are, while others are not, beautiful, and can still reject certain judgements as revealing insufficient perceptual acuity or, although the sense organs are working well enough, a stunted emotional response. Given that means for an appropriate aesthetic reaction are not distributed along any cultural or historical lines, there are, after all, grounds for thinking that decent and reasonable people will agree. And perhaps (although I am not sure he would welcome this defence of his position) Diffey's belief in the undoubted beauty of the Sussex Downs might begin to appear defensible after all.

I don't think that nature's friends should be at all happy about this, however. Just as subjectivism, in personalizing the aesthetic response, diminishes the effectiveness of an appeal to beauty, so too will formalism ill serve the environment's cause, for if the beauty of nature depends simply on the surface appearance of things, then beauty will connect only contingently and haphazardly with what might well be considered other desirable properties, such as goodness, integrity and health. My judgement that, say, a stand of trees is beautiful cannot be overturned by the discovery that they have their present look just because they suffer from some mineral deficiency, or are fighting a losing battle against air pollution, or that their lower branches have all been lopped, and the trees themselves will be felled tomorrow. Indeed, it will connect only contingently and haphazardly with nature at all, as things may well look the same, whatever their origins or internal constitution. The moon is beautiful even if they are not clouds but noxious fumes that drift across its surface in a manner altogether beguiling, and it remains beautiful even if it turns out to be not the moon at all, but a factory searchlight, trained on a scarred and pitted wall. The look is just the same. Although the concern here is, of course, to pursue truth wherever it leads, environmentalists might well hope that formalism turns out to be untenable.

Such hope might be encouraged by what is, for formalism, an obvious difficulty and one to which, in spite of first appearances, there is no equally obvious response. It is all very well to say that where the David is concerned I ought not to take into account that there are within the painting representations of particular Romans, involved in a particular activity. But do I go wrong in identifying the figures even as Romans, or men to the left, and women to the right, or indeed as people at all? Similarly, is an aesthetic response to Tarn Howes to some degree sullied if I identify water as water, trees as trees, and sheep, people, ice-cream vans and orange peel each as what they are, and not another thing? It might be said that identification is all right, as long as I put all this from my mind in reaching at an aesthetic appreciation, but, of course, it may not be psychologically possible to look at people, or trees, and not see them for what they are. There are devices – squinting, the Claude glass, standing on one's head – but they are at best partially successful, and although nothing is laid down either way for nature, art, at least, is not intended to be viewed under duress. Nor can this difficulty be overcome by ruling out our taking into account only particular items of information, yet still allowing our response to be coloured by the kinds of background knowledge and understanding with which we are naturally provided. There are no firm lines here. It may be obvious to those broadly familiar with Western art that there are people within the David, but such familiarity cannot be universally assumed. Equally, the sorts of natural-historical information that I might take for granted could come as news elsewhere. Just as it is easy enough to imagine people who don't find the Sussex Downs beautiful, so is it easy to think of those who have not even a passing acquaintance with a bird, a tree or a blue sky. The deep difficulty for formalism, then, is that it isn't clear either that we can address just the form of a thing, or that there is any non-arbitrary ground for admitting some bits of background information, while prohibiting others.

Certain issues deriving from all this will need to be taken up again later, but having sketched the broad shape of the formalist approach where both art and nature are concerned, I can begin to consider its opposite, and the claim that much more than the look of a thing needs to be considered, where beauty is concerned.

Allen Carlson has argued, in a number of articles, that this appreciation needs to be informed by a scientific understanding of what nature is about. Taking a lead from several persuasive critiques of formalism within the domain of art,[12] Carlson argues that our response to the natural world is similarly unsatisfactory unless it, too, is founded on knowledge of the appropriate kind. The objections to formalism run on broadly parallel lines, but the undeniable differences between art and nature mean that details of what is needed in the latter case can usefully be identified. As Carlson himself puts it:

> First, the relevant order is that typically called the natural order. Second, since there is no artist, not even one assimilated to processes and materials, the relevant forces are the forces of nature: the geological, biological and meteorological forces which produce the natural order by shaping not only the planet but everything that inhabits it. Although these forces differ from many that shape works of art, awareness and understanding of them is vital in nature appreciation, as is knowledge of, for example, Pollock's role in appreciating his action painting, or the role of chance in appreciating a Dada experiment. Third, the relevant account which makes the natural order visible and intelligible is, as noted, the story given by natural science – astronomy, physics, chemistry, biology, genetics, meteorology as well as the particular explanatory theories within these sciences. Awareness and understanding of evolutionary theory, for example, is relevant to appreciating the natural order as revealed in flora and fauna; without such knowledge the biosphere may strike us as chaotic.[13]

Now I think this is quite wrong, but it may seem not to be wrong at all if what I think of as key notions in and behind this passage are overlooked or misunderstood. First, Carlson's claim is not simply that this scientific understanding may alter, may indeed help with, the appreciation of natural objects, but that it is, as he says, "vital". Without it, proper appreciation just cannot go on. Secondly, the levels of understanding appealed to here are far from minimal. Carlson is not claiming, in line with a point I made above, that one needs, in order to appreciate nature, to know that rocks are rocks, trees are trees, or in general that nature is nature. He makes explicit reference to a number of discrete sciences, including some that have only recently developed, in characterizing the kind of understanding needed for appreciation. Thirdly, there are no clear signs that his notion of appreciation is so construed as simply to guarantee the result he is after. Appreciation could be taken as a near synonym for understanding, so that with nature as with art, the claim that one doesn't really appreciate what one is seeing – an action painting, a sea urchin – unless one understands what it is, how it is made and so on, becomes trivially true. But Carlson seems to intend appreciation in an aesthetic sense. I claim, not to understand the scene before me, but simply to find it beautiful, to be moved by it. On Carlson's view, if I am lacking in appropriate understanding, then even here something is amiss.

What is amiss exactly? Carlson surely cannot mean that I am simply unable to think that there is beauty in nature unless I have some substantial and appropriate scientific knowledge. Perhaps he means that my response, without this knowledge, is somehow illegitimate or unjustified, or that although I can think such things, I cannot know them. Or perhaps I can know that something is beautiful, but cannot know what it is, such that there is nothing in particular that I am appreciating. But take it how you will, why this is quite wrong, surely, is that it has the result that for most people, and for most of history, an aesthetic appreciation of nature has simply been unavailable. Scientific knowledge is new-fangled and arcane. Unlike the appreciation of nature, it is a minority pursuit. Insist on it, and much seeming appreciation is rejected. It is worth noticing how what might appear an analogous comment on art appreciation is, in contrast, far less troubling. Art is intended for audiences who share certain of the artist's beliefs about the world. To claim here that an appropriate aesthetic response is tied to some reasonably detailed understanding of what the work is about, such that without doing their homework most people are debarred from such a response is, while far from demonstrable, a very plausible position to maintain. I know virtually nothing about African art and, faced with examples, don't know at all how to respond, or what aesthetic properties are manifest within them. Most Africans, similarly, will be unable to appreciate the art of the Byzantines. But nature isn't in any corresponding manner asking to be looked at in certain ways and with certain understandings. So with nature alone, I suggest, should we be uneasy about dismissing aesthetic reactions on the near-global scale.

Moderate views

Both formalism and its opposite are, I have suggested, profoundly unattractive. Judgements as to a thing's beauty are, as matter of fact, typically influenced by what we know of that thing. To insist on the irrelevance of such knowledge to aesthetic appreciation appears both unmotivated and untenable where both art and nature are concerned. Strong anti-formalism, in insisting that a proper aesthetic response has need of considerable amounts of background information, has appeal within art. But when directed to nature it, too, looks to be hopeless. Are there middling positions? Unsurprisingly there are, and I can offer sketchbook accounts of three.

The first can be understood as a softening of Carlson's line. Rather than any detailed scientific knowledge of what things are, and how they work, it might instead be suggested merely that we need, for a proper aesthetic response, to see nature as nature, and to understand, when we admire the high mountains, or find ourselves moved by the implacable strength and slow pace of deep rivers, that natural forces – even if we are not exactly sure which – are in play here. Without such recognition, this apparently modest claim has it, our belief in our encounter with beauty is inadequately grounded.[14]

This looks to be a reasonable demand, and looks, if anything, the more reasonable when it is considered that a similar demand made for art is very highly plausible. We might give up on the insistence that one knows about painters, styles, influences and the like and yet still want to say that a proper appreciation of art at least involves recognition that it is art, and that one doesn't take a painting of fruit for fruit, or a contemporary installation piece as the children's den. Even here, though, there might be found some difficulty, as it seems possible that the demand that we take art for art derives in part from its being intended that we so take it. It is not at all difficult to imagine pieces of which the point is that they are mistakenly categorized, where what is intended is that the work is not seen as art. If intention is relevant in some such way, then the plausibility of the claim that we should see nature as nature is somewhat undermined, for no one intends that we should so see it.[15] This isn't an effective objection. The thought that we normally need a minimal understanding of what we are appreciating doesn't depend on the claim that someone intends us to have such understanding, and isn't affected by the suggestion that in abnormal circumstances our needs may be different. Less than wholly effective, too, is the objection that someone who believes that nature is designed, realized and held in existence by God doesn't see nature as nature, but isn't on that score disallowed an appropriate aesthetic response. It might be said here either that the theist sees nature as nature nevertheless, or that too much enthusiasm for seeing God in everything does indeed threaten the validity of response. The nature as nature view withstands, then, at least these efforts to undermine it, and so remains, I suggest, as a seemingly viable modification of Carlson's anti-formalist account.

Two further positions, while not reverting to thoroughgoing formalism, hold that formalist and anti-formalist elements can coexist. One insists that any object can be seen either with or without elements of background information, either under or free of the relevant categories, and that there are no grounds for identifying one rather than the other response as appropriate. A botanist and a young child can both believe that snowdrops are beautiful, just as a connoisseur and another young child can equally thrill to the colours and patterns in Andy Warhol's Marilyn prints. Although, of course, the experts have more knowledge of what they are seeing, and might well claim their response to be better informed and more deeply grounded, nevertheless the untutored response, the more or less immediate reaction just to the look of the thing, will, on this account, be no less legitimate.[16]

This free-for-all position challenges, then, even the very modest anti-formalist stance outlined above. We can appreciate nature without appreciating it as nature, perhaps because we have no views about it, or because we falsely believe that it is something else, mistaking lines of pebbles left by the tide as some environmental art piece. There is a difference here, however. A response based on no information is one thing, while one based on false information is another. The pluralist view gives legitimacy to both the innocent and the informed response. It need not treat a reaction based on mistaken or confused beliefs so generously. Suppose it accommodates both. Is this free-for-all view plausible? I will need to return to it below, but for the moment suggest that it is.

This second middling position needs to be distinguished from another, which again allows for both responses, but maintains that they each have their particular object. A version of this is both familiar and to some degree persuasive where art is concerned. Whereas it might be argued that the aesthetic response to a work like Van Dyck's *Cupid and Psyche* is too little grounded in so far as one doesn't pick up on the classical allusions, many twentieth-century works – perhaps within abstract expressionism and op art in particular – explicitly ask that the viewer react simply to the painted surface, and not attempt to probe into the history, symbolism and meaning behind it.[17] Of course, what artists say about their works and what they request of audiences can both be ignored, and it can rightly be pointed out that even with works of this kind, a richer and more satisfying reaction will derive from knowledge of their background. Nevertheless, it is undeniable that where art is concerned formalist theory is, to some significant degree, borne out in practice.

But for nature? One recent suggestion is that there is a relevant distinction here, too, between, on the one hand, those individual living things, and more particularly the parts of things, that might be said to have a purpose or function, and, on the other, the several aspects of nature – rivers, mountains, deserts, ponds – that do not in this sense have a purpose or function. This distinction, which of course corresponds to that between things that do and things that don't have a good of their own, is then said to underscore differences in the plausibility of formalism. Nick Zangwill has argued[18] that the formalist response is appropriate for things of the latter kind, whereas it is, at the least, less appropriate where living things are concerned. As he puts it:

> As a moderate formalist, I partly agree with Carlson about biological nature. It sometimes matters aesthetically what kind of creature we are appreciating, or what part of a creature we are appreciating. If so, we have cases of dependent beauty. But I think that nature also has

purposeless beauty. And about inorganic or non-biological nature, I do not agree at all. Inorganic nature, I say, has only formal aesthetic properties.[19]

The idea, then, is that different kinds of beauty, and different kinds of aesthetic properties, attach to different kinds of thing, and to their parts. Zangwill seems to think that as parts of living things – wings, shells, flowers – have very clearly a function with respect to the whole, then at least a part of their beauty (assuming that they are beautiful) cannot be grasped without understanding that function. I refer here to a part of their beauty just because Zangwill wants to allow that even in these cases two species of beauty might be present: a dependent, non-formal beauty on the one hand; and a free, formal beauty on the other. Even eyes can be looked at simply as if they were pearls. So already, then, this version of moderate formalism is threatening to collapse back into the earlier version, where the formalist and non-formalist responses are not tied to different kinds of objects, but can coexist. Nor is this collapse halted later:

> Extreme formalism about inorganic nature seems obvious to me. Surely, where a natural thing has no purpose, we need only consider what can be immediately present to our senses, and we need not know about its origin. The beauty of an inorganic natural thing at a time is surely determined just by its narrow nonaesthetic properties at that time. Anything else may be interesting but it does not (or should not) affect aesthetic appreciation.[20]

Having introduced the distinction between types of beauty, all that is sure to begin with is that to consider the free beauty of a mountain or a swamp we need only attend to our immediate sensory input. That is a truism. The retort that in this case, as a swamp has no function, this is the only kind of beauty it can have, is ineffective. If there is a kind of beauty that depends only on form, and a further kind that depends on function, why not a still further kind that depends on what a thing is, where it came from, and how it is made? Call it, perhaps, structural beauty. Its detection requires that we take into account the structure and origins of a thing. That, too, is a truism. Where a point of substance might emerge is in the claim that although various things can be looked at in various ways, certain of these ways are, in certain cases, more appropriate than others. It might then be claimed that when looking at and responding aesthetically to mountains, or sunsets, or the differences between wet and dry mud at the side of an estuary, we should not, however we are tempted, concern ourselves with what these things are, or how they came to be. It isn't at all clear how an argument for such a claim might go.

Whereas this third account has, in the end, too little to recommend it, both the nature as nature view, and the view that allows for both formalist and anti-formalist responses to the whole range of appreciable objects, retain more plausibility than either of the extreme positions. Both the extreme positions and the account rejected here have a certain precision and elegance. The more plausible positions are, in contrast, somewhat vague. But that may in part be because the entire question of just what form the appreciation of nature should take admits of no clear and concise answer. All we might do, perhaps, is assemble reminders.

Responding to nature

I am cycling on steep tracks through the woods in early summer. It is the middle of the evening, and there are pockets of cooler air in the hollows, and unexpected warmth on the brows of hills. There is some delicious scent, perhaps honeysuckle, perhaps the last of the azaleas, drifting on the hint of breeze. It is all delightful. But does it matter at all that I don't know how this scent is produced, or why the air is in places so unaccountably warm? It seems at first not to matter at all. Yet this first reaction is under some pressure, perhaps, if it turns out, say, that I smell, not blossom, but cheap perfume on the woman riding behind me, or chemicals from a nearby factory, or strangely mutated rotting flesh. Suppose, as seems likely, I am delighted less. Can it be said that the smell is exactly the same, and that if it was beautiful before, it must remain so now? I have no option, of course, but to agree that the smell is unchanged, but it doesn't follow that my response should be unchanged as well. I can insist, surely, that I took there to be flowers, and that it was the smell of flowers that I judged beautiful. Suppose, in contrast, that my reaction remains the same. Can it be objected that I ought to react differently, given this new information about the true origin of the smell? I go back to a distinction I made above. If I had believed that my response was to the beauty of flowers, then maybe it should change. I had it wrong. But if I had thought only that something, who knows what, smells beautiful, then it can appropriately remain.

This defence of the pluralist view needs several amendments. First, it may often be unclear how far beliefs about the object of experience will figure in the aesthetic response. I may firmly believe that a smell comes from flowers but still react to it just as a smell, so that new information as to origins leaves the aesthetic response unaffected. Or beliefs about origins may be merely implicit, and never formulated, but still play a role in the aesthetic response. Secondly, although both responses are possible, and both are of value, this is not to say that there is nothing to choose between them. Their values may not be equal. Someone who is forever unable to respond just to the look or feel or sound of a thing – someone who cannot simply delight in the play of light on the rippled surface of a lake, indifferent as to whether this is caused by breeze or jet skis – this person is in some measure aesthetically incapacitated, but not as much as someone whose interest is always at the levels of surface. We are typically concerned with more than mere appearances, where beauty is concerned, and this typical concern is, in large measure, the right concern to have. Too much of value is lost, and our range of responses is too thin, if we are not interested in the relationships between the surfaces and the depths of things, if we are not alive to harmonies and incongruities here, and if our interest in beauty is divorced from attendant interests in goodness, health and truth.[21] Thus while it is not always necessary to appreciate nature as nature, and indeed while it might on occasion be important to forget that there is nature there at all, appreciation tied to some sort of understanding ought, or so I claim, to figure in most of our responses.[22]

It might be objected that the appeal here to our typical concern with the informed response can carry little weight against the formalist, who is concerned with the ideal, rather than the real, character of our aesthetic attitude, but remember the dispositional account. A thing is beautiful, we said, if it appears beautiful to normal observers under normal conditions. Something might look beautiful, and yet not be beautiful, just as it might look red, and yet not be red, because of either an internal or an external abnormality. There may be defects in the eyes, or too limited attention, or factors without that prevent our getting a proper look at the thing in question. But, it can be argued, formalism ignores half of this. While insisting on the acuity of our sensory apparatus, it fails to see how the objects with which we are engaged ought not to be disguised. The normal conditions for smelling chemicals are when they are presented to us as chemicals, and not when masquerading as wild flowers, and the normal conditions for encountering the victims of torture is, for most of us, via newspaper reports, documentary film or Amnesty International appeals, and not when disguised as works of art.

Of course, the formalist can retort that we might be interested in merely the surface of a thing, in appearance, rather than the reality of beauty. So we might, but the formalist offers a revisionary account. The onus is on him or her to explain why we should change, and establish as the norm what is so far exceptional. No good argument is yet forthcoming.

The suggestion here, that an appropriate aesthetic response to nature typically but not invariably gets beneath the mere surface of things, connects with views advanced elsewhere. Ronald Hepburn, in a thoughtful and utterly unfrivolous paper,[23] has similarly insisted on the importance of looking carefully and thinking clearly where a full appreciation of nature is concerned, and has argued that intemperate, lazy and muddle-headed responses are so much the worse for that, and less than nature deserves. Failure to acknowledge, for example, the true character of wild animals, and a tendency to see them as human beings in disguise, can lead to an overly sentimental attitude to the natural world.

Perhaps Hepburn is, in the end, a little too rigid in his distinguishing between trivial and serious responses to nature's aesthetic values. His rejection of extremes, and his suggestion that between them "we might find an acceptable ideal for serious aesthetic perception in encouraging ourselves to enhance the thought load *almost* to the point, but not *beyond* the point, at which it begins to overwhelm the vivacity of the particular perception"[24] is arguably right enough, even if it might look impossibly precise.[25] What I have wanted to allow is room for at least the occasional response in which the thought load is more or less absent. Looking long and hard, free of concepts, is not at all like casual looking with the wrong concepts, and is a way of taking nature seriously even if it is not taking it seriously as nature.

Beauty

The question so far has concerned the right response to nature: what ought we to attend to if we are genuinely to appreciate the beauty in nature? But there is a further, and equally important, question concerning just how beautiful nature is, and on just what its beauty depends. In certain respects this question has already been addressed, as I have suggested, against formalism, that there is aesthetic value in nature, as there is in art, that rests on more than merely the surface properties of a thing, and that just as we will need to consider more than the surface of a painting if we hope properly to understand and appropriately respond to its value as art, so, too, with nature more than appearance should help to shape our response. This is a very partial answer, and there are important issues here that need a more detailed consideration. First, some preliminaries.

One view is that the beauty in nature depends just on nature. It is all beautiful. This view might be dismissed out of hand were it not the case that just such a view, as I have noted, is not infrequently advanced. It surfaced among much deep ecological writing and it surfaces again, perhaps more surprisingly, in Carlson, who, taking certain somewhat ambiguous remarks by the Dadaist Hans Arp as a cue, insists that natural objects "to the extent that they are appreciable at all, are more or less equally appreciable – equal in beauty and importance".[26] But the view has nothing to recommend it.[27] We should not be disallowed from finding some animals (hogs, toads, slugs) fairly ugly, some processes (decomposition, the way that snakes eat) repellent, and some views (the sea on a dull day, tundra, land hit by a storm) boring or messy. Are these aesthetic verdicts? They take into account, in most cases, more than the appearance of things, but without formalism that is not in itself an objection. It is, in an important way, to appearance that we are reacting here. Decomposition is worse to see, and to smell, than merely to think about. There is no good reason to deny that our concern here is with aesthetic value.

A view that deserves even shorter shrift is that only nature is beautiful. We should not forget Venice. But this impossible view connects with another: that in general nature is to be preferred, as it is in general more beautiful than artifice. So put, this view is vague and unpersuasive. It could be true, but there is a lot of nature, a lot of artifice and a lot more that is a mixture of the two, and it isn't clear how any overall assessment would proceed. Would we count individual things, see how much beauty there is per square mile, or what? Nor is it clear, even if true, how important a result this would be. Perhaps we would decide that nature has so far had all the breaks, or that we should try harder. There are related views that might be more readily assessed. The first is that for any appearance, it is better if that appearance is produced by natural rather than artificial means. Although clear, this is highly implausible. Why think that a place that looks like Venice would be more valuable if, by some near miracle, it resulted from altogether natural forces? A second, more plausible view is that anything that has the appearance of being produced by natural forces is better if produced by those forces. Conversely, anything that appears to be produced by human ingenuity is more valuable if it is so produced, and isn't a freak of nature. The view, in short, is that it is better if things are as they seem.

This view connects back with ground already covered. I suggested that we might well revise our assessment of a thing's value if we take it for natural and then discover that it is artificial, or vice versa. We admire the Bayreuthian splendour of Thirlmere, the most dramatic and mysterious of the English lakes, only to find that its present appearance is very much due to the activities of water companies, and that it is a genuine lake no longer. This phenomenon is not quite the one under consideration here. Disappointment at revealed confusion is compatible with the artificial lake being in itself as valuable as, or more valuable than, the real lake. It is with a blanket denial of such possible values in the objects, irrespective of our fluctuating valuations of them, that the present view is concerned. Is it plausible? Should we suppose there is something we might think of as an authenticity value where aesthetics is concerned, such that however beautiful a thing is, it is somewhat less beautiful if it is not altogether what it appears to be?

Faking nature

The view arrived at here is closely connected with, but still not quite the same as, one considered and defended in an important paper by Robert Elliott. The connections, and the differences, will emerge:

> Consider the following case. There is a proposal to mine beach sands for rutile. Large areas of dune are to be cleared of vegetation and the dunes themselves destroyed. It is agreed, by all parties concerned, that the dune area has value quite apart from a utilitarian one. It is agreed, in other words, that it would be a bad thing considered in

itself for the dune area to be dramatically altered. Acknowledging this the mining company expresses its willingness, indeed its desire, to restore the dune area to its original condition after the minerals have been extracted. The company goes on to argue that any loss of value is merely temporary and that full value will in fact be restored. In other words they are claiming that the destruction of what has value is compensated for by the later creation (recreation) of something of equal value. I shall call this "the restoration thesis".[28]

Elliott objects to this restoration thesis. His position is not extreme. He doesn't suggest that the value attaching to pristine nature is always so high as to prevent interference. Nor does he even go as far as to insist that real nature is in every case more valuable than seeming nature. One difference between the present view and that outlined above, then, is that it is compatible with the rejection of the restoration thesis to hold that in certain cases nature restored will be of greater value than the original nature. It may be better for a thing not to be as it seems. The target of Elliott's attack is just the contention that restoration makes no difference, leaving the value of nature, be it high, low or non-existent, just as it was.

However, "Faking nature" is a rather loaded title. It implies an intention to deceive. Imagine a company that mines by night and before each dawn obliterates all traces of its work. When asked about its activities in this area it denies any involvement. Another company fully acknowledges what it is doing – it is open with the press and public, and even produces information sheets, brochures and videos on how the restoration is managed. The distinction here is, of course, mirrored in art. There are fakers and forgers on the one hand, and innocent copyists on the other, but the works they produce may in appearance be identical.[29] The differences in intention, though, may be thought to spill over into different values accruing to the works themselves such that forgeries, and not only forgers, may be thought of as in some sense corrupt, and tainted by their origins. Elliott doesn't want any part of his argument to rest on such considerations; restored nature is differently valued from the original even if the restorers have been candid throughout. Something else is presumably irrelevant to Elliott's argument, although his discussion hardly helps make this clear. Just as there are issues as to whether copyists or restorers are out for gain, there are also issues concerning their relationship to the original loss. In Elliott's examples restored nature is nature that has earlier been damaged or destroyed by human hands, but the force of his argument is equally effective when we attempt to repair damage done by nature, as when we replant trees after a storm, landslide or drought.

Fakery, and all that attaches to it, should be put aside, then. What needs to be considered is the case where the restorer is not sullying his or her work with underhandedness, and where the viewer is all along aware of the true character of the area. It had once a certain look, and that was produced by natural forces. It has just the same look today, thanks to the restoration process. And "look" here is to be interpreted generously. No matter how close the inspection, and with what instruments, the original and restored landscapes are indistinguishable from one another. The restoration thesis too easily collapses if we cannot rule out plastic trees, polystyrene rocks and taped bird song where once a natural landscape stood. Similarly for art, the case to consider is not that of a superficial ill-judged copy, executed in inappropriate materials, but patient and skilled repair of a damaged original such that even the expert eye can detect no difference.[30] As the restoration thesis claims that in this case the value of the artwork is preserved, so, too, in the case of nature.

Values

There are, though, many kinds of value. As I have already said, the restoration thesis need not claim that our valuings will be unaffected. Nor need it claim, what is evidently a corollary of this, that monetary values will be unaffected. Nor, again, that certain moral values – suppose the original was stolen from some foreign country whereas the copy was manufactured at home – must be unchanged. There might also be an ingenuity or skill value that is higher in the restored work than the original; replication is more technically demanding, often, than original creation. What is certainly at issue where art is concerned, and just this appears to be the crux for nature as well, is the question of aesthetic value, and what the restoration thesis claims, in both cases, is that however aesthetically valuable an original is, precisely that value is present within a replica or copy. If a seventeenth-century still life is exquisite, so, too, and to equal degree, is a twentieth-century copy.[31] If a lake, high in the mountains and half hidden by pines is, when wholly natural, of unsurpassable beauty, then so, too, does it remain beautiful if restoration work has been needed after damage by floods or storms.

The restoration thesis is defensible. It is defensible even if formalism is abandoned, and it is defensible even if, in spite of first appearances, there may yet be more than aesthetic values in play here.

A by now familiar claim is that the aesthetic properties of a thing derive wholly from its surface appearance. Thus, if in restoration a qualitatively identical surface is constructed, it follows straightforwardly that the original aesthetic properties are preserved. But formalism, I have agreed, is indefensible, and it can be allowed that a richer account of the aesthetically relevant properties needs to be given, such that a thing's beauty or aesthetic value is not simply a function of it surface appearance, and so cannot be assessed simply by a careful investigation of that surface. What a richer, non-formalist account wants to allow is that certain non-intrinsic properties are relevant to aesthetic worth, and while investigation might lead to well-formed hypotheses about such properties, still, the truth or falsity of such hypotheses can substantially affect the value. So I might, for example, believe a little piano trio to be by Dussek. The discovery that it is, in fact, one of Beethoven's lost works will rightly affect my evaluation – authorship matters. Or I might take the cathedral in Prague to be a fine example of late Gothic work. The discovery that it is mostly a nineteenth- and twentieth-century invention will again bear on my assessment – history matters. Although the intrinsic properties, as well as my beliefs about them, are unchanged, new information as to relational properties will, not inappropriately, bring about a reappraisal as to aesthetic value.

Formalism cannot account for this, which is in part why it has to go, but the restoration thesis can. Consider history in more detail. It will be agreed, presumably, that the histories of originals and their copies clearly differ: originals are older. Where art is concerned, an original may be painted by Rubens, and a copy by an unknown Victorian. A virgin forest may have developed gradually over hundreds of years, as the result of natural forces, while a restored forest is planted yesterday, by men with machines. But differences here allow important similarities to survive, and crucially, the causal story behind the genesis of a copy doesn't begin with the copy but reaches back, necessarily, to the original. Otherwise it wouldn't be a copy. Elliott considers a stand of trees, high among the mountains, which has been recently planted, in an effort to recreate an earlier scene: "If value consists of the presence of objects of these various kinds, independently of what explains their presence, then the restoration thesis would seem to hold".[32] There isn't, however, any clear objection to the restoration thesis here, as the new trees are explained more or less as are the old. They are of the kind they are, and are where they are, because that is what nature intended. Admittedly, that isn't a complete explanation of the present scene, but it is essential to an understanding of it. Similarly, copies of paintings are explained by reference to the originals of which they are copies. The putti are in the top left-hand corner because that is where they are found in the original. Thus the restoration or copy can well be seen as preserving the properties of the original, giving us, first, the same historical information as did the original about an artist's style, development and so on, or about how nature worked to transform a scene, and warranting, secondly, the same aesthetic responses. Consider paintings – if the original was lively, well balanced, garish or subtly toned, then so, too, is the copy. More complex aesthetic properties are preserved as well. Suppose the original was innovative, imaginative and stylistically adventurous. Then so, too, is the copy. It would be a mistake to judge all copies as derivative and unadventurous, on the grounds that the copyist is herself uninventive. The judgement is about the work of art, and not about recent activity on the painted surface. It is the same for nature. Carefully restored woodland can cause us to marvel, wholly appropriately, at how nature works, as one species gradually and over time gives way to another. And "gradually" can be appropriate even if these actual trees were planted only recently.

There is an important distinction to be drawn here between accurate copies and restorations on the one hand, and endeavours to make new work in an old style on the other. An objection to the Van Meegeren forgeries is that they distort our picture of Vermeer, of his concerns, influences, development. But imagine that a genuine Vermeer is to be destroyed. A perfect copy would be of immense value, not simply as a beautiful painting, but as preserving the thread of art's history. Similarly, a seemingly natural scene like Tarn Howes, or Yosemite National Park can, if we are ignorant of the extent of human involvement, too easily mislead us about how nature works. Although they may not be straightforwardly less beautiful, certain of our aesthetic evaluations will change, and rightly so, when we realize that nature plays a secondary role, and didn't (and perhaps also couldn't) create or maintain a scene with the look of the one we admire. This is invention, and not restoration. A well-executed restoration project is a different matter, and reinforces rather than undermines our picture of nature's ways, providing just the same phenomenal surface, and demanding just the response of the original scene. So if we value pristine forest "because there is a certain kind of causal history which explains its existence",[33] we might value the restored forest for just the same reason. There are extra links in the causal chain, but restorations of nature, like copies of art, reach back to the source.

Yet Elliott will object to this line of argument. He might admit that a restored forest can be just as beautiful or affecting as the original but insist nevertheless that something is missing. I said that it will appear that we are concernced with aesthetic values here, but Elliott denies this, insisting that his point is not about aesthetic value, but rather about value in some other sense. And it is this value, whatever it is, that is lost under restoration. But what is it? As he says, "part of the reason that we value bits of the environment is because they are natural to a high degree".[34] As it stands, this is a comment on our valuings, and not on value itself. I agree that we will value the untouched woodland more highly than the restored. In the same way, we will value a genuine Vermeer over a perfect copy. But do we have reason to value things just because they are old, or natural, or have been touched by a person of genius? Or is this a sort of fetishism? Imagine that, in the future, the world is hit by an asteroid, and everything is destroyed. But information has been stored on computers and beamed to another distant planet so that our world can be recreated. Jungles, deserts, mountain ranges, Watteaus, Hockneys, Las Vegas and Siena are all reconstituted just as before. (In one version we travel to the new world by rockets, while in another we are beamed there as well.) We will regret the loss of the original world, but it isn't clear to me that anything of value is lost.[35]

Use or ornament

Suppose that we value wild nature. It can be objected that there is no genuinely wild nature left. We put a fence around a park and tell nature to get on with its business. This is artificial, and depends as much on human decision as does restoration. If there are objections to the one, then there are objections to the other. Elliott rejects this:

> What is significant about wilderness is its causal continuity with the past. This is not something that is destroyed by demarcating an area and declaring it a national park. There is a distinction between the "naturalness" of the wilderness itself and the means used to maintain and protect it. What remains within the park boundaries is, as it were, the real thing.[36]

Certainly there is a difference between restoration and preservation, but there are similarities as well. In both cases our link with pristine nature is threatened and then sustained only by human activity. In both cases, that is, we attempt to stave off some of the consequences of development. The difference appears to be no more than that in one case we ring-fence a natural area and prevent further incursions, while in the other we remove and then replace items in their natural setting. Suppose that we agree that in the latter case continuity is broken. That might be said to represent a loss of value. But in the first case continuity is artificially rather than naturally sustained, and, even if to a different degree, that can equally be said to represent a loss of value.

This so far underplays the typical character of preservation projects. Where is Elliott's park? If it is Yosemite, or Ayers Rock, or the Masai Mara, then the real thing included, for centuries, fair numbers of indigenous peoples living a somewhat primitive life. In many cases they have been forcibly removed. Nor do we, in preserving nature, engineer a one-off adjustment to the balance of nature and thereafter let things be, for preservation is typically ongoing, with efforts to regulate population sizes for both plants and wildlife on the one hand, and to make and maintain roads, paths and tourist facilities on the other. Parks are "real" to a degree, but hardly real through and through.

The underlying issue here is that of detaching the look of a thing from its original place within the wider scheme, and the issue is often acute in relation to modified nature. Very many of the landscapes we value are preserved by what are, in certain ways, artificial means: subsidies, stringent planning regulations, and, most especially, the development and demands of the tourist and heritage industries. The traditions of layering hedges, dry-stone walling or maintaining local breeds of farm animals are seriously skewed, even if not quite broken, when an activity that was handed down through generations and pursued because there was no viable alternative is taught in schools and colleges, and promoted because we like things to look old, natural or genuine.

Walling is a good case here. The dry-stone walls that are such a prominent feature of the rural landscape in many upland areas of the UK are not, typically, as old as people think. Most were put up in the late eighteenth or nineteenth centuries. Most are useless, as hill farmers go out of business completely, or amalgamate, or find that they have no particular need for numbers of small fields. But because they are now seen as part of the beauty of the landscape, they are, by various means, preserved.

Or consider churches. In what may seem the best case an old church continues to play its traditional role in village life. It is tolerably full on Sundays, people reserve burial plots and the vicar's wife makes jam. In many other cases a church, even though it is not used, is preserved and restored, with a new roof, new gargoyles, protection for its monuments and stained glass, or is simply closed and deconsecrated, its treasures taken elsewhere and the building and grounds then left to nature. Some people see beauty in ruins and decay, while others shudder, preferring even the old to look like new.

Things are not what they were, and we have different views as to how important is our relationship to the past, and how that relationship is best acknowledged. Elliott believes that the restoration of nature is a second best, but still overall a good thing. Yet in so far as we can understand the attitudes of those who think that without a proper grounding in the life of the community, churches, walls and ancient homes should be allowed or encouraged to crumble, so is there space for similar views where both moderated and wild nature is concerned. Woodland management, through coppicing, pollarding and the selective introduction and control of domestic stock, was once an integral part of the rural scene. Should such practices be reintroduced, even when they are of no economic benefit, or should we simply let them go? Wilder nature found its shape of its own accord. Now that it can survive for the most part only in pockets,[37] and with our near-constant attention, should it, too, be abandoned, with preservation and restoration policies alike viewed as exercises in nostalgia? I am inclined to say no, in both cases, but contrary views should be taken seriously. The present difficulty is in having any clear idea of what living with integrity would be like.

Summary

It matters that we live in a beautiful world. We mostly believe that this matters and, I have suggested, we are right to believe this. Our well-being, our psychological health, in part depends on our living in some sort of proximity to what is beautiful, or otherwise aesthetically valuable. It matters also, and for similar reasons, that we live in some sort of proximity to nature. It is good for us, if not for it, that nature is beautiful.

Still, our particular ideas of what in nature is beautiful are, inevitably, shaped by more than the way nature happens to look. They are shaped, first, by beliefs about the character of the thing we are looking at – what it is for, whether it is young or old, sick or healthy, the degree to which it has been affected by human involvement. That such considerations bear on our responses is undeniable, but should they so bear? I have wanted to steer a middle path here, denying both that we ought, where beauty is concerned, not to penetrate the surface at all, and also that our reactions are inappropriate unless we approach nature fully informed. Our reactions are shaped, secondly, by our culture. This has a bearing on the question, often raised, as to whether beauty is in the mind or in objects. If our judgements didn't vary from time to time, and from place to place, then there would be reason to think either that certain things are beautiful in themselves, or that, as with colour, judgements are a function of something no less general than human nature. But they do vary, and, although I haven't argued this at any length, it is implausible to suppose that some small subset of these judgements is more solidly founded than the others. A shift from valuing the picturesque to valuing the sublime was a shift for neither good nor ill, but something that happened, as culture changed.

We ought, then, to be circumspect about the status of our own tastes, where nature's beauty is concerned. There are environments that I value, and would very much like preserved, but although I am fairly confident that the environment matters, I am less confident that these particular environments matter.

CHAPTER 11

Human Beings

An argument of this book has been that our concern for the environment, even if not straightforwardly a concern for human beings, is nevertheless a concern expressed by human beings, and one that appropriately takes the welfare of human beings as among its central focuses. This leaves several questions unanswered. Some can be addressed here.

A world without people

Could there be reason to destroy, or wish for the destruction of, the human race? Many environmentalists believe that there could. We consign animals to lives of misery, cut down ancient forests, exterminate species on a massive scale and generally trash the planet. It would be better off without us. But this can be meant in one of two ways. In the first, human beings are so wretched, and do such wretched things, that a world containing them is of net disvalue overall. So even if a world without people cannot have value, still, that valueless world would be better than this. In the second, the world without people can have value, but whatever that value is, people make it worse, leaving it with a lesser positive value, or no value either way, or again net disvalue overall. Either way, they make the world a worse place than it would otherwise be. And that is why, according to some, they have to go.

Is it plausible to hold that an unpeopled world must be of neutral value? It surely isn't plausible to hold this. We might think that what is bad about people, and the source of their disvalue, is the evil they do, but much, even if not all, evil is linked with suffering. We are evil in part because we cause other human beings and animals to suffer unnecessarily, and that suffering is

253

another source of disvalue. So, if a world without people nevertheless contains animals, most of which have some moments of pleasure, and others of suffering, then that world is unlikely to be of neutral value.[1]

Set sentience aside. Many environmentalists believe that even without people and animals, there are values and disvalues in the natural world. Not only is water of value to trees, but trees, and perhaps also water, are valuable in themselves. If we believe that people are evil, and disposed often and for no good reason to destroy such things, then we might believe that it would be better if there were no people. A world without us, and without other sentient creatures, might be good in itself. I have wanted in some ways to resist this. Imagine that we can snap our fingers and bring into existence a forested planet, deep in some distant galaxy. Or imagine that such a planet will disappear unless we snap our fingers. Either way, we have no reason to snap. Even though wanton destruction is wrong, there is no obligation on us to create or preserve, for their own sake, more non-sentient things. The mere existence of such things is not valuable in itself. Although this may be conceded for nondescript things, it may be different with beauty. Suppose that merely by snapping my fingers I can bring into existence a beautiful planet. Is there now a reason to snap? Certainly a difference between beautiful and nondescript things is that not only do we, but we ought to, value the former. This doesn't immediately give us a reason to create beauty when, because of its spatial location, it will never be experienced by human beings, but it is enough, I think, to make at least plausible the suggestion that there is some such reason. As I have suggested earlier, it does seem as if it would be wrong not to put some effort into preserving beauty, even when that beauty will not be experienced as such.

Suppose we have a choice. We might want to swap a less beautiful world with people for a more beautiful world without them, even when the first world is of some positive value, and where this value is to some degree contributed to, rather than detracted from, by the people within it. We might think it would be better to remove ourselves, and so enhance beauty. We might even think it would be better if we had never existed, and that God had ended his creation on the fifth day. Could it be reasonable to prefer this beautiful world without people to a less beautiful world that has people within it?

Imagine a last woman who, unlike the last man, is no vandal. She likes things to look good, but she is sick, and needs food and medicine. The only way she can get these is by destroying what looks good, and building a farm and a clinic in their place. These will look less good. Rather than destroy beauty, and extend her life, she allows herself to die, knowing that beauty will be left behind.

Is this last woman irrational? I see no reason to think so. Assume that, although sick, her life is good now, and if she chooses medicine and food, it will be considerably better. Even so, as it is not obviously irrational to sacrifice your life for the welfare of other people, or for animals, so it is not obviously irrational to sacrifice your life for beauty. That is a value, and not obviously a foolish value, to which one might hold. Still, choosing to end your own life is different from choosing to end the lives of others. We might individually or collectively decide to end our lives for the sake of animals, or beauty, and that might not be irrational, but most people would think it clearly wrong to bring about the deaths of those having a different view. Perhaps utilitarians think that if the sums are right then killing should go ahead, and perhaps there are many who think that, given very substantial benefits, killing the innocent is permissible, but only a few will want to say that the preservation of beauty can justify bringing about the death of human beings.[2] So consider a situation where this may not be necessary. Imagine a future war. In preparation for population losses people have produced many thousands of embryos, which are stored in fertilization clinics. One of the weapons of war is a gas that puts everyone into a coma, and arrests the development of the embryos. The gas is released. One woman who has so far avoided the gas has three forms of antidote gas. If she releases the first, those in a coma will wake up, and the embryos will continue to develop. If she releases the second, those in the coma remain, soon to die, but, some time after her own death, the embryos will continue to develop. If she releases the third, her own future will be secured, but both the people and the embryos will soon die. Her own future will be secured, too, with either the first or second gases. Assuming that she wants at least for her own life to continue, she has to choose between the various forms of gas; she cannot simply walk away. She can revive existing lives and start new ones, or start new ones alone, or ensure that there will be no future human beings. The woman, no particularly close friend of humanity, wonders what she should do.

Suppose, first, that her choice is between all three gases. Unless she takes positive action, those in a coma will never again be conscious. I suspect that it may not be as bad to fail to reverse a coma as it is to fail to help someone presently conscious who will otherwise die.[3] Even so, it may seem that if the first form of antidote gas is available, the woman does have some obligation to release it, and to restart the lives of people already in existence. But suppose that only the second and third gases are available. Does she have any obligation to release the second gas, and so start the development of new lives? The question is like, having done his work in five days, and then having had the idea of creating people, did God have any obligation to create us?

Reasons for people

People need people, and they often like them. One reason for ensuring that there are future generations is simply to increase the happiness of the present generation. Most people want to have children. I needn't agree that this is a reasonable desire, but given the desire, it is in some degree reasonable to take steps towards its satisfaction. Even those who don't want children have some reason to assist those who do, simply because it will help make those people (or so they believe) happier. There are further reasons. One may be under some sort of obligation to past generations, having promised parents and grandparents to bring more children into the world. Again, there is a question of whether one should have made any such promise in the first place, but if it is made, then there is of course some obligation to carry it through. Similarly for a promise made to a spouse or partner, or to one's first children. Another reason may involve considerations of prudence. As we get older, and in need first of pensions and later of care, younger people become increasingly valuable. Without them, having to fend for ourselves, our last years would be much worse.

The sorts of reasons adduced here are limited, in the main, to the next generation, where the overlap with ours is considerable.[4] Few people these days promise grandparents that they will do all they can to sustain the family line forever, and whereas many people just want, even if for no good reason, that there be children around, very few just want, even if for no good reason, that there be people around forever. But the reasons adduced here will be reiterated as, presumably, the next generation will also want children, will also need care, and so on. So in so far as we have reasons for wanting there to be a future generation, there are reasons for thinking that there will be future generations, *ad infinitum*.[5] Because of these overlaps, and these various dispositions, it may seem obvious that there should be future people, and that our extinction would be terrible thing.

All such considerations are, however, irrelevant where the somewhat artificial situation of the last woman is concerned. Future people will not help her. Nor has she promised anyone that she will help create future people. Nor is she herself strongly disposed to ensure our species' survival. So the question about future people is here presented in a purer form, and in that form the answer is less obvious. There is a need for a more thorough consideration of the arguments on either side.

Against people

Start with the gloomier view. Could there be reasons against restarting the human race? Various suggestions might be made.

1. Our suffering

It might be thought that this world is a vale of tears. Our lives are subject to so much pain and so much suffering that it would be better had we never been born. Religious believers might hold that, given we have been born, we should bear our lot with fortitude, rather than exit life at our own hands. Perhaps, too, either reason or nature will lead us to have children, and so lead to further cycles of human suffering. The situation facing the last woman is far from a normal situation. Perhaps here, when a conscious decision has to be made whether to preserve or destroy the human race, then, because of suffering, it may be better to end it.

Two versions of this view might be distinguished. Allow that our lives are interspersed with moments of happiness. On the first version, such moments could, in principle, outweigh the suffering. But, unfortunately, there are too few such moments. It is, then, a contingent fact that our lives are so much marked by suffering. On the second view, the natures of suffering and happiness are such that the latter cannot compensate for the former. So no matter how many our moments of bliss, given that we suffer, it would be better had we not been born. This is, as it will seem, an extreme view. But I will need to return to it below, and may then make a related view seem less than extreme.

2. Our wrongdoing

Perhaps our own lives appear to go well. But because of the havoc we wreak elsewhere, it would be better if we ceased to exist. Again, it might be held that even though this is so, it is still not permissible to bring to an end existing lives. The situation is importantly different where what is at issue is not this, but, as with the last woman, the question of whether new lives should be started. In this case, because of the wrong we do, it is appropriate that our species be brought to an end.

Again, aspects of this view need to be unpacked. Perhaps it is certainly, although contingently, true that we will do evil things, and in such quantities that no good that we do, to ourselves, to each other, or to creatures of different kinds, can outweigh this. Can we really believe this? People have believed it. The Old Testament God decided to flood the world, and kill everything, not just the people. But it was people who had wrecked the world, and made it, in God's view, worse than nothing. Perhaps some people still believe it. Perhaps some believe the even more radical view that evil cannot be compensated for by good, so that no matter how little evil, and how much good, given that we do some evil, it would be better had we never been born. This extreme view is not one that we need to revisit.

A further distinction might be made here, for it might be thought that, as with suffering, it is the intrinsic badness of evil that justifies our extinction. Even if there were just the one human being, locked safely in a cell, it might be that because of his or her disposition to evil, it would be better were he or she not to exist. Some will object to killing the innocent, no matter how evil they are, but again the situation this woman faces requires no killing.[6] The alternative view is that the badness of evil lies in the suffering it causes, so although it may be regrettable that we are disposed to evil deeds, the world may be such as to accommodate the tendency to evil with no ill effect. The last woman looks to another world where the last man, the only sentient being left, is busy with his flame-thrower. She has no reason to wish him dead and, in so far as the capacity to generate suffering is limited, no reason to prevent more people like him from being born.

One final point here. Physical suffering figures in both human and animal lives. If that is a reason to wish for our non-existence, it will suggest the same wish for animals as well. But if it matters, too, that we note our psychological suffering (this may be simply our anticipation and memory of pain, or it may take more complex forms), then it may be that animal lives are not in the same way judged to be overall bad, and similarly for evil.

For people

Suppose that there are not, contrary to the gloomy view, reasons for thinking this woman should ensure our destruction. It doesn't immediately follow that she ought, in contrast, to ensure our survival. Perhaps she does nothing wrong in choosing either way. But many will disagree with this, and suspect that she does have reasons to release the antidote gas, and restart the development of the embryos. What are those reasons? Here are some.

1. Species preservation

You might think that there is just no reason at all to create extra people, say on some distant planet, but that isn't the situation facing this woman. She is deciding on the fate, not just of extra human beings, but of the human race. If she doesn't release the gas, there will soon be no human beings anywhere. It may be tempting to believe that extra people is one thing, while the species as a whole is another. So given that it is these embryos or nothing, their development should be restarted.

Nevertheless, as I indicated in an earlier chapter, it isn't clear that this is a temptation to which we should succumb. It may be useful, for the sake of other things, that there are some members of a species still in existence, yet it isn't easy to see how it can be good in itself that a species has some, but only some, representatives. As Jonathan Glover has noted, if we believe that human beings should exist for as long as possible, it seems we should also believe that they should exist for as far as possible.[7] Otherwise we betray an unjustifiable bias in favour of time, and against space. Thus, the argument goes, a concern for species preservation implies a concern to maximize, other things being equal, the number of individuals existing at any one time. Is this a good argument? It may be hard to say what, if anything, is wrong with it, but its conclusion is not one that chimes with many ordinary views. Very few have the intuition that there should, other things being equal, be as many people as possible. But very many believe it would be an enormously bad thing were our species to become extinct.[8]

2. Consistency

Suppose that you think it would be a bad thing if pandas or tigers became extinct. If, without much effort, you can preserve those species, then you should. But then, other things being equal, you ought to preserve our species as well. Otherwise we are guilty, albeit in a less familiar form, of speciesism. The assumption here is that other things are equal, but that might be challenged. As I have noted, we, unlike pandas, are capable of evil.

The argument from consistency might be more broadly construed. Suppose that you think there are reasons for preserving beauty, either natural or man-made, or for promoting more beauty in the future by ensuring that seeds will germinate, trees will grow and rivers will continue to run. Again, if there can be intrinsic value here, then, arguably, there can be intrinsic value in the existence of human beings as well. There may, of course, be various reasons for ranking beauty above people, but it is not at all clear how one could admit value in beauty, and yet insist that the suggestion that there should be a similar value in people cannot even get off the ground. Still, it might not get far off the ground. Beauty is obviously a positive quality, but the jury is still out on people. So perhaps we should agree with this: *if* there is some reason to create beauty, then there is some reason to create people, *if* people are overall good.

3. Preserving and promoting

There is at least a *prima facie* obligation to save lives. But if it is good that we should save lives, it is surely good also that we should start them. For if we can act in such a way as to bring about the past fifty years of good experiences, why not get a life going, and bring about these experiences, along with the thirty or so years of good experiences that precede them?

This isn't persuasive. Even on an intuitive level a distinction between preserving and promoting, or starting and saving, is customarily made, and it has its rationale. I don't want to claim that it is as clear why we should save someone from a sudden and painless death as it is that we should save them from torture, but in so far as it is clear, it is because of thoughts about completion of a life already under way, the fulfilment of plans and projects already formed, but not yet realized. When a life is prematurely[9] curtailed something of value is lost, but this isn't in the same way so when a life isn't started. This isn't a puzzling distinction. It is often better to see none of a film than to be dragged from the cinema half way through.

The distinction between human and animal lives is again relevant here. In so far as animals have neither hopes for the future nor memories of the past, and in so far as they effectively live for the moment, so obligations to start and save are in their case more closely connected. But they are, I suggest, equally weak. Setting instrumental considerations aside, it isn't any more important that animals should die, than that they are never born. This isn't to imply that such things are of no importance, and analogously, nothing here implies that it is of no importance that we should promote new human lives. The claim is only that it doesn't at all follow that we should do this from the relatively clear contention that we should preserve extant lives.

4. A symmetry argument

Suppose that human beings are destined to live wretched lives. It would then be wrong to bring them into existence. Symmetry suggests that if they are destined to live good lives, then it would be right to bring them into existence. And knowledge isn't required here. If we have good reason to believe that a life would be wretched, then it would be wrong for us to start that life. Often, however, we have good reason to believe that life will go well.

The argument here doesn't insist, counterintuitively, that we ought to have many more children, for it readily allows that the case for starting lives can be outweighed by, among other things, the financial and emotional costs that will be incurred. There are no such costs where the last woman is concerned, so, assuming that she has reason to believe that future lives will be good, she ought to do what is needed to help start those lives.

How compelling are these appeals to symmetry? There are, I think, reasons for thinking they carry less weight than at first appears. What, if anything, is obvious is that we shouldn't start lives that are full, and will remain full, of extreme pain. Analogously, then, we should start lives that are full of extreme pleasure. But what is that? The difficulty here is that few, if any, of us have much idea of what such a state would be like. There seems to be an unavoidable asymmetry in the range of our responses. If we consider more complex notions of well-being, then, while symmetry may be restored, the obviousness pertaining to bad lives begins to disappear. It isn't at all obvious to me that we should start the lives of people who will be head over heels in love, but then neither is it obvious that we should refrain from starting the lives of those who will be broken-hearted.

I outlined above the apparently extreme view that no amount of pleasure can compensate for pain. But something like this extreme view has to be in play here, if we are to deny, as I have suggested that we might deny, that symmetry considerations are telling. Perhaps that view is not so extreme, after all.[10]

5. Instrumental reasons

Most of these arguments suggest that there is some sort of intrinsic value in the existence of human beings. But consider the first argument further. One puzzle about species preservation is why it doesn't generate a demand that there be as many people as possible. This puzzle is solved, however, if we think instead in terms of instrumental value, for then the population needed will be a function of demands elsewhere. This might now be more fully explored. Environmentalists may decide that they, too, have reasons to wish for future people. Not only people need people. The natural world, and in particular the plants and animals within it, cannot very well look after themselves without human assistance. If we want beauty, stability, diversity and the rest, then human beings will be needed to act as nature's custodians. On one version of this view, human beings will always be needed, perhaps to maintain a balance between other species, or to protect the rarities from accidental destruction. On another version the need is temporary. Imbalances are our doing, and we should attempt to correct them.

Beauty, too, may be unable to look after itself without human assistance. Perhaps we are needed to minister to the beauties of nature, to the look of deserts or mountains or, on a smaller scale, to the balance of shapes and colours in a woodland grove. And perhaps we will be needed to care for paintings, buildings and other of our creations, which will otherwise crumble into dust.

If, as I am assuming, non-human nature, along with human artefacts, will for a while at least continue anyway, there may be some reason to include human beings, even if they are not valuable in themselves, in order to ensure smooth running. Again, this instrumental argument is linked with one about intrinsicness. If we think it good that the non-human world continue, why not think that human beings themselves are part of, and not merely a means to, that good?

People and value

There is mix of values here. People who just like people, or who just like children, hold people, or children, to have personal value. They value them, but don't thereby claim that they are in any way objectively valuable. People who think we need people, either to look after further people, or to look after the natural environment, hold that people have instrumental value. Presumably, if the old were healthier, and then allowed to end their lives when the quality of those lives began inevitably to diminish, the need for carers would be reduced. The environmentalist who wants people to care for the non-human world also holds people to be instrumentally valuable. If there were no longer nature to nurture, there would no longer be any value in people.

There is also the claim that human beings are intrinsically valuable. If this is so, there will be reason to ensure our survival (and reason, too, to maximize the number of people, other things being equal), quite independently of how we happen to feel about people, and quite independently also of their effects elsewhere. This idea, that human beings are intrinsically valuable, needs to be further explored. For there has been a certain asymmetry in the considerations discussed so far. Our reasons against people focused on certain intrinsic properties of human beings, and the allegation that in virtue of these properties it would be better if we didn't exist. Our reasons for people had a somewhat different emphasis, seeing how we might arrive at a need for

261

people from a consideration of factors (mostly) elsewhere. But as well as arguing, say, that if pandas are intrinsically valuable then so, too, are people, the question of the value in human lives needs to be tackled in a more direct fashion. On intrinsicness, then, there is more still to be done.

Intrinsicness, sanctity and beyond

The widespread view that human beings are, in some way, intrinsically valuable admits of many variations. People who agree on what seems to be a broad principle here can disagree over details, and it is worth exploring something of the range of views. One place to start is with the quasi-religious notion that life is sacred. This itself covers several positions.[11]

First, there is a question of scope. Most people who speak of the sanctity of life are unlike Schweitzer. Although they make no express restriction to human beings, it is usually clear that such a restriction is implied. For the sanctity view, in line with its religious origins, holds us to be apart from the rest of nature. Secondly, many of its proponents hold not that we should start, but that we shouldn't stop, human lives. It is, typically, a view about preservation rather than promotion. And thirdly, although many hold that it is always wrong for us to end lives, or even to hope that they will end, they are often less clear about whether it is always bad when lives come to their (more or less) natural end. So in many cases the sanctity view appears to focus on the disvalue of certain activities relating to life, rather than emphasizing its positive value. It is, I think, a matter only of focus here, for the sanctity view isn't just about the wrongness of killing, but does hold that, at least with premature death, something of value is lost.

Ignore these various qualifications, and in each case the sanctity of life view becomes more extreme. But even with the qualifications the resulting view – that mere human life, irrespective of its content, has value such that our ending it is always wrong – is hardly uncontroversial and will, to many, still seem extreme. This sanctity view seems to involve a number of challenging claims where value is concerned. It suggests, first, that this value in human life is not merely contingently present, depending on further characteristics of that life. It is, with one important reservation, another denial that value depends on properties. It is at heart such a view, as it holds that this value in our lives doesn't depend on whether we are good, rational or even conscious. The reservation is that as the sanctity view is standardly restricted to human beings, it holds that this value does depend on our being human.[12] But it is unclear, once the more striking characteristics of being human are stripped away, why this should matter. It suggests, secondly, that this value in human life cannot be outweighed by values elsewhere, either by competing positive values, or by the disvalue of our own pain.[13] If the choice is between life and relief from agony, then life wins. And if it is a human life, or a thousand animal lives, or the preservation of Venice, then human life wins. It isn't claimed that the sanctity of human life is the only value there is. And the view allows that in respect of further properties one life might be more or less valuable than another, but that this core value is present to the same degree in each of us, and in each of us takes precedence over further values.

This sanctity view, as I have suggested, in putting human beings so high, is a view on intrinsic value that many environmentalists will find hard to swallow. With its insistence that human life has value whatever its condition, it is a view that many humanists find hard to swallow too. It is hard to see how it can be well defended.

Less extreme views on intrinsic value, unsurprisingly, will fare better. One holds that mere life is always of some positive intrinsic value, but allows that it can be outweighed by the disvalue in pain. So while a comatose life is one worth living, an agonized life is not. Another holds that mere life is of no value in itself, but that life as lived has a positive or negative value in virtue of the pleasure or pain (or, on increasingly sophisticated accounts, more complex psychological states and dispositions to such states) that it contains. This view holds, then, that human life is intrinsically valuable when it is constituted a certain way, but not that it is of value irrespective of its condition. Thus, in so holding that value depends on properties, this view, in contrast to the earlier sanctity account, holds that life is contingently of intrinsic value. This, or so I believe, is more plausible than the view that it has such value necessarily. (A variant here holds that value attaches only to the properties – the experiences of pleasure, friendship, beauty may be valuable in themselves[14] – while human life, the existence of a person, has only instrumental value, in allowing for the existence of such mental states. Although I think that this is less plausible than the view that holds that under certain conditions value attaches directly to people, the differences between these variants, and their relative merits, can here be ignored.)

Different positions can be given different names. Call that which holds that human lives have value irrespective of their content the sanctity view. The variant that holds that content matters is the quality view. The latter, I claim, is the more defensible, but remember that the sanctity view is in a further respect typically modest in that it doesn't ask us to start new lives. A concern with quality, in contrast, often does ask us to start new lives, on condition we can expect the content to be right. Call these, respectively, the preservation and the promotion views. Preserving quality lives lies here at one extreme, while promoting lives irrespective of quality is at the other.

Species survival

What should this last woman do? There will be a time when there are no human beings, but, if she presses the right button, after two centuries embryos will be unfrozen, new human beings will be born and, in many respects, life will carry on much as before. There will be Venice, Beethoven, Chekhov and Hume, as well as books on medicine, petrochemicals, horticulture and so on. And there will be greed, envy, war, disease and famine as well. The complex pattern to human existence is likely to continue. Ought she, or ought she not, to press this button? Or, although there will certainly be different consequences either way, is there nothing that she ought to do? One difficulty is in assessing the effects of human survival. Another is in knowing what to make of those effects, and how to adjudicate between the different outcomes. It isn't obvious what we should think of the alleged value in nature, or beauty, or sentience, all of which are sensitive to human interference. Nor is it obvious whether, and to what degree, human beings might be thought intrinsically valuable.

Although much isn't obvious, still, I think certain easy answers can be rejected. It isn't clear, surely, that we are, as the sanctity view urges we are, of such value that irrespective first of our condition, and secondly of what we do elsewhere, it is good that human beings exist. Promoting lives irrespective of quality is not, surely, something that we are obligated to do. Nor is it clear, surely, that we are, as an optimistic version of the quality view might suggest, most of us in such a condition that it is good that creatures like us should exist. Nor is it clear that we have been in the past, or, more important, that we will be in the future, instrumental in improving the overall shape of the world. Similarly for negative views. Someone may hold that human beings are deeply and irreversibly corrupted such that, whatever they do, it would be better were they not to exist. But there is nothing to be said for this view. Nor is there much to be said for a pessimistic quality view. We are not, most of us, in so much pain, or so strongly disposed to evil that it would be better if our kind were not to survive. Nor, again, much for the view that even allowing we might have complex and mixed natures, still our net effect on the non-human world is so clearly negative that it would be better without us.

That leaves space, first, for some fine-grained judgements about the overall character of our lives, and about the effects of those lives both on other human lives and beyond. It leaves space, too, for going a little further than the first of the two extreme positions outlined above. Almost everyone will think that we should preserve quality lives, but we cannot prove that we should do this. Perhaps, as many will also think, we should, other things being equal, promote quality lives as well. I have offered various considerations that give some degree of support for such a view. That we are some way from a proof here ought, perhaps, not to be considered to provide strong grounds for scepticism.

Future generations

The question so far has been, ought there to be future generations? Forget, for now, about war, gases and embryos and think instead about a more likely scenario, and a more practical question. There will be future generations. Some will overlap with those of the present. The later future will overlap with the earlier future. Now the practical question concerns the relationship between these future people and our present practices. We can ask, what is our share of the world's oil? If present population levels are sustained for ten thousand years, and we believe in equal shares, then it is very small. It seems unlikely that these levels will be sustained, for population is increasing, and seems likely to go on increasing, at least in the medium term. So our share of the world's oil is smaller than very small. Or, we can ask, is it safe to dump nuclear waste? It isn't perfectly safe. We might ourselves choose to live with a very small risk, say a one in ten million chance, within twenty years, of catastrophe. Some might think it wrong to impose even this small risk on those in the next generation, who have themselves made no such choice. Yet it might be said against this, first, that the risk is very small, and, secondly, that these people will get some share of the benefit. Allow that the human race will continue. The longer it continues, the more likely it is that this catastrophe will occur. If it continues for ten thousand years, the chances of catastrophe within that period are down to one in twenty thousand. And this is assuming, what seems unlikely, that the chances do not increase over that period, as storage systems deteriorate, and materials begin to escape. Surely it is wrong to impose this sort of risk on people, especially when, as seems likely, they receive no compensating benefit.

Strategies

How, given this long procession[15] of people through time, can we justify our current use of resources, and our current attitudes to risk? There are several strategies. One is to say that we don't know what the future will bring. We don't know that people will need oil, and so don't know that we are using more than our share. Similarly, we don't know that they won't have found a foolproof method of dealing with nuclear waste, and so don't know that we will be imposing any long-term risk on anyone. More vehemently, but less plausibly, we might claim to know that they won't need oil, and will have methods for dealing with waste, and so on. A second strategy is to claim that though we do know they will need oil, the future counts for less, and the further future for much less. Suppose that population levels, within each decade, and the demand for oil both remain the same. One widespread thought is equal shares. But advocates of the second strategy claim that because they live in the distant future their share of the oil is less. Equal shares

265

works for people living at the same time, but not for people living at different times. A third strategy is to change the facts. If we continue as we are, then there will be future generations who can make substantial claims on us. We are already using someone else's oil. But we don't need to continue as we are. We can take steps to reduce future population levels. One reason for doing this might be to improve the quality of life for those future people. Another reason might be to justify our maintaining our own current high quality of life. So we might think either that billions and billions just cannot lead a good life together, or that they cannot lead this good a life as long as we live our good life today.[16]

What can be said for or against these strategies? Consider the first, in both its forms. We might agree that we cannot say, or cannot truly say, that we know people will have no need of oil. The Romans couldn't have said that they knew we would have no need of coal, nor the Celts that we would have no need of flint. Can we say that we don't know they will need oil? Yes, we can say this. No one knows for certain what the future will bring. But we cannot justify present consumption merely by an appeal to lack of certainty.[17] Probabilities matter as well. Suppose that it is, as far as we can tell, unlikely that people in a thousand years will have much need for oil. Does this help to justify present consumption? We need to take into account the consequences of a mistake. We think it unlikely they will need oil, but think also that if we are wrong about this, they will surely find some substitute. With luck, if we are wrong with the first thought, we will still be right with the second. Perhaps we might even run the risk of being wrong on both counts. If we are wrong, they will be inconvenienced. The situation is clearly different, however, where nuclear waste is concerned. Even if it is highly likely that current storage systems are safe, and highly likely, too, that if they are not safe, future generations will be able to remedy any defects, still it may be wrong to leave even this much to chance. A high risk of inconvenience is better than a low risk of calamity. We know that if we get this one wrong, the consequences are serious indeed.

The second strategy has been much discussed. It claims that we are justified in discounting for the future, and in viewing later costs and benefits as less important than costs and benefits occurring now. Suppose we think that radiation leakage associated with a nuclear power station will bring about one hundred deaths. If these deaths occur within the present generation that may well be considered an unacceptable cost, but if they occur generations hence, then, according to advocates of discounting, the cost may well be acceptable. For the future matters less, and the further future less again. This is not, as I note above, simply to rerun the point about uncertainties. In so far as we are ignorant of what the future will bring we can legitimize some level of discounting, but many have claimed that even setting uncertainty to one side, we can still count future people for less. Just the fact that they are temporally distanced is enough to warrant this. If this is right, and we can legitimately care less about future generations than about those alive today, our own lives will be made more comfortable, and the arguments of many environmentalists about the problems we are leaving for others to face can be more or less ignored. For with a discount rate of 10 per cent, a single life today is worth a million lives only 145 years hence.[18]

This view looks strange. How does it even begin to get established? Within the economic sphere the rationale is fairly clear. The promise of a hundred dollars tomorrow is worth more than a hundred dollars in ten years' time. Even discounting inflation I might invest the money now, and have considerably more than a hundred dollars ten years hence.[19] But extrapolating from here to any general discounting position, as has been carefully argued,[20] involves a confusion. Suppose we believe that a certain amount will compensate someone for the harm caused by nuclear radiation. If we want to set aside sums great enough to provide such compensation, we need some idea of when the anticipated harms will occur. For those occurring in the immediate future almost the entire sum will need to be set aside, but for harms occurring in the further future a fraction of that sum, appropriately invested, will guarantee the entire sum will then be available. What we need to do now to compensate for our mistakes decreases, the longer it is until the effects of our mistake are felt. But later effects are felt just as keenly as earlier effects. That is why, when the time comes, the same sums are needed for compensation. Future problems are not less important than present problems, just because they are further away.

What of the third strategy? The problems with resources and risk arise because of the billions of people still to come who, on the face of it, might live worse lives because of present policies. If we knew that the world would soon end, these problems with resources and risk would simply disappear, and they would certainly disappear if we knew that although the world would continue, human beings would soon become extinct.[21] Even if they remain, but with numbers much reduced, the problems become less pressing. Dwindling supplies would more easily go round, and fewer people would be subject to inordinate risk. (Although some might challenge the second point, thinking that whether we site millions or merely hundreds near a suspect reactor, the wrong remains the same.[22] I shall simply assume that numbers make a difference here.) But future numbers are very much in our hands. We can do very little, and allow population increases to continue their dramatic rise, or we can introduce policies to arrest or reverse this increase. If we were to reduce substantially the size of future generations, we would be able help ourselves to more of the earth's resources, and take greater risks with the environment than would otherwise be permissible. Should we introduce such policies?

Numbers

The practical question about population size needs to take certain factors into account. We cannot undo the past. There have been and are human beings in substantial numbers; some resources are gone and most others are available in only limited supply. We cannot yet consider, and may never be able seriously to consider, inhabiting other planets – one of the limited resources is the size of the earth.[23] Nor can we set aside the consequences for present generations of policies designed to affect future numbers. There are overlaps, and a total ban on new people would be both politically unfeasible and, if implemented nevertheless, unpleasant for the old. We cannot, then, talk only of what population size we might want in some ideal world. Perhaps ideally there are billions and billions of people, living wholly risk-free lives, and burning oil as if there is no tomorrow. But that is not an option. Given these several constraints, we can still ask, how many people should there be?[24] Because that is a notoriously difficult question to answer, we might instead focus on a narrower question. Although there might be some advantage to us in restricting future population size, there might be arguments against our introducing such restrictions. Are there such arguments?

Some people will claim that we ought not even to consider questions like this. The very idea of future generations of human beings depending for their size and even existence on present deliberations is too hubristic, too much our playing God, too close to final solutions, for decent people to want to take it seriously. We should let things be. This isn't a defensible attitude. Perhaps we should let things be where other creatures are concerned, and where the consequences of letting be are not apparently calamitous. But, fairly obviously, human populations do not increase without human involvement and, if nothing further is done, numbers are very likely to rise to a level where life as we know it, both for creatures of our own and of different kinds, is seriously under threat. Even if in the end we decide for some or other reason to do little or nothing, that is surely a position that we should reach, rather than occupy merely by default.

One way of reaching such a position is to claim that there ought to be as many people as possible. Not only should we not restrict numbers, but we should encourage growth. The claim here, as it holds that human life is valuable irrespective of quality, suggests a version of the sanctity view, and is, perhaps, the Catholic view on human population size. It has little to recommend it. A related, and more plausible, view is that we should maximize numbers as long as, or as long as we have reason to believe that, most lives will be good. This is more plausible, of course, as it pays attention to quality. Nevertheless, arguments that we ought to promote lives, I have suggested, fail to carry conviction. A further argument, this time against restriction and promotion alike, is that such policies contravene an individual's absolute right to reproduce or not, as they choose. This view, unlike the sanctity view, allows that the upshot of reproduction may be bad both for those who will be born, and for those alive now, but denies that negative consequences can stand in the way of exercising rights. There are not, however, good reasons for thinking there are such absolute rights.

So far it seems that nothing prevents our introducing policies that will restrict the size of future generations, and so permit us more licence than we might otherwise enjoy, where the use of limited resources is concerned. But there is a further consideration. Just as we might think that a reason for restriction is to avoid a drop in the present quality of life, so a reason against might be if there will otherwise be a similar drop in future quality. If there are a billion people, they can mostly have very good lives. But if, because of our demands, numbers drop to a million, the quality of life might fall. A million people aren't enough to do efficiently all that needs to be done, and it might be thought that it is wrong to make them suffer just so that we can live the high life today. But the worry here may need to be refined. Suppose the million still live better lives than ours. It may now seem less wrong that they have been made worse off. The wrongness will be more evident, the more their lives are of lower quality than those lived today.

The reasoning here may just as well lead us to restrict numbers. A billion can have a good life, but if there are a trillion, though worth living, lives will be less good. The billion will be worse off, if we let numbers go to a trillion. So restricting numbers may be to our benefit, and to the benefit as well of those still to be born.

Identities

Perhaps we can have it both ways, continuing with our present rates of consumption, and allowing for large populations in the future, whose lives will be worse than ours. For there is a further factor to be taken into account. This further factor will suggest that there is something amiss in the last of the arguments above.

As several philosophers have noted,[25] we can alter not only the number, but also the identity of people who will be born. Almost any reasonably long-term and wide-ranging government policy, no matter how insignificant it may seem, will have some effect on future identities. We go to war, our boys mix with their girls, with predictable consequences; or there are power cuts, and limited options for cold dark nights; or whole industries are shut down, and tens of thousands migrate to California, Arizona and New Mexico, and make new friends. So we are mistaken in thinking that there are millions of possible people, and depending on what we do, some or all of those people will be born. A better picture is that there are zillions of possible people. If we do one thing some of these people will be born, while if we do another, different people will be born. Both the numbers and identities of actual people are affected by what we do.

What are the moral consequences here? We probably already think it wrong, other things being equal, to reduce the quality of life of someone who is presently alive. It is wrong, other things being equal, to pollute the atmosphere and so increase respiratory disease. We probably already think it wrong, too, adversely to affect the quality of life of those who will be born. My wife is pregnant. My new neighbour belches soot and fumes from his supposedly eco-friendly wood-fired pottery. As far as my wife is concerned, her quality of life is already worse than it was. As far as our new child is concerned, her quality of life is worse than it would otherwise have been. On either count, there is something wrong in what my neighbour does. Across the street other neighbours, sick of fumes, leave their garden and take to the bedroom. Nine months later a child is born. This child wouldn't have existed were it not for pollution. Although he is not altogether healthy, we cannot say that his quality of life is worse than it would have been. So we might ask, as far as this child is concerned, does my neighbour do anything wrong?

The situation here is replicated on the large scale. We use current resources – oil, copper, hardwood, marble – in extravagant ways. We seriously damage the ozone layer, fish herring, cod and tuna to near extinction and obliterate the countryside's familiar face. And we take no steps to reduce future populations. In the future people will be born whose lives will be worse than ours, but who, were it not for environmental despoliation, would never have been born at all. Their parents met when the trees were cut down, or when the fishermen came home or, when the countryside no longer became a place to visit, in airport lounges on the way to Orlando or Las Vegas. Although their lives are worse than ours, they are not worse, or not much worse, than they might have been. Again we can ask, from the point of view of human welfare, do we, in adopting these environmental policies, do anything wrong?

It has been insisted that there is wrong here. Even though my neighbour's child, on the one hand, and these future generations, on the other, live lives that are worse than lives that would have been lived had different policies been adopted, these better lives would not have been theirs. So these particular people are not made worse off by these policies. Does this remove what might otherwise have appeared a strong moral objection to such policies? Parfit insists that it doesn't, for he denies that wrongs require victims.[26] If we can choose between two policies, one of which will bring into existence population group X, while the other will generate population group Y, then if the quality of life for X will be worse than that for Y, there is some objection to choosing the policy that will bring about group X. This is so, Parfit claims, even if we grant that no one is made worse off by choosing this policy.[27] The objection is that we haven't done as well as easily we might have, in choosing the former policy.

Two versions of what is claimed here might be distinguished. What Parfit believes is true, and what is certainly relevant to the present discussion, is the general principle, allowing for variation in both numbers and identities:

A   It is bad if those who live are worse off than those who might have lived.[28]

But he allows that this is by no means a familiar claim, and will be often rejected. And to fully explore and account for A we "would need to go deep into moral theory".[29] Yet if A is put forward in a restricted form, such that while identities differ, numbers are held constant, then the substance of the claim might be more easily grasped, and assent more readily given.[30] Thus:

> B   If the same number of lives would be lived either way, it would be bad if people are worse off than people might have been.[31]

This restricted claim, too, can figure in the present discussion.

Two components within Parfit's position can be distinguished. First, there is the somewhat controversial claim that those made worse off by a certain policy decision ought not to be viewed differently from those who, because they wouldn't otherwise exist, are not made worse off. Consider again the pottery. What the potter does has the result that both my child and my neighbour's child are less than 100 per cent healthy. My child would have existed without the pottery and my neighbour's child would not. But from the moral point of view there is no distinction to be drawn. Call this the parity claim. Secondly, there is the claim that in both cases a child is wronged. Call this the immorality claim. These claims are distinct, although the second follows from the first, given also that my child is wronged by what the potter does. Yet as the components in the argument can be separated in this way, so there emerge two ways in which the thesis that wrongs don't require victims can be challenged. We might deny the parity claim, or we might deny the immorality claim. In what follows I will say something about both.

Equality, more, or less

Notice that in both A and B above no claim is made as to just how bad it is that things are less good than they might have been, or as to what we might be expected to do to improve things. But this needs to be considered.

Think about the decision to begin a new life. Some people insist that we should do everything possible to give those as yet unborn the best possible start in life. This is plainly not a plausible position. There is no obligation on future parents, whether or not their child is yet conceived, to make every possible sacrifice that will further its future.

A second view is that we should, as far as is possible, do what is necessary to give the unborn a life at least equal in quality to ours. This is more plausible, but it is far from obviously true. It may be, either because the child is in some way disabled, or because of external environmental deterioration, that enormous sacrifices are needed to realize equality. Perhaps such sacrifices are not ones that we can reasonably be expected to make.

A third view is that we should better the lives of the unborn when the benefits to them outweigh the costs to us and to others. This consequentialist position is even more plausible, but there can still be objections. One relates to equality. If the unborn will, in any event, be much better off than us, it may be unclear why we should make sacrifices to make them even better off, even when the benefit to them is greater than the cost to us.

None of these views, then, offers a clear and uncontroversial position on our dealings with the unborn. And although in certain ways relevant to it, none offers an evident way forward with the sort of situation Parfit asks us to consider. He claims that we should select, from the unborn, those who will have the highest quality lives. But this seemingly straightforward claim needs immediately to be modified. It is implausible to suppose that we should make every sacrifice to achieve this end, but it is implausible as well to suppose that the claim is we should do this only when other things are equal. Certainly, the thought is, we should be prepared to make some sacrifice in order to start the highest quality lives. So perhaps the claim is that if we can choose between populations X and Y, then if the differences in level between X and Y are greater than the sacrifice needed to bring about the population at the higher level, we should make this sacrifice.

It is hard, however, to see why we should do this. Suppose I must start either world X or Y, each with a billion inhabitants. In X, people's lives are considerably better than mine, while in Y their lives are better still. To start X I need only to snap my fingers, while to start Y I must do fifty push-ups. I don't see that it is in any way wrong for me not to do these push-ups, or in any way bad if world X rather than Y comes into existence. Nor does it make any difference that all the lives here are better than mine. Suppose the level in X is equal to mine, while in Y it is higher. Or suppose it is lower in X, while in Y it is equal. Still I don't see that I need do more than snap. Nor, I think, does it make a difference if the levels are lower in both cases. Why should I have to do push-ups to bring about a population living lives slightly worse than mine, as opposed to one that is worse to greater extent? There is an important proviso here. I am assuming that all these lives are worth living. The question of why we should make sacrifices to choose worthwhile, rather than worthless, lives is more easily answered.[32]

If you are still far from persuaded by any of this, imagine a situation where your own involvement is profound. Suppose you and a friend survive the nuclear holocaust, but a tiger survives as well. Although, in spite of everything, both lives are worth living, your friend's life is somewhat better than yours. But the tiger eats him. Should you now think it bad that he was eaten instead of you, and that it would have been better if the tiger had eaten you instead? It is hard to see why you should think this.

My worry here is not a version of that relatively familiar worry about consequentialism. Both virtue and rights theorists claim, plausibly, that we are not always obligated to bring about the best outcome. The worry here is about the notion of a best or better outcome itself, and not one about what we must do with respect to it. Although world X might be one in which lives are better than they are in Y, I am not sure that it follows from that (even when other things are equal) that it is therefore a better world. And although my friend's life may undoubtedly be better than mine, again I am not sure that it is a better world, or that it would simply be better, were he to survive rather than me. This isn't to suggest that the notion of best outcomes is generally bankrupt. The worry is about the resilience of that notion where wholly different populations are concerned. This difference can take (at least) two forms: one in which we compare two possible populations at a given time; and one in which we compare actual populations at different times. Just as I am unclear that a second future is worse than a first, because lives are less good, so I am similarly unclear that its really a better world in 1450 than in 1250, because lives are going better at the later time.

An obvious objection here is that it must straightforwardly follow, if equal numbers of lives are going better, and nothing is going worse, that it is overall a better world. Similarly it straightforwardly follows that if my friend's life is really better than mine, then it would have been better if I had been eaten in his place. This objection might, I think, be granted, but only if it is insisted that no further concession is being made about what then follows. I might allow that there is some sense in which it would have been better if I had been eaten instead, so long as I am not thereby under any sort of obligation to regret my survival. And I might allow that world X is better than world Y, so long as it isn't suggested that I ought therefore to have done push-ups in order to bring X rather than Y into existence. Only if this notion of better outcome is given an innocuous interpretation ought we to allow that the notion has, where different populations are concerned, any role to play.

Perhaps there's room for a further, and more controversial, claim. I said above that Parfit's position, denying that wrongs require victims, involved both a parity claim and an immorality claim. What I have said so far has focused on the former, but what about the latter? The identities of those who will exist in the medium- and long-term futures depend on what we do now, but the shorter-term future includes those who are born already, or who are about to be born, or whose identities, although not yet fixed, depend more on random events than on any policy decisions that we have still to make. What are our responsibilities towards those people? What will seem much less contentious than either of Parfit's principles above is the following claim:

C   It is bad if those who live are worse off than they might have been.

In contrast to the earlier principles, C implicitly compares not different groups of people, but different situations for the same group of people. Like both A and B, it doesn't yet say how bad this is, or what we should be prepared to do to remedy this bad. It doesn't claim, for example, and implausibly, that we should make every sacrifice to improve the lot of our children and grandchildren. But again, it does, I think, imply that we should be prepared to make some sacrifice to benefit other lives. But is it true? Think about people in the past, and bracket out the bad lives. Suppose that we agree both that the good lives in Roman Britain were less good than the good lives in Britain today, and that those very lives could have gone better. Is it bad that they weren't as good as they might have been? If, as I suspect, this isn't bad, then surely we can say the same of the future. Perhaps because of our extravagant environmental policies our grandchildren will lead less good lives than they might otherwise have led. But should we quickly agree that this is a bad thing? One important difference between the past and future, of course, is that responsibility for the future's shape lies very much with us. If future lives are less good than ours, that may well be our fault. But the whole point is that "fault" may be inappropriate here – we do nothing wrong, with respect to future generations, unless what we do is in some respect bad for them. And I don't think it is clearly true, assuming that they live good lives anyway, that it is bad that their lives are not better. Some lives go very well, but none are perfect, and perhaps none go as well as they possibly could. I am far from sure we should think it bad that our lives are not perfect, and go less well than they possibly could. So I am not sure we should think it bad if people in the future lead less good lives than we lead today.

Environments

Suppose we need to choose between two wide-ranging environmental policies. One somewhat plausible view is, if the same people will be born either way, then we should choose the policy that will do the best for people, but if different people will result from the different policies, we are not obligated to choose the policy that will do the best for people. Parfit objects that in both cases we should do the best for people. I suggested, first, that this objection might not be strong, and secondly, that perhaps, as long as we do good enough, in neither case need we do what is best. Of course, there will be many objections to this last claim.

There will, as well, be objections of a different kind. Many will say that there is more than people to take into account. We need to consider as well how, as a result of our policy decisions, the environment itself will fare. This is right, but much of what has been said about people can be transferred to the wider context.

Consider animals first. As a result of particular policies certain animals will begin to suffer, while others will be born into bad lives from the start. There are reasons here against implementing such policies. But suppose the result is that the lives of future generations, though good, will be less good than they might otherwise have been. As with a corresponding claim about people, there is some vagueness about the details here. In one case, particular animals live lives that are both good and the best that are available to them. With different policies these particular animals just wouldn't have been born. Again, it is hard to see an objection here to our sticking with this policy. In another case, though their lives are already good, these particular animals could have lived better lives, if we had chosen a different policy. This might then be reason to choose differently. But again, we might deny that we are under an obligation always to do the best possible. What matters is that we take steps to avoid creating or sustaining bad lives.

Similarly for the environment's further aspects. As a result of the policies we adopt, the world contains certain items, and is beautiful. Suppose that these items are subject to the best possible arrangement – the world couldn't be more beautiful unless it were to contain more, or fewer, or different things. We might think that although a different world might contain more beauty, that isn't clearly a reason to think it would be better if this more beauty-containing world were to exist. (Think of a simple model. In the first case the world contains one beautiful planet. In the second it contains this planet along with its perfect double. The second world contains more beauty, but it isn't in any obvious way a better world.) Suppose, instead, that the items in the world are arranged so that the world is beautiful, but that they could be arranged so that it is even more beautiful. Still, we might think, although it matters that the world is beautiful, it doesn't matter that it is as beautiful as possible.

Beauty contrasts with diversity. It is hard not to believe that beauty is valuable, but hard as well to have an understanding of beauty that is wholly distinct from human concerns. In contrast, while we can grasp readily enough what diversity itself consists in, it is more difficult to see why diversity, in itself, should be valuable. But suppose we can see this. And suppose that there is a level below which there is insufficient diversity for diversity to be considered good. In the following cases we are above this level. There are still two questions. First, there is more diversity in world X than in world Y, but no overlap between the constituents of the different worlds. Is there reason to try to bring about, or wish for, or welcome the existence of X rather than Y? It isn't easy to see that there is. Secondly, world Y contains what world X contains, but more besides. Look to these extra constituents not as intrinsically valuable, but as simply contributing to diversity. We might still legitimately hold to the view that world X is diverse enough, good enough, and deny we have reason to hope that Y will take its place.

Similarly for other characteristics having environmental value.

Summary

I have been concerned, in this final chapter, to address further certain issues that have been aired earlier. One concerns the question of whether human beings are themselves a good thing. I have argued here for a middling position. Although there aren't good reasons for thinking that people are valuable no matter what they are like, or what they do, there aren't good reasons, either, for thinking that our ill effects on the environment are so pronounced, or so unmitigated by good, that it would be better if we ceased to exist.

A second question concerns the relationships between this and future generations. There are people now, and there are likely to be more. It is rightly thought that we cannot simply be indifferent to the fate of future generations, but it is harder to see precisely what sorts of obligations their lot imposes on us. We exploit natural resources, and add to various forms of pollution at what many believe is an alarming rate, and it is often suggested that we should either reduce our consumption, or, less often, reduce the size of generations to come. There is an evident complication here, when it is realized that to adopt different policies will make for a shift in the identities of those to be born. Against some reputable views, I have wanted to suggest that this counts against our having reason to change our policies. No one will benefit. More controversially, I have suggested that even when particular people will benefit, still there may not be reason to change our policies. Environmentalists will, of course, see this as bad news.

The overall position that I have wanted throughout to defend has two parts. Animals are in important respects like human beings. If future people will ruin their lives, then it may be wrong to bring such people into existence, even if their lives will be worth living. But plants, rocks, deserts and streams are different. Suppose that it is inevitable that future people will ruin the deserts. This doesn't suggest that it is wrong to bring such people into existence. But there are, of course, important corollaries. If ruining deserts affects adversely the lives of present people, or the lives of animals, then we may need to think again. The more the natural world is wrecked by future lives, the less likely it is that such lives will, in the end, remain worthwhile. Environmentalists will, of course, agree.

Afterword

Ruskin's fears for the polluted and darkening skies over Cumbria have proved strangely prescient. A full century after his death, thousands of animal carcasses are burned in open pyres, black smoke covering the same fells. For as I make the final changes to this book, Britain is in the grip of its first foot and mouth outbreak for over thirty years. The government seems impotent, hemmed in by legislation, bureaucratic bumbling, and its obsessive concern, particularly in an election year, to do nothing until certain that its decision will command widespread support. And so, as the science is too little understood, and as the different interests are confused and conflicting, new cases continue to be reported. The very survival not only of livestock farming, but of much of the countryside in anything like its recognisable form, is now seriously under threat.

This isn't hyperbole. Foot and mouth comes when the vast majority of farmers are already feeling the effects of a year-long collapse in prices, when the Europe-wide pattern of subsidies – and this alone protects many from bankruptcy – is being seriously questioned, and when meat-eating, after a string of diseases – BSE, swine fever, now this – is showing signs of a substantial and irreversible decline. There will be sheep and cattle farming in the future, but its scale may well be much reduced.

Is it then fundamentally a problem for agriculture, and for the countryside? Some people have questioned the sense in shutting down much of the country, and supporting the relatively small farming industry while ignoring the far wider implications for tourism. But this is muddled thinking. Without farming, and without animal husbandry in particular, the British landscape is unlikely to pull in the crowds. Sheep and cows, walls, hedgerows, pasture and meadowland are what people want to see, not the limitless expanses of rape and barley, near sterile environments where no birds sing. Nor, despite

277

nature's knowing best, do they want an equally limitless expanse of untended scrub as ancient boundaries, now useless, fall into decay, and bracken, dock, and struggling trees make the land inhospitable.

Does it matter that millions of animals are killed? It has come as a shock to many to discover that foot and mouth is nowhere near a fatal disease, and the reasons for this mass slaughter are essentially economic. The second shock is to be reminded that a farm animal's whole existence is based on economics, and most are in any event killed long before they are ever mature. This isn't, however, to suggest, as the uncharitable and unimaginative would have it, that we should suspect seemingly distressed farmers of merely shedding crocodile tears. A short life can be good, and an early death still timely. And the loss of entire herds, built up and pedigreed over generations and irreplaceable, is as serious as the loss of species.

And does it really matter if the countryside undergoes profound change? It depends how profound. Certainly there are too many sheep – current numbers are a hangover from wartime demand – and there are upland parts where the ecology would be both richer and more appealing without them. But our different concerns – aesthetic, financial, for food, for animal welfare – are in tension, and suggest that the future can only be bleak. A countryside managed to look good, even supposing we could agree on what that would involve, could only be unsettlingly artificial, with both sheep and their farmers playing roles like the actors at Disneyland, while to make this an opportunity to "rationalize" farming and food production could only dehumanize, denature us further.

APPENDIX A

Deep Ecology: Central Texts

Certain of deep ecology's writings have, I suggested, taken on something of the authority of religious texts and, in the manner of several religions, have sought pointedly to emphasize the differences between the preferred and rival views. This is in spite of the insistence of the movement's leaders that they are engaged in a non-hierarchical, non-centralized activity. I give examples here in order to illustrate something of the style of deep ecological writing.

The first represents a somewhat leisurely summary of the contrasts between the so-called dominant and minority world views. Deep ecology is not mentioned explicitly.[1]

Dominant position
- Centralized authority democratic
- Bureaucratized
- Police
- Individualism (radical subjectivism or "deluxe nihilism")
- Leadership by holding instruments of violence (such as police)
- Competitive communalism
- Frequent encouragement to "produce more, consume more"
- More government regulation

Minority tradition
- Decentralized; nonhierarchical;
- Small-scale community
- Local autonomy
- Self-responsibility
- Leadership by example ("not leading")
- Helping others; mutual aid;
- Simplicity of "wants"
- Self-regulation; nonviolent in a "professional" way

• Secular authority	• Respect spiritual–religious mentors
• Churches monopolize religious ritual	• Community fully participates in rituals
• Tends towards monopoly of ideology whether religious or secular	• Tolerance of variety of approaches to being
• Nature perceived as "data" or as "natural resources"	• More open communication with Nature
• Narrow definition of citizenship; all other inhabitants of place are slaves or disenfranchised	• Broader definition of community (including animals, plants); intuition of organic wholeness

A later summary, in which the contrasting position is now explicitly deep ecological, though discernibly similar, is rather more crisp.[2]

Dominant world view	Deep ecology
• Dominance over Nature	• Harmony with Nature
• Natural environment as resource for human beings	• All nature has intrinsic worth/ biospecies equality
• Material economic growth	• Elegantly simple material needs for growing human population (material goals serving the larger goal of self-realization)
• Belief in ample resource reserves	• Earth "supplies" limited
• High technological progress and solutions	• Appropriate technology; non-dominating science
• Consumerism	• Doing with enough/recycling
• Nationalized/centralized community	• Minority tradition/bioregion

This second summary is followed immediately by the movement's "Basic principles", brought back from the desert by Sessions and Naess, and presented, according to Devall and Sessions, in "a somewhat neutral way" in the hope that they might then be widely accepted:

Basic Principles
1. The well-being and flourishing of human and non-human Life on Earth have value in themselves (synonyms: intrinsic value, inherent value). These values are independent of the usefulness of the non-human world for human purposes.
2. Richness and diversity of life form contribute to the realization of these values and are also values in themselves.

3. Humans have no right to reduce this richness and diversity except to satisfy *vital* needs.
4. The flourishing of human life and cultures is compatible with a substantial decrease of the human population. The flourishing of non-human life requires such a decrease.
5. Present human interference with the non-human world is excessive, and the situation is rapidly worsening.
6. Policies must therefore be changed. These policies affect basic economic, technological and ideological structures. The resulting state of affairs will be deeply different from the present.
7. The ideological change is mainly that of appreciating *life quality* (dwelling in situations of inherent value) rather than adhering to an increasingly higher standard of living. There will be a profound awareness of the difference between big and great.
8. Those who subscribe to the foregoing points have an obligation directly or indirectly to try to implement the necessary changes.[3]

Each of these principles is then expanded and commented up by Naess and Sessions,[4] and then again some ten years later, by Naess alone.[5] They are not exactly commandments, but they come close.

APPENDIX B

The Axiarchical View

Why does the universe exist at all? Several writers, including most notably John Leslie and more recent Derek Parfit,[1] have argued that the answer "It just does" is not one that we should willingly embrace. For the argument goes, we know both that this universe contains life, and that the probability of its containing life is, on the face of it, extremely low. It seems that the conditions obtaining at the moment of the universe's coming into being could very easily have been such as to render life impossible. Thus the universe appears to have been "fine-tuned" for life.

How, then, is this fine-tuning to be explained? Two suggestions need to be considered. One is that the universe is, after all, created by God, who purposely fashioned its initial conditions such that life would evolve. The other is that this is in fact one among a very large number of actual universes, most of which are incompatible with life's development. Given this large number, and the randomness of their initial conditions, it is now much less surprising that some small portion will be suited to life. It is unsurprising too that we should find ourselves in such a universe, rather than elsewhere.

Leslie offers a number of analogies that help to illustrate these claims. Imagine coming across a solitary monkey who has just sat down and typed out the words to the Battle Hymn of the Republic. It is unreasonable to treat this as just one of those things. Far better to suppose either that there's some kind of deception – perhaps it is a man in a monkey suit, or perhaps the spontaneity is illusory, and this monkey has been carefully trained – or that there are, across the world, zillions of monkeys, each with a typewriter, each of whose efforts is at this moment being inspected. A special monkey is like a universe created by God, while zillions of monkeys are like zillions of universes.

Consider the God hypothesis further. We might ask, where does God come from? Both Leslie and Parfit go on to suggest that in place of supposing that the universe exists because God, who sees what is good, so wills it, we might suppose instead that the universe exists because it is good that it exists. This they describe as *axiarchism*, where the value within the universe is somehow such as to bring the universe into existence. How on earth this should happen is deeply mysterious, but it isn't obviously more mysterious than either that there should be a God who created the universe, or that there should be zillions of universes, in all styles, each springing from nowhere, or that there should be just one universe, again springing from nowhere, but this time undeniably special.

I don't want to elaborate on these views further, or to make any suggestions as to how plausible they should seem. What I do want to do is consider briefly how the last of the views sketched here connect with the environmentalist's accounts of intrinsic value.

There are evident similarities. Both accounts appear to hold that certain things are good in themselves, quite independently of human concerns. But there are differences. One relates to scale. Environmentalists typically consider intrinsic value to characterize certain things existing on or near the surface of this planet, whereas on the axiarchic view, the universe as a whole is good, or valuable. This difference may be less profound than it first appears. What is not always clear, among those presenting the axiarchic view, is whether it is particularly this fine-tuned, life-containing universe that might be thought to exist because it is good, or whether axiarchism might be put forward of any universe whatever. What is unclear, that is, is whether a discussion that begins as a revisiting of the design argument has, at this stage, slipped back into something more akin to the cosmological argument.

Suppose that there is such a slipping back. Life is no longer privileged, and the value attaching to rocks, stars and clouds of gas[2] is hardly one that we can hope to grasp. But suppose that this slipping hasn't happened. Then the relationship between intrinsic value accounts and this axiarchic view is close. Both suggest that goodness is peculiarly local; it is in virtue of the value around here and around now that the whole universe exists. So much for the Copernican Revolution. Of the two views, axiarchism is perhaps somewhat narrower, and somewhat more puzzling. For the intrinsic value view might)allow that there could be even greater value in a significantly different world, while axiarchism, in contrast, loses its pull if it doesn't insist that this universe is the best there could be. Suppose that we allow that some other universe could be better. We would then ask, why this one, and not that one?

Gaia

James Lovelock began to formulate his ideas about Gaia in the 1960s, and has written about them, often alone, and often in collaboration with others, on many occasions since. The term itself was suggested to Lovelock by the novelist William Golding, and has undoubtedly helped to encourage an interest in subtle and complex scientific theses among a wider public. So, what do those who believe in Gaia believe? And is what they believe true?

Some people misunderstand views that are themselves cogently stated. We cannot straightforwardly hold proponents of a certain view responsible for confusions elsewhere, but there are times when we can do this, and it is not unreasonable to think that Lovelock is himself in part responsible for the wilder interpretations of his Gaia view, even if he does not hold, and never has held to such interpretations himself.

First, there is the word. Gaia is the Greek name for the earth goddess. Use this name, and it is unsurprising if you are taken to be suggesting that the earth is importantly like a person, with, like a person, knowledge, beliefs, purposes, and a sense of the future and the past. There is a noticeable irony, of course, in this choice of name, and what it suggests. For Gaians and deep ecologists, although they should not be identified, have much in common. On the one hand is a rejection of anthropocentrism, and on the other this tendency to see the whole earth as if it is a person.

Secondly, there is what the word refers to. Lovelock often speaks simply of Gaia, as if Gaia undoubtedly exists, and just as often of the Gaia hypothesis, as if what is under consideration is merely a theory, which may turn out to be true or false.[1] The tension here might seem easily resolved. Gaia is the earth, which undoubtedly exists, and the Gaia hypothesis a theory about the workings of the earth. But things are not this simple. Gaia isn't simply the earth, but the earth in so far as it is, at least, a self-regulating system. Lovelock

285

is explicit that the history of the earth is older than the history of Gaia. Nor can we date Gaia's creation to the moment that life appeared. Gaia exists as long as the earth's various components, living and non-living, interact in appropriate ways.[2] Until this idea of appropriate interaction is further explicated, and it is made clear that this is in fact occurring, there is space for a question about whether Gaia actually exists. It cannot be assumed that it does, just because the earth exists.

This isn't to say that the distinction between Gaia and the Gaia hypothesis therefore collapses. We might suppose there to be characteristics of Gaia's working that go beyond the minimum needed for its existence, so that even when existence is established there are still questions as to whether the Gaia hypothesis is true. But then, what is hypothesized about Gaia? Various claims might be distinguished.[3]

1. The earth is a whole system whose various parts interact with and have influence on each other.
2. The earth's system is self-regulating.
3. The earth as a whole is a living being.
4. The earth is a living being that (normally) maintains itself in a healthy condition, and that is able (to some extent) to resist both external and internal interference with that condition.

The first of these claims is weak. Suppose, somewhat artificially, we distinguish between the earth's living and its non-living components. Who will deny that there is mutual influence here? Weather, earthquakes and radiation have effects on life, and vice versa. As Lovelock tellingly reminds us, there would be no limestone were it not for living things. There is nothing here that can be considered a hypothesis, and nothing that distinguishes a believer in Gaia from any reasonably well-informed person.

The last claim is strong, but it could be stronger. Nothing here suggests that Gaia knowingly maintains its condition, and Lovelock has denied ever making any such suggestion: "never was it considered to regulate by foresight in the way of an intelligent animal".[4] So much for Gaia as a person, then. But even if nothing like this has been claimed, something very like it has been speculated on:

> We are sure that man needs Gaia but could Gaia do without man? In man, Gaia has the equivalent of a central nervous system and an awareness of herself and the rest of the universe. Through man, she has a rudimentary capacity, capable of development, to anticipate and guard against threats to her existence.[5]

This does make Gaia sound much like an intelligent animal. Yet perhaps we should agree that assertion is one thing, and speculation another.

The more moderate claim of point 4 is that Gaia is something like an animal, even if not an intelligent animal. Any animal is, to some extent, able to maintain its condition, resist threats from outside and ward off disease. Can Gaia do this? Or, more cautiously, can we hypothesize that it might? A difficulty here is that we understand the difference between health and sickness where animals and indeed plants are concerned, but have no corresponding understanding for planets. The point is not simply one about statistical information. We count living things healthy, in good condition, at least in part in so far as they are able to reproduce. Planets, obviously, don't do this, so any analogy between Gaia and more familiar living things is hard to sustain.

Does this mean that point 3 is unsustainable too? My suggestion here is that the earth is not a living thing in anything like the ordinary sense. Perhaps Lovelock has no quarrel with this. His more or less standard claim is that Gaia is not an organism but a superorganism, just as a bees' nest is a super-organism.[6] He would say the same about other complex wholes, and take issue with my earlier suggestion that a forest, unlike its trees, isn't itself alive. Is he right about this? One thing he is certainly right about is the difficulty in giving a precise account of what life consists in. So perhaps we ought not to be dogmatic about just what is, and what is not, alive. Still there is a difficulty with the superorganism idea, especially if the analogy with a bees' nest is to have any purchase. Presumably a bees' nest is in a good condition when the bees are in good condition, but it is unclear how this helps with Gaia. Certainly it is hard to see how any species or groups of species – microorganisms on the one hand, or megafauna on the other – might be privileged. Perhaps all we should say is that Gaia is in a good condition when it is supportive of life. There are two difficulties here. First, it gives us very little guidance as to how to welcome or regret current environmental changes, for although particular species and styles of life are under threat, life itself isn't. Secondly, the claim is tautologous. Were we to say that the earth is in good condition when it supports life, then we would be making a claim of some substance, but Gaia isn't the earth, but, by definition, a system that involves and supports life.

Is the earth's system self-regulating? As we can think of one environment or many, so with ecosystems. Ponds, deserts, cities and mountain ranges are not isolated wholes but connect with and influence one another. Innocuously, then, we can allow that there is one large ecosystem on and near the surface of the earth. It isn't regulated from outside, even if outside forces – the sun's energy, the orbits of asteroids – play a not inconsiderable role in determining its condition. Perhaps to claim that the system is self-regulating is innocuous enough.

There is a relationship between views about Gaia, and the fine-tuning views that connect with axiarchism. The new design arguments have an advantage over the old in that they identify complex phenomena that cannot be explained in Darwinian or neo-Darwinian evolutionary terms. All apparent evidence of design *post* the first few moments of the universe's existence is in the end not puzzling, as it can be given a straightforward causal explanation, given the materials of the universe along with the laws governing their combinations. And thus Gaia is not puzzling. It may not at first be clear just how the earth manages to be a self-regulating system, but nothing that we know to happen or to have happened here is resistant to ordinary scientific explanation.[7] Regulation, purposes and goals can all be allowed, as long as they are given a familiar and naturalistic explanation.

Such criticisms of the Gaia idea are not new, nor are they always welcome. Lovelock insists that many of them miss the point, and are relevant, if at all, only to an earlier and long-abandoned version of the Gaia hypothesis. But this earlier version (if indeed distinctions between its versions can be made) still has influence, and so criticisms of that version might still usefully be made. Nor can later versions simply duck criticism. Lovelock writes:

> By 1988 Gaia theory had proved its worth by initiating a new study of Earth's atmosphere and climate . . . In its testing, Gaia theory had already opened several new fields of research, each with its own literature. This is what measures its worth, not arguments about whether it is right or wrong.[8]

Gaia theory cannot be worthwhile simply in virtue of generating new fields of research. What is needed, and what Lovelock surely believes, is that these new fields of research prove their worth by uncovering truths about the way the world works. Truth, even if not everything, is certainly one of the things we value. And it is difficult to see how it can be inappropriate to ask of any scientific or quasi-scientific theory precisely what it claims, and whether or not those claims are true.[9]

Notes

Introduction

1. From the preface to *The Queen of the Air*, J. Ruskin, *Works*, 39 vols, E. T. Cook & A. Wedderburn (eds) (London, George Allen, 1903–12) and in K. Clark, *Ruskin Today* (London, Murray, 1964), p. 118.
2. For much on the relationship between environmentalism and Romanticism, see J. Bate, *Romantic Ecology* (London and New York, Routledge, 1991).
3. See particularly *The Storm Cloud of the Nineteenth Century* in Ruskin, *Works*, vol. 37.
4. Although Bate, consciously breaking new ground, describes him as an ecologist.

Chapter 1: Problems

1. British government White Paper, *The Reorganization of Local Government* (London, Department of Environment, 1970).
2. See, for example, K. Lee, "Awe and humility: intrinsic value in nature: beyond an earthbound environmental ethics", in *Philosophy and the Natural Environment*, R. Attfield & A. Belsey (eds) (Cambridge, Cambridge University Press, 1994) and E. C. Hargrove (ed.), *Beyond Spaceship Earth: Environmental Ethics and the Solar System* (San Francisco, CA, Sierra Club Books, 1986).
3. Until well into the second half of the twentieth century the standard dictionary meaning of "environmentalist" referred to those taking the former side in the nature/nurture debate. It had little currency beyond academic psychology.
4. See, in favour of multiple environments over the one environment, and for something like these reasons, J. Benson, *Environments, Ethics and Human Concern* (Milton Keynes, Open University, 1999), and D. E. Cooper & J. A. Palmer, *The Environment in Question* (London and New York, Routledge, 1992). For the contrary view, see N. Dower, "The idea of environment", in *Philosophy and the Natural Environment*, Attfield & Belsey (eds).
5. Although it can be said that very few terms are amendable to precise definition, and that the vagueness around "environment" and its cognates is thus nothing special, there may be more danger and less consistency here than elsewhere. One example: my hunch is that we typically

289

think of nuclear power as raising a number of environmental issues, but that we less typically think of nuclear weapons this way. Obviously, however, there would be serious consequences for the environment were any of them to be used. The distinctions in nature that our terms suggest may be almost altogether wanting.

6. AIDS is, of course, very bad in Africa. Still it is, globally, less bad than many predicted in the 1980s.

7. This is merely a sketch of what ecology involves. I discuss this in more detail in Chapter 8. See J. R. DesJardins, *Environmental Ethics* (Belmont, CA, Wadsworth, 1993), p. 166, and P. J. Bowler, *The Fontana History of the Environmental Sciences* (London, Fontana Press, 1992), pp. 309–10 for useful first accounts.

8. How entrenched are the distinctions to begin with? In *The Environmental Revolution*, E. M. Nicholson refers to ecology as "the study of plants and animals in relation to their environment and to one another. But it is also much more than that: it is the main intellectual discipline and tool which enables us to hope that . . . man will cease to knock hell out of the environment on which his own future depends" (London, Hodder & Stoughton, 1970), p. 43. In A. Bullock & O. Stallybrass, *The Fontana Dictionary of Modern Thought* (London, Fontana, 1977), this account is described as "debased". Thus the attempt at a revisionary account is here rejected. But in *Nature's Economy*, Donald Worster argues that ecology's distance from straight science is long-standing, and that whether it is primarily "a science or a philosophy of interrelatedness has been a persistent identity problem" (Cambridge, Cambridge University Press, 1994), p. 471.

9. I use "moral" here in a familiar broad sense. But as I go on to explain, moral philosophy might appropriately be seen as a component within a still broader range of value issues.

10. I am using these terms here as if they are transparent enough, but, as will emerge, particularly in Chapter 9, but also in various places along the way, that is not so.

11. See, for example, Libby Purves in A. Barnett & R. Scruton, *Town and Country* (London, Jonathan Cape, 1998), pp. 199–205.

Chapter 2: Causes

1. This story, along with many others relevant here, is well told in J. Diamond, *The Rise and Fall of the Third Chimpanzee* (London, Vintage, 1992).

2. See, for a justly well-known account, W. G. Hoskins, *The Making of the English Landscape* (London, Hodder & Stoughton, 1955).

3. A. Mitchell & A. Coombes, *The Garden Tree* (London, Seven Dials, 1999), p. 10.

4. Human beings have, for example, been responsible for the extinction of species.

5. See Hoskins, *English Landscape*, and O. Rackham, *The History of the Countryside* (London, Dent, 1986).

6. I don't want to exaggerate the stability in human nature, so the suggestion is that short-sightedness, greed, and self-interest are not new, but can be seen to have flourished in a variety of cultures and periods. Nevertheless, such traits are not universal, and might with reason be viewed as products of particular economic and political milieux. It has to be recognized, however, that such traits are disappointingly easy to introduce into cultures where they might seem to have no natural home.

7. L. White, "The historical roots of our ecologic crisis", *Science* 1, 1967, 1203–7, claims, for example, that "somewhat over a century ago science and technology – hitherto quite separate activities – joined to give mankind powers which, to judge by many of the ecologic effects, are out of control. If so, Christianity bears a huge burden of guilt", and, more bluntly, "modern Western science was cast in the matrix of Christian theology".

8. Genesis i, 26.

9. Genesis i, 28.

10. J. Passmore, *Man's Responsibility for Nature* (London, Duckworth, 1980). See also, for further criticism of White, Lewis W. Moncrieff, "The cultural basis of our environmental crisis", in L. Pojman (ed.), *Environmental Ethics* (Boston, MA, Jones & Bartlett, 1994).
11. But see K. Thomas, *Man and the Natural World* (Harmondsworth, Penguin, 1984), Ch. 1, for a subtler account of the theological underpinnings of our attitude to nature.
12. Worster, *Nature's Economy*, and Bate, *Romantic Ecology*, each tell parts of the story here.
13. See Montaigne's essay, "On cannibals", in M. Montaigne, *The Essays of Michel de Montaigne*, M. A. Screech (trans.) (London, Allen Lane, 1991) and Shakespeare's exploration of the same themes in *The Tempest* (Act II, Scene i).
14. Nor does one possible retort here, that of these different ways some are better than others, have much to recommend it, for what would make for a ranking between these various ways, if it were not, in the end, something to do with their relation to certain seemingly relevant facts?

      Also, what White misses about Christianity is any awareness of that religion's extreme adaptability. A plausible view is that the seedbed for intellectual and technical advancement was laid in Europe before and quite independently of Christianity's success. Climate and geography encouraged the growth of trade and movement between populations in, initially, the Mediterranean basin, but then in lands further north, well before the Romans' subjugation of Palestine. Christianity, with its multiple and sometimes conflicting roots, proved able to accommodate several of its doctrines to prevailing hegemony.
15. Passmore, *Man's Responsibility*, especially Chs 1 and 2.
16. It might be conceded that it is impossible to prove that human activity plays no part in bringing about such events, but this is a sign, not so much of appropriate caution, as of a grandiloquent belief in our fallen natures. As Voltaire observed, many believed that the Lisbon earthquake of 1747 was a punishment for human ills. Similarly for Montaigne, and reactions to France's religious wars.
17. White, "The historical roots", p. 1206.
18. An awareness due very much to Rachel Carson's classic, *Silent Spring* (Boston, MA, Houghton Mifflin, 1962).
19. See, for much of value here, Worster, *Nature's Economy*, Ch. 16.
20. Noted in R. Mabey, *Flora Britannica* (London, Chatto & Windus, 1997).
21. Note, for example, the subject matter of films and literature. A concern with history is, of course, hardly recent, but it was, typically, intended to illuminate, rather than offer an escape from, the present. Future concern, and science fiction, are, with some notable exceptions, recent phenomena.
22. See D. Pearce & E. Barbier, *Blueprint for a Sustainable Economy* (London, Earthscan Publications, 2000), Box 1.2, p. 3 and Table 5.4, p. 113, for two instances of such variation in predictions.
23. For a recent, and in some ways important, example of this sort, see R. Scruton, *England, An Elegy* (London, Chatto, 2000).
24. This may be considered an uncharitable summary of White's argument, but I think it fair. He insists that "we shall continue to have a worse ecologic crisis until we reject the Christian axiom that nature has no reason for existence save to serve man", in "The historical roots", p. 1207. Can we suppose that we might be rid of this troublesome axiom, yet leave the rest intact? Hardly. It is clear that White thinks this central to Christianity in any form.

Chapter 3: Solutions I: Voting and Pricing

1. There are rough but still useful comparisons with religion. We distinguish theists, atheists and agnostics; only the last are doubters. It is sometimes suggested that the others can be described as holding to dogmatist and negative dogmatist positions respectively.
2. Whether or not the Internet, along with attendant new technologies, will allow for an expansion of town-hall politics still remains to be seen.

3. There are two questions. The first is whether reason can discover moral truth, and the second whether it can motivate us to pursue it. There isn't space to engage with these questions here.

4. Although there are serious issues of principle here. In many countries the party of government has less than majority support. And there are always in fact more than two options; we can be for, against, or neutral on any proposal.

5. The distinction here mirrors, more or less, that explored in Plato's *Euthyphro*, where Socrates is concerned to explore whether god or the gods discover or (merely) stipulate what is right.

6. The suggestion here, that morality as much as science is in need of experts, is long-standing. It starts, famously, with Plato's *Republic* and has continued, more or less unabated, ever since.

7. See J. S. Mill, *On Liberty* (Indianapolis, IN, Hackett, 1978 [originally published 1859]), and, for a good recent discussion of several of the issues here, J. O'Neill, *Ecology, Policy and Politics* (London and New York, Routledge, 1993), especially Chs 6 and 8.

8. Although my underlying assumption here, that there is at least the hope of discovering some such relationship, might be challenged, with the claim that democracy aims at nothing more elevated than a political solution to a political problem. Moral truth, by such views, is something of a chimera.

9. For penetrating discussions of the issues here, see especially S. Blackburn, *Essays on Quasi-Realism* (Oxford, Oxford University Press, 1993) and J. McDowell, *Mind, Value and Reality* (Cambridge, MA, Harvard University Press, 1998).

10. For a fuller discussion of this question than I can provide here, see John Dryzek, *The Politics of the Earth* (Oxford, Oxford University Press, 1997).

11. Particularly in English speaking countries, the UK, the USA, and also Australia and New Zealand, statist interventionist politics have been put on the back burner, and electable parties have abandoned any explicit commitment to intervention, agreeing that market forces are best able to look after the country's and its citizens' interests.

12. W. F. Baxter, *People or Penguins: The Case for Optimal Pollution* (New York: Columbia University Press, 1974), p. 17.

13. Or as is often said, to compensate us for losing something. These come to the same: to keep something is to forego what you could get for selling it.

14. For more detailed discussion see R. Stavins & B. W. Whitehead, "Market based incentives for environmental protection", *Environment* 34, 1992, 7–42.

15. It is worth noting that there is potential damage in the siting of a reservoir, and in the management of its environment. Not only does privatization cut demand, but it can lead to improvements in amenity value.

16. Even though there is still considerable impetus behind the "right to roam" campaign, it is evident that the countryside, especially in popular areas like the English Lake District and the Derbyshire Dales, has in many ways been impoverished by permitting unrestricted access. The alleged historical right to the countryside, typically taken up if at all by small and local populations, is a poor model for present times, when cars, motorways, advertising and increased leisure time permit and encourage unsustainable levels of use. One solution, adopted within US national parks like Yosemite, is to restrict usage by controlling the number and locations of ancillary facilities such as shops and hotels, but that is hardly viable in the UK, where parks are not government owned.

17. For discussion of this and similar issues, see D. Parfit, "Future generations: further problems", *Philosophy and Public Affairs* 11, 1982, 113–72, and *Reasons and Persons* (Oxford, Clarendon Press, 1984), Part IV.

18. "If the buffalo is not mine until I kill it and I cannot sell my interest in the living animal to another, I have no incentive – beyond altruism – to investigate others' interest in it. I will do with it as I wish. But if the buffalo is mine and I may sell it, I am motivated to consider others' value estimate of the animal. I will misuse the buffalo only at my economic peril", Richard Stroup & John Baden, *Natural Resources, Bureaucratic Myths and Environmental Management* (San Francisco, CA, Pacific Institute for Public Policy Research, 1983), quoted in DesJardins, *Environmental Ethics*, p. 52.

19. "Organic growers receive subsidies of £70 per hectare, declining to £25 after five years, and nothing after that. Barley barons polluting the groundwater with nitrates and the rivers with pesticides get a steady 'arable area payment' of £269 a hectare", George Monbiot, *Guardian*, 1997.
20. One complication goes back immediately to the question of altruism. Perhaps I ought to consider other people, not so as to further their well-being in a way that is wholly distinct from my own, but because my well-being and theirs are not altogether separable.
21. See M. Sagoff, *The Economy of the Earth* (Cambridge, Cambridge University Press, 1988) for this first. It is noted and discussed in O'Neill, *Ecology, Policy and Politics*, pp. 112–22, which is in turn noted and further discussed in Benson, *Environments*, pp. 50–51.
22. D. Pearce, A. Markandya & E. B. Barber, *Blueprint for a Green Economy* (London, Earthscan Publications, 1989).
23. Quoted in Benson, *Environments*, p.189.
24. O'Neill, *Ecology, Policy and Politics*, p. 120.
25. Sagoff, *Economy of the Earth*, p. 37.
26. *Ibid*.
27. And arguably they would be much worse under a direct democracy than under a market governed society. We would be very likely to vote for incompatible policies: lower taxes and more schools and hospitals. Markets, reasonably or not, would at least prioritize.

Chapter 4: Solutions II: Moral Theory

1. Although, in fact, there was a surprising amount of agreement, at least so far as the higher level public voice was concerned, that it would have been wrong.
2. I am deliberately vague here. Allow that people in Kosovo have a real need. We might say that because of this we ought to help them, or that we have an obligation, but not an overriding one, to help, or that, although the need is real, there is no obligation on us (although perhaps there is on some others) to help. See especially Peter Unger's provocative discussion in *Living High and Letting Die* (Oxford, Oxford University Press, 1996).
3. See especially Bernard Williams, *Moral Luck* (Cambridge, Cambridge University Press, 1981).
4. See S. Scheffler, *The Rejection of Consequentialism* (Oxford, The Clarendon Press, 1982).
5. J. Narveson, "Utilitarianism and new generations", *Mind* 76, 1967, 62–72.
6. For this and many related points, see Aristotle's *Nicomachean Ethics*, T. Irwin (trans.) (Indianapolis, IN, Hackett, 1985).
7. Although useful, this distinction is not always perspicuous. I say more about it in Chapter 9.
8. See J. Bentham, *An Introduction to the Principles of Morals and Legislation* (London, Methuen, 1970); J. S. Mill, *Utilitarianism* (Indianapolis, IN, Hackett, 1994); and C. Dickens, *Hard Times* (Harmondsworth, Penguin, 1994).
9. So whereas Bentham, in *Principles of Morals*, notoriously insisted that pushpin was not intrinsically less valuable than poetry, Mill, in *Utilitarianism*, made serious efforts to distinguish between higher and lower pleasures. How successful he was is a matter for debate.
10. See, again, Aristotle, *Nicomachean Ethics*.
11. More accurately, it is indifferent to mere spatial location. But, of course, the consequences of differences in location have to be taken into account. There may well be greater efficiencies in attending to local, as opposed to distant, problems.
12. "Nor were these hills high and formidable only, but they had a kind of unhospitable terror in them. Here there were no rich pleasant valleys between them, as among the Alps; no lead mines and veins of rich ore, as in the Peak; no coal pits, as in the hills about Hallifax [sic], much less gold, as in the Andes, but all barren and wild, of no use or advantage either to man or beast". So wrote Daniel Defoe, in *A Tour through the Whole Island of Great Britain* (quoted in N. Nicholson

(ed.), *The Lake District: An Anthology* (Harmondsworth, Penguin, 1978)), betraying here a rather narrow view of use and advantage.

13. It will be addressed further, if not solved, in Chapter 11.
14. Of course, even the most hedonistic utilitarianism needs to take future generations into account, and so there will be some limits to the levels of present environmental degradation.
15. See O'Neill, *Ecology, Policy and Politics*, and his linking of such a view with Aristotle. This is undoubtedly right, but there is again a connection with Christianity as well. Some believe that the Bible encourages the view that the earth is put here for our benefit. That view, they claim, encourages environmental damage, as we look on the non-human world as a mere resource, here for our material benefit. But these people overlook an important point. We can benefit from the earth in many ways. One benefit derives simply from admiring its beauty. After all, it was God who first looked at the world, and saw that it was good. And, of course, many people have connected nature experience with religious experience.
16. Rights theorists, in so far as they are concerned to protect autonomy, emphasize permissions above requirements. But it is a notably libertarian position that consistently avoids mention of obligation.
17. A related claim, that there are things one ought not to do that the law permits, does not in the same way suggest that the law should be changed. Very few want the law to prohibit all immoral behaviour.
18. As well as legal and moral rights, mention ought, perhaps, to be made of those notions of human rights and civil rights that, particularly in the international arena that is so often the stamping ground for large-scale environmental disputes, are so often discussed today. But there is not the space here, so see J. Waldron (ed.), *Theories of Rights* (Oxford, Oxford University Press, 1984) and R. Dworkin, *Taking Rights Seriously* (London, Duckworth, 1978) for this.
19. J. Bentham, "Anarchical fallacies", in J. Bowring (ed.), *The Works of Jeremy Bentham* (Edinburgh, 1843), vol. II, p. 491 and J. Mackie, *Ethics, Inventing Right and Wrong* (Harmondsworth, Penguin, 1977), Ch. 1.
20. See Rawls's insistence on the separateness of persons in J. Rawls, *A Theory of Justice* (Cambridge, MA, Harvard University Press, 1971), pp. 22–7.
21. See especially I. Kant, *Groundwork of the Metaphysics of Morals*, H. J. Paton (trans.) (New York, Harper & Row, 1964).
22. For subtle and sophisticated defence of the Kantian position see, especially, C. Korsgaard, *Creating the Kingdom of Ends* (Cambridge, Cambridge University Press, 1996).
23. H. L. A. Hart, "Are there any natural rights?", *The Philosophical Review* **64**, 1955, 175–91 and Waldron, *Theories of Rights*.
24. To deny that it has rights is not to say that we can do with it as we will. This may need insisting on.
25. See, for some central figures here, T. Hobbes, *Leviathan* (Harmondsworth, Penguin, 1968 [originally published 1651]), J. J. Rousseau, "The social contract", in D. A. Cress (trans.), *The Basic Political Writings* (Indianapolis, IN, Hackett, 1987 [originally published 1762]), T. Scanlon, *What We Owe to Each Other* (Cambridge, MA, Belknap Press, 1998) and also Scanlon's "Contractualism and utilitarianism", in A. Sen & B. Williams (eds), *Utilitarianism and Beyond* (Cambridge, Cambridge University Press, 1982).
26. The point is to describe rather than endorse what a rights theorist might say. One objection that surfaces at just this point is that there may be things one ought (in some soft sense) to do, even though, in not doing them, no one's rights are infringed. While we might not want to go the whole consequentialist hog, perhaps we ought, for example, to give something, and perhaps more than we do, to charity. Thus a duty? And thus an end to the correlation? Well, we can carve up the discourse in various ways.
27. It isn't enough here to agree that there would be something wrong in killing this person, for that agreement might be easily given and the killing still might still go ahead. What is needed, on this strong rights position, is the claim that it would still be overall wrong, or wrong all things considered, or some such.

28. Current UK debate about the so-called "right to roam", although in many ways welcome, perhaps doesn't give enough consideration to changed patterns of access to and use of the countryside. Footpaths and bridleways were originally the natural and convenient routes on which small numbers of mostly local people would move around their own districts, doing their everyday business, and not components in a national or international tourist industry. This isn't an argument against a "right to roam" but a complaint that the argument for it needs considerably more than an appeal to some alleged historical precedent.

29. It has to be stressed that the questions here are about priorities and emphasis rather than about black and white differences. Just as a rights-based theory has to take consequences into account, so, too, a virtue approach can hardly dispense with the notions of right and wrong action, simply replacing them with reference to good and bad character. See, for a well-argued rejection of black and white differences, R. Hursthouse, *On Virtue Ethics* (Oxford, Oxford University Press, 1999).

30. Although this may not be quite the right way of putting it. For a virtue theorist may well insist that generosity, kindness and so on are revealed as a matter of course or not at all. A consequentialist, concerned to maximize overall good, may simulate kindness, but no more.

31. It is easy enough to copy the action, harder to copy the motive. The virtuous person does what they do in a certain way from certain motives, habitually, and without calculation. Acquiring new dispositions is not easy, but it can be done. See again Aristotle, *Nicomachean Ethics*, and discussion of this in Hursthouse, *On Virtue Ethics*.

32. Although it is worth noting that act utilitarianism is also concerned with a situation's precise details. An unsatisfactory characterization of the virtue account emphasizes here the distance from the deontological position, but neglects the proximity to consequentialism.

33. For this see especially "Moral luck" in B. Williams, *Moral Luck* (Cambridge, Cambridge University Press, 1981) and "Moral luck" (same title, different paper) in T. Nagel, *Mortal Questions* (Cambridge, Cambridge University Press, 1979).

34. See P. Benn, *Ethics* (London, UCL Press, 1998) for a good discussion of this.

35. This is in some ways a Machiavellian point. It isn't, as he is supposed to have said, simply that the ends justify the means, but rather, as Trotsky is supposed to have said, that the ends justify the means when something justifies the ends.

36. Virtuous in what ways? What I have been assuming here is that the traditional views are just the ones under consideration where the environment is concerned. But it has been suggested, particularly by Rosalind Hursthouse in thus far unpublished work, that there may be distinctively environmental virtues, notably wonder at and respect for nature. I consider both, in Chapters 10 and 6 respectively, although I don't there pursue in any detail the question of whether they are virtues, or something else.

37. Someone sympathetic to a Darwinian or socio-biological approach might suggest that the evolutionary pay-off in being able habitually to trust (at least) those human beings with whom we are in day-to-day contact is not replicated in the situations obtaining between distant tribes, or distant governments, where a back-up to trust (guarantees, checks and balances, deterrents, etc.) is in order, and appropriate.

38. See, for presentation of and comparison between all three, N. Baron, P. Pettit & M. Slote, *Three Methods of Ethics* (Oxford, Blackwell, 1997).

39. Rawls, *Theory of Justice*.

40. Although, as I have suggested, the ensuing discussion is full of subtleties, Rosalind Hursthouse begins her recent book with an insistence on just this, claiming that virtue ethics has moved through the stage of being "the new kid on the block" to having acquired "full status, recognized as a rival to deontological and utilitarian approaches, as interestingly and challengingly different from either as they are from each other", *On Virtue Ethics*, p. 2.

Chapter 5: Animals

1. By "animals" I mean, of course, non-human animals. There is no need to keep spelling this out.
2. Someone might think that, particularly where animals are concerned, if cruelty isn't wanton, it isn't cruelty at all. Certain of the issues here are taken up below.
3. Singer first brought philosophical considerations into the wider public debate in his justly famous article "Animal liberation", *The New York Review of Books*, April 1973. See also P. Singer, *Animal Liberation* (London, Jonathan Cape, 1976) and P. Singer, *Practical Ethics* (Cambridge, Cambridge University Press, 1993).
4. Although not universally, perhaps. Pain is in some way bad whenever it occurs, but if the choice is a painful operation or immediate death, pain may be in one's interests. This suggestion, as will become clearer in a discussion below, is more persuasively made of human beings than of animals, however. For it isn't clear why animals should undergo present misfortune for future gain.
5. The term is not his, having been coined by Richard Ryder in 1970. See R. Ryder, *Speciesism: The Ethics of Vivisection* (Edinburgh, Scottish Society for the Prevention of Speciesism, 1974).
6. Singer, *Practical Ethics*, Ch. 3. See also his "summary statement" in P. Singer, "The ethics of animal liberation: a summary statement", in *On the Side of Animals: Some Contemporary Philosophers' Views* (RSPCA Information, 1996).
7. Although, along with many so-called negative utilitarians, his emphasis is on reducing pain, rather than increasing pleasure.
8. Of course, what utilitarianism allows for in principle, even if it seems to its proponents unlikely to be justified in practice, is the use of human beings for the benefit of animals.
9. See Singer, *Practical Ethics*, pp. 60–61.
10. To say it has appeal where human beings are concerned is not to say that the argument in its support is watertight. Nor, I think, is it clear that Singer thinks it is. See here Singer, *Practical Ethics*, Ch. 2. What can be urged is that those bodies whom one might reasonably expect to be impartial – police, judges, doctors – should act in accordance with the principle. But it is hard to see why it should be extended to cover all relationships among human beings, and so hard to see at all why it should be extended to animals. My suspicion is that in so far as the principle has appeal, this is in part because Singer makes relatively little of the shift from consideration to equal consideration. Nor is the appeal buttressed by the suggestion that it might soon appear as incredible that we should see animals as things to eat as it now appears that we should see blacks as fitted for slavery. So it might, but that isn't a justification.
11. The claim need not be anywhere near so crude as, for example, that all men are more aggressive than all women (the least aggressive man is more aggressive than the most aggressive woman?) but just that in suitably sized samples, broad tendencies can be discerned.
12. Although Singer allows that precision in measuring pains is not needed (and so the unavailability of precision is no obstacle) he does claim that "Pain and suffering are bad and should be prevented or minimized, irrespective of the race, sex, or species of the being that suffers. How bad a pain is depends on how intense it is and how long it lasts, but pains of the same intensity and duration are equally bad, whether felt by humans or animals" (*Practical Ethics*, p. 61).
    My point here is not that the differences between human beings are morally irrelevant, where those between our and other species may not be. Grant pleasure and pain matter in human beings, there is no justification for saying they matter less elsewhere. But without greater understanding of animals, this is of theoretical interest. And it isn't to rescind on an earlier point. For something may matter, or be important, in itself without generating moral obligations in us.
13. See especially T. Regan, *The Case for Animal Rights* (Berkeley, CA, University of California Press, 1983), but see also his papers, "The moral basis of vegetarianism", *Canadian Journal of Philosophy* 5, 1975, 181–214 and "The case for animal rights", in *In Defence of Animals*, P. Singer (ed.) (Oxford, Blackwell, 1985) and the collection, T. Regan & P. Singer (eds), *Animal Rights and Human Obligation* (Englewood Cliffs, NJ, Prentice-Hall, 1976).

14. This might suggest that a rights account will do more for animal welfare than will consequentialism or utilitarianism. But, as will emerge, there are several reasons for doubting this. And it is worth noting, too, that although I often bracket these rival accounts, it might be insisted that strictly a rights account is not directly concerned with welfare at all, but with the rigorous upholding of a means/ends distinction. And this is perfectly compatible with leaving animals simply to fend for themselves in an often hostile world. Yet a side effect of attention to rights will often be an increase in welfare, and as that side effect will, for most animal rightists, at the very least be welcome, the bracketing can stand.

15. For a hard-hitting presentation of this objection, see R. Hursthouse, *Humans and Other Animals* (Milton Keynes, Open University, 1999), Ch. 4.

16. See Lawrence Johnson, *A Morally Deep World* (Cambridge, Cambridge University Press, 1991), Ch. 2 for discussion.

17. See P. Carruthers, *The Animals Issue* (Cambridge, Cambridge University Press, 1992) for illuminating detail on this.

18. Regan, "The case for animal rights", p. 13.

19. The best attempt at an answer will again appeal to some version of the contractarian account. But this hardly does Regan any favours.

20. Recent years have revealed a number of cases in both the USA and the UK (tests on prisoners, blacks, soldiers, all unwitting) where the outrageous has occurred. But, of course, it has stopped now.

21. P. Singer, "Animal rights and human obligation", in Pojman, *Environmental Ethics*, p. 36.

22. Regan, *Case for Animal Rights*, p. 243.

23. See especially Bernard Williams, "The Makropoulos case", Jeff MacMahan, "Death and the value of life" and other papers in *The Metaphysics of Death*, J. M. Fischer (ed.) (Stanford, CA, Stanford University Press, 1993). And see also C. Belshaw, "Death, pain and time", *Philosophical Studies* 97, 2000, 317–41. The imperfection in this answer lies in its giving us an account of what we, as opposed to most other animals, lose in death, while not fully explaining why, when death is unannounced, this loss should be thought of as bad.

24. At best. It should be noted that even if we agree that some animals are, in the appropriate sense, subject-of-a-life, it won't follow from this that they have any absolute right to life. It doesn't follow for people either. One claim is descriptive, the other normative.

25. Regan's list of characteristics is complex. Some are evidently possessed by many animals, while for others the attribution is problematic. We might think that if they have most of the characteristics, we can give them the benefit of the doubt over the remaining few, but that isn't a good policy. The remaining few may be critical.

26. A further difficulty in this approach is that there are human beings who are not, in this rich sense, subjects-of-a-life. How, if at all, do they get the right to life? One standard response – they belong to a species the normal members of which are subject-of-a-life – explains nothing.

27. T. Regan, "The radical egalitarian case for animal rights", in Pojman, *Environmental Ethics*, p. 45 (also published as "The case for animal rights").

28. J. Baird Callicott, "Animal liberation, a triangular affair", *Environmental Ethics* 2, 1980, 31–8.

29. R. Elliott, *Environmental Ethics* (Oxford, Oxford University Press, 1995), p. 53.

30. See, for a puzzling argument on this point, the very end of "Death", in Nagel, *Mortal Questions*, pp. 9–10 and in Fischer, *Metaphysics of Death*, p. 69.

31. Thomas Aquinas, *Summa Contra Gentiles* (New York, Benziger Brothers, 1928 [originally published 1259–64]), Bk. 3, Pt. 2, Ch. 112.

32. I. Kant, *Lectures on Ethics (1780–81)*, H. Louis Infield (trans.) (New York, Harper & Row, 1963), pp. 239–40, where he goes on to note, "In England butchers and doctors do not sit on a jury because they are accustomed to death and hardened".

33. M. Midgley, "Sustainability and moral pluralism", in *The Philosophy of the Environment*, T. D. J. Chappell (ed.) (Edinburgh, Edinburgh University Press, 1997), pp. 94–5.

34. As J. Passmore puts it, "To understand why human beings behave as they do, we shall do better in very many cases to appeal by way of explanation to their ignorance, fear, vanity, greed, bigotry,

their lust for power – and sometimes, fortunately, to their generosity, affection, courage and creativity – than to moral principles to which they officially subscribe. Not, of course, in every instance. It would be absurd to deny that moral and metaphysical principles ever have any effect on human conduct, if only to justify courses of action which might otherwise arouse qualms. But their effect is a great deal less than is sometimes suggested" (*Man's Responsibility*, p. x).

35. See Carruthers, *The Animals Issue*.

36. An objection to this view, though, is that it seems to allow little space for someone's coming to realize that what they did was cruel, even though they didn't realize it, and didn't intend it, at the time. The account might be supplemented, then, by some reference to pain being inflicted carelessly, thoughtlessly, at too high a level, even though there is no malice.

37. "Once we realise that insects feel no pain, the only remaining motive for discouraging children (from pulling their wings off) is that their activities are sort of play-acting for real cruelty" (Carruthers, *The Animals Issue*, p. 57). It is unclear here who "we" are. If children, too, realize that there is no pain, then pulling wings off butterflies (without some complicated story to the contrary) is no more cruel, and no more play-acting cruel, than pulling petals off flowers, and reciting, "She loves me, she loves me not". If they don't realize this, then they may well be intending to be cruel. And this isn't play-acting, either, even if they don't succeed.

38. He might agree that we can harm the dog, but deny that this is to do anything wrong. This isn't, in general, a completely spurious distinction, as I argue in later chapters. But it is hard to see how it can be applied where sentient creatures are concerned. As Carruthers, *The Animals Issue*, pp. 108–9, notes, throwing darts at a cat is importantly different from throwing darts at the Mona Lisa.

39. "It all sounded rather grand, when Aristotle said that we have reason and they don't. But under pressure, the Stoics retreated to the position that at least they don't have syntax. The moral conclusion seems to be 'They don't have syntax so we can eat them'", R. Sorabji, *Animal Minds and Human Morals: The Origins of the Western Debate* (London, Duckworth, 1993), p. 2.

40. R. Descartes, *The Philosophical Writings of Descartes*, J. Cottingham, R. Stoothoff & Dugald Murdoch (trans.) (Cambridge, Cambridge University Press, (vol. II) 1984 & (vol. I) 1985); see especially vol. I, pp. 139–41, "Discourse on method".

41. See, for discussion, Johnson, *A Morally Deep World*, Ch. 2, and, for a negative account, R. G. Frey, *Interests and Rights: The Case Against Animals* (Oxford, Clarendon Press, 1980) and *Rights, Killing and Suffering* (Oxford, Blackwell, 1983). See also S. Clark, *The Moral Status of Animals* (Oxford, Clarendon Press, 1977).

42. See, for example, Carruthers, *The Animals Issue*.

43. See D. Hume, *Enquiries Concerning Human Understanding and Concerning the Principles of Morals*, 3rd edn, L. A Selby-Bigge (ed.), P. H. Nidditch (rev.) (Oxford, Clarendon Press, 1975), especially Section XII. As Hume puts it, "Nature is always too strong for principle" (p. 160).

44. See Callicott, "Animal liberation".

45. Callicott, "Animal liberation", quotes John Muir's description of domestic sheep as "hooved locusts" (in J. Muir, "The wild sheep of California", *Overland Monthly* 12 (1874), 359).

46. See, for detailed discussion of a particular case, Kate Rawles, "Conservation and animal welfare", in *The Philosophy of the Environment*, T. D. J. Chappell (ed.) (Edinburgh, Edinburgh University Press, 1997), 135–55.

47. See, for much valuable detail, L. Alderson, *The Chance to Survive* (Bromley, Helm, 1989).

48. As noted and then explored by Callicott, "Animal liberation", p. 311.

49. Somerset Council, at least, takes the former view, referring to camels as "dangerous wild animals" (author's conversation with camel owner, Bridgwater Sands, September 1999).

50. If (to rephrase Narveson's distinction) we are concerned to make happy animals, rather than simply to make animals happy, then it can be allowed that the utilitarian might have instrumental reasons for wanting to preserve species. It won't be straightforward. We could get rid of pandas and fill their reserves with rabbits.

51. Real in that there are uncontentiously cases of either kind. I don't suggest that there isn't a whole range of borderline cases.

52. We might enjoy watching the kill. Or we might enjoy the existence of the animals that need to

kill to survive. Someone might think that the first kind of pleasure is perverse. Notoriously, utilitarians rarely take such considerations into account.

53. Singer, *Animal Liberation*, pp. 238–9.
54. It might seem that it need not. We might say that the tiger has a right to life but no right to kill to live. The absence of a right here is not to imply that the tiger does wrong in killing, but just that its rights do not extend this far. So even without a right, killing is permitted. And this isn't overruled by the prey's right to life.
55. See T. Regan, "Animal rights: what's in a name?", in *Animal Welfare and the Environment*, R. Ryder & P. Singer (eds) (London, Duckworth/RSPCA, 1992), pp. 53–5.

Chapter 6: Life

1. Even though some will claim that viruses are not, strictly, alive.
2. C. Stone, "Should trees have standing? Towards legal rights for natural objects", *Southern California Law Review* 45, 1972, 450–501.
3. Stone, "Should trees have standing", reprinted in Pojman, *Environmental Ethics*, 177–85, p. 181.
4. *Ibid.*, p. 182, original emphasis.
5. Some will think this a little fast. But I suggest that a lawn wants a drink in a manner analogous to that in which (to refer to a well-known example) a thermostat knows the temperature. We can speak in these ways, and we will be understood. Nevertheless most of us, if pressed, will agree that these are extensions of standard uses. Or at least this: lawns don't want in a way similar to that in which human beings want. Sometimes I need a drink but don't realize it and it would be odd to say that I want a drink on such occasions. Because this is odd, it seems that we ought to accept that a lawn has wants only in a non-literal fashion.
6. Singer, *Practical Ethics*, p. 57.
7. R. Dworkin, *Life's Dominion* (New York, Knopf, 1993), p. 16, original emphasis.
8. So I am inclined to think. I may be so ill that it is in my interests to die, but this isn't an interest in turning into a corpse. A corpse isn't a kind of thing. Suppose I die and turn into a gnat or a toad. And suppose toads live the longer and happier life. Still it isn't in my interest to turn into a toad as, if the turning here is complete, the toad is not me. Against this, it might be said that we can have an interest that is not self-interest. It is in my interest that my family does well. They might do better (although we need not bother to explain why) if I turn into a toad.
9. See "Death" in Nagel, *Mortal Questions*. There is a reply. Undiscovered betrayal is against my interests as it is the sort of thing that would cause pain, were I to discover it. There may be some mileage in this reply but there is still available the counter that it would have this effect simply because it is, antecedently, a bad thing to be betrayed.
10. It may be said that some machines have similar characteristics. Will I claim that they, too, have interests? Why not? They don't have interests in the sense that human beings do, but then neither do trees. As will emerge, both here and in Chapter 7, an important part of my argument is that once past sentience, there are no further important distinctions to be drawn.
11. My claim here is not emphatically that plants do have interests, and that those who will not sever the link with sentience have simply got it wrong. It is, somewhat more tentatively, that although both positions may be defensible, I incline to the former. Further, what may be defensible are not two accounts of the true nature of interests, only one of which in the end will turn out to be right. It is rather, and merely, that there might be two positions on how the term is standardly or most appropriately used.
12. "Severe" here will be the kind of pruning or training that weakens the plant, or shortens its life. Coppicing can appear severe, and is hardly natural, but, as it is able to extend life almost indefinitely, it stands in an intellectually challenging relationship to a tree's interests.
13. A. Schweitzer, *Civilization and Ethics* (London, A. & C. Black, 1923), reprinted in part as "Rev-

erence for life" in Pojman, *Environmental Ethics*, 65–70, p. 66, original emphasis.

14. *Ibid.*, p. 66.
15. *Ibid.*, p. 69.
16. There are similarities between Schweitzer's position here and that of certain deep ecologists. See Chapter 8.
17. P. W. Taylor, *Respect for Nature* (Princeton, NJ, Princeton University Press, 1986).
18. *Ibid.*, pp. 99–100. And an equivalent formulation in P. W. Taylor, "The ethics of respect for nature", *Environmental Ethics* 3, 1981, 197–218.
19. Taylor, *Respect for Nature*, pp. 133–4, original emphasis.
20. At some places, seemingly cautious, Taylor claims only that respect for nature is a stance that we might consistently adopt. But his prevailing view seems to be that we should adopt it; that although the arguments in its favour are not watertight, they are nevertheless weighty, and so constitute powerful even if non-conclusive reasons for thinking that we have responsibilities towards all forms of life. And there is room for an intermediate position. For a view might be that we have practical but not theoretical reasons for adopting the view; it would be good for us, even though there is no evidence in its favour.
21. Mill, *Utilitarianism*.
22. "Just as animals and plants can be neither good nor bad scientists, engineers, critics, or Supreme Court justices, so they can be neither good nor bad moral agents. More precisely it is meaningless to speak of them as morally good or bad. Hence it is meaningless to say either that they are morally inferior to humans or that humans are morally superior to them", Taylor, *Respect for Nature*, pp. 132–3.
23. *Ibid.*, p. 133, original emphasis.
24. Carruthers seems to come close to advancing such a view in *The Animals Issue*.
25. Taylor, "The ethics of respect", p. 201. There are questions here about the distinction, if any, between inherent worth and intrinsic value. See Chapter 9 for more on this.
26. Taylor, "The ethics of respect", p. 201.
27. Although there is as yet an ambiguity in this. We might be able always to put an individual person before an individual plant, but if the values are on the same scale then it will surely be that some number of plants outweighs the value of one person.
28. Taylor, "The ethics of respect", p. 217.
29. *Ibid.*, p. 152.
30. *Ibid.*, p. 153. The overall structure of the argument here is dubious. In rejecting arguments that are supposed to establishes our superiority, Taylor makes use of rather strict notions of entailment. None of the cited arguments establish our superiority. But then in the positive argument against superiority rather looser criteria are employed: "I am not arguing that a strict formal deduction can be made here", p. 154.
31. In the same way, a lot of people will think that one has greater obligation to help a young infant than an adult, without at all thinking that the infant is the superior creature. Of course, sentience is connected in fact with further advantages, such as mobility, but imagine that this is not so, and that trees do feel pain. They would be wretched things, and arguably we'd have a strong obligation to care for them.
32. It is, perhaps, possible to offer some sort of defence of Taylor's equal inherent worth view. A distinction needs to be made between what we ought to do with respect to starting existence, on the one hand, and preserving it, on the other. It is because animals can feel pain, I have suggested, that they make more telling demands on us than do plants, but they win out here in cases where they and the plants already exist. Sentience is no obvious reason for bringing animals into existence rather than plants. If there is anything good or valuable about life itself, such that, other things being equal, there is reason to want new life to begin, then both animals and plants can have some sort of claim advanced on their behalf. It may well now be an equal claim; the peacock is, to us, prettier than the sedge grass, but it is neither inherently superior nor, prior to its coming to exist, more needful of our ministrations.

This is both a limited and contentious defence of the biocentric view. It is limited in that such a construal of the equality of inherent worth says almost nothing about our everyday interactions with the world. No radical rejigging of morality is called for, if our concern is only with creating. It is contentious, as many will want to challenge even this. For is there really no justification for preferring the creation of people to grass? Is it merely a prejudice, an unwillingness or inability to adopt a neutral and disinterested position, to suppose that there is no more reason to bring a (fairly ordinary) human being into existence than a (fairly ordinary) plant? This is a question that will surface again in a later chapter, but for the moment I want to distinguish three positions. On the first, people are more valuable. On the second, people and plants are equally valuable. And on the third, the whole business of assigning inherent value to things is found puzzling and unsatisfactory. (A fourth position, that plants are more valuable, will have appeal only to the unredeemable misanthrope.) I don't want to claim that the first position is, in fact, correct, but only that it is not obviously hopeless. And I want to claim also that while one may sympathize with the third position, the second, which is Taylor's, is actually more problematic than the first, for in defence of this first position one might appeal to the wide range of powers and properties that human beings exhibit. Many plants, in contrast, are noticeably uniform. What, now, could support the claim that these very different things have exactly the same value?

33. Taylor, *Respect for Nature*, Ch. 6. But I cannot go into these here.
34. Although, as I have suggested, allowing that plant value is individual by individual lower will not in itself justify us in eating a whole plate of salad.
35. Taylor, *Respect for Nature*, pp. 67–8.
36. K. Goodpaster, "On being morally considerable", *Journal of Philosophy* 75, 1978, 308–25.
37. See "Death", in Nagel, *Mortal Questions*.
38. I am being evasive here about the nature of the connection involved. Is it a logical connection? Is it part of the concept of pain that it is, other things being equal, wrong to bring it about? I want as yet neither to assert not deny this.
39. It may be objected (and I refer back to Schweitzer here) that there is no difference, and that life should be understood as including all that is the product of natural forces. That is a poor objection in several ways, and it won't salvage the life-centred view. First, it is not clear that breaking icicles is worse than breaking down a fence, or that in general nature has anything over artifice. Secondly, to go down this route is to undercut what is hardly peripheral to Taylor's argument: the claim that, in having directedness, in pursuing a good of their own, living things have a case for inclusion within the moral domain.

Chapter 7: Rivers, Species, Land

1. And it is worth noting that the writers discussed in the previous chapter all blur this, referring to streams (Stone, in Pojman, *Environmental Ethics*, p. 180), ice crystals (Schweitzer, in Pojman, *Environmental Ethics*, p. 66) and a rather undifferentiated nature (Taylor, passim).
2. There is room for a group of exceptions where diminution increases the chances of a thing's longer-term survival. Trees can benefit from being pruned.
3. Johnson, *A Morally Deep World*, pp. 145–6.
4. There are ancillary points to make here. I set the cat aside because it is bad that animals should suffer. Someone may allow this, but insist that the wrongness of wanton destruction is no worse in this case than it is with, say, the icicles. Assume, though, that our destroyer believes that the cat will suffer, while the icicle will not. Then it is reasonable to distinguish between the wrongness of the destroyer's acts. We can make a further observation. Destroying stalactites, knowing them to be ancient and rare, is worse than destroying icicles. What I am denying is that wrongness is stepwise increased between living and non-living, or between natural and artificial.
5. See, for this, Richard Routley & Val Routley, "Human chauvinism and environmental ethics", in *Environmental Philosophy*, D. Mannison, M. McRobbie & R. Routley (eds) (Canberra, Australian

National University, 1980). And see Benson, *Environments*, Ch. 1, for useful discussion.

6. See again "Death" in Nagel, *Mortal Questions*. Although I believe that such a view is defensible, it is, *prima facie*, less plausible than the view that death's badness varies with the goodness of life and that this can be at zero or below.

7. I don't, of course, want to suggest that there is anything wrong with sentiment.

8. Nothing further is implied here, I think. In particular, unless we were also to think that starting to exist is good, we wouldn't have to think "the bigger the better". Indeed, a smaller universe might be better than a bigger one, if the former is stable or expanding, while the latter is beginning to shrink.

9. P. Sarre & A. Reddish (eds), *Environment and Society* (London, Hodder & Stoughton in association with the Open University, 1990).

10. An objection is that there are no pre-theoretical facts at all, and that even a claim as apparently straightforward as that such and such is an animal is not given in nature. This point can in one way be conceded. Differences are given in nature, but it isn't given which of these differences are important, or where lines are to be drawn. This doesn't suggest, however, that there is, in every case, any real issue about where the lines are drawn. And on the occasions where there is an issue there will be lower level facts where, again, matters are not up for grabs. The claim that there are pre-theoretical facts is supposed here to be true, but not deeply true.

11. E. Sober, *The Philosophy of Biology* (Boulder, CO, Westview, 1993), p. 148, original emphasis.

12. Sarre & Reddish, *Environment and Society*, p. 198.

13. For someone to be prepared to concede that there are, in these circumstances, two kinds of tiger still seems grudging, to my mind. There is some water on Mars. But there are not two kinds of water, earth water and Martian water. A difference here is that no one is tempted to make the historical (or geographical) claim for water. But if, where species are concerned, this claim is undermined, why not leave it at that, rather than cling to the wreckage?

14. In one version they can breed with Martians, Earthlings or each other, while in another they breed only among themselves. I am not sure that this makes for any overall difference in what we want to say here.

15. Satisfy most of our tiger interests, but not all. Our interest in tigers as examples of earth's biggest carnivores will not be served by creatures from space.

16. These cases are all ones involving the same species. But in others, saving one individual is claimed adversely to affect the well-being of different species.

17. For a contrary view see Johnson, *A Morally Deep World*, pp. 162–3.

18. Is the first innocuous? Someone might insist that genuine tigers need to be produced in the normal way. It may seem clear that thawing of embryos is normal enough, but then if the production of these beasts depends not on the preservation of appropriate material, but on information stored in a computer program, it might be thought that even though the causal connections are sustained, they are now too circuitous. For a related discussion on personal identity, see Parfit, *Reasons and Persons*, Pt. III.

19. According to D. H. Meadows, "Biodiversity: the key to saving life on Earth", *Land Steward Letter*, 1990, and reprinted in Pojman, *Environmental Ethics*, 156–8, p. 157.

20. This is claimed, but it can be objected that the notion of potential is abused here as, although we may not be able to sort the wheat from the chaff, some species offer no benefits, and no potential benefits, whatsoever.

21. In "Why do species matter?", *Environmental Ethics* 3, 1981, 101–12, Lilly-Marlene Russow makes a similar point about zebras, suggesting that if they were being hunted for their distinctive coats, we might, in the interest of species preservation, selectively breed out the stripes. We'd have zebras, but an indifferent appearance.

22. Although some of the complications in species resurface here. If breeds are construed historically, then once lost they are forever lost. But if they are understood in terms of appearance (near the surface, as with roses, or going deeper, as with the taste of pork), then founding the kind again becomes a possibility, even if remote.

23. Consider, for example, coastal erosion in East Yorkshire, or Mirror Lake at the head of the

Yosemite Valley. In these case we can be sure enough that the alteration is (more or less) the upshot of natural processes. In others, as with the disappearance of urban sparrows, the causal factors are harder to discern.

24. A. Leopold, *A Sand County Almanac* (New York, Oxford University Press, 1949).
25. *Ibid.*, p. 204.
26. *Ibid.*, pp. 215–16.
27. *Ibid.*, pp. 216–17.
28. *Ibid.*, p. 217.
29. *Ibid.*, p. 218.
30. Although it might be asked, could the pyramid be inverted, or placed on its side? The particular spatial metaphor could be different.
31. Leopold, *Sand County Almanac*, pp. 224–5.
32. *Ibid.*, pp. 203–4.
33. *Ibid.*, p. 204.
34. *Ibid.*, p. 210–12.
35. J. B. Callicott, "The conceptual foundations of the land ethic", in *In Defense of the Land Ethic* (New York, SUNY Press, 1989), and reprinted in Pojman, *Environmental Ethics,* 92–102, p. 92.
36. Reprinted in Pojman, *Environmental Ethics,* 92–102, p. 95.
37. *Ibid.*, p. 99.
38. *Ibid.*, pp. 98–9.

Chapter 8: Deep Ecology

1. They include Arne Naess, George Sessions, Bill Devall, Warwick Fox, Michael Zimmerman and (although here with reservations) Val Plumwood and Richard Sylvan.
2. Among others, the physicist Fritjof Capra, the writer and poet Gary Snyder and the social and political analyst Theodore Roszak.
3. A. Naess, "The shallow and the deep, long-range ecology movements", *Inquiry* **16**, 1973, 95–100.
4. "Ecology is a *limited* science which makes *use* of scientific methods. Philosophy is the most general forum of debate on fundamentals", Naess, "The shallow and the deep", p. 99. He goes on to offer the term *ecosophy,* "a philosophy of ecological harmony or equilibrium", as a way of bringing into sharp focus this connection between science and wisdom, or what the world is like, and how we ought to live. See here also A. Naess, "Identification as a source of deep ecological attitudes", in *Deep Ecology*, M. Tobias (ed.) (Santa Monica, CA, IMT Productions, 1985).
5. See, for example, B. Devall & G. Sessions, *Deep Ecology: Living as if Nature Mattered* (Salt Lake City, UT, Peregrine Smith, 1985).
6. This is most clearly seen in what was for a long time viewed as a kind of deep ecology manual: Devall & Sessions, *Deep Ecology*.
7. *Ibid.*, pp. 65–6, original emphasis.
8. Notably in Naess, "Identification as a source".
9. An attitude perhaps encouraged by the movement's key figures. Devall and Sessions offered lengthy commentaries on the principles, with Naess later joining them in this quasi-scriptural activity. See Devall & Sessions, *Deep Ecology*, pp. 70ff. and A. Naess, "The deep ecology: 'Eight Points' revisited", in *Deep Ecology for the 21st Century*, G. Sessions (ed.) (Boston, MA, Shambhala, 1995), pp. 213–21.
10. See, for this last in particular, Capra's discussion of paradigm shifts, in "Deep ecology: a new paradigm", in Sessions, *Deep Ecology*, pp. 19–25.
11. See here Benson, *Environments*, pp. 21–3, and R. Sylvan & D. Bennett, *The Greening of Ethics* (Tucson, AZ, The University of Arizona Press, 1994).

12. See, for example, Sylvan & Bennett, *Greening of Ethics*, pp. 34–5.
13. This is not to say that we can draw no lines. We can describe in all necessary detail both the relationships and distinctions between a fish, its food and the shoal within which it lives. And even allowing that a desert gives out only gradually, we can nevertheless correctly say of most of the land what is desert and what is not. Even without a clear use for the distinction between individuals and wholes, then, appropriate discriminations can be made.
14. W. Fox, "Deep ecology: a new philosophy for our time?", *Ecologist* 14, 1974, 194–200.
15. DesJardins, *Environmental Ethics*, pp. 221–2, although, to be fair, it isn't altogether clear that DesJardins is endorsing this argument.
16. Callicott, *In Defense of the Land Ethic*, p. 87.
17. Although it has been argued that ecosystems often play a very minor role: "Britain's golden eagles are confined to the Highlands . . . not because they are fans of Landseer but because in the lowlands, which on the whole offer easier pickings, they were shot", Colin Tudge, *London Review of Books*, 21 June 2001, 38–9.
18. H. Morowitz, "Biology as a cosmological science", *Main Currents in Modern Thought* 28, 1972, quoted and discussed in J. B. Callicott, "The metaphysical implications of ecology", *Environmental Ethics* 9, 1986, 300–15, and in DesJardins, *Environmental Ethics*, p. 222.
19. DesJardins, *Environmental Ethics*, p. 182, original emphasis.
20. To "You cannot really understand anything unless you understand everything" one might be tempted to reply, "You cannot really know what 'really' means."
21. This is, of course, a fairly crude statement of the three positions, but only the central one is particularly problematic, inviting questions as to the ranking procedures employed when both kinds of entity count, but to different degrees.
22. As Callicott remarks, in "The search for an environmental ethic", in *Matters of Life and Death*, T. Regan (ed.), 318–424 (New York, Random House, 1980), "the extensionist approach to an environmental ethic is utterly incapable of countenancing intrinsic value or moral considerability for wholes". One sees what he means, but again it is unnecessarily strident – for why not see a consideration of wholes as yet a further extension?
23. See their tabular summary of two opposing "world views", Devall & Sessions, *Deep Ecology*, p. 69.
24. Unless, that is, our being thoroughly a part of nature implies that all we do is determined and, further, determinism is thought incompatible with our being able to make genuinely free and morally responsible decisions. There are more than purely philosophical issues in play here, for it is at the centre of many religious perspectives that our having moral lives is bound up with our being made, unlike the rest of nature, in the image of God.
25. I am tempted to resist John Benson's suggestion that there is here a third sense of "nature"; Benson, *Environments*, pp. 124–5. People hold that what is natural is good, without, I think, holding that a positive evaluation is included as part of the meaning of nature.
26. Both P. W. Taylor, "Are humans superior to animals and plants?", *Environmental Ethics* 6, 1984, 150, with his community of life view, and, more especially, Fox, "Deep ecology", who urges that we identify not only with other human beings, but with trees, mountains and the cosmos as a whole, fall prey to this. But it is quasi-Romantic, only. Both Wordsworth and Ruskin on occasion, and increasingly as they grew older, felt themselves alienated from nature. Ruskin, for example, writes to a friend, "Do you know Susie, everything that has happened to me is *little* in comparison to the crushing and depressing effect on me, of what I learn day by day as I work on, of the cruelty and ghastliness of the *Nature* I used to think so divine", cited in Clark, *Ruskin Today*, p. 119. This doesn't get things right, but one might be impoverished never to feel something similar.
27. B. Commoner, *The Closing Circle: Nature, Man and Technology* (New York, Bantam, 1971), p. 41.
28. Regan, *Case for Animal Rights*, pp. 361–2, where the particular target is Leopold.
29. See, for example, Naess, "Some critics tell me that I must enter the professional philosophical debate about what exactly might be meant by terms like 'intrinsic value,' 'inherent value' and

'value in itself' . . . But . . . entering this discussion would be misplaced", cited in Sessions, *Deep Ecology*, p. 216.

30. Callicott, "Search for an environmental ethic", pp. 409–10.
31. *Ibid.*, p. 415, original emphasis.
32. Johnson, *A Morally Deep World*, pp. 175–8.
33. Devall & Sessions, *Deep Ecology*, p. 67.
34. Naess, "The shallow and the deep", p. 95. Although, perhaps, the best sense of what it is to exploit something suggests that exploitation is avoidable.
35. See Naess's "Eight points revisited", in Sessions, *Deep Ecology*.
36. Devall & Sessions, *Deep Ecology*, pp. 148–9.
37. A similar situation now obtains along the English/Scottish borders, where it is claimed that only if fishing is restricted to traditional methods can stocks of wild salmon survive.
38. Devall & Sessions, *Deep Ecology*, p. 71. For a fuller discussion of some of the issues here, see J. B. Callicott, "Whaling in Sand County", in Chappell, *Philosophy of the Environment*.
39. I have put standard in scare quotes because, of course, it is deep ecology's fiction that there is any such thing as the standard or mainstream view.

Chapter 9: Value

1. Some will insist that we could expect nothing more than the appearance of choice in such cases. But then it might be countered that there could be nothing more that this in the case of human beings. And see Steven Luper, "Natural resources, gadgets and artificial life", *Environmental Values* 8(1), 27–54, for more on the relationship between nature and artifice.
2. T. Regan, "Does environmental ethics rest on a mistake?", *The Monist* 75, 1992, 161–82, p. 164.
3. See Dworkin, *Life's Dominion*. For discussion see C. Belshaw, "Abortion, value and the sanctity of life", *Bioethics* 11, 1997, 130–50.
4. H. Rolston III, "Value in nature and the nature of value", in *Philosophy and the Natural Environment*, R. Attfield & A. Belsey (eds) (Cambridge, Cambridge University Press, 1994).
5. That isn't to say that there's no argument for going down this idealist route, but it isn't one that can be pursued here, and isn't one, either, to which many are inclined.
6. R. Attfield, "Environmental ethics: overview", *Encyclopedia of Applied Ethics*, vol. 2 (London, Academic, 1998).
7. Taylor, "Are humans superior?", pp.150–51. The preceding terms 1–4, concerning instead value, merit or excellence, and the immediately good, are dealt with much more briskly. A pity, perhaps, as a little more time on 3 and 4, in particular, would have helped illuminate further Taylor's comments on 5 and 6.
8. Although in "Does environmental ethics rest on a mistake?" Regan appears to hint that the inherent/intrinsic distinction might have some substance. Regan, "Does environmental ethics?", p. 163.
9. Regan, "The case for animal rights", and in Pojman, *Environmental Ethics*, p. 45. (See also J. B. Callicott, "The search for an environmental ethic", in *Matters of Life and Death*, T. Regan (ed.) (New York, Random House, 1980b) for discussion of Regan's position here.)
10. R. Elliott, "Intrinsic value, environmental obligation and naturalness", *The Monist* 75, 1992, 138–60.
11. *Ibid.*, p. 140.
12. *Ibid.*
13. The opening comments certainly suggest that Elliott believes, standardly, that the intrinsically valuable should exist for its own sake. But the intrinsic/instrumental distinction implied here gets lost, or so it seems to me, in the later discussion.
14. E. C. Hargrove, "Weak anthropocentric intrinsic value", *The Monist* 75, 1992, 138–207.

15. *Ibid.*, p. 187.
16. *Ibid.*
17. O'Neill, "Varieties of intrinsic value". See also O'Neill, *Ecology, Policy and Politics* for a very similar account. It isn't altogether clear that O'Neill endorses this view, but nothing he says suggests that he takes exception to it.
18. As, arguably, O'Neill fails to do. Among other things, he sets out in "Varieties of intrinsic value" to defend the claim that "natural entities have intrinsic value in the strongest sense of the term, i.e. in the sense of value that exists independently of human valuations" (p. 119). On this account, given owls and their digestion, mice are intrinsically valuable. That won't do.
19. I don't say that only this is claimed. I can bring to mind no reputable thinker who denies that human beings are also intrinsically valuable and, as will become clearer below, it has sometimes been suggested that domesticated animals, non-native plants and semi-natural features possess such value as well.
20. "To say a kind of value is 'intrinsic' means merely that the question whether a thing possesses it, and in what degree it possesses it, depends solely on the intrinsic nature of the thing in question", G. E. Moore, *Philosophical Studies* (London, Routledge & Kegan Paul, 1922), p. 160.
21. O'Neill, "Varieties of intrinsic value", p. 124.
22. A similar point can be made in relation to artworks, where one cannot always tell, from an inspection of the work alone, that it is the work of a particular artist. The difference here is that the claim that the value of artworks depends solely on intrinsic properties doesn't even begin to look plausible.
23. Attfield, "Environmental ethics", p. 73.
24. For similar criticisms of Regan's position see M. A. Warren, "Difficulties with the strong animal rights position", *Between the Species* 2, 1987.
25. Naess, "The shallow and the deep", p. 95, original emphasis. Nor is the shift between value and rights merely a slip. Elsewhere Naess explicitly identifies the one with the other. See, for example, Naess, "Identification as a source".
26. Although something approaching the very odd is put forward in John Taurek's famous and controversial paper, "Should the numbers count?", *Philosophy and Public Affairs* 6(4), 1977, 293–316.
27. Real, because the sort of relationship between food and flourishing will figure in an account of the mind-independent furniture of the world. But should we think that mental states are less than real? Elliott objects ("Intrinsic value", p. 142) and one can understand why. Nevertheless there is something to be said for a distinction between the aspects of the world that can be understood from some absolutist, detached point of view, and those graspable only from the inside. But there is also something to be said for questioning this entire realist/anti-realist dichotomy.
28. Callicott, *In Defense of the Land Ethic*, 133–4, original emphasis.
29. Hume exegesis is never easy, and his real views are hard to pin down. I make no commitment here to whether either reading is fair to Hume.
30. Hume, *Enquiries*, pp. 291–2.
31. So dinosaurs, although extinct, might be valuable now, but they weren't valuable then. Elliott, "Intrinsic value", struggles with this.
32. Given this, we might avoid the relativism inherent in Elliott's account.
33. John O'Neill captures the essence of this account in making a distinction between (a) properties that cannot exist independently of an observer, and (b) those that cannot be characterized independently of an observer. Only in the first case should we say that properties are therefore subjective; in the second, O'Neill speaks of weak objectivity. Although Callicott's account of value is surely committed to subjectivism, his "altogether independent" at the close of the quoted passage is consistent with the dispositional account, and O'Neill's weak objectivity.
34. So the question, "Is beauty/colour in the mind or in the objects?" ought, for as long as possible, to be resisted. The apparently related questions, "What things are beautiful/red?" are, in contrast, easily answered.
35. See, for much of and on this, Blackburn, *Essays on Quasi-realism*.

36. O'Neill, "Varieties of intrinsic value", p. 128.
37. Although one important difference here is that it is harder to see how differences in colour perception (assuming that they make a similar number of discriminations in similar places) would emerge. Someone of an empiricist or positivist bent might want to capitalize on that.
38. This is one of the areas where more time is needed, for a frequent complaint is that the analogy between colour and value breaks down even here: "Morality applies to angels and to other possible life forms and intelligences. But in a sense beauty is relative to kinds of sensory experiences", N. Zangwill, *The Metaphysics of Natural Beauty* (Ithaca, NY, Cornell University Press, 2001), p. 9.
39. Indeed, the first difficulty might, if the second were solved, itself disappear, for if I could see that it is good in itself that the desert survive, rather than simply good for cacti, or scientists or even for the desert, then I might see that I had reason to care for that good. The problem is in getting anywhere with the antecedent.
40. Well known, at least since Plato's *Euthyphro*.
41. My conclusion here does, in the end, very much match that drawn by O'Neill. Our routes are different, however, with O'Neill finding developments of and extensions to the neo-Aristotelian account of flourishing and well-being that which is more rewardingly travelled.

Chapter 10: Beauty

1. Although, as I have said elsewhere, if there are better reasons, their seeming cuddliness might be put to tactical use.
2. This is not pure invention. Just these sorts of claims are made about some of the works of, respectively, Alban Berg, Mark Rothko and Jean Sibelius.
3. See, for such claims and apposite criticism, M. Montaigne, *An Apology for Raymond Sebond*, M. A. Screech (trans.) (Harmondsworth, Penguin, 1987). Of course nature (as opposed to representations of nature) can be used by us for representational or expressive purposes. See works by environmental artists such as Richard Long, Andy Goldsworthy and David Nash, and, in a different vein, recent work by Jeff Koons.
4. For information on eighteenth- and nineteenth-century endeavours to counter this see M. Andrews, *The Search for the Picturesque* (Aldershot, Scolar Press, 1989).
5. Architecture constitutes an exception here, but it has had to fight for status within the hierarchy.
6. D. Mannison, "A prolegomenon to a human chauvinistic attitude", in *Environmental Philosophy*, D. Mannison *et al.* (eds) (Canberra, Australian National University, 1980), pp. 212–13, 216. R. Elliot gets close to making a similar point, denying that responses to nature can "count as aesthetic responses" in "Faking nature", *Inquiry* 25, 1982, 81–93.
7. See A. Berleant, "The aesthetics of nature and art", in *Landscape, Natural Beauty and the Arts*, S. Kemal & I. Gaskell (eds) (Cambridge, Cambridge University Press, 1993).
8. E. Burke, *A Philosophical Enquiry into the Origin of our Ideas of the Sublime and the Beautiful* (Oxford, Oxford University Press, 1990, originally published 1756). For discussion, see Andrews, *Search for the Picturesque*.
9. I am certainly not alone in noting how cutting exhaust emissions in Southern California has led to a reduction in the number of garish, kitschy but still deeply attractive sunsets, and I am surely not alone in regretting their loss.
10. T. Diffey, "Natural beauty without metaphysics", in Kemal & Gaskell, *Landscape, Natural Beauty and the Arts*, original emphasis.
11. Is the beauty of the human form an exception here? There may be broad areas of agreement, but variation across time and through cultures is notable.
12. Including views advanced, in various writings, by Jerome Stolnitz, Paul Ziff and Kendall Walton.
13. Allen Carlson, "Appreciating art and appreciating nature", in Kemal & Gaskell, *Landscape,*

Natural Beauty and the Arts, p. 220.

14. The modest claim here relates to another, that even while not needing detailed scientific under-standing, still a proper appreciation requires that we understand the natural kinds in which the things we are considering belong. This is much too stringent as it stands – how many of us can identify more than a handful of kinds of tree? – but modified – we must see birds as birds, trees as trees, mountains as mountains, and so on – it is, perhaps, plausible enough.

15. Or no appropriately authoritative person intends it. Certainly I might hope that you see the forest as natural. Could I also intend that you so see it? I have doubts.

16. In "On being moved by nature", Noel Carroll sometimes appears to be offering just such a view. While there is certainly space for appreciating nature "under the suitable scientific categories", there is space too for "certain very common appreciative responses to nature – responses of a less intellectual, more visceral sort", in Kemal & Gaskell, *Landscape, Natural Beauty and the Arts*, pp. 244–5. But Carroll's advocacy of this alternative response is perhaps half-hearted, and his understanding of Carlson perhaps incomplete. His "being moved by nature" might appear at first to be the untutored, category-free, reaction to nature that formalism enjoins, but the ensu-ing discussion strongly suggests that minimal understanding is still present; we are at the least moved by nature as nature. Nor, surely, does Carlson at all want to rule out the kind of emotional response with which Carroll is concerned. His point is only that the emotional response is inappropriate in so far as the nature that moves us is too little understood. The differences here are of degree, then, rather than kind.

17. Famously, if not altogether seriously, Stravinsky remarked that his music was for children and animals.

18. Zangwill, *Metaphysics of Natural Beauty*.

19. *Ibid.*

20. *Ibid.*

21. I am suggesting only that there is some significant correspondence here, and not that there is any thoroughgoing alignment of values. Given even moderate sympathy for Darwinian explana-tions, the correspondences here are not at all hard to explain.

22. There is arguably a moral dimension here too. It might be said that the formalist response is wholly inappropriate, given certain objects.

23. R. W. Hepburn, "The trivial and serious in aesthetic appreciation of nature", in Chappell, *Philosophy of the Environment*. See also R. W. Hepburn, *Wonder and Other Essays* (Edinburgh, Edinburgh University Press, 1984).

24. Hepburn, "The trivial and serious", p. 71. And note the anti-Carlson flavour: "I need to say here that 'seriousness' or 'depth' in aesthetic appreciation of nature cannot be correlated in any simple way with intensity and fullness of thought content. Some thoughts (perhaps of causal explanation of the phenomena at the level of particle physics) might not enrich but neutralise the experience, or at least fight and fail to fuse with its a perceptual content", *ibid.*, p. 68.

25. I am reminded of the early injunction to lutenists to tune the top string so high that it almost, but not quite, breaks.

26. Carlson, "Appreciating art", p. 221. Arp's claim, "in nature a broken twig is equal in beauty and importance to the clouds and the stars", may mean that nature itself has no truck with beauty and importance.

27. That things are equally appreciable is uncontroversial, if it means that they can equally be considered from the point of view of aesthetic merit. That natural things equally manifest the natural order is, arguably, also uncontroversial. It might even be allowed that the beauty of natu-ral things depends on their manifesting this order. Still, it won't at all follow that they are equally beautiful.

28. Elliott, "Faking nature", p. 81.

29. If a fake can have different aesthetic values from the original, so presumably it can differ from the innocent copy.

30. There are questions as to whether it is possible. Nelson Goodman, particularly in *Languages of Art* (New York, Bobbs Merrill, 1968), makes much of this. I assume that it is possible, for

practical purposes, at least in art. There are questions, too, about decisions as to whether to repaint (as recently at Assisi) or to leave blanks, when damaged works need to be restored.

31. Compare replacement and duplication. In the second case the original survives, but it may, now that it is duplicated, be less valuable.
32. Elliott, "Faking nature", p. 84.
33. *Ibid.*, p. 88.
34. *Ibid.*, p. 85.
35. Suppose that every thousand years the universe disappears and then reforms. There is, in a clear sense, a loss of continuity here, but it is hard to see that this matters at all.
36. Elliott, "Faking nature", p. 88.
37. Although to say this may be an indication of bias. Much in the oceans is still wild, and it is still wild on the moon, Mars and beyond.

Chapter 11: Human Beings

1. Unlikely, but not impossible, as there could be a wholly fortuitous balance between good and evil. Even so, a neutral value so achieved will be of a different kind from one resulting from the impossibility of things' having value.
2. Only a few will want to say this, but, implicitly at least, we do rank animals and beauty over human life, when, as is not uncommon, we give money to donkeys, or to Venice, before famine relief.
3. This is not simply the point that our duties to assist are not as strong as our duties not to harm. It may be worse to push someone into a lake than to stand and watch them drown when they fall accidentally, but I am not claiming that here. The claim is about the special case where conscious life is already, because of the coma, on hold.
4. See P. Laslett & J. S. Fishkin, *Justice Between Age Groups and Generations* (New Haven, CT, Yale University Press, 1992), pp. 6–11, on the vagueness in the notion of a generation.
5. I claim only that there are reasons here, not that they are strong. There may be reasons for doubting that future generations will resemble ours in all relevant respects, and we can imagine that the desire for children and the need for carers might both dwindle.
6. At least, no killing of innocent people. The assumption here, of course, is that in terminating the development of human embryos this woman is not killing human beings.
7. J. Glover, *Causing Death and Saving Lives* (Harmondsworth, Penguin, 1977), p. 70.
8. For example, "Other people, including me, think that to end the human race would be about the worst thing it would be possible to do. This is because of a belief in the intrinsic value of there existing in the future at least some people with worthwhile lives", Glover, *Causing Death and Saving Lives*, pp. 69–70.
9. I am making here only the modest claim that premature death is bad. As is evident, many very old people have hopes and plans for the future. Arguably, death is bad whenever it occurs. See again several of the papers, and perhaps especially Nagel and Williams, in Fischer, *Metaphysics of Death*.
10. Perhaps. Within the one life, denial of the compensation view will still seem extreme, but for many non-utilitarians, compensation across different lives will be found problematic. How far these intuitive responses can be sustained, and what is involved in their reconciliation, are matters that might be explored elsewhere.
11. On this see Belshaw, "Abortion, value and the sanctity of life", and, behind that, Dworkin, *Life's Dominion*. Glover, *Causing Death and Saving Lives*, Ch. 3, also addresses several of the issues here.
12. Suppose that it is not restricted in this way. Just as there is a question about the importance of being human, so there is a question, as we have seen, about the importance of life. Mere life, and

mere human life, lack evident importance, in a way that, for example, mere consciousness, or mere beauty, do not.

13. Either the intrinsic value of mere life is so great that it outweighs the disvalue in pain, no matter how great the pain, or how long it lasts; or the value of life, and the disvalue in pain are not the same scale. On this see "Death", in Nagel, *Mortal Questions*.

14. Three related positions can be distinguished. A few people create things of enormous beauty or make discoveries of tremendous worth. Think of Mozart or Einstein, the Prado or the Tate, Venice or Rome. More than a few people understand the value of, and appreciate, such things. One view is that such accomplishments are intrinsically valuable, and should no more be destroyed than should objects of natural beauty. A second view is that the ability to make such accomplishments is valuable. A third is that the appreciation of such things is valuable. This is surely a plausible view. If pleasure is intrinsically valuable, so, too, is the appreciation of such achievement. Not a few will want to go further, holding that such appreciation is more valuable than mere pleasure, and thinking that while it might not be a terrible thing if there were no more pleasant states of mind, it would indeed be a terrible thing were such appreciation to cease to occur.

    Thus there are three candidates for value here, and three losses that we might regret: the likes of Mozart; the listeners to Mozart; and the scores of Mozart. For my part, and against some reputable contrary views, I am not sure if having lost the first and second, it would be particularly bad to lose also the third.

15. See, for the presentation and development of this image, the introduction to Laslett & Fishkin, *Justice*.

16. Although what needs to be remembered here is that those living the good life today are already a very small percentage of the world's population. There are issues of intergenerational justice, but there are issues of intragenerational justice as well.

17. This cuts both ways. We cannot justify conservation just on the grounds that it is possible that someone may at some time have an unsurpassing need for what we might otherwise destroy.

18. T. Cowen & D. Parfit, "Against the social discount rate", in Laslett & Fishkin, *Justice*, p. 145.

19. "It may often be morally permissible to be less concerned about the more remote effects of our social policies. But this would never be because these effects are more remote. Rather it would be because they are less likely to occur, or would be effects on people who are better off than we are, or because it would be cheaper now to ensure compensation, or it would be for one of the other reasons we have given. All these different reasons need to be stated and judged separately, on their merits. If we bundle them together in a social discount rate, we make ourselves morally blind", Cowen & Parfit, "Against the social discount rate", pp. 158–9.

20. Especially in *ibid*., pp. 150–52. But see also O'Neill, *Ecology, Policy and Politics*, for useful further discussion.

21. Very much, rather than completely, because although animals won't need oil, they might suffer from leakages of radioactive materials.

22. See, famously, John Taurek's "Should the numbers count?", and, a little less famously, Parfit's trenchant reply in D. Parfit, "Innumerate ethics", *Philosophy and Public Affairs* 7(4), 1978, 285–301.

23. Contra Keekok Lee, "Awe and humility". Space travel on any serious scale seems much less likely now, in 2001, than it did thirty or so years ago, when *2001* was made.

24. There are different questions here. As Jan Narveson has observed, we might want to maximize the total number of people in existence, or we might want to perpetuate the human race for as long as possible. These are different aims. Perhaps, if we cut the human population to a few hundred thousand, we will be able to go on for millions of years. If, on the other hand, we continue to allow for the creation of billions, we will make ourselves extinct within decades. There is a third consideration, which becomes increasingly relevant as it becomes increasingly possible to extend human life. If we are aiming for the maximum number of human years, it might be better to have a few very long lived people, rather than more short lived people. But I will assume that lives are of normal length, and that we can consistently aim for both maximization and perpetuation.

25. See especially Parfit, *Reasons and Persons*, Pt. IV. Several of the themes and arguments of this book have appeared, often in less detail, in journal articles. My discussion here is drawn, in the main, from D. Parfit, "Energy policy and the further future: the identity problem", in *Energy and the Future*, D. MacLean & P. G. Brown (eds) (Totawa, NJ, Rowman & Littlefield, 1983), reprinted in Pojman, *Environmental Ethics*, 2nd edn, pp. 289–96.
26. *Ibid.*, p. 291. See also Parfit, *Reasons and Persons*, Ch. 16.
27. Assume all lives are worth living. Group X isn't made worse off. It can't be worse to be born and have a good life than not to be born. Nor is group Y made worse off. Even if you think it would be better for them to have been born, it can't be worse for them not to be born. On this last point, see Parfit, *Reasons and Persons*, Appendix G, "Whether causing someone to exist can benefit this person".
28. Parfit, "Energy policy", p. 294.
29. *Ibid.*
30. It is more complex where different numbers are involved. A clear case is that involving the 14-year-old girl (*ibid.*, pp. 290, 293). If she can have a later child, her choice to have a child now is reprehensible in a way that it would not be if it were now or never. Suppose that she can have twins now, or one child later. If we ask, one now, or a better one later, the choice, for Parfit, is clear. But if we ask, twins now, or a better *one* later, it may be less clear. See Parfit, *Reasons and Persons*, Ch. 16.
31. Parfit, "Energy policy", p. 295. As Parfit noted, B can apply in cases both where identities differ, and where they are the same.
32. The connection between these and some earlier claims might be explored elsewhere. Earlier I questioned whether we have any kind of obligation to bring new worlds into existence. Many people will agree that there is no obligation here, but think that when it is a choice between worlds, we ought to choose the best. It is similar on the domestic scale. It is not true that I ought to have a child, but if I am to have a child, I ought to choose the best. My strong suspicion, however, is that the two sorts of case cannot so easily be separated.

Appendix A: Deep Ecology: Central Texts

1. Devall & Sessions, *Deep Ecology*, pp. 18–19.
2. *Ibid.*, p. 69.
3. From *ibid.*, p. 70, original emphasis.
4. From *ibid.*, pp. 70–73.
5. See "The Deep Ecology 'Eight Points' Revisited", in Sessions, *Deep Ecology*, pp. 213–21.

Appendix B: The Axiarchical View

1. See J. Leslie, *Value and Existence* (Oxford, Blackwell, 1979) and D. Parfit, *Environmental Ethics*, 2nd edn (Boston, MA, Jones & Bartlett, 1998).
2. Assuming that what is of value is *this* universe, which undoubtedly does contain such things. As Leslie makes clear, other possible universes wouldn't contain even this much.

Appendix C: Gaia

1. It is often suggested that there is no genuine hypothesis here at all, and Gaia is little more than a metaphor. This and the previous criticism are bluntly if tellingly combined by Anthony O'Hear – "the notion functions far more like a personified dogma", in "The myth of nature", in Barnett & Scruton, *Town and Country*, p. 78. For more detail see James W. Kirchner, "The Gaia hypotheses: Are they testable? Are they useful?" in Pojman, *Environmental Ethics*, 146–54.
2. J. E. Lovelock, *The Ages of Gaia* (Oxford, Oxford University Press, 1995), p. 40.
3. In part I follow Kirchner here, "The Gaia hypothesis".
4. Lovelock, *The Ages of Gaia*, p. 15.
5. J. E. Lovelock & S. Epton, "In quest for Gaia", *New Scientist*, February 1975, reprinted in Pojman, *Environmental Ethics*, 142–6, p. 145.
6. For example in Lovelock, *The Ages of Gaia*, p. 15.
7. I think Pojman goes wrong here, and succumbs to the temptation to think that something supernatural is claimed. He writes "if the earth were governed simply by geochemical systems (rather than by biological systems) like Mars and Venus, its atmosphere would have been largely carbon dioxide and nitrogen, as on Mars and Venus, in which case life would not have appeared", Pojman, *Environmental Ethics*, p. 141. But Earth wasn't governed by biological systems prior to the appearance of life.
8. Lovelock, *The Ages of Gaia*, p. 213.
9. How should we interpret these claims? Bowler, *The Fontana History*, p. 546, sees Lovelock as yet another prophet of doom, whereas J. B. Callicott, *Earth's Insights* (Berkeley and Los Angeles, CA, University of California Press, 1994), p. 41, believes that Gaian self-regulation may "kick in to save us from runaway global warming". Such optimism may be welcome to George W. Bush, who has recently signalled the USA's reneging on the Kyoto Treaty to limit climate change.

Bibliography

Alderson, L. (1989) *The Chance to Survive*. Bromley: Helm.

Andrews, M. (1989) *The Search for the Picturesque*. Aldershot: Scolar Press.

Aquinas, Thomas (1928) *Summa Contra Gentiles*. New York: Benziger Brothers [originally published 1259–64].

Aristotle (1985) *The Nicomachean Ethics*, Terence Irwin (trans.). Indianapolis, IN: Hackett.

Attfield, R. (1983) *The Ethics of Environmental Concern*. Oxford: Blackwell.

Attfield, R. (1998) "Environmental ethics: overview", *Encyclopedia of Applied Ethics*, vol 2. London: Academic.

Attfield, R. & Belsey, A. (eds) (1994) *Philosophy and the Natural Environment*. Cambridge: Cambridge University Press.

Barnett, A. & Scruton, R. (eds) (1998) *Town and Country*. London: Jonathan Cape.

Baron, M., Pettit, P. & Slote, M. (1997) *Three Methods of Ethics*. Oxford: Blackwell.

Bate, J. (1991) *Romantic Ecology*. London & New York: Routledge.

Baxter, W. F. (1974) *People or Penguins: The Case for Optimal Pollution*. New York: Columbia University Press.

Belshaw, C. (1997) "Abortion, value and the sanctity of life", *Bioethics* **11**: 130–50.

Belshaw, C. (2000) "Death, pain and time", *Philosophical Studies* **97**: 317–41.

Benn, P. (1998) *Ethics*. London: UCL Press.

Benson, J. (1999) *Environments, Ethics and Human Concern*. Milton Keynes: The Open University.

Benson, J. (2000) *Environmental Ethics*. London: Routledge.

Bentham, J. (1843) "Anarchical fallacies", in *The Works of Jeremy Bentham*, J. Bowring (ed.). Edinburgh.

Bentham, J. (1970) *An Introduction to the Principles of Morals and Legislation*. London: Methuen [originally published 1789].

Berleant, A. (1993) "The aesthetics of nature and art", in *Landscape, Natural Beauty and the Arts*, S. Kemal & I. Gaskell (eds). Cambridge: Cambridge University Press.

Blackburn, S. (1993) *Essays on Quasi-Realism*. Oxford: Oxford University Press.

Bowler, P. J. (1992) *The Fontana History of the Environmental Sciences*. London: Fontana Press.

Bullock, A. & Stallybrass, O. (1988) *The Fontana Dictionary of Modern Thought*. London: Fontana Press.

Burke, E. (1990) *A Philosophical Enquiry into the Origin of our Ideas of the Sublime and the Beautiful*. Oxford: Oxford University Press [originally published in 1756].

Callicott, J. B. (1980) "Animal liberation: a triangular affair", *Environmental Ethics* **2**: 311–38.

Callicott, J. B. (1980) "The search for an environmental ethic", in *Matters of Life and Death*, Tom Regan (ed.). New York: Random House.

Callicott, J. B. (1985) "Intrinsic value, quantum theory, and environmental ethics", *Environmental Ethics* **7**: 257–75.

Callicott, J. B. (1986) "The metaphysical implications of ecology", *Environmental Ethics* **9**: 300–15.

Callicott, J. B. (1989) "The conceptual foundations of the land ethic", in *In Defense of the Land Ethic*. New York: SUNY Press.

Callicott, J. B. (1994) *Earth's Insights*. Berkeley & Los Angeles, CA: University of California Press.

Callicott, J. B. (1997) "Whaling in Sand County", in *The Philosophy of the Environment*, T. D. J. Chappell (ed.), pages?. Edinburgh: Edinburgh University Press.

Capra, F. (1995) "Deep ecology: a new paradigm", in *Deep Ecology for the 21st Century*, G. Sessions (ed.), 19–25. Boston, MA: Shambhala.

Carlson, A. (1993) "Appreciating art and appreciating nature", in *Landscape, Natural Beauty and the Arts*, S. Kemal & I. Gaskell (eds). Cambridge: Cambridge University Press.

Carroll, N. (1993) "On being moved by nature: between religion and natural history", in *Landscape, Natural Beauty and the Arts*, S. Kemal & I. Gaskell (eds). Cambridge: Cambridge University Press.

Carruthers, P. (1992) *The Animals Issue*. Cambridge: Cambridge University Press.

Carson, R. (1962) *Silent Spring*. Boston, MA: Houghton Mifflin.

Chappell, T. D. J. (ed.) (1997) *The Philosophy of the Environment*. Edinburgh: Edinburgh University Press.

Clark, K. (1964) *Ruskin Today*. London: Murray.

Clark, S. (1977) *The Moral Status of Animals*. Oxford: The Clarendon Press.

Commoner, B. (1971) *The Closing Circle: Nature, Man and Technology*. New York: Bantam.

Cooper, D. E. & Palmer, J. A. (1992) *The Environment in Question*. London & New York: Routledge.

Cowen, T. & Parfit, D. (1992) "Against the social discount rate", in *Justice Between Age Groups and Generations*, P. Laslett & J. S. Fishkin (eds) (1992). New Haven, CT: Yale University Press.

Descartes, R. (1984, 1985) *The Philosophical Writings of Descartes*, vols I, II, J. Cottingham, R. Stoothoff & D. Murdoch (trans.). Cambridge: Cambridge University Press.

DesJardins, J. R. (1993) *Environmental Ethics*. Belmont, CA: Wadsworth.

Devall, B. & Sessions, G. (1985) *Deep Ecology: Living as if Nature Mattered*. Salt Lake City, UT: Peregrine Smith.

Diamond, J. (1992) *The Rise and Fall of the Third Chimpanzee*. London: Vintage.

Dickens, C. (1994) *Hard Times*. Harmondsworth: Penguin.

Diffey, T. J. (1993) "Natural beauty without metaphysics" , in *Landscape, Natural Beauty and the Arts*, S. Kemal & I. Gaskell (eds). Cambridge: Cambridge University Press.

Dower, N. (1994) "The idea of environment", in *Philosophy and the Natural Environment*, R. Attfield & A. Belsey (eds). Cambridge: Cambridge University Press.

Dryzek, J. (1997) *The Politics of the Earth*. Oxford: Oxford University Press.

Dworkin, R. (1978) *Taking Rights Seriously*. London: Duckworth.

Dworkin, R. (1993) *Life's Dominion*. New York: Knopf.

Elliott, R. (1982) "Faking nature", *Inquiry* **25**: 81–93.

Elliott, R. (1992) "Intrinsic value, environmental obligation and naturalness", *The Monist* **75**: 138–60.

Elliott, R. (1995) *Environmental Ethics*. Oxford: Oxford University Press.

Fischer, J. M. (ed.) (1993) *The Metaphysics of Death*. Stanford, CA: Stanford University Press.

Fox, W. (1974) "Deep ecology: a new philosophy for our time?", *Ecologist* **14**: 194–200.

Frey, R. G. (1980) *Interests and Rights: The Case against Animals*. Oxford: Clarendon Press.

Frey, R. G. (1983) *Rights, Killing and Suffering*. Oxford: Blackwell.

Glover, J. (1977) *Causing Death and Saving Lives*. Harmondsworth: Penguin.

Goodman, N. (1968) *Languages of Art*. New York: Bobbs Merrill.

Goodpaster, K. (1978) "On being morally considerable", *Journal of Philosophy* **75**: 308–25.

Hargrove, E. C. (1992) "Weak anthropocentric intrinsic value", *The Monist* **75**: 183–207.
Hargrove, E. C. (ed.) (1986) *Beyond Spaceship Earth: Environmental Ethics and the Solar System*. San Francisco, CA: Sierra Club Books.
Hart, H. L. A. (1955) "Are there any natural rights?", *The Philosophical Review* **64**: 175–91.
Hepburn, R. W. (1984) *Wonder and Other Essays*. Edinburgh: Edinburgh University Press.
Hepburn, R. W. (1997) "The trivial and serious in aesthetic appreciation of nature", in *The Philosophy of the Environment*, T. D. J. Chappell (ed.). Edinburgh: Edinburgh University Press.
Hobbes, T. (1968) *Leviathan*. Harmondsworth: Penguin [originally published in 1651].
Hoskins, W. G. (1955) *The Making of the English Landscape*. London: Hodder & Stoughton.
Hume, D. (1975) *Enquiries Concerning Human Understanding and Concerning the Principles of Morals*, 3rd edn, L. A. Selby-Bigge (ed.), P. H. Nidditch (rev.). Oxford: Clarendon Press [originally published 1748, 1751].
Hume, D. (1978) *A Treatise of Human Nature*, 2nd edn, L. A. Selby-Bigge (ed.), P. H. Nidditch (rev.). Oxford: Clarendon Press [originally published 1739–40].
Hursthouse, R. (1999) *On Virtue Ethics*. Oxford: Oxford University Press.
Hursthouse, R. (1999) *Humans and Other Animals*. Milton Keynes: The Open University.
Johnson, L. (1991) *A Morally Deep World*. Cambridge: Cambridge University Press.
Kant, I. (1963) *Lectures on Ethics (1780–81)*, H. Louis Infield (trans.). New York: Harper & Row.
Kant, I. (1964) *Groundwork of the Metaphysics of Morals*, H. J. Paton (trans.). New York: Harper & Row [originally published in 1785].
Kemal, S. & Gaskell, I. (eds) (1993) *Landscape, Natural Beauty and the Arts*. Cambridge: Cambridge University Press.
Korsgaard, C. (1996) *Creating the Kingdom of Ends*. Cambridge: Cambridge University Press.
Laslett, P. & Fishkin, J. S. (eds) (1992) *Justice Between Age Groups and Generations*. New Haven, CT: Yale University Press.
Lee, K. (1994) "Awe and humility: intrinsic value in nature: beyond an earthbound environmental ethics", in *Philosophy and the Natural Environment*, R. Attfield & A. Belsey (eds). Cambridge: Cambridge University Press.
Leopold, A. (1949) *A Sand County Almanac*. New York: Oxford University Press.
Leslie, J. (1979) *Value and Existence*. Oxford: Blackwell.
Leslie, J. (1996) *The End of the World*. London & New York: Routledge.
Lovelock, J. E. (1995) *The Ages of Gaia*. Oxford: Oxford University Press.
Lovelock, J. E. & Epton, S. (1975) "In quest for Gaia", *New Scientist*, February.
Luper, S. (1999) "Natural resources, gadgets and artificial life", *Environmental Values* 8(1): 27–54.
Mabey, R. (1997) *Flora Britannica*. London: Chatto & Windus.
McDowell, J. (1998) *Mind, Value and Reality*. Cambridge, MA: Harvard University Press.
Mackie, J. (1977) *Ethics, Inventing Right and Wrong*. Harmondsworth: Penguin.
MacMahan, J. (1993) "Death and the value of life", in *The Metaphysics of Death*, J. M. Fischer (ed.), 233–6. Stanford, CA: Stanford University Press.
Mannison, D. (1980) "A prolegomenon to a human chauvinistic attitude", in *Environmental Philosophy*, D. Mannison, M. McRobbie & R. Routley (eds). Canberra: Australian National University.
Meadows, D. H. (1990) "Biodiversity: the key to saving life on earth", *Land Steward Letter*.
Midgley, M. (1979) *Beast and Man: The Roots of Human Nature*. Brighton: Harvester Press.
Midgley M. (1983) "Duties concerning islands", in *Environmental Philosophy*, R. Elliot & A. Gare (eds), 166–81. Milton Keynes: Open University Press.
Midgley, M. (1997) "Sustainability and moral pluralism", in *The Philosophy of the Environment*, T. D. J. Chappell (ed.). Edinburgh: Edinburgh University Press.
Mill, J. S. (1978) *On Liberty*. Indianapolis, IN: Hackett [originally published in 1859].
Mill, J. S. (1995) *Utilitarianism*. Indianapolis, IN: Hackett [originally published in 1863].
Mitchell, A. & Coombes, A. (1999) *The Garden Tree*. London: Seven Dials.
Montaigne, M. (1987) *An Apology for Raymond Sebond*, M. A. Screech (trans.). Harmondsworth, Penguin.
Montaigne, M. (1991) *The Essays of Michel de Montaigne*, M. A. Screech (trans.). London: Allen Lane.

Moore, G. E. (1922) *Philosophical Studies*. London: Routledge & Kegan Paul.

Morowitz, H. (1972) "Biology as a cosmological science", *Main Currents in Modern Thought* **28**.

Naess, A. (1973) "The shallow and the deep, long-range ecology movements", *Inquiry* **16**: 95–100.

Naess, A. (1984) "A defense of the deep ecology movement", *Environmental Ethics* **6**: 265–70.

Naess, A. (1985) "Identification as a source of deep ecological attitudes", in *Deep Ecology*, M. Tobias (ed.). Santa Monica, CA: IMT Productions.

Naess, A. (1995) "Eight points revisited", in *Deep Ecology*, G. Sessions (ed.), 213–21. Boston, MA: Shambhala.

Nagel, T. (1979) *Mortal Questions*. Cambridge: Cambridge University Press.

Narveson, J. (1967) "Utilitarianism and new generations", *Mind* **76**: 62–72.

Nicholson, E. M. (1970) *The Environmental Revolution*. London: Hodder & Stoughton.

Nicholson, N. (ed.) (1978) *The Lake District: An Anthology*. Harmondsworth: Penguin.

O'Neill, J. (1992) "The varieties of intrinsic value", *The Monist* **75**: 119–37.

O'Neill, J. (1993) *Ecology, Policy and Politics*. London & New York: Routledge.

Parfit, D. (1978) "Innumerate ethics", *Philosophy and Public Affairs* **7**(4): 285–301.

Parfit, D. (1982) "Future generations: further problems", *Philosophy and Public Affairs* **11**: 113–72.

Parfit, D. (1983) "Energy policy and the further future: the identity problem", in *Energy and the Future*, D. MacLean & P. G. Brown (eds). Totawa, NJ: Rowman & Littlefield.

Parfit, D. (1984) *Reasons and Persons*. Oxford: Clarendon Press.

Passmore, J. (1980) *Man's Responsibility for Nature*, 2nd edn. London: Duckworth.

Pearce, D. & Barbier, E. (2000) *Blueprint for a Sustainable Economy*. London: Earthscan Publications.

Pearce, D. Markandya, A. & Barber, E. B. (1989) *Blueprint for a Green Economy*. London: Earthscan Publications.

Pepper, D. (1989) *The Roots of Modern Environmentalism*. London & New York: Routledge.

Plato, *The Republic*.

Plato, *the Euthyphro*.

Pojman, L. (ed.) (1994) *Environmental Ethics*. Boston, MA: Jones & Bartlett.

Pojman, L. (ed.) (1998) *Environmental Ethics*, 2nd edn. Boston, MA: Jones & Bartlett.

Rackham, O. (1986) *The History of the Countryside*. London: Dent.

Rawles, K. (1997) "Conservation and animal welfare", in *The Philosophy of the Environment*, T. D. J. Chappell (ed.). Edinburgh: Edinburgh University Press.

Rawls, J. (1971) *A Theory of Justice*. Cambridge, MA: Harvard University Press.

Regan, T. (1975) "The moral basis of vegetarianism", *Canadian Journal of Philosophy* **5**: 181–214.

Regan, T. (1982) *All that Dwell Therein*. Berkeley, CA: University of California Press.

Regan, T. (1983) *The Case for Animal Rights*. Berkeley, CA: University of California Press.

Regan, T. (1985) "The case for animal rights", in *In Defence of Animals*, P. Singer (ed.). Oxford: Blackwell.

Regan, T. (1992a) "Animal rights: what's in a name?", in *Animal Welfare and the Environment*, R. Ryder & P. Singer (eds). London: Duckworth/RSPCA.

Regan, T. (1992b) "Does environmental ethics rest on a mistake?", *The Monist* **75**: 161–82.

Regan, T. & Singer, P. (eds) (1976) *Animal Rights and Human Obligation*. Englewood Cliffs, NJ: Prentice-Hall.

Rolston III, H. (1988) *Environmental Ethics*. Philadelphia, PA: Temple University Press.

Rolston III, H. (1989) *Philosophy Gone Wild*. Buffalo, NY: Prometheus Books.

Rolston III, H. (1994) "Value in nature and the nature of value", in *Philosophy and the Natural Environment*, R. Attfield & A. Belsey (eds). Cambridge: Cambridge University Press.

Rousseau, J. J. (1987) "The social contract", in *The Basic Political Writings*, D. A. Cress (trans.). Indiana, IN: Hackett [originally published 1762].

Routley, R. & Routley, V. (1980) "Human chauvinism and environmental ethics", in *Environmental Philosophy*, D. Mannison, M. McRobbie & R. Routley (eds). Canberra, Australian National University.

Ruskin, J. (1903–12) *The Works Of John Ruskin*, 39 vols, E. T. Cook & A. Wedderburn (eds). London: George Allen.

Russow, L. (1981) "Why do species matter?", *Environmental Ethics* 3: 101–12.

Ryder, R. (1974) *Speciesism: The Ethics of Vivisection*. Edinburgh: Scottish Society for the Prevention of Vivisection.

Sagoff, M. (1988) *The Economy of the Earth*. Cambridge: Cambridge University Press.

Sarre, P. & Reddish, A. (eds) (1990) *Environment and Society*. London: Hodder & Stoughton in association with the Open University.

Scanlon, T. (1982) "Contractualism and utilitarianism", in *Utilitarianism and Beyond*, A. Sen & B. Williams (eds). Cambridge: Cambridge University Press.

Scanlon, T. (1998) *What We Owe to Each Other*. Cambridge, MA: Belknap Press.

Scheffler, S. (1982) *The Rejection of Consequentialism*. Oxford: The Clarendon Press.

Schweitzer, A. (1923) *Civilization and Ethics*. London: A. & C. Black.

Scruton, R. (2000) *England, An Elegy*. London: Chatto.

Sen, A. & Williams, B. (eds) (1982) *Utilitarianism and Beyond*. Cambridge: Cambridge University Press.

Serpell, J. (1986) *In the Company of Animals*. Cambridge: Cambridge University Press.

Sessions, G. (ed.) (1995) *Deep Ecology for the 21st Century*. Boston, MA: Shambhala.

Sessions, G. (1969) *Reverence for Life*. New York: Harper & Row.

Sikora, R. (1978) "Is it wrong to prevent the existence of future generations?", in R. Sikora & B. Barry (eds), *Obligations to Future Generations*. Philadelphia, PA: Temple University Press.

Singer, P. (1973) "Animal liberation", *The New York Review of Books*, April.

Singer, P. (1976) *Animal Liberation*. London: Jonathan Cape.

Singer, P. (ed.) (1985) *In Defence of Animals*. Oxford: Blackwell.

Singer, P. (1993) *Practical Ethics*, 2nd edn. Cambridge: Cambridge University Press.

Singer, P. (1994) "Animal rights and human obligation", in *Environmental Ethics*, L. Pojman (ed.). Boston, MA: Jones & Bartlett.

Singer, P. (1996) "The ethics of animal liberation: a summary statement", in *On the Side of Animals: Some Contemporary Philosophers' Views*. RSPCA.

Smart, J. J. C. & Williams, B. (1973) *Utilitarianism For and Against*. Cambridge: Cambridge University Press.

Sober, E. (1993) *The Philosophy of Biology*. Boulder, CO: Westview.

Sorabji, R. (1993) *Animal Minds and Human Morals: The Origins of the Western Debate*. London: Duckworth.

Stavins, R. & Whitehead, B. W. (1992) "Market based incentives for environmental protection", *Environment* 34: 7–42.

Stone, C. (1972) "Should trees have standing? Towards legal rights for natural objects", *Southern California Law Review* 45: 450–501.

Stroup, R. & Baden, J. (1983) *Natural Resources, Bureaucratic Myths and Environmental Management*. San Francisco, CA: Pacific Institute for Public Policy Research.

Sylvan, R. (1985a) "A critique of deep ecology I", *Radical Philosophy* 40: 2–12.

Sylvan, R. (1985b) "A critique of deep ecology II", *Radical Philosophy* 41: 10–22.

Sylvan, R. (1990) *In Defence of Deep Environmental Ethics*, preprints in environmental philosophy. Canberra: Australian National University.

Sylvan, R. & Bennett, D. (1994) *The Greening of Ethics*. Tucson, AZ: The University of Arizona Press.

Taurek, J. (1977) "Should the numbers count?", *Philosophy and Public Affairs* 6(4): 293–316.

Taylor, P. W. (1981) "The ethics of respect for nature", *Environmental Ethics* 3: 197–218.

Taylor, P. W. (1984) "Are humans superior to animals and plants?", *Environmental Ethics* 6: 149–60.

Taylor, P. W. (1986) *Respect for Nature*. Princeton, NJ: Princeton University Press.

Thomas, K. (1984) *Man and the Natural World*. Harmondsworth: Penguin.

Unger, P. (1996) *Living High and Letting Die*. Oxford: Oxford University Press.

Waldron, J. (ed.) (1984) *Theories of Rights*. Oxford: Oxford University Press.

317

Warren, M. A. (1987) "Difficulties with the strong animal rights position", *Between the Species* 2.
White, L. (1967) "The historical roots of our ecologic crisis", *Science* 1: 1203–7.
Williams, B. (1981) *Moral Luck*. Cambridge: Cambridge University Press.
Williams, B. (1993) "The Makropoulos case", in *The Metaphysics of Death*, J. M. Fischer (ed.), 73–92. Stanford, CA: Stanford University Press.
Wordsworth, W. (1974) "A Guide Through the District of the Lakes", in *The Prose Works of William Wordsworth*, vol. II, W. J. B. Owen & J. W. Smyser (eds). Oxford: The Clarendon Press [originally published 1835].
Worster, D. (1994) *Nature's Economy*, 2nd edn. Cambridge: Cambridge University Press.
Zangwill, N. (2001) *The Metaphysics of Natural Beauty*. Ithaca, NY: Cornell University Press.

Index